EUGENICS
AND THE
WELFARE STATE

EUGENICS
AND THE
WELFARE STATE

STERILIZATION POLICY IN DENMARK, SWEDEN, NORWAY, AND FINLAND

EDITED BY GUNNAR BROBERG AND NILS ROLL-HANSEN

Michigan State University Press

East Lansing

⊚ The paper used in this publication meets the minimum requirements of ANSI/NISO Z39.48-1992 (R 1997) (Permanence of Paper).

 Michigan State University Press
East Lansing, Michigan 48823-5245

Printed and bound in the United States of America.

11 10 09 08 07 06 05   1 2 3 4 5 6 7 8 9 10

ISBN to the revised paperback edition 0-87013-758-1
The 1996 hardcover edition was originally catalogued by the Library of Congress as follows:

LIBRARY OF CONGRESS CATALOGING-IN-PUBLICATION DATA
Eugenics and the welfare state : sterilization policy in Denmark, Sweden, Norway, and Finland / edited by Gunnar Broberg and Nils Roll-Hansen
p. cm.
Includes bibliographical references and index.
ISBN 0-87013- (alk. paper)
1. Eugenics—Scandinavia—History. 2. Sterilization, Eugenic—Government policy—Scandinavia—History. 3. Welfare state—History. I. Broberg, Gunnar, 1942– . II. Roll-Hansen, Nils, 1938– .
HQ755.5.S34E94 1995
363.9'2'0948—dc20
95-17633
CIP

Uppsala Studies in History of Science, Volume 21.

Eugenics and the Welfare State: Sterilization Policy in Denmark, Sweden, Norway, and Finland was produced with the financial support of the Uppsala Studies in the History of Science Series.

Cover design by Heather Truelove Aiston.

g green press INITIATIVE   Michigan State University Press is a member of the Green Press Initiative and is committed to developing and encouraging ecologically responsible publishing practices. For more information about the Green Press Initiative and the use of recycled paper in book publishing, please visit *www.greenpressinitiative.com.*

Visit Michigan State University Press on the World Wide Web at *www.msupress.msu.edu*

Contents

Preface to 1996 Edition

This book, *Eugenics and the Welfare State*, is the first real attempt to cover the story of the Scandinavian, including Finnish, history of eugenics. It has been told in rather similar ways to make comparisons possible. The book starts with a general introduction, which is followed by separate chapters on Denmark, Sweden, Norway and Finland. Finally, there is a conclusion bringing the Scandinavian experience into a broader European context. Considering that so much of our story has been unknown, we have allowed ourselves rather extensive descriptions and documentation. As Scandinavian welfare has often been given prominence in European and American discussions we feel that this story warrants attention. Clearly, it offers a different picture of Scandinavian history than is generally known.

We would like to thank those who have checked our English (Dag Blanck and others) as well as NOS-H for a generous grant and Wissenschaftskolleg zu Berlin for funding a seminar on eugenics and the welfare state.

Gunnar Broberg
Nils Roll-Hansen

Preface to the 2005 Edition

The science of human heredity is unavoidably tied to social politics. In our experience, this also very much applies to the historiography of the subject. A year after this book was first published, its story—the practice of sterilization in the Scandinavian welfare state—was sensationalized in the world's mass media. This media event in the autumn of 1997 demonstrated both how historical interpretation can be a powerful weapon in political struggles and how a combination of political fashion and media attention can distort historical accounts. The event raised, in a sharp and interesting way, questions concerning truth, honesty, and appropriate behavior for scientists and politicians as well as for journalists. This time the focus was not on the social responsibility and moral integrity of natural science (in this case genetics), but on that of humanistic sciences. Perhaps the event can be taken as a reminder of the close interdependence of natural and humanistic sciences: that they will fall or stand together and that the widening ideological gulf between them is a serious threat to a productive social role for the Western scientific tradition—taking science in the broad continental enlightenment sense including the natural as well as the humanistic sciences.

On 20 August 1997 *Dagens Nyheter,* one of Sweden's most influential national newspapers, announced that tens of thousands of Swedes were sterilized under compulsion; across Europe only Nazi Germany has exceeded these numbers.[1] The somewhat more restrained article substantiating this claim was based on the well-known fact that 63,000 Swedes were sterilized in the period between 1935 and 1975 in accordance with the sterilization law that was enacted by parliament in 1934 and modified in 1941, and that similar laws and policies were typical of Denmark and Norway. This story and the comparison to Nazi Germany caught like wildfire during the following weeks. The *Wash-*

ington Post wrote about "a 40-year Nazi-style campaign of forced sterilization." A Reuter telegram asserted that "Social democratic Swedish governments sterilized 60,000 women to rid society of 'inferior' racial types and to encourage Aryan features." "The laws . . . could have come out of a Nazi text book" declared the *Guardian*. The *Times* explained that "Most damning of all was the Swedish government's willingness to sterilize women because they did not conform to the Aryan image of blonde hair and blue eyes."[2]

Apparently the willingness to associate Scandinavian social democracy with Nazism was inspired by a trend of criticism of the welfare state, exposing its authoritarian and anti-liberal aspects. The political message impacted more than a transitory public opinion; the view that Scandinavian countries, led by social democratic regimes, carried out large scale compulsory sterilization as part of a eugenic population policy is now widespread in scholarly literature.[3]

The spectre of Nazi eugenics hovers over today's public debates on genetic technologies in human reproduction. Since the 1970s the word eugenics has become strongly associated with Nazism. To characterize a practice or idea as eugenic has been to condemn it as totally unacceptable. Only recently have many philosophers, medical doctors, and others begun to argue for a broader view of eugenics. They have pointed out that new techniques that are now rapidly being introduced have effects, more or less consciously aimed for, that can properly be called eugenic. Some have claimed that policies and practices that improve the genetic quality of a population can be for the greater good, provided they are based on a well-informed free choice by the individuals involved.[4]

But so far the willingness or interest among historians to approach the complexity in the history of eugenics has been limited. An influential exception is Daniel Kevles, who wrote a 1985 treatise on eugenics in America and Britain.[5] He emphasized the difference between what he called mainline and reform eugenics; he defined the former as the segment dominated by authoritarian politics and negligent of the new science of genetics, and the latter as more liberal and observant of individual rights as well as eager to base its policies on the most advanced genetic knowledge.

In America mainline attitudes and laws about sterilization dominated from the early twentith century until eugenics went out of fashion by the late 1930s, and in England no sterilization laws were enacted. Scandinavian sterilization laws were introduced mainly in the 1930s under Social Democratic regimes in close consultancy with scientific experts, and the practice of sterilization continued at a high rate there well after WWII. This raises important questions about the nature of the eugenics that was associated with Scandinavian sterilization laws and about the nature of Scandianvian sterilization practices. Were sterilizations there based on free choice or coercion? Were the criteria for them primarily eugenic in a biological sense or were they primarily social, linked to central goals of welfare policy, like proper care and upbringing of children, family planning, and women's liberation? It seems obvious to make a comparison with Nazi Germany, where a sterilization law was introduced in 1933. How did the content of laws and the practice of sterilization in these places differ? What was the effect of different political and legal regimes—liberal democracy versus authoritarian dictatorship?

A main goal of our 1996 book was to shed some light on these questions and to stimulate further research.[6] A number of substantial new studies on Scandinavian sterilization and eugenics have been published since, but unfortunately they have so far been published only in Scandinavian languages; only summaries have been published in English. In *Racehygiejne i Danmark 1920–56* Lene Koch outlines the history of Danish lawmaking and the involvement of scientific and social institutions in sterilization practice, in particular in the sterilization of the mentally retarded. On the scientific side Tage Kemp played a central role. He became head of the Institute of Human heredity at the University of Copenhagen when it was established in 1938, and in 1956 he organized the First International Congress of Human Genetics in Copenhagen. Koch also describes and discusses extensively the relation of sterilization to social causes other than eugenics, as well as the problematic and changing balance between free choice and coercion. The paternalist moralism that still reigned in the 1930s gradually gave way to a liberal emphasis of individual rights that by the 1960s and '70s produced new sterilization laws and quite different practices.[7]

Steriliseringar i folkhemmet (Sterilizations in the peoples home) by Maja Runcis focuses on the situation of women. More than 90 percent of the 63,000 people sterilized in Sweden were women. Runcis shows how sterilization was linked to the social status and role of women, and in particular to the suppression of female sexuality. She presents gripping and tragic stories about young women who were sterilized. Runcis also argues that there was a strong connection between the rise of the Swedish welfare model, on one hand, and the sterilization program, on the other.[8]

In 1997 a Swedish government commission was set up to investigate sterilization practices between 1935 and 1975. This led to a parliamentary decision in 1999 to give restitution to persons who had been subjected to compulsory sterilization. As part of the commission's investigation Mattias Tydén conducted a thorough historical study *Från politik till praktik. De svenska steriliseringslagarna*

1935–1975 (From politics to practice: The Swedish sterilization laws, 1935–1970). Tydén claims there was a gradual change in attitude starting in the 1950s. A widespread culture of paternalistic coercion gave way to free individual choice, and motives shifted from eugenic and biological to individual and social: "sterilizations in the interest of society were replaced by sterilizations in the interest of the individual."[9] Mental retardation often was a main criterion in cases where a person was deemed not capable of making a voluntary decision or where coercion was applied to a degree that today is considered unacceptable. Tydén points out that officially the Swedish sterilization laws were based on voluntary consent. Forced sterilization like that in Nazi Germany was repudiated by the Swedish parliament, and the National Board of Health in its regulations emphasized voluntary cooperation. But clearly the standards for voluntary consent nevertheless were different in the 1930s and '40s, with less emphasis on protecting the rights of the individual, than they were toward the end of the twentieth century. For instance, in the earlier period sterilization was frequently set as a condition of release from institutions for the mentally retarded.[10] A central theme in Tydén's study is the way in which the sterilization policy was transformed throughout the policymaking process. In part, the personnel at the National Board of Health implemented the laws at their own discretion, as did various officials and groups and individuals at the local levels.

A similar study was commissioned by the Norwegian government. In *Sterilisering av tatere 1934–1977* (Sterilization of traveling people, 1934–1977) Per Haave presents a corresponding description and analysis of Norwegian lawmaking and sterilization practice that contains a similar story of change from sterilization as a means of social control to sterilization as a means of individual freedom. From the 1960s there was a very rapid increase in Norwegian sterilizations as they became a popular method of birth control. This trend was not limited to Scandinavian countries; in the United States in 1988 close to half of all women between the ages of 35 and 44 either had themselves been sterilized or had partners who were.[11] One conclusion of Haave's Norwegian study is that at no point had there been a government policy of eugenic sterilization: "there was never a systematic sterilization of mentally retarded based on political decisions or political administrative instructions."[12] Tydén similarly concluded that "the sterilizations in Sweden in 1935–75 cannot be understood as the outcome of one specific political program or goal."[13] Consequently, both Haave and Tydén reject the now common view that Norwegian and Swedish sterilization practices were the result of eugenic policies launched by Social Democrats in the 1930s and the post-war period.[14]

In a study of eugenics in Finland, *Kansamme parhaaksi* (In our nation's best interest), Markku Mattila points out that eugenic sterilization there peaked around 1960, considerably later than in the other Nordic countries. Different socio-political conditions could be one explanation. A civil war after the Russian revolution where "whites" suppressed "reds," followed by wars with the USSR in 1939–44, shaped a more authoritarian political climate there than in the other Nordic countries.[15]

All the Nordic countries introduced quite similar sterilization laws in the period from the late 1920s into the 1930s. But there are important differences in the practice of these laws. For instance, sterilization for medical reasons was included in the Swedish law but not in the Norwegian law. And while the Norwegian law allowed sterilization for purely personal purposes, like birth control, the Swedish law did not. Denmark had two laws: one for sterilization of the mentally retarded, and one for sterilization of people with normal mental faculties. This pluralism makes it difficult to compare statistics in the four countries, but it also provides interesting comparative insights.

An important statistical investigation of Danish sterilizations of the mentally retarded has been carried out by Lene Koch and published in her book *Tvangssterilisation i Danmark 1929–67*. The 1934 law about treatment of the mentally retarded included rules for sterilization, and altogether 5,579 sterilizations were registered under this law from 1934 to 1968. Koch classified these sterilizations into three categories according to motivation: purely eugenic, partially eugenic, and non-eugenic. Eugenic was defined in a restrictive sense as referring to assumptions about possible hereditary properties of potential offspring. Non-eugenic motivations were "too many pregnancies, poverty, exhaustion, amoral or asocial behaviour, etc."[16] The analysis showed that the number of purely eugenic sterilizations was very low throughout the period. The number of mixed cases ("partly eugenic") grew until around 1950, remained at a level of about half until 1960, and then fell to about a quarter by the end of that decade. The total number per year was relatively stable until 1950 and fell quickly from then on. These two developments together indicate an increasing belief in hereditary causation of mental retardation as well as belief in the practicability of eugenics as social policy up to around 1950, which apparently corresponds with developments in Sweden and Norway.[17]

Sterilization was not the only field of social policy where eugenic considerations played a role. The effects on legislation about marriage and abortion in Norway has been studied by Øyvind Giæver. The Norwegian marriage act of 1918 contained a clause prohibiting marriage for the insane. This clause appears to have been based mainly on social considerations. Medical expertise had warned that eugenic arguments were highly uncertain and should not be taken into serious consideration. But when the law came up for revision in the 1950s, the government commission preparing the law proposed a prohibition clause that included the mentally retarded and drug addicts in addition to the insane; exceptions could be made on condition of sterilization. This proposal was supported by a statement from the commission's psychiatric expert, demonstrating a strong belief in the important role of heredity in various forms of insanity and mental retardation. By the time the law was passed in 1969, skepticism about sterilization and eugenics, as well as paternalistic health and other social policies, was growing, and as a result the sterilization proviso was dropped and the marriage ban remained virtually unchanged. In a 1991 revision the marriage ban for the mentally ill was finally discarded.[18] A parallel paper on abortion legislation claims that arguments about eugenic effects were largely absent from Norwegian abortion debates but appear to have been more important in Sweden and Denmark.[19] However, a high point in the belief of hereditarianism among psychiatrists around 1950 appears well documented. An extreme example is a project launched in 1945 that attempted to reveal detrimental hereditary dispositions among traitors and others disloyal to the country during the 1940–45 war with Germany.[20]

Switzerland has special comparative interest because of similarities to Scandinavia. It shares cultural as well as geographical borders with Germany and has a strong liberal democratic tradition. In the 1990s political concerns about abuse of sterilization on eugenic grounds resulted in a number of government-commissioned studies of sterilization practices. News from Sweden had a stimulating effect on public debate here as it did in other countries. The lack of comprehensive national statistics of the kind that exits in Scandinavia is a serious limitation in assessing both the total number of sterilizations and their distribution on different motivations. Nevertheless, there are indications that total numbers as well as the distribution of indications were comparable.

Geneviève Heller and collaborators in *Rejetées, rebelles, mal adaptées* investigate public debate and practice of nonvoluntary sterilization through the twentieth century in Francophone Switzerland. They define cases where the proposal to sterilize comes from someone other than the person to be sterilized as nonvoluntary. The typical nonvoluntary case is an inmate of an institution for the mentally ill or handicapped. The canton of Vaux in 1928 adopted a law regulating such sterilizations, which had been practiced for some years before. This was the first such law in Europe, and the only one in Switzerland. Other cantons, like Geneva, where the problem was also much discussed, introduced no such laws. Here the situation was analogous to England: "Sterilization, even that of persons with limited powers of judgment, was considered an entirely private problem, where the decision falls on the doctor alone." While Geneva tended towards political and medical liberalism, Vaud "was quite favourable to state control of the individual."[21] It is not sterilization as such that is problematic, state the authors, noting that, after all, it is the most used method of contraception in the world today. It is the motives and procedures leading to the operation that can be problematic.[22] They stress that nonvoluntary sterilizations always had multiple motives. Eugenic concerns about the risk of transmitting hereditary disease were important in the interwar period, but even during this period they were neither sufficient nor dominant. Lacking ability to take care of children was a central motive throughout the whole period.[23] It was also found that in the majority of cases of nonvoluntary sterilization the file indicated that the person had agreed—for example, by signing a document. However, the validity of this consent was often contested.[24] Altogether, the picture is very similar to the Scandinavian one.

In a study of compulsion ("*Zwang*") and eugenics in psychiatry and social welfare in the canton of Zürich, Thomas Huonker found that in the period from 1920 to 1934 the maternity hospital of Zürich alone carried out 1,957 abortions, 1,395 (71%) of which were combined with sterilization.[25] These cases belong to a different category from the nonvoluntary sterilizations of Heller et al., since it was not the institutionalized, mentally ill, or retarded that were being sterilized. These sterilizations were based on medical indications, ostensibly efforts to protect the life and health of the women. To what extent such operations were voluntary or done under some degree of compulsion or coercion is unclear and disputed. Medical sterilizations were regulated by law only in Sweden and Finland, and they made up more than two thirds of the 63,000 lawful Swedish sterilizations during the period from 1934 until 1975. Huonker's numbers raise questions about the frequency of medical sterilizations in countries other than Sweden and Finland. Haave has estimated that in Norway the number of sterilizations performed outside the law was probably much larger than that of those within,[26] and Koch indicates that around 1960 the number of medical sterilizations outnumbered by several times those carried out under the sterilization laws.[27] This begs the question how many sterilizations were performed, with medical or other justifications, in countries that had no sterilization law?

In *Eugenics and the Welfare State* we wanted to explore the role of eugenics and sterilization in the development of the Scandinavian systems of social welfare in the middle decades of the twentieth century. We felt that comparison with Germany both before and after the Nazi takeover in 1933 would yield interesting insights into the relationship between scientific expertise and politics under both liberal democratic and totalitarian regimes. Comparisons to Scandinavia, in particular between Sweden and Nazi Germany, are frequently mentioned in the scholarly literature, though detailed comparisons are still few. What we find distressing is that the picture of Scandinavia in this literature is so highly influenced by the mass media distortions of 1997 and so little informed by the detailed research briefly reviewed above. There is a language barrier since most of the research is only published in Scandinavian language. But even a careful reading of what is published in English, including our 1996 book, ought to make authors more sensitive of precise information and important differences. This, we think, is a good reason for this reissuing of our book.

For example, a passing reference in a Swiss official report to the fact that "in social democratic Sweden in the period 1935 to 1976 around 63,000 mentally handicapped persons, mainly women, were sterilized"[28] is simply not correct. Less than a quarter of this number were mentally handicapped.[29] This mistake may be an accidental slip, but it fits the mass media picture of large scale eugenic sterilization. Similarly, a generally very sober and balanced discussion of ethical questions in the application of gene technology to human reproduction mentions the "tens of thousands of Swedes" that fell victim to eugenic sterilization.[30]

We hope that the strong politicization of the history of sterilization and eugenics in Scandinavia will stimulate new careful scholarly research from a comparative international perspective. It is our opinion that a thorough and nuanced analysis of the disagreements, the general debates, the lawmaking, and the changing practices of sterilization in the Scandinavian countries can provide useful background knowledge for handling parallel problems likely to be raised in the future, such as the problems that arise with respect to the regulation of applications of genetics in human reproduction, in balancing individual rights and interests against common social goals in the distribution of public social welfare, etc. One area where there is a serious lack of data and precise knowledge is the extent of sterilizations, in particular the "medical sterilizations" carried out at the discretion of medical doctors. There are indications that such sterilizations have been common in most countries in Europe and North America. Perhaps the total number of sterilized people, relative to the population, through the period from 1935 to 1975, and particularly in the period after the second world war, was not so very different in Sweden, England, The Netherlands, France, the United States, etc.? The extensive use of sterilization in third world countries also needs investigation. More generally the history of sterilization and eugenics is a good place for developing an understanding of the interaction between science, ideology and politics—not least the role of liberal democratic discourse as a brake on the distortion and misuse of scientific results and authority.

NOTES

1. The text on advertising leaflets for the paper said: "Sverige tvångssteriliserade 10,000-tals— endast Nazi-Tyskland var värre i Europa" (Compulsory sterilization of 10,000s of Swedes— only Nazi Germany was worse). The title of a prominently placed summary on the paper's front page was: "Rashygien i folkhemmet. 60,000 steriliserades. I Europa tillämpade endast Nazi-Tyskland en hårdare politik än Sverige mot oönskade medborgare" (Racehygiene in the peoples home. 60,000 sterilized. In Europe only Nazi Germany adopted a harsher policy towards its citizens).

2. For more details see Gunnar Broberg and Mattias Tydén, "När svensk historia blev en värdsnyhet. Steriliseringspolitiken och media," *Tvärsnitt. Humanistisk och samhällsvetskaplig forskning,* no. 3 (1998): 2–15.

3. Peter Weingart in his paper "Science and Political Culture: Eugenics in a Comparative Perspective," *Scandinavian Journal of History* 24 (1999): 163–77, finds "a virtual identity of the eugenic and race-hygiene discourse in Sweden and Germany as well as a striking similarity in the sterilisation practice." Weingart's historical account, particularly his use of statistics, has been critically examined in N. Roll-Hansen's "Eugenic Practice and Genetic Science in Scandinavia and Germany: Some Comments on Peter Weingart's Comparison of Sweden and Germany," *Scandinavian Journal of History* 26 (2001): 75–86. Similar interpretations of sterilization practice in Sweden and other Nordic countries as the result of eugenic social policy promoted by ruling Social Democrats can be found in T. Etzemüller, "Sozialstaat, Eugenik und Normalisierung in Skandinavischen Demokratien," *Archiv für Sozialgeschichte* 43 (2003): 492–509; A. Spektorokowski, "The Eugenic Temptation in Socialism: Sweden, Germany, and the Soviet Union," *Comparative Studies in Society and History* 46 (2004): 84– 106; and P. Zylberman, "Eugenique à la scandinave: le débat des historiens," *Medicine/ Sciences* 20 (2004): 916–25.

4. See, for instance, A. Caplan, G. McGee, and D. Magnus, "What Is Immoral about Eugenics?" *British Medical Journal* 319, no. 1–2 (13 November 1999); A. Buchanan et al., *From Chance to Choice: Genetics and Justice* (Cambridge: Cambridge University Press, 2000); and D. Gems, "Politically Correct Eugenics," *Theoretical Medicine and Bioethics* 20: 201–213.

5. D. Kevles, *In the Name of Eugenics: Genetics and Uses of Human Heredity* (New York: Alfred Knopf, 1985).

6. See also N. Roll-Hansen, "Eugenic Sterilization: A Preliminary Comparison of the Scandinavian Experience to that of Germany," *Genome* 31 (1989): 890–95.

7. Lene Koch, *Racehygiejne i Danmark 1920–56* (København: Gyldendal, 1996).

8. Maja Runcis, *Steriliseringer i folkhemmet* (Stockholm: Ordfront, 1998).

9. Matthias Tydén, *Från politik till praktik. De svenska steriliseringslagarna 1935–1975* Stockholm Studies in History, 63 (Stockholm: Almquist and Wiksell International, 2002), 584–90.

10. Ibid., 528f, 586ff.

11. Tydén, *Från Politik till praktik,* 12, quotes this information from John M. Last and Robert B. Wallace, *Public Health and Preventive Medicine,* 13th ed. (Norwalk, Conn., 1992), 1104.

12. Per Haave, *Sterilisering av tatere 1934–1977* (Oslo: Norges Forskningsråd, 2000), 388.

13. Tydén, *Från Politik till praktik,* 588.

14. This means that Tydén's interpretation partly has changed since the original publication of *Eugenics and the Welfare State* in 1996.

15. Markku Mattila, *Kansamme parhaaksi* (Helsinki: Bibliotheca Historica, 1999), 421–29.

16. Lene Koch, *Tvangssterilisation i Danmark 1929–67* (København: Gyldendal, 2000), 32–33, (English summaries) 343–55.

17. See *Bibliotek for Læger 193* (2001): 190–252 for a discussion of Koch's book.

18. Øyvind Giæver, "Marriage and Madness: Expert Advice and the Eugenics Issue in Twentieth-Century Norwegian Marriage Legislation," *Science Studies* 16 (2003): 3–21.

19. Øyvind Giæver, "Abortion and Eugenics: The Role of Eugenic Arguments in Norwegian Abortion Debates and Legislation, 1920–1978," *Scandinavian Journal of History* 30 (2005): 267–92.

20. Øyvind Giæver, "The Psychiatry of Quislingism: Norwegian Psychiatric Research On the Collaborators of World War II," *Science in Context* 17 (2004): 267–92.

21. Geneviève Heller, Gilles Jeanmonod, and Jacques Gasser, *Rejetées, rebelles, mal adaptées. Débats sur l'eugénisme. Pratiques de la sterilisation non volontaire en Suisse romande au XXe siècle* (Paris, 2002), 414.

22. Ibid., 2, 131.

23. Ibid., 419.

24. Ibid., 420.

25. Thomas Huonker, *Anstaltsanweisungen, Kindewegnahmen, Eheverbote, Sterilizationen, Kastrationen. Fürsorge, Zwangsmassnahmen, "eugenikk" und Psychiatrie in Zürich zwischen 1890 und 1970,* Bericht von Thomas Huonker verfasst im Auftrag des Sozialdepartements der Stadt Zürich (Zürich 2002), 127.

26. Haave, *Sterilisering av tatere,* 277–81. Haave's judgement is based on a study of medical journals at some of the largest maternity hospitals. It would be interesting to see corresponding studies from countries like France, The Netherlands, England, Italy, Germany after 1945, the United States, Canada, etc.

27. Koch, *Tvangssterilisation,* 312–17, 326, and fig. 29.

28. J. Tanner, M. Meier, G. Hürlimann, *Zwangsmassnahmen in der Zürcher Psychiatrie 1870–1970* (Zürich: Ende Dezember 2002), 5.

29. Broberg and Roll-Hansen, *Eugenics and the Welfare State,* 109–10.

30. A. Buchanan, D. W. Brock, N. Daniels, and D. Wikler, *From Chance to Choice: Genetics and Justice* (Cambridge: Cambridge University Press, 2000), 35. The Eugenics Issue in Twentieth-Century Norwegian Marriage Legislation," *Science Studies* 16 (2003): 3–21.

Scandinavia: An Introduction

Gunnar Broberg

Scandinavia is often looked upon as a unit, yet surprisingly little has been written about the common history of its various countries. Historically and ethnically, the area is comparatively homogeneous, in part because the Scandinavian peninsula provides natural borders. It also gives rise to separate centers: the Norwegian population looks out on the Arctic Ocean, while the Swedish face the Gulf of Bothnia; between Norway and Sweden lies a range of mountains. Contacts between towns on the east coast of Sweden and those on the west coast of Finland have occurred, with the sea forming a link—and for hundreds of years Finland was a part of Sweden. A large number of Swedes (or Finnish Swedes) also live in Finland, where they often have had eminent positions. Denmark, projecting southward from the mainland, took part in the cultural life of the continent earlier than did its neighbors to the north.

Ethnically, the population has remained relatively homogenous, especially in Sweden and Norway; the exception in those countries, as in Finland, has been the Sami, who live in the north and number 30,000-40,000 people. Finland also has had its Swedish community, which sometimes was compared with the "Asiatic" Finns. Denmark's ethnic profile has been rather unmixed, and possibly that is why eugenic endeavors never came to play the same role there as in other Scandinavian countries. In Iceland—which lies outside this survey—the Nordic idea was at least equally prominent, a result, in part, of the country's Viking history.

The notion of a "pure" Nordic race was a myth exploited with great persistency in propaganda. Historically, however, Scandinavia, particularly Sweden and Denmark, has seen a great deal of immigration. Germans, Walloons, Scots, and many other groups have settled there from the Middle Ages to the present. German immigrants and trade with German cities were especially important factors in determining the development of Scandinavian culture. The large number of borrowed German words is evidence of those links; even so, Swedish, Danish, and Norwegian can be seen, basically, as dialects of the same

1

language. There have been viable Jewish minority groups in Denmark since the seventeenth century and in Sweden since the end of the eighteenth century. Nevertheless, with few exceptions, the impression of Scandinavia until recently is one of relative ethnic homogeneity.

Politically, the countries have been allied in a number of different ways, with Denmark dominating during the Renaissance and Sweden taking over during the seventeenth century. Denmark, Norway, and Sweden formed a union from 1389 to 1521, with some interruptions. Finland and Sweden had been joined since the early Middle Ages; Denmark-Norway was one country until Norway became Swedish through the Congress of Vienna in 1815, a union that was dissolved after a referendum in Norway in 1905 (368,200 Norwegians voted for dissolution and 184 against). Pan-Scandinavianism was strong around the middle of the nineteenth century, but it met with a severe setback when Bismarck's Prussia seized the Danish provinces of Schleswig and Holstein in the 1864-65 war.

With the celebration of a "Gothic" past, a significant patriotic ideology emerged during the era of the great wars of the seventeenth century and, *mutatis mutandis*, developed into speculations about a German or Nordic "master race." Racism is partly the consequence of colonial struggle, but only Denmark had colonies in the modern era; the last one, in the West Indies, was relinquished in 1917. Greenland, however, is still a Danish dominion. By the twentieth century, nationalism and racism had become intricately interrelated concepts.

In regard to religion, Scandinavia as a whole has been primarily Lutheran. Beside the faith of the majority, Finland also harbored the Greek Orthodox church, unlike the other countries. The Protestant churches are state establishments, a fact of vital importance for an understanding of Scandinavian history. The development of an efficient state organization was made possible by the cooperation of spiritual and secular authorities. In the context of this book, it is important to note that consensus and cooperation are paramount in medical affairs as well as in other areas.

The church has favored literacy, insisting that the whole population should be able to study the Holy Writ. Over a period of time this has resulted in the attainment of a high level of education in secular areas as well. Around the year 1900, typical Scandinavian plans for popular education (Swedish *folkbildning*) were in evidence with roots in the Danish movement for centers for adult education started by N. E. S. Grundtvig. "Physical education" in the form of Lingian gymnastics was widespread beginning in the mid-nineteenth century. For both Grundtvig and Henric Ling, Nordic mythology, combined with an interest in folklore, was a central tenet. Academics involved in popular lecturing on a comprehensive scale struck a nationalistic tone while also embracing the belief in science that was typical at the turn of the century. The Scandinavian willingness to compromise might have had something to do with this combination of nationalistic ideals and hopes for modernization and democratization.

◆   ◆   ◆

The changes which took place in the whole of the Western world around 1900 came about in a particularly striking way in Scandinavia. Denmark and Sweden, especially, moved very rapidly from an old-fashioned agrarian economy to an industrial one. We could even speak of a Scandinavian "wonder." Copenhagen, Stockholm, Oslo, and Helsinki all took on their present character at this time, growing into metropolises, Copenhagen with a population of half a million, Stockholm with a population of 400,000, and Oslo (Christiania until 1924) with a population of a quarter of a million, and Helsinki with nearly 100,00 inhabitants.

Urbanization was only one side of the demographic change that occurred at this time; the other was emigration. Rural areas in particular lost many of the younger generation. Approximately two million Scandinavians emigrated to the United States, but there were also those who went to South America, Australia, and Germany. For a while, Chicago came to be the second largest "Swedish" city, while there was a viable Norwegian colony in New York. Many Finns moved to St. Petersburg, Florida. Despite the drain, the population in the Scandinavian countries increased to over twelve million people at the turn of the century, a figure that should be compared with Germany's fifty-six million and France's thirty-eight million.

With new railroads, modernization of transport, and the telephone, distances diminished. The Oslo-Bergen line, which reached an elevation of 1,300 meters, was completed in 1909. The mining in the north of Sweden put new life into the economy; it also gave rise to a feeling that there were almost inexhaustible natural resources. The rising price of timber favored both Swedish and Finnish industry. In Denmark, the Schleswig War (1864) had resulted in the last of a series of military defeats. What followed was intensive reclamation of moor land and land won from the sea. Scandinavia shrank and stretched at the same time, both geographically and as a mental concept. The modern era, characterized by both nationalism and a belief in science and technology, had reached the north.

During the latter part of the nineteenth century, the labor movement became established in the Nordic countries—a movement which was to direct the course of society in the twentieth century. Its characteristics are the collaboration of the Social Democratic parties, the cooperative movement, and the fairly unified trade unions. In its early stages, social democracy was torn between revolutionary and parliamentary ideologies, but a few years into the new century Scandinavian social democracy, with its willingness to compromise, had taken form. As early as 1920, Sweden saw its first Social Democratic government, with the same formation coming into power in Denmark in 1924 and Norway in 1935.

The Norwegian independence from Sweden in 1905, Finnish opposition to Russia, and various social problems of the period are reflected in the cultural debate that occurred around the turn of the century. In the area of literature, the Danish literary historian, Georg Brandes, preceded the new era with his demand that literature should "put problems under debate" and thus be oriented toward contemporary questions and naturalism. Writers who dealt with problems in Brandes's sense were Henrik Ibsen and Björnstjerne Björnson (Nobel Prize winner) in Norway and August Strindberg in Sweden. In music we find nationalism mingling with political radicalism in the works of Edward Grieg, Carl Nielsen, Jean Sibelius, and Vilhelm Stenhammar. And in the fine arts the Nordic light animated a series of works that now are considered classical. Having been more or less assimilators in the cultural exchange until then, the Nordic countries displayed an impressive number of cultural figures in their own right, a factor of importance for both self-reflection and self-esteem.

The advance in science is particularly striking and exemplified in people such as the chemist Svante Arrhenius and the inventor Alfred Nobel (Sweden), the philosopher Harald Höffding and explorer Knud Rasmussen (Denmark), the explorer A. E. Nordenskiöld and the sociologist Edvard Westermark (Finland), the explorers Roald Amundsen and Frithiof Nansen and the meteorologist Vilhelm Bjerknes (Norway). The explorers, whose struggles against the arctic environment extended man's horizons as never before, were those who attracted the greatest attention. The organization of science gives evidence of similar advances at the turn of the century, as shown in the building of the "City of Science" in Stockholm and the various institutes of the Carlsberg Foundation in Copenhagen. The Nobel prizes, given since 1901, added money and status to science, the arts (literature), and internationalism (the peace prize). Thus, there were many good reasons to believe in progress when World War I changed conditions.

Except for Finland, Scandinavia was spared active involvement in the war. During the Finnish civil war, government forces received aid from Germany and the socialists received aid from Russian Bolsheviks; it ended with the victory of government troops under General Carl Gustaf Mannerheim in May 1918, and the following spring, Finland became an independent republic. The war years meant a general consolidation of social democracy in the Nordic countries, but they also meant the postponement of social improvements. Thus, universal suffrage was introduced in Finland in 1906, in Norway in 1913 (1898 for men), in Denmark in 1915, but not until 1918 in Sweden. In general, the end of the war involved a number of social changes in Scandinavia as in other parts of the world. Scandinavian eugenic laws belong to the interwar period, during the phase which, in this book, is called "reform eugenics" and connected with the beginning of the welfare state.

Swedish peace—in sharp contrast to the earlier history of the country—was put to the test in 1922 when the unpopular decision was taken to follow the recommendations of the League of Nations and let the Åland Islands become Finnish. In the 1920s the Universal Economic Conference was held in Stockholm, not only as a sign of the central position held by the archbishop and Nobel Prize winner Nathan Söderblom but also of the continued secularization of the country. The welfare state came to the forefront when P. A. Hansson, a Social Democrat, launched the concept of a "people's home" in 1928. The tranquil development in Sweden was not the least result of the harmony that came to characterize the relations between employers and trade unions, as in the basic agreement signed in 1938, regulating negotiations and strike actions. That other countries took an interest in Scandinavia is apparent. For instance, *Sweden: The Middle Way* (1935), by the American journalist Marquis Childs, had some influence on Roosevelt's New Deal, with its praise of Swedish welfare policies. A country with rational, organized education, light veneer or steel furniture, kindergartens, cleanliness, and order—that is how Sweden looked, at least from a distance.

Development in Denmark, under the direction of a strong Social Democratic party, more or less paralleled that of Sweden. As early as 1920, Minister of Justice (later Minister for Social Affairs) K. K. Steincke outlined the future welfare state. Transportation within this island kingdom was simplified by bridge constructions, making life easier for, among others, farmers. Agrarian products were, and are, fundamental for the Danish economy and the Danish "good life." Denmark was no doubt the least puritanical of the Scandinavian countries. The temperance movement never gained political power, and so, to the consternation of other Scandinavians, Danish women drank beer and smoked a cigar now and then.

Such extravagances were rare in Norway. Much less centralized, the economy depended on traditional agriculture—though Norway's geography allowed less than 3 percent of the total area for farm land. The fishing industry was, and is, important. Whaling in its modern phase is very much a Norwegian specialty. In the far north, Norway incorporated after international agreement the isles of Spitzbergen (Svalbard) in 1925. In contrast, in 1933 parts of east Greenland were lost through negotiations with Denmark. But, despite its distinct profile, Norway took part in the same social programs as the other Scandinavian countries.

In Finland, legislation was introduced in the 1920s stipulating public education, military service, and freedom in matters of belief. The Finnish-Swedish population nourished fond hopes of greater political freedom, which did not pay off but meant continual tensions with the Finnish nationalists. Between 1919 and 1934 a Prohibition Act was in force. In a new situation the old economic bonds with Russia remained a problem. Finland entered a non-aggression pact with the Soviet Union in 1932 but underlined in 1935 its Scandinavian orientation. This geographical duality, as well as Findland's being the one republic in Scandinavia, gave Finnish history its own dramatic individuality.

◆   ◆   ◆

The favorable Nordic development came to an abrupt end with the German occupation of Norway and Denmark on 9 April 1940; again, Sweden was spared active involvement in the war. Swedish neutrality could only be kept up by means of certain concessions to the superior German forces, however, such as allowing the transit of German troops through Sweden. On the other hand, Sweden provided humanitarian aid for its neighbors both during and after the war. Thus, practically the whole Jewish community (some 7,000) of Denmark escaped to Sweden in October 1943. In Norway, the Nazi regime under Vidkun Quisling left a bitter aftertaste, while in Denmark, the Danish Nazis were kept from political power—at the price of collaboration, however, which was extensive at times. All the same, it was only in the last phase of the war that the Germans and their Danish henchmen took over the state administration. In general, Nazism only attracted minor groups in the Nordic countries during the war years. Finland came to suffer much more, losing a large part of its male population in the devastating war against the Soviet Union in the winter of 1940. In the "War of Continuation," Finland allied itself with Germany; successful at first, it then had to cede large territories in eastern Karelia as well as the northerly Petsamo area in the peace of 1944, and pledge to pay substantial war reparations. The war went on into 1945 in the north, now against German troops—again, a complicated turn in Finnish history.

After the war, Scandinavia received aid through the Marshall Plan, and Norway and Denmark joined NATO. The discussion of a Nordic alliance, which had been lively at times, died out. Finnish foreign policy was characterized by careful balancing in the shadow of the Soviet Union; the two countries signed an Agreement of Friendship, Cooperation, and Mutual Assistance in 1948. Sweden continued on a neutral course, with economic ties to the Western world. Lately, discussions about joining the European Economic Community have been more and more intense, with Denmark in, Finland and Sweden entering, and Norway staying out. There were few employment restrictions for Scandinavians moving between the Nordic countries, but in the early 1990s the situation changed because of economic turbulence in Scandinavia as well as in Europe as a whole.

In the eyes of the rest of the world, Scandinavia probably still represents peace and prosperity. Its welfare program continued and accelerated after the war. People live longer and are wealthier than elsewhere. In many areas, the Nordic countries have come to stand for "quality"—Finnish glassware, Danish furniture, Swedish cars, and Norwegian scenery. While not altogether positive, concepts like Swedish and Danish (but not Norwegian) "sin" have become current; in fact, such conceptions can perhaps be traced to population policies of the kind that are described in this book. On the dark side is an exceptionally high suicide rate, especially in Sweden; this criticism is dismissed in Sweden, however, as based on an erroneous interpretation of statistics. One could argue that there are too many statistics and too much cold rationalism in the north—and answer that modern society and modern science are conjoined twins. All the same, in a world where the alternatives were often depicted in black and white, where East and West were seen as irreconcilable, the Scandinavian model often appeared as a reasonable middle course.

◆   ◆   ◆

Summing up and looking ahead, we could say that Sweden has enjoyed the most peaceful way through the twentieth century. Finland's history has been the most dramatic, while Norway has had the clearest "Nordic" profile and Denmark the most European. Iceland, far off in the Arctic, is a microcosm of its sister countries. The countries were wrenched apart during the wars, but that their affinity is still great will be apparent from the studies presented here. The purpose of this short introduction is simply to underline their common ground.

Here, then, is a brief summary of the themes in this book, some of which have already been hinted at: one is the importance of homogeneous geography and history for political and social solutions. Another is the effect of "middle-of-the-road" politics so typical for twentieth-century Scandinavia and the Nordic consensus which often makes pure political analysis uninteresting; a third is the role of science in the modernization of the Nordic countries, bringing about both economic prosperity and a particular "mentalité." Large-scale social experiments are typical of the welfare policies we are studying, making medical politics a "scientific" part of modernism in a sometimes risky way. Finally, the rather long perspectives in these essays clarify questions of continuity in eugenics and twentieth-century biomedical politics.

All in all, eugenics and sterilization policy are part of modern history and reflect important aspects of it in Scandinavia and the Western world. The history of eugenics is thus a challenging study, bringing together a number of themes connected with contemporary history and future development.

Something Rotten in the State of Denmark: Eugenics and the Ascent of the Welfare State

Bent Sigurd Hansen

How important it is to trace the development of eugenics in each Scandinavian country can be debated. Still, a reasonably good case can be made for examining Denmark, which in many ways offers useful contrasts to the other countries that so far have been studied in detail: the United States, Great Britain, and also, in recent years, Germany[1]—all countries that were great powers at the beginning of the century, and where eugenics had a considerable following.

The fact that a country considered itself a great power, or a power sliding from first to second rank, was in itself a factor that affected the development of eugenics. Certainly, the defeat of Germany in World War I strongly affected the German attitude toward eugenic measures; another example is the striving for "national efficiency" in Great Britain in the years before this war.[2] In contrast, Denmark was not, and did not aspire to be, a great power. Its last pretensions in this direction were lost, together with the fleet—and Norway—in the Napoleonic Wars, a conflict that literally bankrupted the country. And the area of Denmark was further depleted when Holstein and Schleswig were, in effect, ceded to Prussia after the Second Schleswig War (1864-66).

At the beginning of the twentieth century, Denmark was a country with a small homogeneous population, without the antagonism between different ethnic groups that influenced the eugenics movement in other countries. Denmark was the only Scandinavian country with colonies. But her West Indian colonies were transferred to the United States during World War I, and her remaining colony, Greenland, was so remote, so sparsely populated, and of such little economic importance, that its effect on Danish attitudes toward other races and peoples was negligible.[3]

After the first World War, during which Denmark remained neutral, the Social Democrats slowly gained ascendancy without violent political confrontations. Labor relations were also peaceful during the lean years immediately after the war, at least when compared to those in other European

9

countries. A kind of truce developed between the Social Democrats and the traditional parties of the center and right and, as a consequence, a large number of reform laws could be carried out during the 1920s and 1930s, not unanimously, but without violent confrontations. Chief among these laws was the great social reform law complex that marks the beginning of the Danish welfare state.

The preconditions that have been postulated for the development of the eugenics movement—ethnic antagonism, social unrest, conservative opposition to social relief—seem to have been absent, or only weakly represented in Denmark. Yet Denmark was the first European state to introduce national legislation concerning eugenic sterilization in 1929.

BIOLOGICAL DETERMINISM IN DENMARK: THE NINETEENTH CENTURY

Most of the powerful biological myths prevalent in the Western world in the nineteenth century can be found represented in Denmark. There was a general belief in the strong influence of heredity, coupled with an almost complete ignorance of actual genetic mechanisms. A picture of the confusion in this area can be gained from the prize-winning essay *Arvelighed og Moral* (Heredity and Morals), which appeared in 1881. The author, Karl Gjellerup, was not a scientist but a poet and novelist, who was later awarded a Nobel Prize in literature. Today, he is almost completely forgotten, even in Denmark. The essay was entirely derivative, with Prosper Lucas, Augustine Morel, Herbert Spencer, and Charles Darwin as main sources, and strongly influenced by a contemporary book by Théodule Ribot.[4] Much of the essay was anecdotal material, concerning alleged examples of what Ernst Mayr has called "soft inheritance,"[5] cases where heredity was supposed to have been directly influenced by the environment, the so-called Lamarckian heredity. Though not a professional scientist, on this point Gjellerup reflected the general consensus of contemporary medical and biological expertise.

A particular version of hereditary determinism, the belief in degeneration, was widely shared in Denmark. It was given scientific legitimacy by the French psychiatrist Augustine Morel, but the concept itself is much older. The psychiatrist Frederik Lange, who himself belonged to a well-known liberal, patrician family, introduced the ideas of Morel in his doctoral thesis of 1881.[6] His last book, published two decades later, reminisces about his experience as the leader of Middelfart Psychiatric Hospital, and is a strange and haunting description of the last representatives of the declining great families he observed.[7] More a work of art than a scientific treatise, it has been overshadowed by a work of fiction that conveyed the same melancholic impression, Herman Bang's *Håbløse Slægter* (Descendants Without Hope) published in 1882, a poignant, partly autobiographical, account of a young man who regards himself as the last degenerate member of such a declining family.[8] This theme was popular in nineteenth-century fiction, and other examples from Danish literature can be cited. Belief in degeneration, of course, presupposed belief in hereditary determinism, and, at the same time, belief in the—mostly negative—effects of bad behavior, drinking, sexual excesses and so on.

References to Darwin and Darwinism were widespread, but mostly in association with evolution in general and what Darwin himself called "descent with modification." Phrases such as "struggle for existence" and "survival of the fittest" were bandied about in the contemporary literature and applied, rather vaguely, to humans and human society. But no complete account of social Darwinism—selectionist ideas applied to social relations and social stratification—can be found before J. B. Haycraft's *Darwinism and Social Improvement* appeared in translation in 1894.[9] The main thesis of this work was that the most valuable parts of the population reproduced at the lowest rate, while the part of the population that was "inferior," mentally and physically, reproduced at the highest rate—the concept of differential reproduction. Furthermore, this tendency was characteristic of civilized, as opposed to "natural," society and was reinforced in particular by the progress in medicine and various types of social relief. References to Herbert Spencer, regarded by many as the original inventor of social Darwinism, can of course be found much earlier. But it is characteristic that a work from 1881, where he was one of the primary sources, used his ideas of a general organic evolution and connected these ideas with the German theories of the cell-state.[10] What has often simply been called Darwinism was, in Denmark, as in other countries, a confusing web of partly overlapping and partly conflicting biological ideas and myths.

Virtually all of the authors that used or referred to these ideas were regarded, and regarded themselves, as liberals or progressives. Many were radical followers of Georg Brandes, the great European literary critic, who was the leader of what has been called "the Modern Breakthrough" in Denmark—both a literary and a political movement directed against romanticism and reaction. A surprising number of the intellectuals attracted to biological determinism were also attracted to the ideas of Henry George. Gustav Bang, the major intellectual ideologue of the Danish Social Democrats, who at that time represented the extreme left in the political spectrum, wrote a doctoral thesis on the decline and degeneration of the old Danish nobility. Another young socialist intellectual arranged lectures for the workers of Copenhagen during the great lockout in

1899. And what were the lectures about? Darwin, Spencer, and Weismann, of course.[11] Denmark had its share of cultural pessimists, and they could find plenty to be pessimistic about, from the defeat in the Schleswig Wars and the subsequent loss of territory to the general decline in taste, literacy, and morals. But there were no examples of the blend of cultural pessimism, conservatism, chauvinism, and biological and racial determinism that could be found further south, nor of the exaltation of "Nordic" ideals combined with political reaction.

Physical Anthropology

A certain legitimating of this worship of the "Nordic" physical and mental type can be found in the discipline of physical anthropology, which had been established as a legitimate science in the last half of the nineteenth century with the Swede, Anders Retzius, as one of the founding fathers. A review of the development of this discipline in Scandinavia noted that Denmark was poorly represented compared to other Scandinavian countries, and attributed this to the generally mixed character of the Danish population that made studies of racial characteristics so unrewarding.[12] Most of the work that was done was statistical in nature, and several papers were very critical toward some of the accepted methods, in particular the use of the cranial index established by Retzius.[13]

Physical anthropology was never established as an independent scientific discipline at the university. A Danish anthropological committee was established in 1905 with the physician Søren Hansen, first as secretary, then as chairman of the committee. Søren Hansen was the closest Denmark came to a full-time physical anthropologist. He obtained grants to study physical anthropology, visited several of the famous European anthropologists, and published numerous works on physical anthropology. But the point is that he never actually had the opportunity to be a full-time anthropologist. He never achieved an academic position; he was forced to do his doctoral work in a completely different field and to support himself as a police doctor. In Denmark, physical anthropology never achieved the prestige it had in other countries.[14]

Physical anthropology could be regarded as the biological science about man, correlating physical and mental characteristics of the different races and types of man. Eugenics was defined by many as human biology, applied with special regard for future generations. So it was not surprising that there was a great overlap between physical anthropologists and eugenicists. Søren Hansen was only one of the many physical anthropologists who attended the First International Eugenics Conference, an experience that converted him to a prolific advocate of eugenics. But, as he was the only physical anthropologist in Denmark, he was almost the only eugenicist. One of the reasons for the absence of a more broadly based eugenics movement in Denmark might be the weak standing of physical anthropology.

Eugenics and the Institutions

Unfortunately, only a very small part of the literature on eugenics deals explicitly with institutions for the mentally retarded and the mentally ill—the hospitals, prisons, and schools—where an increasing number of these people were segregated from normal society. But institutional leaders were among the first to use eugenic arguments. Not only were the "inferior" kept in an isolated and protected environment where they could do no harm and could be put to some use, but they were also prevented from transmitting their "inferiority" to any progeny. Surgery for eugenic or partly eugenic purposes was first performed in the institutions, and it was the institutionalized groups who remained the primary target of eugenics legislation in most countries. Institutional staff occupied a unique position where they could provide the observations and the scientific data that justified eugenic measures, put the eugenic proposals into practice, and even evaluate the benefits of the eugenic measures they performed.[15]

In several cases the medical experts at the institutions challenged the existing legislation. In some cases they simply carried out sterilizing operations without the sanction of the law, as Edwin Hedman, the head of an institution for the mentally retarded in Finland, did in 1911. In Denmark, it was the leader of the institution for the mentally retarded in Thisted that, more cautiously, forwarded the first formal application for eugenic sterilization.[16]

Of course, the institutional leaders were also in a position where they could effectively block eugenic measures, if they disapproved of them for religious or humanitarian reasons. Certainly, the early sterilization data for the United States, as depicted in the surveys of Harry F. Laughlin and J. H. Landman, shows that institutions in the same state differed widely in the zeal with which they carried out sterilizations. This trend proceeded well into the 1950s, as the example of Sonoma State Home in California demonstrates.[17]

It is generally accepted that the first to carry out eugenic sterilization (vasectomy) was Harry Sharp, who performed these operations at the Jeffersonville State Prison in Indiana. But these first operations were performed primarily for non-eugenic purposes, namely, to suppress excessive masturbation. According to Sharp, the operation seemed to repress not only masturbation but also other kinds of sexual activity. He emphasized that the operation, as an additional benefit, would prevent reproduction.

Sharp carried out a large number of such operations even before 1907, when his experiences became the basis of a sterilization law in Indiana, the first modern eugenic sterilization law. It is interesting to note that virtually all experts since 1920 have claimed that the effects of vasectomy on sexuality are minor and mainly psychological. It could have been this psychological effect on the prisoners that Sharp observed; alternatively, he himself might have been deluded by his expectations.[18]

Even before Sharp's first operation in 1899, however, straightforward castrations had been performed at several institutions for the mentally retarded: at Elwyn in Pennsylvania under Isaac Kerlin and later under Martin W. Barr; in Winfield, Kansas, under F. Hoyt Pilcher, and in other American institutions.[19] Of Sharp, Barr wrote:

> Much distressed by the debasing habits rife among the children of this institution, and having exhausted every means of reformation through discipline, he, after consultation, castrated fifty-eight boys, with a resulting gain in almost every case of marked improvement both mental and physical.[20]

But, in all cases the immediate reason for the operation was masturbation. Revulsion toward the various kinds of emerging sexuality that were possible under the conditions imposed by the institutions made the radical intervention of the surgeon's knife acceptable. And, later, other benefits, among them the eugenic effects of asexualization, added to the rationale for the operation. No doubt the institutions for the mentally retarded, like many other organizations, were easier to run without the further complications of sexuality, but ironically, the problem that was solved by the operation was created by the very nature of the institution.[21]

Barr and his coworkers from Elwyn also submitted a law proposal dealing with the castration of the mentally retarded. They stressed the double advantage of the operation: both that the individual operated on became "more docile, more tractable . . . a gelding or an ox loses nothing but becomes in every respect more docile, more useful and better fitted for service" and that reproduction was prevented: "It must be remembered that these idiots always must be dependents . . . the state therefore has a right to act in place of a parent and also to take measures to prevent their propagation."[22] The eugenic benefits expected from this law can also be seen from the fact that Barr called it a proposal "for the prevention of idiocy." It was passed by both the legislative chambers of

Pennsylvania, but was then vetoed by the governor in 1904, to the great dismay of Barr.

In the same period, the psychiatrist and sexual reformer August Forel also experimented with castration at the psychiatric hospital of Burghölzli in Switzerland. The targets were violent patients, whose behavior he hoped to modify and control with the operation. It was also in the 1890s that the new operation ovariectomy, female castration, was used as a cure against hysteria by the inventor of the operation, the professor of obstetrics at Freiburg, Alfred Hegar.[23] Another example of this conjunction between mentally ill patients and radical interventionist surgery was the craniectomy operations that enjoyed a brief popularity. For some time, several eminent neurologists had maintained that mental retardations could be caused by a too early closing of the cranial sutures. Craniectomy, the reopening of these sutures, was suggested as a method to restore normalcy. The operation was widely promoted in the popular press, and in 1890 about fifty operations were undertaken in Europe and the United States. The operations were a dismal failure; about 15-25 percent of the patients did not survive the operations, and no significant improvement could be detected in the surviving group.[24]

During the last years of the nineteenth century, the utopian hopes of educating and essentially curing the mentally retarded had largely been abandoned. More and more, the institutions became places where the inmates were kept isolated from the rest of society, where they could be trained in certain skills according to the way they had been classified, and where a reasonable amount of work could be extracted from them, under humane conditions and for the benefit of society. The teacher and the amateur philanthropist became subordinate to the physician, the expert who could classify the mentally retarded and determine the extent of mental retardation, and subsequently the amount of instruction required.

The social niches where the mentally disabled could maintain an existence were slowly disappearing, and more and more people were being flushed out into a strange world where accelerating industrialization and urbanization made them helpless. The mentally retarded were no longer figures of fun; the old crude ways were disappearing, succeeded by the modern, "humanitarian" attitude—that they should be kept out of the way. The result was that pressure on the institutions increased; and to most observers, it appeared that the number of the mentally retarded was increasing.[25] Craniectomy meant that the last hope of curing the mentally retarded had to be abandoned; but other, less dangerous types of surgical intervention still held out the hope that the feared increase in their number could be checked.

THE INSTITUTIONS IN DENMARK—CHRISTIAN KELLER

At the turn of the century, the Danish institutions for the mentally retarded formed a small, close-knit community. They had all started out as privately funded philanthropic organizations, but now an increasing part of their budget was being provided by the state. They formed a loose organization, Abnormvæsenet (care of the abnormal), with the schools and institutions for the deaf and blind, but there was very little cooperation with the psychiatric institutions, which had much closer ties to the regular hospitals— and much higher prestige within the medical community.

The institutions for the mentally retarded were slowly being secularized and professionalized; physicians were gaining ascendancy as experts, while the philanthropic clergymen and the far-too-optimistic educators were being relegated to minor roles. Nevertheless, for a long time these institutions retained an old-fashioned, nonprofessional air compared to the regular medical world. Leadership of the institutions tended to run in families in a rather feudal way. The Keller family is a good example of this: the father and founder, Johan Keller, a philanthropic clergyman, had established institutions for the mentally retarded, the "Keller-institutions," which later were moved to Jutland, where the large modern institution Bregninge was founded. When he died, the institutions, at that time still officially private property, were divided up among his family, with the main responsibility resting with his son, Professor Christian Keller, who was to become the acknowledged leader in the field in Denmark. Other sons and relatives were put in charge of minor institutions. With these strong family ties in mind, it was perhaps not surprising that Christian Keller remained a convinced hereditarian all his life.[26]

Though these institutions remained isolated from the regular hospital world and the centers of medical research in Denmark, close links to similar institutions in other countries were maintained. There was widespread cooperation between the different Scandinavian institutions but also much contact with institutions in other countries. In many places, Bregninge was regarded as a model institution, and international visitors were frequent.

The Danish institutions were confronted directly with the problem of asexualization in 1897, when a group of doctors from Elwyn, headed by Dr. Barr, circulated a questionnaire on asexualization,[27] addressed to sixty-one institutions in the United States and Europe, including the Scandinavian countries:

1. In what proportion of the inmates of your institution do you consider procreation advisable?
2. In what proportion of the inmates of your institution do you consider procreation possible?
3. What would be the probable effect of asexualization upon their mental and moral condition?
4. What effect upon their physical condition?
5. What operation would you advise upon a male—removal of the testes, ligation of the cord, or ligation of the vas deferens?
6. What operation would you advise upon females?
7. At what age would the operation be most effective?
8. Have you had practical clinical experience in this matter?
9. Should a state law be enacted to legalize this operation? If so, what would you suggest in regard to such a law?[28]

Unfortunately, only twelve institutions responded, three European and no Scandinavian. When Christian Keller chose to comment on this reaction some years later in a short review of Barr's book *Mental Illness and Social Policy*, he suggested that one of the reasons for the poor response was that Europe did not have experience with operative asexualizations on a larger scale, but he also considered the possibility that Europeans were much more reticent toward asexualization and sexuality in general than the Americans:

> The American reasoning—that the already existing mentally retarded cannot be cured, and that all effort therefore should be directed towards inhibiting the production of a new generation of the mentally retarded—can probably obtain general approval in Europe. But the chosen road leaves the Europeans wondering and doubting, as long as one does not realize, that the American institutions to a large degree are dominated by "moral imbeciles" either with or without a defect in intelligence. With regard to the mentally retarded according to European usage, confinement—eventually for life— should be enough. Their role in the procreation of the race is not so important that it justifies the radical American therapy. We can get through with less.[29]

This negative reaction from the leading representative of the Danish institutions apparently caused some consternation on the other side of the Atlantic Ocean. Keller was answered by Dr. S. D. Risley in the *Journal of Psycho-Asthenics*, and in an editorial by Barr in the same issue.[30] Barr described his experience with eighty-eight cases of emasculation of the mentally disabled patients: violent and dangerous individuals became mild and docile; for the epileptics, seizures were considerably reduced; sexual "perversions"—not specified—disappeared, and sexuality as such was much reduced—obviously a good thing. Again, without using the word eugenics, Risley accurately summed up the eugenic point of view: the mentally retarded and the habitual criminal should not be allowed to perish according to the law of natural selection, but modern altruistic treatment of these unhappy persons should not include a free license to procreate. Society must be allowed to hinder their unlimited propagation which would lead to even more degenerate progeny. To this, Risley added that masturbation, widespread among the mentally retarded, was generally recognized as an ethiological factor in epilepsy, neurasthenia, and other nervous disorders. He also commented darkly on other aspects of the lack of sexual restraint among the mentally retarded. Asexualization, which in the case of Elwyn meant castration, could remove the troublesome sexuality and, at the same time solve the problem of the increasing number of the mentally retarded.

Risley and Barr were quoted extensively by Keller. He himself added only a brief comment on the pessimism and fatalism that characterized the American position, but he was not impressed and certainly not convinced by the American arguments.

Neither Keller nor anybody else from Abnormvæsenet chose to argue directly against asexualization. Perhaps it was self-evident to him and to others why internment was preferable to more radical measures; or perhaps he and others were simply reluctant to write about a subject so closely connected with human reproduction. Some years later, however, one of Keller's colleagues from Bregninge, Hother Scharling, brought up the subject again. Scharling accepted both the eugenic indication for asexualization and the other reason, the violent and unrepressed sexuality of some of the mentally retarded. He did not completely agree with Keller's abrupt rejection of the American practices, but he could not accept surgical castrations—the operation was far from harmless, particularly with regard to women (this was before antibiotics and contemporary statistics bore him out on this point). Furthermore, the operation might interfere with functions of the sexual glands other than the maintenance of reproductive capacity. Finally, he admitted to a certain revulsion toward the removal of a healthy functioning organ.[31]

Scharling touched on an important point. Castration, and particularly male castration, was a subject that was difficult to approach with a rational, enlightened spirit. Many people would regard it as mutilation, a barbaric penalty rather than a mere medical intervention; in principle, it was equivalent to the cutting off of an ear or a finger, only more cruel. Later critics of sterilization and castration used the same arguments repeatedly, and always it was male castration that seemed most objectionable.

Instead, Scharling advocated x-ray treatment for women and vasectomy for men. He found this operation "rather attractive" and no doubt less frightening than complete castration. He maintained that the operation did not interfere with sexuality, but he did not submit any references as proof. However, it is unlikely that his main source was Sharp, since Sharp's argument for the operation was exactly the reverse: that it did suppress sexuality.

In 1910 a young female physician working at Bregninge, Bodil Hjort, obtained a grant that allowed her to visit several of the more famous American institutions for the mentally retarded. Elwyn was among them, but probably her most important visit was to Vineland, Massachusetts, where Henry H. Goddard resided.

Several articles by and about Goddard subsequently appeared in *Nyt Tidsskrift for Abnormvæsenet*. The subject of eugenics was not mentioned directly, but heredity was emphasized as the most important factor in the etiology of mental retardation. Though the usual family trees made their appearance, Mendelian factors were not yet mentioned. In general, the influence of Goddard strengthened the scientific approach toward the mentally retarded, as could be seen in the use of advanced texts (for example, the Binet-Simon intelligence tests), strong emphasis on family research, and the introduction of advanced pedagogical methods. The important thing was to accurately determine the type and extent of mental retardation; then the amount of education could be adjusted accordingly.[32]

Goddard became one of the authorities most frequently quoted by the Danish eugenicists during the following decades, with the Kallikak family featured prominently. Although his work was seriously criticized during this period, and he himself admitted to misgivings about the strong hereditarian views in his earlier works, no Danish source has been found that reflects this criticism.[33]

The subject of eugenics was brought up again before a much broader audience at the 6th Nordic Conference on the Welfare of the Handicapped in 1912 in Helsinki. Edwin Hedman, leader of the Bertula institution for the mentally retarded near Helsinki, underlined the importance of eugenics in his speech. The Finnish psychiatrist Björkman argued strongly for sterilization as the only effective prophylactic against the threatening increase in the number of the mentally retarded. At the very end of the meeting, a third Finnish speaker, Professor Georg von Wendt, was scheduled to speak on "A theoretical view of defective-support, seen in the light of eugenics." According to Hedman, hardly an unbiased observer, the subject seemed incomprehensible to most of the audience, in particular to the numerous clergymen and those in the audience mainly concerned with the blind and the deaf. Not many registered that von Wendt, at the end of his speech, put forward a resolution calling for eugenics legislation, support of eugenic research, and commitment to the eugenic cause.[34]

Hedman later did his best to obtain support for this resolution in the pages of *Nyt Tidsskrift for Abnormvæsenet*. He received a negative reaction from Sweden. The leader of the Swedish delegation did not reject eugenics outright; instead he opposed the resolution for more formal reasons: this was outside the scope of the meeting, the participants had not been chosen for such a purpose, etc. Hedman did receive an enthusiastic reply from Bodil Hjort, but not the much more important endorsement of Professor Keller, who for the moment remained silent on the subject.[35]

There is no explanation for the strong interest in eugenics in Finland, which at that time enjoyed semi-autonomous status as a Russian principate. It is perhaps important that all the advocates of eugenics belonged to the Swedish-speaking minority.[36] In 1915 Hedman described eugenic operations that had been carried out at Bertula since 1912. The operations were vasectomies, performed on male inmates; the purpose of the operation was sterilization as well as a reduction of sexuality, just as originally recommended by Dr. Sharp.[37]

The period 1911-12 can be regarded as the first breakthrough for the eugenic ideas in Denmark. Apart from the meeting in Helsinki and the fresh impulses that Bodil Hjort brought to the institutions for the mentally retarded, the first Danish book on the subject appeared in 1912. This was *De Velbårne og de Belastede*, a slim tract by the dentist Alfred Bramsen, whose earlier production included similar works on correct diet and on the correct method of chewing. In 1913 August Forel's *The Sexual Question*, which also introduced the concept of eugenics, was translated.[38]

What was most important was probably that the anthropologist Søren Hansen, at that time promoted to chairman of the Danish anthropological committee, participated in the First International Eugenics Conference and returned a convinced eugenicist. From then on, he became almost a one-man eugenics movement. He gave interviews, lectured, and wrote, both to the specialist periodicals and the daily newspapers.[39] His writings touched on all aspects of human heredity, population science, and eugenics. He consistently campaigned for more scientific research into human heredity; among the projects he wanted support for was, naturally enough, his own anthropological laboratory, a collection of anthropological and genetic data that he had been accumulating and that he imagined would one day grow into a permanent general registration of all hereditary afflictions. (This goal was finally achieved when the Institute of Human Genetics was founded in 1938 under the leadership of Tage Kemp.[40])

When considering the eugenic methods that should be applied, Søren Hansen was much less consistent. In some of his earliest writings on the subject he seemed to favor sterilization—but in other contributions he pulled back and found it was still premature to consider this remedy. In the same way, he sometimes seemed to favor eugenically based restrictions on marriage, then later argued that marriage laws of this kind so easily could be circumvented that the eugenic effect was negligible. (The subject turned up in 1911 when the Interscandinavian Marriage Commission actually introduced the official use of the concept of eugenics in its very cautious recommendations.[41])

A persistent motive in Søren Hansen's writing was the declining birthrate. Since this decline took place among the best-educated and most intelligent groups, even a small decrease in the population might constitute a large decrease in its quality. For this reason, he also opposed any kind of birth control and even argued that the use and dissemination of contraceptive devices and methods should be legally restricted.[42]

In 1915, a supporter of eugenics, the educator Vilhelm Rasmussen, entered the Danish Parliament. He was a member of the Social Democrats, but in temper and conviction seemed closer to the radicals who had gathered around Georg Brandes at the end of the nineteenth century. He espoused a number of slightly outdated ideas like Darwinism and atheism and must have been something of an embarrassment to the former radicals who, at this moment, were leading the government (Brandes's brother was secretary of finance). Vilhelm Rasmussen was bright and had very advanced ideas, but unfortunately not very much common sense. He repeatedly annoyed his parliamentary colleagues, lecturing, pontificating, and digressing during the yearly budgetary debates. In him, eugenics had gained a spokesman, but perhaps not a very effective lobbyist.[43]

Nineteen-fifteen was also the year when Hedman again brought up the subject of eugenics in the pages of Nyt Tidsskrift for Abnormvæsenet by announcing that he had performed several vasectomies since 1912. He proceeded to prod and pressure his Danish colleagues, particularly Keller, to declare themselves for eugenics. There is evidence that, during this period, Keller was becoming convinced of the benefits of eugenics, but in public he remained silent.[44]

Two groups of patients particularly interested Keller. One was the dangerous and violent, sexually aggressive male, the other the female counterpart, the sexually irresponsible, promiscuous female. These two groups corresponded very well to the two types of surgical therapy that later were included in the Danish law of 1929. Males became the main target of castration, while females predominated in the group that was sterilized. For the latter group, one often gets the impression that this behavior in itself became one of the indications of mental deficiency; that poor and ignorant females ran a greater risk of being committed if they gave birth to too many illegitimate children or in other ways proved sexually active.

These two groups often ranged in the upper intellectual scale of mental deficiency. They were too active and too normal to be kept under strict supervision in a closed section of an institution, and if they were placed in open wards, they very often ran away and caused trouble, each in their fashion. Keller found the solution to the problem: an island, not too big and not too small, would accommodate each of these groups of troublemakers. Here they could walk freely among the surroundings, yet it was impossible to get away. He succeeded in securing such an island for the males in 1910 but was not able to obtain a similar island for the females until 1920, and, by that time, he had abandoned the idea that this or any other kind of isolation could be regarded as an alternative to castration and sterilization.[45]

Apart from these special categories of inmates, the biggest problems for the institutions were overcrowding and lack of space. So, beside the more distant idealistic goals of eugenics—reduction of the number of the mentally retarded and general improvement of the population—the surgical solution offered some immediate advantages to the institutions, including the possibility of releasing some of the inmates or at least relaxing the strict and expensive controls.

In 1917 Keller chose to translate a lecture by the famous Walter Fernald, superintendent of the Massachusetts School for the Feeble-Minded. He painted a dismal picture of the number of paupers, prostitutes, and criminals that could be characterized as the mentally retarded. To him, it was indisputable that the majority of the mentally retarded had inherited their defects—and they would go on multiplying, pampered and protected in our civilized society, if they were not segregated and ultimately sterilized.

This was, of course, the standard type of eugenic argument, not very different from the arguments of Barr and Risley in 1906. But this time Keller did not dismiss it with a few adverse remarks; he just let it stand. One of the consequences—perhaps not quite unintended—was that several people, including K. K. Steincke, took it to be Keller's own opinion.[46]

Then, in 1918, the leader of one of the smaller provincial institutions asked whether he was allowed to sterilize one of the inmates for eugenic reasons. The application was rejected. According to the authorities, this kind of operation could not be regarded as a normal therapeutic procedure, and it could not be allowed without special legislation. With this decision, Denmark joined the majority of the countries that had considered the question of eugenic sterilization. Only in some of the Swiss cantons was it accepted that eugenic sterilizations and castrations could be regarded as a part of the doctor's individual responsibility. It was with this background that in 1920 Christian Keller forwarded his application: on behalf of all the institutions for the mentally retarded, he asked that an expert commission be assembled to consider the question of their sterilization.[47]

WILHELM JOHANNSEN

Wilhelm Johannsen was not only the leading Danish expert in genetics, he was one of the principal architects of the new Mendelian genetics that arose after the rediscovery of Mendel's works at the turn of the century. Famous all over the world for his work on the pure lines of the brown bean, he also coined the expressions gene, genotype, and phenotype.

In his book, *Arvelighed i Historisk og Eksperimentel Belysning* (Heredity in historical and experimental light), published in 1917, Johannsen devoted a full chapter, forty pages, to the subject of eugenics. In the historical introduction, he mentioned Plato and his utopian eugenics, and he did not hide his distaste for the idea of "human stockbreeding plans with systematic control, fraudulently organized marriage lottery, abortion and exposure as eugenic measures—dreamers and fanatics from the prohibition and eugenics movements of our own period can see themselves as in a mirror."[48]

This negative attitude also pervaded the chapter that dealt directly with eugenics. Johannsen emphasized the fact that eugenic ideas had developed before the advent of modern genetics. For that reason the eugenic literature was full of outdated concepts such as stigmata, atavism, telegony, Lamarckian inheritance, and, not the least, the expressions degeneration and degenerate. He showed that the use of these terms could be traced back to Morel's theories and similar sources. Their use was extremely subjective and often implied a doubtful value judgment, and the application of these terms was particularly inappropriate when humans were compared to domesticated animals and plants. In that type of comparison—a favorite with many eugenicists—the term degenerate was used both to designate the supposedly weak and inferior human and organism (animal or plant) that had reverted from domesticated to the natural form—that is, in most respects, the superior organism.[49]

Johannsen made a distinction between Mendelian eugenics and what he called Galton eugenics, the eugenics of Pearson and his biometrical school.

When Johannsen published his work on beans, demonstrating that a stable genotype can correspond to a continuous variation in phenotype, Pearson regarded it as a personal insult and published a violent rejection of the work. Furthermore, when Johannsen visited England and asked to see Pearson, he received an arrogant reply. So Johannsen had no particular reason to be gentle in his criticism of Pearson and his colleagues when he provided several examples of how flawed arguments had led them to false conclusions. According to Johannsen, their use of sophisticated statistical techniques was meaningless as long as the data were collected on the basis of faulty and outdated ideas of inheritance. He also found Pearson's eugenic arguments callous in the extreme: "The whole idea of heredity is wrong . . . there is no reason to assume that the weak and the sickly would represent the genetically inferior stock—they might be individuals possessing the same value as children from higher social classes, who are better cared for."[50]

But Johannsen also expressed skepticism toward the attitude of the Mendelian eugenicists. He especially criticized Charles Davenport for trying to fit all the different kinds of pathological symptoms into simple patterns of dominant or recessive inheritance. Since these symptoms, in most cases, could be regarded as an interaction between the genotype and the surrounding conditions, they should not automatically be treated as hereditary units or unit-characters. The distinction between genotype and phenotype provided his main arguments against eugenics. The genotype could not always be derived from the phenotype, not even in cases where one looked at only a single set of characters with a simple pattern of inheritance. How much more difficult then to make estimates of the genotype, when so little was known of human genetics in general and of the inheritance of mental illness in particular.[51]

And then there might be cases of false inheritance: transfer of some pathological trait in a manner that mimicked true heredity but in reality represented a completely different mechanism. This was one of Johannsen's favorite subjects, and for several pages he tried to demonstrate that the familiar examples of the transfer of alcoholism in families and the degeneration of family lines due to alcoholism represented instances of false inheritance.[52]

Johannsen's arguments were only partly technical. In many cases he applied common sense arguments, appealing to the reader's own experiences from daily life. And he tried to make even the more technical arguments easy to understand by illustrative examples, often from plant physiology, his original specialty:

various hereditary malformations in some poppies can be avoided if the earth is changed for the young plants . . . we are here contemplating a sensitive period during the development where the surrounding conditions have a decisive influence on the phenotype acquired by the individual. A closer investigation of these matters does not exist for humans, but we are approaching the problem of education.[53]

Johannsen was very much against all attempts to favor the propagation of the "better, healthier, nobler—in short, ideal members of humanity. But what is the ideal? Who shall be responsible for the decision? The complexity of society makes it impossible that one single human type should be the best. We need all different types of humanity."[54]

This was what he called positive eugenics. He was more inclined to accept negative eugenics, where the procreation of individuals with strongly flawed genotypes was inhibited. But he emphasized that it would be very difficult and complicated to carry this out in a responsible fashion. He certainly did not approve of "the haphazard surgical sterilization methods" applied in the United States:

> There can be no doubt that negative eugenics has a future. That will come when first the medical profession accepts the responsibility and tries to cover all the different aspects. But a general legislation will easily be premature and might cause much unhappiness and injustice. Legitimate individual rights are here irrevocably opposed to the interests of society as a whole.[55]

It is tempting to cast Johannsen as the chief adversary of eugenics in Denmark because of his polemics against the eugenicists. Yet, as we have seen, he was not opposed to eugenics as a whole but to the part of eugenics that was founded on wrong or outdated ideas. Thus, when he joined the Permanent International Commission on Eugenics in 1923, his membership was not inconsistent with his views. One of the most active members of the commission, the Norwegian Jon Alfred Mjöen, celebrated it as a great triumph. According to a review of Scandinavian eugenics written by Mjöen in *Nationalsozialistische Monatshefte* in 1930, Johannsen experienced a complete conversion, and from then on defended eugenics with the same zeal as he had attacked it.[56] Mjöen is not a particularly truthful or reliable witness, and the written sources certainly give no indication of this sudden conversion.

What we do know is that in these years Johannsen became more involved with eugenics and human genetics. In 1922 he assumed responsibility for a special government grant that would cover the preliminary investigation of the possibility of establishing Danish research in "human genetics and eugenics."[57] The first example of Danish eugenics legislation, the marriage law, was carried through in 1922, and other forms of eugenics legislation were being considered. In 1924 Johannsen actually was asked to join the commission on castration and sterilization, and accepted. With this development in mind, it was a clear advantage to have a Danish member of the International Commission on Eugenics, and Johannsen was the obvious choice.

In Johannsen's writings on eugenics in the 1920s he hardly appears as a zealot for the cause. He toned down his criticism of the biometrical school but devoted some effort to demonstrating how little effect even very strict selection would have on recessive genetic diseases. He still rejected what he called positive eugenics but found negative eugenics acceptable, when it was applied with caution.[58] The same attitude is apparent in his contributions to the negotiations of the commission on castration and sterilization.[59]

DANISH GENETICISTS AND EUGENICS

Several other Danish scientists were interested in genetics and eugenics. The pathologist Oluf Thomsen introduced human genetics into the medical curriculum and also did research into the inheritance of blood types. After Johannsen's death, Thomsen took over the responsibility for the university grant set up to establish research in genetics and eugenics in Denmark. He became deeply involved in the negotiations with the Rockefeller Foundation that eventually led to the establishment of the University Institute of Human Genetics in 1938. It was also Thomsen who, earlier, had handpicked Tage Kemp as the prospective leader of Danish research into human genetics. The psychiatrist August Wimmer was among the first to introduce the concept of eugenics in Denmark, but not without a certain skepticism; and he attempted Mendelian analysis of mental illnesses as early as 1920.[60] In 1918 and 1922 he represented Denmark in the Permanent International Commission on Eugenics. Both Thomsen and Wimmer were convinced hereditarians. Thomsen was much impressed by the works of the German criminologist Johannes Lange, but both were initially skeptical about eugenics. On the sterilization commission, Wimmer—like Johannsen—seems to have been a moderating influence; but later he came out strongly in favor of eugenic measures, and Thomsen also argued in favor of eugenics at the beginning of the 1930s. Wimmer played an important role as a member of the medico-legal council, where he was able to influence the revision of the sterilization legislation in 1935 as well as participate in the decisions on individual sterilization cases.

After Johannsen's death, the mycologist Øivind Winge was regarded as the leading Danish geneticist. He came out in favor of eugenics in the 1930s, when the Danish sterilization law was revised, but his textbook and other publications contained very little about human genetics and eugenics.[61]

The psychiatrist Jens Christian Smith should also be mentioned. He cooperated with Johannsen in a short paper on the connection between alcohol and heredity, a paper that argued against the widespread belief in hereditary degeneration caused by alcohol. The paper did not directly attack eugenics, but it attacked people like August Forel and Agnes Blum, who were well-known eugenicists. Considering the well-established connection between the propaganda for teetotalism, prohibition, and eugenics, this review could be regarded as another, more oblique attack against the exaggerated propaganda for eugenics, but not against the eugenic principle itself. Smith was also responsible for the first genetic investigation of twins in Denmark and published several papers on the inheritance of mental illnesses. Later he became the genetic expert on a special board that ruled on sterilization of the mentally retarded, a powerful position where he became responsible for the major portion of eugenic sterilizations in Denmark in the years prior to World War II. From his surveys of these sterilizations it was clear that eugenic considerations played a major role, and he also argued for the introduction of a more undisguised eugenic indication in connection with the sterilization of the mentally retarded. Though Smith never seems to have been involved in the political side of the eugenics issue, it was he, together with the institutional leaders, who shaped the eugenics policy that would be carried out within the framework of the law of 1934 concerning the mentally retarded.[62]

K. K. STEINCKE, THE POLITICIAN

The professionalization of the institutions was only one example of a general trend in the social sector, where the philanthropist, the amateur busybody, and do-gooder—often with ecclesiastical affiliations—gave way to the professionals: the physicians, of course, but also the professional reformer, planner, and administrator. As noted, it was a change that took place at a different pace in different parts of the social system; and there were great differences between the Scandinavian countries, with Denmark as the most secularized, and—for obvious geographical reasons—the most centralized.

K. K. Steincke was one of the new breed of administrators. As a young man, he had joined the Social Democrats when they were still regarded as a party of uncouth trade unionists. He was one of the few intellectuals in the party at that time, but unlike most of them, he always identified with the reformist wing of the party. When he obtained his law degree, he started out by administering municipal poor relief and made a spectacular career at a time when membership in the Social Democrats still constituted a handicap for a civil servant. The Byzantine system of poor relief, with its numerous different boards and its jungle of paragraphs, made a strong impression on him, and in 1920 he single-handedly produced a blueprint for a general streamlining and rationalization of the social sector, *Fremtidens Forsørgelsesvæsen* (Social relief of the future), in reality, a general outline of the coming welfare state.[63]

Of the 200 pages that constituted the book, twenty-eight pages were devoted to eugenics. And Steincke was not a recent convert to the cause. He was a hereditarian from the beginning, pontificating about population theory, Malthusianism, and the dangers of differential reproduction, in *Socialisten,* the monthly review for socialist intellectuals. He believed that the duty of the more intelligent part of the population—a group in which he definitely included himself—was to produce as much progeny as reasonably possible, at least more than the average two children which he believed to be a bane to civilized society.

Practicing what he preached, he consulted a specialist, the psychiatrist August Wimmer, before his own marriage in 1907. He was worried about a neurasthenic strain running in his own family; but Wimmer, sensibly enough, advised him to go on with the marriage. The sound peasant stock of his fiancée would more than compensate for his own nervous frailties. So Steincke married and subsequently went on to father five children, doing his part against the dangers of differential reproduction.[64]

The most important foreign source for Steincke's book was Geza von Hoffman's *Die Rassenhygiene in den Vereignigten Staaten von Nordamerika,* a glowing recommendation of American eugenic practices. He also quoted Søren Hansen's *Retten og Racehygiejnen* (Eugenics and law) from Denmark; and he quoted extensively from *Biologiske Causerier* (Biological essays) by the Swedish author Robert Larsson, an entertaining little book, translated into Danish in 1918, that popularized most of the recent advances in genetics but also came down firmly on the side of eugenics.[65]

But Steincke was also strongly influenced by Wilhelm Johannsen. A large part of the chapter on eugenics is simply a paraphrase of Johannsen's negative views on Darwinian selection, his rejection of Lamarckian inheritance, his criticism of the prevailing myths regarding the connection between alcoholism and heredity, and his account of Mendelian genetics and the fundamental difference between genotype and phenotype. No wonder this chapter met with Johannsen's approval.

Steincke also paraphrased many of Johannsen's critical remarks against eugenics. Still he made no attempt to reconcile the violently conflicting views of Johannsen and Geza von Hoffman and the other eugenicists he quoted. He started by introducing the concept of eugenics and the American experience, echoing the views of von Hoffman. H followed with a remark to the effect that there is some truth in this, but it might be exaggerated, and then switched to the views of Johannsen. The effect is that Steincke, after the first reading, appears moderate and cautious, critical toward the extreme eugenicists, but nevertheless convinced that eugenic measures will be important and necessary. Undoubtedly, this was how Steincke saw himself, but the overall result was an impressive piece of eugenic propaganda. Only a close reading reveals that Steincke in fact accepted the eugenic premises completely, a position very far from Johannsen's skepticism.

Steincke and most of the Danish followers of eugenics can be regarded as moderate or "reform" eugenicists, since they openly stated that they disapproved of the more violent eugenics propaganda and of the early American practice of sterilization, particularly as it was done in California. But when we take a closer look at their views—the belief in horror stories about the "Jukes" and the "Kallikaks," the acceptance of the dangers of differential reproduction, and their uncritical hereditarianism—they do not appear particularly moderate.

However, Steincke differed from the more extreme eugenicists in one way. He did not regard eugenics as an alternative to social relief and social legislation. Rather, he regarded the two concepts as complementary. Just to abandon the unfit and helpless would be callous; allowing them to breed unhindered would be folly—but eugenics solved the problem. You could afford to be humane and generous toward them, feed them and clothe them, as long as eugenic measures ensured that they did not increase in number. Steincke was a self-proclaimed anti-Darwinist, more or less because he identified Darwinism with social Darwinism; but though he did not accept the social Darwinist conclusion that selection should be allowed to proceed unhindered by social legislation, it appears that he accepted the premise that social relief in itself was dysgenic, harmful for future populations.

Steincke also differed from the extremists in his view on the value of eugenic propaganda:

> Now when some people regret that the great part of the population is too ignorant to be interested in eugenics, then I am tempted to regard it as a big advantage. For could anything be more fatal to both a responsible effectuation of the sensible part of these ideas (the practice steps toward future race improvement) and to maintaining a

healthy outlook among the population, with conservation of the ethical values—than if large segments of the population became infatuated with eugenics.

If we shall advance in a responsible way, it has to be on an irreproachable scientific basis, free from emotions, agitation and stockbreeding arguments; whereas these ideas, freely disseminated and discussed in newspapers and at public meetings, doubtless would have a brutalizing effect, when the prevailing intellectual level of the population is taken into consideration.[66]

These sentiments were not uncommon at the time, yet it is surprising to find them expressed by a Social Democrat and politician. Though Steincke was a great seeker of publicity for himself, he maintained, through his long political career, that the majority of the population was stupid and ignorant, and that the mass media were sensational and corrupting. This attitude also contained a strong puritanical element. Interference with reproduction was still, in 1920, a delicate matter, not something to be bandied about in the press and on every street corner. This puritanism also influenced his attitude toward eugenics and sterilization. If he disapproved of sexual license, then he was revolted by "the bestial scenes that take place in the mental hospitals and the asylums" as well as the "horrible and saddening examples of the unlimited breeding that takes place among the inferior strata."

The revolting acts and their equally revolting consequences were fused together in an emotional argument for eugenics. This extreme revulsion at the thought of the sexual activity of the mentally retarded has already been mentioned in connection with the first American castrations. Sentiments similar to Steincke's can be found among his fellow eugenicists and in many other contemporary sources. In these cases, sterilization, the surgeon's knife, could not be regarded as inhumanity; true inhumanity would be to disregard "the unhappy descendants . . . allowing all kinds of irresponsible and defective individuals to propagate freely. . . ."[67]

Eugenics was necessary, but had to be left to the experts. Therefore, Steincke's final suggestion was that a special commission should be set up consisting of representatives of the various institutions—the medical, legal, and genetic experts. This idea was not new; similar suggestions had been put forward since 1915 by Vilhelm Rasmussen. But Steincke carried more weight than Rasmussen, both within the Social Democratic Party and in general; and he had also chosen a more opportune moment. In 1920 Keller had forwarded an official proposal, similar to Steincke's, on behalf of the Danish institutions for the mentally retarded; in that same year, radical surgical solutions to social problems were put forward from another front.

THE WOMEN'S PETITION

In his application, Keller had not specified the exact character of the asexualization operation but left it to the medical experts. While this application was still pending, the parliament received a petition, signed by more than 100,000 people from the Women's National Council which was much concerned with the increase in the number of sexual offenses.

Whether, as these women claimed, there had been an actual increase in sexual offenses is still unclear; perhaps only the number of reported cases was increasing as society became more civilized and genteel. But the distinction between the dangerous, violent sexual offender and more harmless exhibitionist types was hopelessly confused in the subsequent discussion. The women regarded the offenders, in particular the recidivists, as a perpetual threat to women and children, and they wanted something done about it. They were not interested in draconian or spiteful solutions, for they were not out for revenge but wanted something that could neutralize the offenders permanently; here, castration was mentioned as an alternative to internment for life.[68]

It was still a daring thing for a woman to give public support to a demand for asexualization, and those who signed the petition were not extremists and fanatics, but members of the solidly middle-class core of the Danish women's movement. Some physicians—such as the prison doctor Georg C. Schrøder—also supported them, but the public prosecutor August Goll had grave reservations, as did other legal experts. The whole problem was referred to the commission on criminal law reform (the third since 1905). This commission again asked for advice from the medico-legal council (which counted August Wimmer among its members); it was told that only castration would be of any use toward sexual offenders, and that the unpredictable side effects of this operation made the medical experts regard it in a very negative light.

Consequently, the commission gave a negative reply. It could not recommend castration as a penalty or as a substitute for a penalty. In his thoughtful review of the problem, August Goll left a door open. The commission had not ruled out castration in all cases; it had just rejected it as a part of criminal law. Use of this and other operations in a medical and social framework was not excluded by the decision.[69]

This same year, 1923, actually saw the first Danish example of eugenics legislation. The mentally retarded and the seriously mentally ill would have to obtain permission from the minister of justice in order to marry. Though the law could be seen as an inducement to live together without a marriage license, still a very serious thing at that time, there were not many protests. If any party could be regarded as the eugenics party, it was the Social Democrats, but the government accepted the recommendations of the experts.

"Social Measures" and "Degeneratively Disposed Individuals"

In 1924 the first Social Democratic government took office. The secretary of justice was K. K. Steincke, and he soon succeeded in putting together a commission in accordance with the principles he had outlined in 1920. The commission was to consider Christian Keller's request regarding sterilization of the mentally retarded, as well as the castration of certain groups of sexual offenders.

As Steincke had suggested in 1920, the commission included physicians, scientists, and legal experts. Wilhelm Johannsen represented the legal expertise together with the psychiatrist August Wimmer. Christian Keller became a member of the commission, and another member, the physician Estrid Hein, had close links to the Women's National Council, even though she officially represented expertise in social insurance. Therefore, both groups that had pressured for radical surgical procedures were represented on the commission. Denmark's greatest expert on reproductive endocrinology, the physician Knud Sand, was not originally a full member of the commission but functioned as its secretary. He joined the commission as a full member when he became a full professor in forensic science. Along with Keller, five members of the commission represented institutions concerned with various deviant groups. There were four physicians and four legal experts, including August Goll. The only politician, and the only member that could be regarded as a layman, was the mayor of Copenhagen, a peaceful, elderly Social Democrat who was not likely to disagree with this awesome collection of experts. As it turned out, he certainly had fewer misgivings about sterilization than Johannsen and Wimmer, the experts in genetics.

The report from the commission was finished and published in 1926. Today, the title of the report seems curiously euphemistic: *Betænkning Angående Sociale Foranstaltninger Overfor Degenerativt Bestemte Personer* (Social measures toward degeneratively predisposed individuals). After all, the subjects were castration and surgical sterilization, eminently biological forms of intervention—which of course could have various social effects. Deliberate dissimulation was probably not intended, but "social" was just a handy, vague phrase that could be used to cover a variety of purposes, including those intended by eugenics. On the other hand, it was probably intentional that the phrases sterilization and castration were not used in the title.[70]

"Degeneratively" could not be considered a very happy choice. It had no precise meaning in human genetics. "Degenerate" was used popularly as a catch-all, covering everything from declining nobility to the mentally retarded, and very often used to designate unorthodox sexual behavior. In any case, it was confusing that the commission was considering two very different types of surgical operations, with very different effects, directed against different groups. The ambiguous title of the report only increased the confusion and reinforced the popular opinion that all sexual offenders were genetically afflicted or that all the mentally retarded were potential sexual offenders. It was Johannsen who argued against using the word "degenerate" and instead had suggested "degeneratively afflicted." Initially, this caused more confusion, since some members of the commission took it to mean that all carriers of afflicted genes should be considered targets of the legislation; and for the layman, "degeneratively" still carried the same connotations as "degenerate."

Most of the report consisted of factual information. A large section reviewed the law, proposals, and reports concerning eugenics in other countries. Characteristically, the Danish commission could draw not only on American or Swiss experience, but also on government reports from Norway, Finland, and Sweden, for Denmark was the last of the Scandinavian countries to consider the sterilization question in detail. In the United States, the survey of Harry F. Laughlin in 1922 demonstrated that the situation there was much more complicated than described by Geza von Hoffmann and other propagandists; several laws had been repealed, found unconstitutional, or been very difficult to administer.

In the two sections of the report written by the genetic specialists, Wilhelm Johannsen reviewed Mendelian genetics in general, and August Wimmer, the heredity of mental illness, including mental retardation.

Johannsen's contribution contained his usual mixture of moderation and common sense. Again he emphasized the distinction between genotype and phenotype, and the consequences for eugenics—that manifest abnormal individuals could be genetically healthy and, conversely, that seemingly normal and healthy people could be genetically afflicted. He briefly tried to illustrate the numerical relationship between the afflicted and the carriers of a recessive disease: if only one in ten thousand was afflicted, carrying two copies of the harmful gene, then one in one hundred would be carrying one copy of the gene and be normal and healthy. This was in fact a very brief summation of what is known today as the Hardy-Weinberg rule, and the consequences for human genetics had been realized by several Mendelians, notably by R. C. Punnet in 1917; but it was not discussed in most of the contemporary eugenics literature, and it was also absent from the Danish writings on eugenics.[71] Johannsen concluded: "Calculation of this type demonstrates in a disquieting fashion the extent of the genotypical deficiencies in the population; and it shows the enormous difficulties inherent in carrying out eugenic measures. It is one thing to attempt to change the race, but an entirely different thing to intern and sterilize people with a degenerative phenotype in order to keep them from doing any harm to society."[72] So Johannsen did not rule out sterilization but emphasized that the purely eugenic benefits of the operation would be very small.

August Wimmer listed the different types of mental disorders and the type and pattern of inheritance that they followed. According to him and his sources—no references were given—the manic-depressive psychosis followed a well-defined pattern close to the dominant mode of inheritance. Schizophrenia exhibited a much more complex picture because no direct inheritance from parent to progeny could be detected, while uncles, aunts, and siblings often exhibited the disorder. Wimmer concluded that schizophrenia showed an "extremely recessive" mode of inheritance. Epileptics, the mentally retarded, and psychopaths did not as groups exhibit well-defined patterns, yet his conclusion was that at least in some cases these afflictions were inherited: the majority of the psychopaths had probably inherited their "defects," while perhaps only a small percentage of the epileptic cases observed were hereditary in character. For the mentally retarded he referred to a Danish survey—probably the observations of H. O. Wildenskov that were published in an extended version in 1931—where the conclusion had been that about 50 percent of the cases were inherited, but he also noted that recent German sources gave lower numbers. For these three groups he concluded that the total amount of mental illness in the family should be taken into account.

He finished his survey with a cryptic paragraph:

> For mental defectives, habitual psychopaths, and epileptics, the limited possibilities of a general hereditary prognosis should be evident. But it must be emphasized for these, as for the well-defined disorders, that estimates over the more theoretical possibilities not in practice have to be decisive or relevant, for example, with regard to eugenic measures. It is the balanced judgment in the concrete cases that must be of importance. And with the necessary regard for all the individual facts, evaluated on the basis of our general knowledge of the laws of heredity, one should in many cases be able to reach a decision with such a degree of probability that it should be justified to use it as a basis for certain eugenic measures, including sterilization if necessary.[73]

It is not very clear what Wimmer was trying to say here, or what he meant by "theoretical," "in practice," and "balanced judgment." But what worried him was the lack of certainty in the genetic prognosis. Should a decision be reached based on probabilities and could this be explained to the public? The only thing that was clear was that Wimmer, after listing all the doubt and all the difficulties, reluctantly came down on the side of an active, negative eugenics, i.e., sterilization.

From all these deliberations the commission concluded that what it called "legislation directed towards a general racial improvement" was not feasible at the time. Sterilization and other types of eugenic measures directed against the procreation of certain classes of the phenotypically afflicted—it again used the expression "degeneratively" disposed—would not significantly decrease these afflictions. On the other hand, the commision held, it should be legitimate to sterilize certain groups, including mentally ill persons who were incapable of raising and educating their progeny under acceptable conditions, progeny that also had a great probability of being genetically harmed:

> Such a progeny, badly equipped from birth and equally badly raised, would often be predestined to a dismal existence, a burden to themselves and to society, not contributing anything of value to the common good, on the contrary representing a heavy social load on society, and a reservoir of prostitution, crime and shiftlessness.[74]

Clearly, in the commission's view, society was better off without these people. By suggesting this mixed social and eugenic indication for sterilization, the commission dodged a very important argument against eugenic sterilization: the fact that it was difficult to distinguish with any certainty the genetically sound from people with a flawed genotype, a fact that Johannsen had pointed out and one that had worried Wimmer. Given a purely eugenic indication for sterilization, it would have been necessary either to lie about the certainty of the genetic prognosis or to introduce the concept of probability into the legislation, a difficult thing to explain properly or perhaps even to justify. But now, instead of saying that a woman would have a 50 percent probability of giving birth to mentally retarded children, one could argue in this fashion, following the commission: this woman is slightly mentally retarded, shiftless, lazy, and sexually promiscuous; clearly, she will be unable to raise the children who may also become mentally retarded. In this way eugenic considerations were let in through the backdoor, though "legislation directed towards a general racial improvement" was rejected.

The commission suggested further restrictions. Sterilization should be limited to people confined to institutions. This was not strictly logical, since this group already was subjected to a fair dose of control, enough to make procreation a difficult affair. And even if pregnancy occasionally occurred at these places, this was hardly the group that constituted "a reservoir of prostitution, crime, and shiftlessness." However, when sterilization was introduced at the institutions, supervision and control could be relaxed and the load on institutional resources reduced. Furthermore, sterilization of citizens leading a normal life would have been much more controversial than sterilization at these remote places.

The other half of the same law proposal covered castration. It was suggested that sexual offenders could be castrated if their sexual disposition was so strong or so abnormal that repeated offenses were to be expected, and if they or their guardians applied voluntarily. No distinction between violent sexual offenders and other types, such as homosexuals and exhibitionists, was made in the proposal (and this continued to be the case both in the final text of the law of 1929 and in the subsequent, revised law of 1935), and several individuals from this latter category were sterilized according to the law in the following years. The proposal distinguished between castration (for sexual offenders) and sterilization (for social and partly eugenic reasons), but the public continued to confuse the two concepts. This was not surprising given the preoccupation with the sexuality of the mentally retarded in the discussion of eugenics.

It was also proposed that the law was to be regarded as an experimental law, scheduled to be valid for at most five years before revision. Perhaps for this reason the applications for sterilization had to follow a rather complicated route before a decision could be reached. The secretary of justice had to give every case his approval, and, prior to that, two authorities, the medico-legal council and the department of health, had to give recommendations. The doctor in charge of the institution or the local medical officer had to forward the application; and in all cases where the persons to be sterilized could understand the effect of the operation, they had to give their consent. If they were unable to understand it, a special guardian acting on their behalf had to be appointed.

With respect to the indications for sterilization, that is, the types of mental illness and their severity, the text of the law provided no details. Of course the original report gave some advice, but there was much room for interpretation and only advice was offered, not specific guidelines. In effect, the doctors forwarding the application, those from the medico-legal council and the health department, were free to formulate their own rules, with the minister of justice as the only controlling party.

The voluntary character of the sterilization or castration operations was not questioned (neither in the proposal nor in the definitive law text). This aspect of the law was later regarded as one of the fundamental differences separating it from the German law "Zu Verhütung Erbkranken Nachwuchses" passed in 1933.[75] But what does it really mean that an act is voluntary? Completely free will is not present when one is in a school, a military camp, a prison, or a similar institution. A person may be asked to make his or her own decisions, but if those decisions are not made in accordance with the powers that be, that person will sooner or later have to face the consequences. And who, in this case were the people expected to reach such a complicated decision? They were not even average ignorant laymen, but people who were seriously mentally disturbed or who had marked difficulties of comprehension. Nevertheless, they were expected to stand up to the considerable authority invested in the medical profession as well as the very real pressures of their confinement.

PARLIAMENTARY DEBATES AND THE PASSING OF THE STERILIZATION LAW

Though the commission's report with the proposal for the law appeared in 1926, political complications, unconnected with the problems of eugenics and sterilization, delayed the final approval of the law to 1929. The Social Democrats stepped down in 1926 and were followed by a government of the Agrarian Party, Venstre. This was the last government in Denmark to represent the landed interests, and it has generally been regarded as the most reactionary government in the twentieth century. But when first the new government had been established, the progress of the sterilization and castration law was not impeded, demonstrating the bipartisan character of the issue. As far as the record shows, the only really convinced eugenicists in the Danish Parliament were K. K. Steincke and Vilhelm Rasmussen, now in opposition, and Steincke frequently complained about the lack of interest in eugenics among his fellow politicians. What in particular irritated him was the indifference of the members of the Agrarian Party; they especially should know the value of good stock and sensible breeding. Their indifference was not due, however, to any underlying aversion, and the great majority of the Danish Parliament accepted the arguments of the experts and eventually was convinced.

The debate in the Parliament in 1928 shows that the only real opposition came from a very small group within the Conservative Party—led by the young clergyman Alfred Bindslev. He was one of the young Conservatives who had gathered around the movement called Det Unge Danmark (The Young Denmark), and for a period he had been editor of the movement's periodical *den Ny Tid* (The New Times). He was also a popular priest in Copenhagen and something of a society figure. In his attack on the law, Bindslev succeeded in touching on a number of sore spots:

> I would recommend, on behalf of a minority within my own party, that Parliament not approve this legislation because of the instinctive aversion that one experiences towards this type of experiment, whicht interferes with the most secret riddles of life itself; and also because knowledge still has not advanced further than the experimental stage with respect to eugenics. We know too little about these things; we have not yet thoroughly explored the human world, nor the human psyche.[76]

Bindslev also quoted the statement by Wimmer about the limited amount of knowledge concerning the different kinds of mental illness. And he reserved his strongest attack for the part of the law dealing with castration.

The minister of health and welfare answered that the law actually showed great restraint; it was formulated as an experimental law with a limited duration precisely because so little was known. He stated emphatically that it could not be regarded as a eugenics law, a law that used eugenic indications for sterilization. Several other speakers used the same argument. A similar interpretation was offered by August Goll, the director of public prosecutions who had been a member of the commission.[77]

It was true that the commission had emphasized that "legislation directed toward a general racial improvement" was not feasible at the moment. Nor did the word "eugenic" appear in the text of the law. It was not directly stated in the law that people could be sterilized for eugenic reasons; instead, the following words were used: " . . . where suppression of reproduction must be regarded as being of great importance to society." Certainly, however, considerations about the heredity of various mental illnesses were very much part of the law, and when we look at the way it was carried out, it must be regarded as a eugenics law. This was definitely the impression of Knud Sand in 1935 when he reviewed the cases of sterilization performed according to the law of 1929. He stated xplicitly that all decisions regarding sterilization had been based on three ty₁ ; of considerations: eugenic, social (the potential benefits for society), and individual (potential advantages for the person involved—for example, release from confinement). Tage Kemp arrived at similar conclusions when he discussed the law in 1933.[78] What was remarkable was that some of the people that had put together the text of the law disagreed among themselves about the interpretation. But the importance of this disagreement must not be exaggerated; it was about the meaning of words, notably the word "eugenic," not about what actually could be done according to the law. The vagueness of the law's text may not have been deliberate, but it certainly assisted in making the law acceptable to the majority in 1929.

Bindslev voted against the law, as did five of his colleagues from the Conservative Party, but to no avail. The law was passed by both chambers of the Danish Parliament, with only minor and unimportant modification. Bindslev proceeded in the following years to fight the various eugenics laws that were presented to the Danish Parliament—but always in vain. The Danish version of eugenics seemed to command agreement among all political parties.

THE MENTALLY RETARDED: THE LAW OF 1934

While the experimental law was still valid, a complex law dealing with all aspects of the mentally retarded and their institutions—including sterilization—was put forward by K. K. Steincke, who was functioning as minister of health and welfare. So far, the confinement of the mentally retarded had been voluntary—it was the family or the guardian that decided whether the mentally retarded should be committed—but the new law listed a number of indications for commitment, and it now became the rule that all the mentally retarded covered by these rules should be committed. Furthermore, it became the duty of teachers, medical officers, and other social authorities to report suspected cases of mental disability.

Two conditions for sterilization were included in the new law. The mentally retarded could be sterilized if they were judged unable to raise and support children, or if the sterilization could facilitate their release from confinement or their transfer to a more relaxed kind of supervision.

This law differed from the law of 1929 on a number of points: minors could be sterilized according to the new law, sterilization of the mentally retarded was no longer limited to people confined to institutions, and consent from the mentally retarded was not needed. The decision to apply for sterilization was made by the doctor in charge and had to be approved by an appointed guardian. It was forwarded through the department for the mentally retarded and, if approved, put before a specially appointed board of three including one medical expert—a psychiatrist or a physician associated with institutions for the mentally retarded.

The law did not explicitly contain any eugenic indication, nor even a mixed indication such as the 1929 law. But one of the criteria for forcibly maintaining confinement was, "if there existed a clear danger that they [the mentally retarded] might have children." This was a sweeping statement covering, in theory, all the mentally retarded of a fertile age. Taken together with the indications for sterilization, it meant that all the mentally retarded could be forcibly confined from the onset of puberty and then sterilized because sterilization might facilitate their release—and the sterilization could be performed without their consent.[79]

The word eugenics had been purged from the law, but the idea remained. The danger not only of bearing children but of bearing mentally retarded children was included in the considerations when compulsory confinement was discussed. The hereditary disposition was taken into account when applications for sterilization were considered. Most of the physicians associated with the department of the mentally retarded were strong hereditarians and positive toward eugenics; certainly, this was true of H. O. Wildenskov, who had followed Christian Keller as the leader of the asylums in Jutland. Wildenskov had a strong influence on the formulation of the law; it was according to his recommendations that sterilization of the mentally retarded was dissociated from the general law on sterilization and castration (to be revised in 1935), and that the decision should be approved by an independent board, not by the medico-legal council. The first physician to sit on this board, Jens Christian Smith, was also favorably inclined toward eugenics. In his later evaluation of the law, he recommended the introduction of a direct eugenic indication.[80] Finally, the minister of health and welfare was one of the most dedicated eugenicists in the country.

There was some opposition to the passing of the law, but not very much. Bindslev cast the single vote against the law in the lower chamber; in the more conservative upper chamber there were three votes against. The representative of the Agrarian Party did not like the fact that people could be forcibly sterilized, but accepted it, characteristically, because the law concerned only the mentally retarded. The medico-legal council was dissatisfied because the mentally retarded were removed from its authority, but its protests were in vain.

It must be emphasized that the largest number of sterilizations occurred under this law and not the revised Sterilization Act of 1935. Until 1945 about 78 percent of those sterilized were the mentally retarded, and of these there were twice as many women as men.

But people were never entirely reconciled to the law. Teachers were worried when slow but otherwise normal pupils fell below the IQ minimum and were removed to an institution, and there were difficulties when parents refused to leave their children to the authorities—in one case, the forcible removal of two children caused a small riot because the local population felt the children were completely normal.[81] In these cases, the reaction was against the forcible internment, rather than against the eugenic aspect of the law; but awareness of the sterilizations that took place tended to reinforce the opposition. The authorities ascribed reactions such as these to ignorance, and the physicians who made the decisions insisted on their expertise in the face of all criticism.

THE REVISION OF THE STERILIZATION LAW IN 1935

Finally, in 1935 the scheduled revision of the law took place. The new law still covered castration as well as sterilization, but the distinction between the character and the effect of the two types of operations was emphasized more strongly in the new law. The new law made compulsory castration possible in certain cases. Apart from this, the greatest difference between the two laws was that the mentally retarded were covered by the Mentally Handicapped Act of 1934. More than 90 percent of the people sterilized from 1929 to 1934 belonged to this category. The indications for sterilization were described with the same vague phrases as in the former law; sterilization could be undertaken "with regard to the interests of society," but a distinction was made between the "normal" and the "abnormal" applicant. The mentally "normal" applicant could be sterilized if special reasons favored the operation, particularly if a danger existed that progeny could be genetically afflicted. For the mentally "abnormal" the criteria were even vaguer, but the operation could be undertaken only if it would benefit the applicant. This meant that the operation could not be undertaken with sole regard to the interests of society and against the interests of the individual.

The final decision concerning each application was still left in the hands of the minister of justice, but now he could act on advice from only one side, the medico-legal council. The applicant had to be advised of the consequences of the operation and give consent. In cases where persons were unable to comprehend the effects of sterilization, a guardian could be appointed to act on their behalf.

The purely eugenic criterion had been accepted at last, but only for people who were judged mentally "normal." Actually, the majority of the people to be sterilized were not members of this group, but they could be sterilized anyway, in accordance with the vaguer criteria applied to the mentally "abnormal," and the eugenic benefits could be achieved without use of the eugenic criterion. In fact, all applications for sterilization had to be accompanied by— among other relevant information—an estimate of the hereditary disposition. And later reviews of the law have agreed that eugenic considerations played an important part in decisions regarding the mentally "abnormal." But the provocative concept of eugenics was not used more than necessary in the text of the law and, at the same time, the difficult question of the hereditary character of the different mental afflictions was circumvented. The law did not provide detailed guidelines for what constituted an existing danger, what kinds of hereditary afflictions were covered by the law, or what was meant by the general interests of society and the benefits to the individual.[82]

This information was provided in a lengthy review undertaken by the medico-legal council and signed by the chairman of the council, Knud Sand. In addition to chairing this council, Sand was also a professor of forensic medicine and at that time generally regarded as Denmark's greatest expert on the endocrinology of the sexual glands, a subject that included the effects of sterilization and castration. Consequently, he could influence the cases of castration and sterilization in a double capacity, as chairman of the advisory board and as medical specialist. Other prominent members of the medico-legal council during this period were the psychiatrist August Wimmer and the leader of the institutions for the mentally retarded in the eastern part of Denmark, Johannes Nørvig.[83]

The review covered both the experience of five years of castration and sterilization and recommendations for the future. During the five years, 108 persons had been sterilized, eighty-eight women and twenty men. Of these 108, 102 were mentally retarded patients from the institutions, the group that in the future would be taken care of by the special law for the mentally retarded passed in 1934. The rest, all six of them, represented the group that in the future would be covered by the revised sterilization law of 1935.

Because of the small sample, the sterilization experience from the experimental law of 1929-35 was not particularly relevant for the future application of the revised law. Nevertheless, the authors stated that the experience with sterilizations had been positive, and proceeded to make a number of sweeping recommendations in their review: schizophrenics and certain cases of epilepsy as well as a number of well-defined hereditary neurological diseases, including Huntington's chorea, should provide indications for sterilization. The authors would also have preferred to include hereditary blindness and hereditary deafness in this group, but realized that this might be too extreme to be acceptable to the general public. With respect to psychopaths, alcoholics, and even habitual criminals of normal intelligence, the authors found that sterilization in many cases would be preferable:

> [the psychopaths] are often—to a larger extent than for example, the mentally retarded—asocial or antisocial (criminal); and their erotic activity and

inventiveness, considered together with their fertility—often extramarital—is considerable. . . . With respect to hereditary tainted progeny the psychopaths are comparable to the more well-defined mental diseases, even though the pattern of inheritance is still unknown.[84]

The review maintained therefore that the law should allow for the sterilization of the most extreme of these cases, especially where hypersexuality was indicated "by the existence of several illegitimate children supported by society."[85]

The same considerations applied to the habitual alcoholics. According to the authors, available documentation (not supplied) demonstrated that the marriages of such persons tended to be more fertile than average, and their sterilization, concurrent with their release from prison, work-house, or institution, would seem a reasonable measure. Criminals of normal intelligence, they stated, were often genetically afflicted and provided very bad conditions for their often numerous progeny. Sterilization of this group should under no conditions be used as a kind of supplementary penalty or a penalty substitute, but was preferable for both social and humanitarian reasons.[86] The authors also recommended that sterilization be performed as early as possible and the age limit imposed by the law of 1929 be removed.

Finally, they considered the consent demanded by the law. They found the inclusion of this condition understandable. They would have preferred to modify it, so consent could be dispensed with in special cases, but again they realized that this was more than the general public would accept.[87]

The whole document is a curious mixture of a review of the Sterilization Act of 1929 with recommendations and guidelines for the revised law of 1935 and criticism of this law with suggestions for further revisions. And the authors were the very same people that constituted the final authority with respect to castration and sterilization. In effect, the medico-legal council used the opportunity to make their intentions clear with regard to the new law.

The document demonstrated that the leading medical experts in 1935 were ready to go very far in their pursuit of eugenic goals and social control of the marginal groups of society. When the review appeared in the periodical of the Danish Medical Association (*Ugeskrift for læger*), there were no adverse reactions. In 1929, when the first sterilization law was introduced, the editors received a few letters in protest, but this time the medical world seemed to agree with the conclusions.

EUGENICS AND SOCIAL CONTROL—DEVELOPMENTS IN THE 1930S

There was indeed evidence for a hardening attitude among the eugenicists as well as growing public support for eugenics in the period from 1929 to 1935. A number of books appeared at this time. August Wimmer's *Sindsygdommenes Arvegang og Raceforbedrende Bestræbelser* (The heredity of mental diseases and racial improvement) and Knud Hansen's *Arvelighed hos Mennesket* (Human heredity) are two examples. Hansen's book strongly emphasized race biology, the superiority of the white race, and the threats against its dominant position; the considerable number of references in the book revealed a strong inspiration from German sources.[88]

Axel Garboe, a clergyman with an enduring interest in social work, wrote *Arvelighed og Socialpolitik* (Heredity and social policy) in 1931. During the same period, he wrote numerous reviews for *Socialt Tidsskrift* that demonstrated his extensive knowledge of the international eugenic literature, and he also wrote accounts of the development of eugenics in Germany, the fate of Boeters' eugenic proposals—the famous "Zwickauer Gesetze"—and the eugenics legislation of the National Socialist government.[89]

Oluf Thomsen published a textbook of human genetics in 1932, which covered eugenics in considerable detail. And finally, as a crowning achievement, *Arv og Race* (Heredity and race) appeared in 1934, followed one year later by Theodor Geiger's *Samfund og Arvelighed* (Society and heredity). In addition, there were numerous shorter articles and reviews by Wildenskov, Wimmer, Steincke, August Goll, Tage Kemp, and Søren Hansen, both in the specialist periodicals and in the more popular media. But there was not very much real debate, apart from a few conservative and Catholic dissenters.[90]

The book *Arv og Race* was a celebration of this Danish consensus. Here, eminent authorities laid down the law on genetics, eugenics, and social policy, and on race and racial biology. Included were Øjwind Winge who was the expert in genetics, Oluf Thomsen the specialist in human genetics, August Goll the legal expert and criminologist, August Wimmer the psychiatrist (who was also regarded as an expert on the genetics of mental illness), Axel Garboe the clergyman and social worker, and finally, K. K. Steincke. It would demand more than a normal amount of courage to dissent from the combined weight of these authorities.

The National Socialists' concept of race and particularly their anti-Semitism was criticized in this book, but there was no comparable criticism of the German sterilization law. Authors such as Wimmer and Goll, who earlier had recommended extreme caution with regard to eugenics, came down in favor of the German law and were ready in certain cases to accept compulsory sterilization also in Denmark. Everybody seemed to agree that a eugenics policy was an urgent necessity in a modern society but that eugenics should complement rather than replace the social security system, thereby concurring with Steincke's original argument.

Even though *Arv og Race* was a popular book, meant to be read by the layman, it is curious that almost no new scientific evidence was presented. The famous criminal families who had served the case of eugenics so well—the Jukes, the Kallikaks, and their companions—were discussed again, and a certain amount of anecdotal material was offered, along with loose estimates of the number of people that should be sterilized in different countries. Though a major reevaluation of eugenic premises was taking place in the English-speaking countries in these years, no trace of this debate can be found in *Arv og Race*.

Another strange omission was that not one of the authors considered that the eugenics legislation might be biased against the poor and the lower classes. On the surface the laws seemed indifferent to economic status but whether you were an alcoholic, a psychopath, or bordering on mental retardation, you were much more likely to become a client of the social apparatus—and subsequently to become eligible for sterilization—if you were poor. Only one author seemed to note this aspect of eugenics, the German sociologist Theodor Geiger, who had emigrated to Denmark in 1934. Geiger also questioned the widespread assumption that only the public social security system was a burden on society, and claimed that people maintained by their family or by private philanthropic organizations placed the same drain on national resources.

Though Geiger was a convinced eugenicist, his book *Samfund og Arvelighed* criticized many of the eugenic assumptions. Of all that was written in Denmark in these years, it must be considered the most original contribution to the eugenic literature. But though Geiger was a sociologist of international stature, his opinions on eugenics did not have much impact on the Danish debate and the Danish legislation. In this area he remained an outsider.[91]

Changed attitudes toward eugenics can be registered both in the eugenic literature and in the parliamentary debates of the 1930s. Compulsory sterilization of the mentally retarded was now regarded as acceptable, together with compulsory castration of sexual offenders. And there were many, including the medico-legal council and several of the leading experts, that recommended compulsory sterilization for other groups. While everybody up to and during the passing of the 1929 law had recommended caution, they now spoke of eugenics legislation as something that was urgently needed.

This corresponded to a general hardening of attitudes toward the poor and the working class (two groups that were often confused), and the marginal members of society in general. Unemployment had risen dramatically following the world crisis in the early 1930s, the new carefully prepared social legislation came under attack, and there was a clamor for more draconian measures including the death penalty. There was much talk about Denmark is being a feeble and dying nation with a declining population. Unemployment relief was criticized; female emancipation was attacked, and it was also viewed as a direct cause of unemployment.

The cost of maintaining the unproductive segment of the population became a favorite topic. Supporters of the new social legislation, a group which included most of the eugenicists, did in many cases accept the argument that such people imposed a heavy burden on society, but argued that the social legislation actually represented a more rational management and control of the marginal members of society, and that eugenics was needed to ensure that the problem and the burden did not increase with time.

The same attitudes were present in the other Scandinavian countries at this time, and also in Germany. In the last years of the Weimar Republic, politicians from most parties, even from the Catholic Center Party, adopted a more positive attitude toward eugenics; a eugenic policy was officially accepted by the Protestant relief organization Innere Mission at the Treysa Conference in 1932. Here, too, the cost of maintaining the retarded was much discussed, and the participants endorsed the policy of the "social minimum," the concept that the retarded should not cost more than the lowest amount spent on the healthy and able-bodied. These beliefs were accepted in a very broad segment of the population. They were not only associated with national socialism, though the Nazis provided the most demagogic version of the argument.[92]

The difference between Denmark and these other countries should not be exaggerated. In all cases, preparations for eugenics legislation were begun well before the onset of the world crisis, and everywhere the crisis made state intervention and resolute legal measures more acceptable. However, only in Denmark did the supporters of eugenics succeed in squeezing a eugenic sterilization law through the legislative apparatus before the crisis had made itself felt.

STRANGE BEDFELLOWS: EUGENICS AND BIRTH CONTROL

Most of the Danish eugenicists mentioned thus far were eminently respected people, occupying relatively high and influential positions in Danish society. They were involved with eugenics in a professional capacity as psychiatrists, geneticists, social workers, institutional leaders, etc. Even though many had a medical education, there is not enough evidence to conclude that eugenics was particularly attractive to physicians as a professional group, only that many physicians in their work became directly or indirectly occupied with eugenic problems.

But other eugenicists were less respected. Thit Jensen was already well-known as an author and feminist lecturer when she became acquainted with Margaret Sanger and her work for birth control in 1923. Thit Jensen became probably the most effective propagandist for the cause in Denmark, for a period touring the Danish provincial towns almost continuously. She cooperated with the Danish League for Sexual Reform, and through it, with the parallel communist organization. Her agitation also led to a break with the Danish feminist organization (Dansk Kvindebevægelse), where the majority did not want to be too closely identified with sexual reform and birth control.

Eugenics was more of a side issue for Thit Jensen, but right from the start she used the eugenic argument for birth control and information about birth control: that it would reduce the number of births of afflicted children. This argument was used in conjunction with other arguments: that birth control liberated women from the perpetual fear of conception and from dependence on men, that it functioned as a check on the threatening overpopulation, and that it secured a well-planned and prosperous family with better opportunities for the children. She became quite notorious during this period, and to the anti-feminists she epitomized everything that was wrong with feminism. She was also, quite wrongly but not unexpectedly, accused of encouraging loose morals and promiscuity.

For Thit Jensen, the eugenic argument and the argument for the small, but prosperous, family occasionally merged; she seemed to believe that the better-fed, better-raised, and better-educated children would also be genetically superior—or, rather, she was not aware of any distinction between the physical and mental health of a person and his or her hereditary potential, between phenotype and genotype. In this way her arguments acquired a Lamarckian flavor which did not make them less convincing to the layman, but set her further apart from the official professional consensus.

Another radical eugenicist was held in even lower esteem. Jonathan Høgh Leunbach, a physician and cofounder of Magnus Hirschfeld's League for Sexual Reform, was also a fervent agitator for birth control and sexual education, so much so that for a period he formed his own Sexual Reform Party, loosely affiliated with the Communist Party. He himself ran twice on the Communist ticket.

He started courses in sexual physiology and birth control in the 1920s, and later, after he had received many requests for abortions, he founded a clinic where pregnancies could be terminated. This brought him into conflict both with his fellow physicians and with the law, and in 1930 the authorities, after several attempts, secured a conviction and three months of imprisonment.

Since that time many commentators have had difficulty understanding why two such progressive and courageous people were attracted to the "reactionary" idea of eugenics. But as we have seen, hereditary determinism and eugenics were supported by progressives, both moderate reformers and radicals. Indeed, there are numerous examples of radical supporters of birth control and sexual emancipation who were strong eugenicists: Victoria Woodhull, August Forel, the Drysdales, Havelock Ellis, Margaret Sanger, and Marie Stopes. They believed that women and men were rational beings that should be allowed to control reproduction—then why not the quality of the progeny?

Leunbach published a book in 1926 called simply *Racehygiejne*, a rather crude tract even when compared to most of the contemporary literature, advocating both positive and negative eugenics and with the usual arguments based on social Darwinism and the degeneration concept. Leunbach later denied that the word "race" in "racehygiejne" had anything to do with the superiority and inferiority of the different races and maintained that the word race denoted the human race. It is true that the expressions race and racial were used with this meaning—that racial quality in many cases simply meant biological quality, and had nothing to do with racism, and that "racehygiejne" as used by many eugenicists simply meant the (genotypical) health of the human race. But Leunbach left himself wide open for charges of racism when he spoke of the struggle between the races, the inferiority of the colored races, and the dangers of miscegenation.[93]

To the more respected eugenicists, people such as Leunbach and Thit Jensen were an embarrassment: they brought eugenics into disrepute by associating it with abortion, free love, and communism: they were the types of people Steincke had in mind when he warned against irresponsible propaganda. But the disagreement was not only a question of style. Both Søren Hansen and Steincke were pronatalists; they firmly believed that the declining birthrate represented a grave danger, not only because the total number of people declined but even more because the decline of the "superior" part of the population was believed to be disproportionately high, since the "inferior" segment of the population was less likely to use birth control. Propaganda for birth control could only accelerate this process of differential reproduction. In a quite violent letter that appeared in the periodical published by the association of Danish physicians, Søren Hansen attacked Leunbach: he did not know what he was saying and doing, and the best thing he could do was to close up shop as soon as possible.

Leunbach's reply was that all forms of eugenic policy had to be voluntary to be successful; as long as only the educated strata knew how to control reproduction, the effect would be dysgenic, but balance would be restored when everybody knew how to do it.

Given the premises that these opponents shared, premises that are not regarded as valid today, Søren Hansen probably got the better of the argument. But the interesting thing is that Leunbach, a Communist and presumably a dedicated collectivist, stressed the importance of individual free choice, while Søren Hansen, much more orthodox politically, was ready to resort to coercion, primarily indirect coercion based on maintaining ignorance, but in some cases even direct coercion, for instance, the suppression and prohibition of the use of contraceptives. Here, he put the interests of the collective, the state, higher than the right of the individual to free information. Søren Hansen's attitude cannot be said to be typical of the Danish eugenicists, who rarely discussed eugenics in these terms, but most of them did agree with the pronatalist argument, and most of them favored a strengthening of the state apparatus and the possibilities of state intervention for eugenic purposes.

One reason for these differing viewpoints could be the different pictures the opponents had formed of the woman that used contraception. To Søren Hansen—and Steincke—she was the modern pampered and spoiled woman who preferred enjoyment and luxuries to children; to Leunbach and other supporters of birth control, she was the poor and prematurely aged woman who lived in perpetual fear of yet another conception.

In defense of the respected eugenicists, it must be said that their lack of confidence in people such as Thit Jensen and Leunbach can appear reasonable in view of their other activities. Thit Jensen was notoriously eccentric and difficult to work with, and became increasingly preoccupied with spiritualism. Leunbach appeared sounder, and he did not become a follower of Wilhelm Reich, as did many from his circle. But he did introduce Hans Hörbiger's *Welteislehre* in Denmark—an eccentric cosmological theory that all respectable scientists regarded as a flagrant piece of pseudoscience.[94] It is not completely unjustified to say that Leunbach and Thit Jensen, together with the earlier Alfred Bramsen and perhaps Vilhelm Rasmussen, represented the eccentric and cranky side of eugenics in Denmark.

RACE AND EUGENICS

With the exception of the book by Knud Hansen in 1929, and perhaps Leunbach's *Racehygiejne* in 1926, the Danish literature on eugenics was remarkably free from racial considerations and racial nationalism. In Germany this was certainly not the case, but even compared with the other Scandinavian countries, the Danish eugenicists seemed fundamentally uninterested in race and seemed to consider it irrelevant to eugenics.

There is one prominent exception, which, when examined closely, actually confirms this impression. In 1919 the periodical *Det Nye Nord* was founded. Originally it represented a form of "modern" businesslike conservatism with a strong emphasis on Scandinavian cooperation. Beginning in 1920, a special section, "Den Nordiske Race," was added. This section was edited by the Norwegian Jon Alfred Mjöen and covered two of his favorite subjects, eugenics and race. The section was very well written, contained contributions from most of the world's leading geneticists, and demonstrated Mjöen's talent as a journalist and propagandist—after all, he had represented his own eugenic ideas as "The Norwegian Program" at the meetings of the International Federation of Eugenics, despite having been ostracized by the professional Norwegian geneticists.

Nevertheless, "Den Nordiske Race" fell flat in Denmark. There were very few Danish contributions and none from the prominent Danish eugenicists, while Harry Federley from Finland and Herman Lundborg from Sweden contributed several times. There were also remarkably few references to "Den Nordiske Race" in the contemporary Danish literature. After a while, more and more of the content was written by Mjöen himself, his family, and his coworkers at his own private research institute.[95]

Later attempts to interest the Danes in their racial heritage did not meet with much success. The contributions to *Arv og Race* in 1934 that dealt with the concept of race were uniformly negative toward race-nationalistic ideas, and Søren Hansen even repudiated the National Socialist concept of race. The attempt by the National Socialists in Germany to stimulate Nordic ideals through the establishment of "Nordische Gesellschaft" was not successful in Denmark. In general, the Danes were not much interested in race, and the eugenicists were actively trying to dissociate the concept of eugenics from all association with race biology and race nationalism.[96]

Opposition to Eugenics

After "Casti Connubii," the papal bull of 1930, Catholics everywhere turned strongly against eugenics. Many Catholics had already expressed criticism of the eugenics movement; G. K. Chesterton's *Eugenics and Other Evils*, published in 1922, is one of the more entertaining examples.[97] In Denmark the Catholics, a very small minority, were virtually the only organized group that persistently criticized eugenics and the sterilization acts.

The attacks were led by the science historian Gustav Scherz, who had a background in biology and a good eye for the scientific shortcomings of eugenics. Scherz maintained that the knowledge of heredity, particularly human heredity, was still very incomplete. He also underlined the principal Catholic argument against sterilization, that it violated the body created by God. This must not be confused with the humanitarian argument. Catholics were quite ready to accept castration as a penalty, just as Alfred Bindslev, another consistent adversary of eugenics, defended capital punishment; but they were not ready to accept inactivation or removal of a healthy part of the body as a therapeutic measure. Another familiar argument, also used by Scherz and other Catholics, was that immorality and promiscuity would increase when the fear of pregnancy disappeared. Obviously, this argument applied mainly to women. It was also taken seriously by the eugenicists. Both Søren Hansen and Steincke warned against sterilization as being "abused" or used for frivolous reasons by people who did not want to marry or have children. The sexually irresponsible woman with a string of illegitimate children constituted a heavy economic burden but with her reproductive capability removed, the same woman might present an even graver moral danger, threatening the very foundations of society, marriage, and the family. Leunbach, of course, believed that the option of sterilization should be completely free.[98]

Finally, Scherz and other Catholics argued that it was inconsistent to suppress reproduction in any way when the population already was declining at an alarming rate. Scherz used strong words such as "the white death" and "national suicide," and admitted he found the National Socialists' policy more consistent; although they introduced sterilization, at least they made an effort to encourage population growth.[99]

It is striking that the Catholic critics in many ways shared the outlook of the more respected Danish eugenicists. They did not disagree with the hereditary determinism of the eugenicists, which was essentially conservative; and like Søren Hansen and Steincke, they were pronatalists. In fact, eugenics without sterilization could be quite acceptable to Catholics, and they had quite early

(1928) translated and printed a series of lectures on family and reproduction given by the Jesuit geneticist Father Muckermann, at that time leader of the eugenics department at the Kaiser Wilhelm Institut in Berlin. Several of these tracts espoused eugenic principles, but Muckermann passed over the controversial subject of sterilization and emphasized positive measures such as greater family allowances and the value of stable, fertile families.[100]

It must also be noted that the attacks on eugenics legislation took place against a background of extreme conservatism, not only vehement anticommunism but also a general antisocialism that even included the very moderate Danish Social Democrats. The political heroes of the Catholic weekly *Nordisk Ugeblad for Katolske Kristne* were Antonio Salazar, Gil Robles, Ignatz Seipel, and Engelbert Dollfuss. Parliamentarism was frequently alluded to as "the dictatorship by numbers," and the organic corporative state recommended in its place. In many contributions, though not in the writings of Scherz, an unmistakable undercurrent of anti-Semitism is discernible.

One often has the impression from the arguments of Scherz that the real target was not so much the Danish eugenics legislation but all the phenomena that he associated with eugenics: female emancipation, free love, state socialism, general secularization, and the concepts of "modern" and "progressive." His attitude toward eugenics legislation was shared by a few conservative columnists who also seemed to aim their attacks against the eugenics of Leunbach rather than against the respected Danish eugenicists. But this conservative opposition never amounted to much, and it certainly never dominated the Conservative Party or the Agrarian Party, the two leading parties of the Right.

There was no trace of an organized opposition to the sterilization acts from the Lutheran Danish state church. Bindslev, who was against them, was, of course, a member of the clergy, but so was the pro-eugenic Axel Garboe. Neither could be regarded as typical or representative of the Danish religious community. Of greater importance was the attitude of the physician H. I. Schou. Schou was the leader of one of the few Danish institutions where religious attitudes still predominated. Schou himself was an unorthodox but devout believer, but he had argued in favor of the law of 1929 when he was consulted by the parliamentary politicians. According to several statements during the parliamentary debates, many people who initially had grave reservations were convinced because a man such as Schou could sanction eugenics.

Some opponents argued against the legislation from a humanitarian position. To them sterilization and particularly castration were mutilations and represented a return to an older, more barbarous legislative tradition, whether they were called therapy or not.[101] The people who defended the sterilization laws called this an emotional argument, as opposed to their own realistic, no-nonsense approach. From the parliamentary debates we know that many speakers admitted that they initially had shared this revulsion, but that they had been converted by the careful arguments of the experts.[102] Castration evoked more revulsion than sterilization, and sterilization of disabled but "normal" blind and deaf people inspired more compassion than operations on the mentally disabled. Very few people seemed to be able to sympathize with this group. One who did raise her voice on their behalf, the pedagogue Sophie Rifbjerg, did not really try to argue against the sterilization of the mentally retarded. Though she had extensive experience with late developers, she considered it futile to argue in the prevailing climate of opinion, but she did emphasize that these people could have a full and happy life in spite of their disability.[103]

THE GERMAN STERILIZATION LAW IN DANISH PERSPECTIVE

In 1933 the new National Socialist government in Germany issued a barrage of new laws. One of them, *Gesetz zur Verhütung Erbkranken Nachwuchses* (Law concerning the prevention of hereditarily afflicted progeny), concerned eugenic sterilization. Later, commentators such as Tage Kemp strongly emphasized the difference between the German law and its Danish counterpart.[104] The German sterilization law was founded on coercion which was exerted by a quasi-legal apparatus of local courts made up of experts in human genetics and legal advisers; people could be sterilized against their will, if the decision from the *Erbegerichtshof* (Hereditary Court) and the succeeding appeal to the *Erbeobergerichtshof* (Hereditary Upper Court) went against them. The indications for sterilization were also much more formalized than in Denmark. No fewer than nine different categories covering sterilization for eugenic reasons were outlined in the law.

Commentators after World War II have characterized the law as a typical Nazi law, and have seen it as the first step down the road to euthanasia and genocide, but most of the contemporary Danish eugenicists regarded the law favorably, an attitude that in no way could be interpreted as sympathy with the Nazi policy in general. In the month before the passing of the German law, the Danish newspaper *Politiken* published a series of features on eugenics by Tage Kemp, August Goll, and Søren Hansen.[105] All had taken pains to dissociate the concept of eugenics from the Nazi doctrines of race, and Søren Hansen had severely criticized the Nazi concepts of racial purity and anti-Semitic propaganda. His later reaction to the German sterilization law was quite different:

[it has been expected] . . . that Germany without doubt in the near future would acquire a sterilization law, which has been carefully prepared by prolonged and detailed deliberations—and this has come to pass. The law was accepted the 14 July and was as good as expected. . . . Already the title *Gesetz zur Verhütung Erbkranken Nachwuchses* demonstrates that this is a purely eugenic measure, and that is all it is. A number of hereditary diseases are listed as indications for sterilization, where medical expertise might decide that imminent danger exists of progeny with severe physical or mental "Erbschaden." It is doubtful whether a substantial improvement of the racial quality of the German people can be expected from the application of the law, but it must be acknowledged that the law is carefully considered and clearly and distinctly phrased.[106]

August Goll, who had lectured about the Danish law in Germany, admitted that "There is a connection between the law and the new national socialist idea of racial purity," and he did not approve of the compulsory sterilization of the deaf, the blind, and the physically invalid, that could be carried out according to the German law. But he did believe that following the German law and introducing the compulsory sterilization of chronic alcoholics and psychopaths would be preferable in certain cases. Finally, he claimed that "there can be no doubt that at least the younger generation among the German physicians are supporting the law, which thus can be regarded as evidence of the enormous progress of the movement for sterilization in the last five years."[107]

This was also the impression of H. I. Schou, the pious director of Filadelfia, an institution for epileptics. He quoted the famous German psychiatrist Bumke as approving the law and another, anonymous German psychiatrist who had confirmed that the majority of his colleagues supported the law and that the law was carried out slowly and carefully.[108] Steincke commented on Schou's article, but merely to correct the impression that the Danish law—as opposed to the German—only allowed for voluntary sterilization. As Steincke correctly stated, the law of 1934 concerning the mentally retarded actually contained provisions for carrying out sterilizations against the will of the individual.[109]

Tage Kemp thought the German organization with local courts preferable to the more cumbersome Danish decision process, but he did not comment on the German provisions for compulsory sterilization at that time.[110] Even Leunbach, the revolutionary socialist, could not find anything to criticize in the German law except the fact that sterilization without the consent of the *Erbegerichtshof* was expressly forbidden.[111]

August Wimmer, who a few years before and only with extreme reluctance had come out in favor of sterilization, now thought that Denmark should adopt at least part of the German practice—the compulsory sterilization of psychopaths, alcoholics, and criminals. Without sterilization of this group, it would not be possible to effect the "purification of the social body of inferior elements" (an expression he had borrowed, with obvious approval, from the German psychiatrist Robert Gaupp).[112]

Axel Garboe was condescending, but also impressed by the German efforts:

> That this contains correct ideas cannot be doubted. That difficulties are ignored and [that] the impact of genetical research for the present is overestimated are also easy to see. . . . But a grand experiment seems to be on the way. Time will tell what the results will be. When the high-sounding phrases and the naiveté that causes affront are removed, there will still be left something to learn and apply, with the necessary modifications, in our own country.[113]

The most critical reaction came from Professor H. O. Wildenskov, usually regarded as a hardliner in his attitude toward eugenics. In his commentary, written before the Danish Mentally Handicapped Act of 1934 had been approved by Parliament, he criticized the German law on two principal points. First, he protested that by insisting on the strict eugenic indication, the law demanded the impossible from the medical authorities. The hereditary character of the different afflictions listed in the German law could be proved with certainty only in very few instances. Second, he opposed the part of the German law allowing for compulsory sterilization. In a more practical commentary, he stipulated that, according to the text of the law, Germany would need around 2,600 physicians with expertise in human genetics, and he doubted that so many were available or could be available at short notice.[114]

Wildenskov's comments are interesting when seen in the light of the 1934 law on which he had been a major influence . In the Danish law there was no eugenic indication—the word eugenic was not mentioned once—though there definitely was a eugenic intention. And, of course, the same law actually did allow for compulsory sterilization, though in a more circumspect way than the German law.

The Danish reaction is not really surprising when we concentrate on the letter of the German law, without using hindsight. True, the German law did specify that the hereditary the mentally retarded, schizophrenics, manic-depressives, hereditary epileptics, hereditary deaf, hereditary blind, people suffering from Huntington's chorea, and alcoholics could be sterilized. The Danish laws of 1929, 1934, and 1935 did not specify anything as detailed. But if we look at the recommendations of the Danish medico-legal council from 1934, we find a similar list, excluding only the manic-depressives. Together with the sterilization of habitual alcoholics, the Danish group also found sterilization of psychopaths, and even mentally "normal" habitual criminals, desirable.[115]

The German law did contain a provision for compulsory sterilization, but so did the Danish law of 1934 concerning the mentally retarded. If we reexamine the commentary of the medico-legal council on the 1935 legislation, we see it quite openly states that compulsory sterilization would be desirable for some categories of criminals and psychopaths. Individual comments from different experts show the same tendency; attitudes hardened considerably in the interval from 1929 to 1935, as even earlier skeptics such as August Goll and August Wimmer now seemed to approve of more draconian measures. We must conclude that the differences between the German law and the Danish legislation were smaller than we have since been led to believe. And the differences were even smaller between the German law and the wishful thinking of some of the Danish eugenicists.

It is difficult to envision a development analogous to the German practice in Denmark. Even if the effects of the world crisis had increased in severity and the political situation had been more polarized, mass sterilization of large groups in the population that were not institutionalized would not have been acceptable to the majority. However, if we consider the rhetoric of the leading experts, it is not quite as impossible to imagine a situation in which institutionalized groups, habitual criminals, psychopaths, and alcoholics could have been subjected to sterilization, compulsory or partly compulsory, on a large scale. The example of Hamburg is not encouraging. This part of Germany had been closest, in attitudes and administration, to the Scandinavian model. Even during the Nazi years, racial ideology played a minor role in Hamburg compared to the rest of Germany. Yet Hamburg was also the area that carried out the largest proportion of sterilizations and deportations of "antisocial individuals" to concentration camps.[116]

From their German colleagues the Danish eugenicists received the impression that the German law was applied cautiously, and that in reality it represented continuity with the Weimar administration which actually had set up a commission to consider proposals for a sterilization law in 1932. There is some truth in this view; the sterilization law that was enacted after the Nazi takeover owed much to work done in the last period of the Weimar Republic, even though the Weimar commission had considered only voluntary sterilization.[117]

The real difference between the German law and the various Danish sterilization laws lay in the way they were applied. In Denmark 1,380 people had been sterilized from 1935 to 1939, 1,200 of them mentally retarded. In

Germany about 200,000 people were sterilized from the beginning of 1934 to the middle of 1937, a staggering 7,000 per month. But neither these facts—which can have been no secret to the Danish medical community—nor the passing of the Nuremberg Laws of 1935 "To Safeguard German Blood and Honor," caused any of the Danish eugenicists to reevaluate or criticize the German sterilization program in public.

FURTHER EUGENICS LEGISLATION

One of the most controversial laws of the 1930s was the abortion law first put forward in 1937 and then, after extensive revision, passed in 1939. The law was an offshoot of the many recommendations of the Myrdal-inspired population commission. It did contain a provision for eugenic indication: the right to have an abortion performed when imminent danger existed that the child would be suffering from mental illness, mental deficiency, severe neurological illness, epilepsy, or severe somatic illness due to hereditary causes. In connection with an abortion, a woman could be sterilized if she was genetically afflicted. But the debate about this issue, which normally would have been quite controversial, was overshadowed by the violent public debate about abortion in general, and about the social indication for abortion in particular.[118]

Nineteen thirty-eight saw a revision of the marriage law. By this time, the law of 1922 was regarded as inefficient with respect to eugenics by some of the medical experts, and together with Steincke, still minister of health and welfare in 1938, they wanted to widen the indications for prohibition of marriage to include the hereditary blind and the hereditary deaf. At the same time, this group wanted to include a provision for compulsory divorce in cases in which married couples, who fulfilled the general requirements for sterilization according to the law of 1935, refused to be sterilized. This proved too much. There was an outcry in the press and among the more conservative politicians; and finally, Steincke had to settle for a clause specifying that marriage could be prohibited if people who fulfilled the sterilization requirements refused to be sterilized. Sterilization and castration could be accepted, but an established marriage was still sacrosanct.[119]

TAGE KEMP AND THE UNIVERSITY INSTITUTE OF HUMAN GENETICS

In the 1930s Tage Kemp gradually rose to become the acknowledged expert on human genetics in Denmark. As previously mentioned, he was handpicked for this position by his mentor, the pathologist Oluf Thomsen.

The government grant that was instituted in 1922 to prepare for the establishment of teaching and research in "racehygiejne" at Copenhagen University had passed into the custody of Thomsen in 1927 when Wilhelm Johannsen died. At that time part of the grant was set aside for the specific purpose of educating a prospective candidate for a chair in eugenics and human genetics. Thomsen chose the thirty-one-year-old medical researcher Tage Kemp, who had already done some work on chromosome cytology but not on anything related to eugenics. In 1932 Kemp started publishing work of this type beginning with the biosocial treatise, "A Study of the Causes of Prostitution, Especially Concerning the Hereditary Factors." Kemp presented this work at the Third International Congress of Eugenics in 1932 and later published it as a monograph.[120]

In this period, Kemp's research career was funded largely by the Rockefeller Foundation. This foundation had more or less saved genetic research in Germany during the lean years after the war and was also supporting genetic research in other places in Europe, notably the Galton Laboratory and Penrose's Institute at Colchester.[121] In 1932 Kemp received a grant that enabled him to study genetics in the United States and Europe, and in 1934 he received another grant that allowed him to visit various institutes of genetics in Europe. During these visits he also functioned as an observer for the Rockefeller Foundation which had voiced concern about the ideological commitment of some of the German researchers. Kemp visited, among others, Othmar von Verschuer, famous for his use of twin methods in human genetics, and stated that he was "a keen national socialist, completely honest, however, I feel, so one can rely upon his scientific research as being objective and real. He works especially with twin investigations, and is doing this research very thoroughly and systematically."[122]

From 1933 on, Kemp wrote regularly on the subject of human heredity and eugenics. In accordance with Johannsen's ideas, he was skeptical of positive eugenics and thought more concrete results could be obtained by concentrating on negative eugenics, preventing the propagation of harmful genes. Like Søren Hansen, he regretted the declining birthrate and considered it part of eugenic policy to encourage childbirth, although he did not recommend state interference with the distribution and use of contraceptives and other drastic measures. He did not criticize the German laws openly at the time of their appearance, but he maintained a certain distance. He spoke of the sterilization law that "was applied very energetically" and stressed the difference between the dictatorship, where the interests of the state overruled the interests of the individual, and the democracies, where it was accepted that society owed all individuals a tolerable existence. He was also very critical of the different American state laws and found that many of them had been carried out too hastily and without the proper genetic insight.[123] Kemp did not, as a rule, advocate coercion and perhaps did not realize that the law of 1934 in effect was compulsory. Instead he emphasized the need for more specific information about the nature of heredity and eugenics, advocating specific prognoses in individual cases so people could judge the risk of having children with hereditary disabilities. Once people had been given proper information, they could be expected to act in conformity with the general interests of society.[124]

In 1938, after prolonged negotiations in which Oluf Thomsen and Tage Kemp were very involved, the Rockefeller Foundation founded the Institute of Human Genetics and immediately handed it over to Copenhagen University. Tage Kemp became the first director and, in accordance with his ideas, it became the center for the registration of genetic diseases and genetic investigations. Denmark had an honorable tradition in genetics but was not particularly strong in the area of human genetics. The Rockefeller Foundation chose Denmark for the establishment of the institute more for its social organization than for its research tradition. Denmark, along with the other Scandinavian countries, offered unique opportunities for research into human genetics. The civil records were almost complete, the population was stable and homogeneous, and the distances small; and together with the advanced state of the social health programs, these factors made family studies and larger surveys easy to complete. With the foundation of this institute, Denmark was chosen to be the major human genetics laboratory in the world.

Genetic registration became the central activity of the new institution. This was supported by the government, which in 1939 recommended that all people who were admitted to the institutions for mental disabilities and mental illnesses fill out questionnaires and forward them to the Institute for Human Genetics. In a way, this work represented a continuation of Søren Hansen's anthropological registration, and the archives of his anthropological laboratory were incorporated into the new institute. Indeed, the institute represented what he had fought for, for more than a quarter of a century.

Along with the genetic registration, the institute conducted family research and other types of research into human genetics; more traditional anthropological research was also carried out, to a limited extent. Finally, the institute also performed experimental research into pathological genetics, primarily on mice. Besides being a research institution, it functioned as a center for genetic counseling—probably the first in the world—dispensing advice on marriage, sterilization, abortion, and other problems of genetic interest.[125]

While research into human genetics was firmly established, interest in the subject of eugenics faded after 1935. Kemp gave popular lectures on the subject, and Søren Hansen published occasional articles. There was some debate in the press about the eugenic changes in the marriage law in 1938, but the controversy was more about the violation of marriage than the subject of eugenics. The eugenic laws took their course, independent of the general interest in the subject: in the five-year period from 1929 to 1935, 108 people were sterilized; during the next five years the number was 1,380. As tables 1-3 show, more than twice as many women as men were sterilized, and far more the mentally retarded than all the other categories put together. And these numbers probably underestimate the true proportion of the mentally retarded. A later survey by Kemp, covering sterilization from 1945 to 1950, demonstrates that the more seriously retarded and those bordering on mental retardation constituted about 40 percent of the people sterilized according to the law of 1935, the law that primarily covered sterilizations not connected with the institutions for the mentally retarded.[126]

Table 1. Total number of legal sterilizations in Denmark 1929-50.

Period	Women	Men	Total
1929-34	88	20	108
1935-39	975	405	1,380
1940-45	1,510	610	2,120
1946-50	1,771	561	2,332

Source: T. Kemp, *Arvehygiejne, Københavns Universitets Årsskrift* (Copenhagen: Københavns Universitet, 1951), 45.

Table 2. Legal sterilizations in Denmark (mentally retarded excepted).

Period	Women	Men	Total
1929-34	4	1	5
1935-39	150	30	180
1940-45	510	110	620
1946-50	902	96	998

Source: T. Kemp, *Arvehygiejne, Københavns Universitets Årsskrift* (Copenhagen: Københavns Universitet, 1951), 45.

Table 3. Legal sterilizations in Denmark of the mentally retarded.

Period	Women	Men	Total
1929-34	84	19	103
1935-39	825	375	1,200
1940-45	1,000	500	1,500
1946-50	869	465	1,334

Source: T. Kemp, *Arvehygiejne, Københavns Universitets Årsskrift* (Copenhagen: Københavns Universitet, 1951), 45.

LATER DEVELOPMENTS: EUGENICS AFTER WORLD WAR II

Denmark was occupied by Germany from 1940 to 1945, but the occupation did not lead to any change in the Danish eugenic policy. The German occupying power did not interfere in this area, and though the Danish government to a certain extent collaborated with Germany, it was ideologically very far from national socialism. There was no equivalent to the Norwegian Quisling government and its introduction of a more extreme eugenics legislation.

After World War II, the word "racehygiejne" had outlived its usefulness, and even the word eugenics was not used very often. But the horrible revelations of the genocidal racial policy of the Third Reich did not lead to any recriminations against the Danish eugenics legislation and the Danish eugenicists. Eugenics disappeared as a concept that was at least occasionally discussed in public, a gradual process that had already started before the war.

There was criticism against the Mentally Handicapped Act of 1934, but the criticism was not in any way connected to the condemnation of the German sterilization policy. There had always been a certain resentment against the administration of the law and its compulsory character, provoked mostly by the summary removal of children from their homes but also by the knowledge of sterilizations that took place in the institutions. There had also been unfortunate publicity about some cases of late developers who had been released and reclassified as normal—after sterilization had been performed. A claim for damages in such a case had been rejected by the courts, but it all contributed to the general dissatisfaction with the law.

This dissatisfaction had already led to an inquiry in 1941, and in 1954 it became possible to appeal decisions (mostly regarding compulsory institutionalization) to the regular court system, where previously this decision had rested with the minister of health and welfare. The same year another commission was founded to consider the problems of the mentally retarded; and in two reports, from 1957 and 1958, the commission recommended that most of the compulsory elements in the Mentally Handicapped Act be eliminated.[127]

According to the law of 1934, the mentally retarded could be interned against their will if there existed immediate danger that they would have children. The commission had this comment:

> About this indication it should be noted that the text makes it very extensive, making compulsory confinement possible for every nonsterilized the mentally retarded person of fertile age. In practice, the clause has only been applied in very few cases, while it may have been of great importance indirectly. The possibility that a patient could be detained at the institution with a view to sterilization, or just the knowledge that such a detainment was legal, probably has facilitated many sterilization applications.[128]

The commission recommended that this special indication be discarded, so the only condition for compulsory confinement was if nonconfinement implied a major disadvantage for the mentally retarded person. About the conditions for sterilization in the Mentally Handicapped Act of 1934 the commission commented:

> The committee finally wants to emphasize that the rules concerning sterilization allow for compulsory sterilization, but that direct compulsion never has been used and never ought to be used in the future.[129]

This was true enough, but even in Nazi Germany direct compulsion was used only in very few of the sterilization cases. A rule allowing for compulsion did not have to be used to be useful. The comments of the commission made it clear that it did not approve of involuntary sterilization and would have preferred to have the paragraph removed, but this revision of the law was postponed because another commission was set up in 1958 in order to consider the whole problem of sterilization and castration. With this exception, the revision of the law regarding the institutions for the mentally retarded was passed in 1959. Sterilization still remained, but the part of the law that had opened the way for eugenic sterilizations, namely the possibility of compulsory confinement for all mentally retarded individuals of fertile age, had been removed.

In 1956 the First International Congress of Human Genetics met in Copenhagen. Among the luminaries present were J. B. S. Haldane, L. S. Penrose, and H. J. Muller, the discoverer of the genetic effect of ionized radiation. Tage Kemp was chairman of the organizing committee and gave the opening speech:

> Within recent years very much attention has been drawn to the dangers which our load of mutations involves for the human race; the risk of reduced fitness and even the perils of genetic death have been strongly emphasized. Beyond a definite intensity, further increase in radiation presents a potential danger to the human race as well as to plant and animal life. The most serious and effective precautions to prevent and control this risk and this danger must be taken. On the other hand, the danger must not be overestimated and unnecessary anxiety ought to be avoided. This is why the study of hereditary lesions is of such great consequence. The knowledge of the conditions effected makes it possible to follow and control their development and fluctuation in the population, and to ascertain the behavior of hereditary diseases down through the ages.[130]

There was no mention of eugenics, no mention of the dangers of differential reproduction, and the baby boom after the war had made all talk about the dangers of depopulation obsolete. "Load of mutations" was one of the expressions of the new age, and it indicated another way of looking at the genetics of human populations. It also expressed the new threat against humanity that had been conjured up in the last days of the war—the atomic bomb. Kemp still believed that moderate negative eugenics was possible and preferable,[131] but he did not think that the survival of nations or the fate of the human race depended on it.

THE FINAL ACT: THE REVISION OF THE STERILIZATION LAW

The commission regarding sterilization and castration delivered its final report in 1964, and the law was revised in 1967. The most obvious change from the earlier laws was that all sterilizations were put under the same law, but what was regarded as the most important change was that compulsory sterilization (and compulsory castration) was removed from the law, on recommendations from the commission.[132] The disappearance of direct coercion from the law was approved by all the political parties, though the smaller parties were more outspoken in their condemnation of the older law. The commission pointed out that it would still be possible after the revision of the law to exert a certain indirect pressure on the mentally retarded to make them apply for sterilization, since release from the institutions, according to the law, could still depend on previous sterilization. This was noted and approved by the minister of health and welfare and by several of the other party representatives. Only representatives of the smaller parties worried about the possibilities of indirect coercion.[133]

The revision of the law was an indication of a general change in the attitude toward the mentally retarded, and probably this change was more important than the actual change in the law. The number of mentally retarded sterilized declined rapidly, from 275 in 1949 to 80 in 1962. During the same period, the safeguards concerning sterilization of this group had been improved. Appeal to a judge had been instituted as well as legal guardians (who could not be associated with the institutions). The organization of friends of the mentally retarded, *Evnesvages Vel*, had been actively involved both in the revision of the sterilization law in 1967 and in the earlier revision of the laws concerning the mentally retarded in 1959. It was now becoming accepted that the mentally retarded should also be allowed the right to a full sexual life.[134]

One thing that was not discussed in the parliamentary debates in 1967 was the topic of eugenics. The closest the discussion came to the subject was a remark from the representative of the Popular Socialist Party, a smaller party to the left of the Social Democrats:

> You will see that the racial hygienic value of sterilization and the value of racial hygiene as such were debated with complete seriousness in 1928. The discussion proceeded in 1934 and 1935, even though the more sober-minded regarded all that race talk as a passing fad.[135]

It is clear that the speaker associated racial hygiene with race biology and racism in general; one can assume from the debate that eugenics had been completely left behind, but this was not the case. The eugenic indication was maintained for mentally normal, and eugenic considerations still had to be included in the considerations for the sterilization of the mentally abnormal. The University Institute of Human Genetics also maintained a moderate negative eugenics as part of its objective, in so far as it was compatible with "democratic conditions with the high degree of personal freedom we prefer."[136] Eugenics therefore continued to be a part of the health policy in Denmark.

Still, eugenics was not a very important part: the number of sterilizations with eugenic indication compared to social indication was declining long before the law revision in 1967. In 1973 free sterilization and abortion were legalized: everybody who wanted to be sterilized or have an abortion could do so, which meant that the possibilities for exerting a eugenics policy were reduced even further. The introduction of chemical alternatives to sterilization also reduced the importance of the sterilization legislation.

Eugenic sterilization was introduced in Danish legislation with the utmost caution in 1929; some would say it was done by stealth. It seems to have disappeared from the Danish consciousness in the same clandestine way. There was no general debate, no confrontation when the sterilization law was revised in 1967; not even the introduction of amniocentesis tests in Denmark in 1970 sparked any discussion. Later, in the wake of the general debate on biotechnology in the 1970s, Denmark joined in the discussion, but by that time everybody seemed to have forgotten that eugenics also had a history in Denmark.

NOTES

The classical review of the development of eugenics in Denmark is T. Kemp, *Arvehygiejne, Københavns Universitets Årsskrift* (Copenhagen: Københavns Universitet, 1951). This has been treated more briefly in G. Koudahl, *Om Vasectomi med Sterilisation for Øje,* dissertation (Copenhagen: Munksgaard, 1967). A more recent treatment of the subject is B. S. Hansen, "Eugenik i Danmark, den Bløde Mellemvej," *Niche* 4 (1984): 85-102. The subject has been treated in connection with the general attitude toward the mentally retarded in B. Kirkebæk's detailed *Abnormbegrebet i Danmark i 20.erne og 30.erne med Særlig Henblik på Eugeniske Bestræbelser og Særlig i Forhold til Åndssvage,* dissertation (Copenhagen: Danmarks Lærerhøjskole, 1985) and in her "Staten og den Åndssvage 1870-1935, fra Filantropi til Kontrol," *Handicaphistorie* 1 (1987): 45-56.

Another work that treats the concept in an institutional setting is F. E. Andersen's "Diskurs og Discrimination," *Agrippa* 3 (1982): 338-60. An extremely interesting discussion of the relationship between eugenics and the other social biological ideologies and the development of social hygiene in general is presented in L. H. Schmidt and J. E. Kristensen, *Lys, Luft og Renlighed: Den Moderne socialhygiejnes fødsel* (Copenhagen: Akademisk Forlag, 1986), esp. 89-114.

The related concept of castration has been treated by L. LeMaire in his dissertation *Legal Kastration i Strafferetslig Belysning* (Copenhagen: Munksgaard, 1946).

1. For an overview of the literature dealing with the United States and Great Britain, see D. J. Kevles, *In the Name of Eugenics: Genetics and the Uses of Human Heredity* (New York: Alfred E. Knopf, 1985); L. Farral, "The History of Eugenics: A Bibliographical Review," *Annals of Science* 36 (1970): 111-23; for literature on Germany, see P. Weindling, *Health, Race and German Politics between National Unification and Nazism, 1870-1945* (Cambridge: Cambridge University Press, 1989); P. Weingart, J. Kroll and K. Bayertz, *Rasse, Blut un Gene. Geschichte der Rassenhygiene in Deutschland* (Frankfurt: Suhrkamp Verlag, 1988); R. N. Proctor, *Racial Hygiene: Medicine under the Nazis* (Cambridge: Harvard University Press, 1988); G. Bock, *Zwangssterilisation und Nationalsozialismus. Studien zur Rassenpolitik und Frauenpolitik* (Opladen: Westdeutscher Verlag, 1986); J. Müller, *Sterilisation und Gesetzgebung bis 1933* (Husum: Matthiesen Verlag, 1985).

2. For examples, see G. Searle, *Eugenics and Politics in Britain* (Leyden: Noordhoff International, 1976); S. F. Weiss, *Race Hygiene and National Efficiency: The Eugenics of Wilhelm Schallmayer* (Berkeley: University of California, 1987).

3. The Danish administrators in Greenland often behaved in the high-handed and condescending way that Europeans used toward native populations, but the effects in Denmark of these attitudes were marginal and cannot be compared to the effects Belgian and Dutch colonies had on their mother countries. In some ways, Greenland and the Greenlanders can be compared to the northern parts of the other Scandinavian countries and their indigenous population, the Lapps. But while there are examples of eugenic literature in both Sweden and Norway, which are concerned about the effects of miscegenation with the Lappish population, I have not been able to find similar examples in the Danish literature with respect to the Greenlanders. Perhaps the generally positive attitude toward these people was partly a result of the immense popularity of the explorer and ethnographer Knud Rasmussen, who himself was partly descended from a Greenlander family. Of course the Danish are not immune against racist prejudice. As a large number of young Greenlanders started moving to Denmark in the sixties and seventies, the accompanying social problems have caused a decidedly racist reaction.

4. K. Gjellerup, *Arvelighed og Moral* (Copenhagen: Andreas Schous Forlag, 1881); T. Ribot, *Sjælsevnernes Arvelighed* (Copenhagen: Gyldendal, 1899).

5. E. Mayr, *The Growth of Biological Thought* (Cambridge: The Belknap Press, 1982), 687-92.

6. F. R. Lange, *Om Arvelighedens indflydelse på Sindsygdommene* (Copenhagen: Gyldendal, 1881).

7. F. R. Lange, *Slægter, Iagttagelser fra en Sindssygeanstalt* (Copenhagen: Gyldendal, 1904). This was translated as *Degeneration in Families: Observations in a Lunatic Asylum* (London: Kimpton, 1906).

8. H. Bang, *Håbløse Slægter* (Copenhagen: Gyldendal, 1882).

9. J. B. Haycraft, *Darwinism and Social Improvement* (London: S Sonnenschein and Co., 1894). This was translated the same year into Danish as *Darwinism og Raceforbedring* (Copenhagen: Jacob Lunds Forlag, 1894).

10. C. Wilkens, *Samfundslegemets Grundlove* (Copenhagen: Wroblewskys Forlag, 1881).

11. G. Bang, *Den Gamle Adels Forfald* (Copenhagen: Gyldendal, 1897); O. Hansen, *Udviklingslære* (Copenhagen: Gyldendal, 1900).

12. J. P. Steensby, "Foreløbige betragtninger over Danmarks Raceantropologi," *Meddelelser om Danmarks Antropologi* 1 (1907-1911): 83-172.

13. See, for example, W. Johannsen, "Über Dolichocephalie und Brachycephalie. Zur Kritik der Index-Angaben," *Archiv für Rassen und Gesellschafts-Biologie* 4 (1907): 171-88; C. Burrau, "Om Hovedets Form og Størrelse," *Meddelelser om Danmarks Antropologi* 1, no. 2 (1908): 241-74.

14. The fate and status of other Danish scientists who demonstrated an interest in physical anthropology exemplify this lack of prestige. The economist K. A. Wieth-Knudsen tried to merge economics, population science, and physical anthropology

in his dissertation *Formerelse og Fremskridt. Økonomisk-Demografisk-biologisk Syntese* (Copenhagen: Julius Gjellerup, 1908), but the biological part of his argument was criticized strongly. Wieth-Knudsen felt that he was being excluded from scientific positions in Denmark and ended up as a professor at the business school in Trondheim, in what he himself considered an exile from Denmark. K. A. Wieth Knudsen, *Mit Videnskabelige Livs Drama eller Universitetets Besættelsesregler og professor L. V. Birck* (Copenhagen: Reitzel, 1930). Fr. C. C. Hansen had a scientific position as professor of anatomy at Copenhagen University and he had cooperated with the famous Swedish anthropologist Carl Fürst, but he was also a notable eccentric and his later works of anthropology—attempts to reconstruct the physiognomy of Danish medieval notables based on the skeletal remains—did not enhance the prestige of the discipline. Fr. C. C. Hansen, *Identifikation og Rekonstruktion af historiske Personers Udseende på Grundlag af Skelettet* (Copenhagen: Københavns Universitet, 1921).

15. P. Reilly, "The Surgical Solution: The Writing of Activist Physicians in the Early Days of Eugenical Sterilization," *Perspectives in Biology and Medicine* 26 (1983): 637-56.

16. For Hedman's role, see E. L. Hedman, "Sterilisation, Nogen Erfarenhetsrön," *Nyt Tidsskrift for Abnormvæsenet* 17 (1915): 107-15; O. E. Hedman, "Några Rön ur den i Praktiken tillämpade Sterilisation," *Nyt Tidsskrift for Abnormvæsenet* 26 (1924): 127-28. For the Danish example, see C. Keller, "Kønsløsgørelsens Problem," *Nyt Tidsskrift for Abnormvæsenet* 23 (1921): 6-9.

17. H. Laughlin, *Eugenical Sterilization in the United States* (Chicago: Chicago Psychopathic Laboratory, 1922); E. S. Gosney and P. Popenoe, *Sterilization for Human Betterment: A Summary of 6,000 Operations in California* (New York: MacMillan, 1929); J. H. Landman, *Human Sterilization* (New York: MacMillan, 1932). An American example of a powerful institutional leader was F. A. Butler, the medical director and superintendent of Sonoma State Home in California, where 4,310 inmates were sterilized from 1919 to 1943; see F. A. Butler, "A Quarter of a Century of Experience in Sterilization of Mental Defectives in California," *American Journal of Mental Deficiencies* 50 (1945): 508-13; see also Reilly, "The Surgical Solution."

18. H. C. Sharp, "The Severing of the Vasa Differentia, and Its Relation to the Neuropsychiatric Constitution," *New York Medical Journal* (1902): 411-14.

19. F. E. Daniel, "Emasculation of Masturbators—Is It Justifiable?" *Texas Medical Journal* 10 (1894): 239-44; see also M. W. Barr, *Mental Defectives* (Philadelphia: P. Blakiston's Son and Co., 1904), 196.

20. Barr, *Mental Defectives*, 196.

21. This criticism against surgical sterilization had already been raised by Prince Krapotkin at the First International Eugenics Congress. Krapotkin spoke with a certain authority, since he was without doubt the only participant who had extensive experience with penal institutions observed from the other side of the bars. See *Problems in Eugenics 2: Report of Proceedings of the First International Eugenics Congress* (London: Eugenics Education Society, 1912), 50-51.

22. Barr, *Mental Defectives*, 194.

23. A. Forel, *Det sexuelle spørgsmål* (Copenhagen: Gyldendal, 1913), 451-52; Weindling, *Health, Race and German Politics*, 84-87; Müller, *Sterilisation und Gesetzgebung bis 1933*, 37; P. Näcke, "Die Kastration bei Gewissen Klassen von Degenerirten als ein wirksamer socialer Schutz," *Archiv für Kriminalanthropologie und Kriminalistik* 3 (1900): 58-84. A. Mayer, *Alfred Hegart und der Gestaltwandel der Gynäkologie seit Hegar* (Freiburg: Herder, 1961).

24. A. Rogers, "Futility of Surgical Treatment," *Journal of Psycho-Asthenics* 3 (1898): 93-95. See also Barr, *Mental Defectives*, 182-88. I have not been able to find a recent historical treatment of this interesting episode.

25. For a characteristic expression of this sentiment, see H. M. Boies, *Prisoners and Paupers* (New York: Putnam, 1893). For a Danish example, see C. Keller, "Hvad Kan der Gøres for at Forringe de Åndssvages Tal," *Nyt Tidsskrift for Abnormvæsenet* 19 (1917): 19-24, 33-37.

26. The general development and character of the Danish institutions for the mentally retarded is described in B. Kirkebæk, "Staten og Den Åndssvage 1870-1935, fra Filantropi til Kontrol," *Handicaphistorie* 1 (1987): 45-56 and in B. Kirkebæk, *Da de Åndssvage blev Farlige* (Copenhagen: Socpol, 1993). The strong ties between the institutions and the Keller family have been detailed in the same manuscript (20-21, 103).

27. Barr, *Mental Defectives*, 192.

28. Ibid., 196.

29. C. Keller, "Åndssvaghed," *Nyt Tidsskrift for Abnormvæsenet* 7 (1905): 104-7.

30. M. W. Barr, "Sterilization of the Unfit. Asexualization—Attitudes of the Europeans: Results of Asexualization," *Journal of Psycho-Asthenics* 9 (1905): 127-29; S. D. Risley, "Is Asexualization Ever Justifiable in the Case of Imbecile Children?" *Journal of Psycho-Asthenics* 9 (1905): 92-98 (partly translated in C. Keller, "Den Åndssvages Kønsløsgørelse," *Nyt Tidsskrift for Abnormvæsenet* 8 [1906]: 161-71).

31. H. Scharling, "Bidrag til Diskussionen om Åndssvages Kønsløsgørelse," *Nyt Tidsskrift for Abnormvæsenet* 11 (1909): 188-92. For the development of the idea of x-ray sterilization, see Müller, *Sterilisation und Gesetzgebung bis 1933*, 22-25.

32. Examples of the articles dealing with or directly translating Goddard's work are C. Keller, "Studiet af Normale og Abnorme Børn," *Nyt Tidsskrift for Abnormvæsenet* 13 (1911): 1-12; H. H. Goddard, "Åndssvaghedens Arvelighed" (translated by B. Hjort), *Nyt Tidsskrift for Abnormvæsenet* 13 (1911): 257-70; B. Hjort, "Familien Kallikak," *Nyt Tidsskrift for Abnormvæsenet* 15 (1913): 1-7; and C. Keller, "Fra Vineland Laboratoriet," *Nyt Tidsskrift for Abnormvæsenet* 15 (1913): 125-26.

33. W. Fernald, "After-care Study of the Patients Discharged from Waverley for a Period of Twenty-five Years Upgraded," *American Journal of Mental Deficiency* 4 (1919): 62-81; H. H. Goddard, "Feeblemindedness: A Question of Definition," *Journal of Psycho-Asthenics* 33 (1928): 219-27. For examples of the kind of criticism directed against Goddard's results and against eugenic sterilizations in general, see R. Pearl, "The Biology of Superiority," *American Mercury* 47 (1926):

257-66; and A. Myerson, "Some Objections to Sterilization," *Birth Control Review* 12 (1928): 81-84.

34. A. Björkman, "Om Forekomsten af Svagsintheten i Finland og Några där av Föranledda Reflexioner," *Nyt Tidsskrift for Abnormvæsenet* 15 (1913): 72-73; E. L. Hedman, "Andesvagsvårdens Betydelse och Uppgift i Social och Rashygienisk Avseende," *Nyt Tidsskrift for Abnormvæsenet* 15 (1913): 73-78; Från Helsingforsmödet, "Sammendrag af Forhantlingarna vid Andesvagesektionerne," *Nyt Tidsskrift for Abnormvæsenet* 15 (1913): 65-71.

35. See the exchange in *Nyt Tidsskrift for Abnormvæsenet* 14 (1912): 241-45 (Hedman), 284-285 (Bodil Hjort), 328-29 (Åstrand); and in *Nyt Tidsskrift for Abnormvæsenet* 15 (1913): 24-26 (Hedman), 83-84 (Åstrand).

36. For the development in Finland, see M. Hietala, "From Race Hygiene to Sterilization: The Eugenics Movement in Finland," in this volume.

37. Hedman, "Sterilisation, Nogen Erfarenhetsrön". See also Hedman, "Några Rön ur den i Praktiken tillämpade Sterilisation." Hedman's vasectomy operations were first reported in Denmark in a brief notice in *Nyt Tidsskrift for Abnormvæsenet* 15 (1913): 29.

38. A. Bramsen, *De Velbaarne og de Belastede* (Copenhagen: Martins Forlag, 1912); Forel, *Det sexuelle spørgsmål.*

39. See, for example, S. Hansen, "Eugenicsbevægelsen," *Ugeskrift for Læger* 35 (1912): 3-7; S. Hansen, "Om Raceforbedring," *Nationaløkonomisk Tidsskrift* (1912-13): 11-30; S. Hansen, "En Undersøgelse af Døvstumhedens Arvelighed i Racehygiejnisk Øjemed," *Månedsskrift for Sundhedsvæsen* (1913): 97-106; S. Hansen, "Degenererer Overklasserne?" *Månedsskrift for Sundhedsvæsen* (1914): 97-99; S. Hansen, "Racehygiejne," *Månedsskrift for Sundhedsvæsen* (1915): 163-71.

40. S. Hansen, "Om en Registrering af Åndssvage," *Nyt Tidsskrift for Abnormvæsenet* 17 (1915): 82-85; S. Hansen, "Det Racebiologiske Laboratorium," *Naturens Verden* 4 (1920): 271-75; see also J. Mohr, "Human Arvebiologi og Eugenik," in *Københavns Universitet 1479-1979,* vol. 7, *Det Lægevidenskabelige Fakultet,* ed. J. C. Melchior et al. (Copenhagen: Copenhagen: Københavns Universitet, 1979), 241-52.

41. See S. Hansen, "Åndssvages Giftermål," *Ugeskrift for Retsvæsen* (1923), 153-56, and compare this with S. Hansen, "Retten og racehygiejnen," *Juridisk Tidsskrift* 1 (1915): 761-80, 2 (1916): 8-23, 66-81.

42. See Hansen, "Retten og racehygiejnen," 766-67.

43. V. Rasmussen, *Rigsdagstidende, Folketinget* (1915-16): 196-97.

44. Hedman, "Sterilisation, Nogen Erfarenhetsrön." See also E. L. Hedman, "Öppet Brev til Herr Doktor Søren Hansen," *Nyt Tidsskrift for Abnormvæsenet* 17 (1915): 22-23. For Keller's attitude toward eugenics, see V. Rasmussen, *Rigsdagstidende, Folketinget* (1915-16): 196-97.

45. C. Keller, "Livø-Mænd," *Nyt Tidsskrift for Abnormvæsenet* 14 (1912): 1-13, 42-45, 79-91, 142-65; C. Keller, "Livø. Mændenes Ø," *Nyt Tidsskrift for Abnormvæsenet* 22 (1920): 93-95; C. Keller, "'Sprogø' som Kvindernes Ø," *Nyt Tidsskrift for Abnormvæsenet* 22 (1920): 95-98; C. Keller, "Sprogø," *Nyt Tidsskrift for Abnormvæsenet* 23 (1921): 43-47, 129-30.

46. C. Keller, "Hvad Kan der Gøres for at Forringe de Åndssvages Tal," *Nyt Tidsskrift for Abnormvæsenet* 19 (1917): 19-24, 33-37 (translated from W. Fernald, "The Burden of Feeble-mindedness," *Journal of Psycho-Asthenics* 17 [1912]: 89-111); K. K. Steincke, *Fremtidens Forsørgelsesvæsen* (Copenhagen: J. H. Schultz, 1920), 241.

47. C. Keller, "Kønsløsgørelsen's Problem" (with a copy of Keller's petition), *Nyt Tidsskrift for Abnormvæsenet* 23 (1921): 6-9. For development in Switzerland, see Müller, *Sterilisation und Gesetzgebung bis 1933*, 37-40; B. Zurugzoglu, "Die Probleme der Eugenik Under Besondere Berüchsichtigung der Verhütung Erbkranken Nachwuchses," in *Verhütung Erbkranken Nachwuchses*, ed. S. Zurugzoglu (Basel: Birkhaüser, 1938).

48. W. L. Johannsen, *Arvelighed i Historisk og Eksperimentel Belysning* (Copenhagen: Gyldendal, 1917), 4-5.

49. Ibid., 259-68, esp. 264.

50. Ibid., 269-74. For the controversy between Johannsen and Pearson, see N. Roll-Hansen, "The Death of Spontaneous Generation and the Birth of the Gene: Two Case Studies of Relativism," *Social Studies of Science* 13 (1983): 481-519.

51. Johannsen, *Arvelighed i Historisk og Eksperimentel Belysning*, 268, 275.

52. Ibid., 278-87.

53. Ibid., 277.

54. Ibid., 287-88.

55. Ibid., 289.

56. J. A. Mjøen, "Rassenhygiene in den Nordischen Landern," *Nationalsozialistische Monatshefte* (6 October 1935): 874-85, 875-76 (remarks about Johannsen).

57. Mohr, "Human Arvebiologi og Eugenik."

58. W. Johannsen, *Arvelighed i Historisk og Eksperimentel Belysning. 4. omarbejdede og forøgede udgave* (Copenhagen: Gyldendal, 1923); W. Johannsen, "Racehygiejniske Problemer," *Naturens Verden* 11 (1927): 214-35.

59. *Betænkning Angående Sociale Foranstaltninger Overfor Degenerativt Bestemte Personer* (Copenhagen, 1926), 20-23; material from "Kommissionen Angående Sociale Foranstaltninger overfor Degenerativt Bestemte Personer," Danish National Archive.

60. O. Thomsen, "Sterilisering med Racehygiejnisk Formål, Nordisk Tidsskrift for Videnskab," *Kunst og Kultur* 11 (1935): 115-23; O. Thomsen, "Forbrydelse som Skæbne," *Politiken,* 22 December 1928, 4; A. Wimmer, "Ægteskabslovgivning og Racehygiejne," *Gads Danske Magasin* (1911-12): 91-96; A. Wimmer, *Sindsygdommenes Arvegang og Raceforbedrende Bestræbelser* (Copenhagen: Levin og Munksgaard, 1929).

61. Ø. Winge, "Er der Fare for Samfundets Arvelige Degeneration," *Naturens Verden* 17 (1933): 106-19.

62. J. C. Smith, "Dementia Præcox og Maniodepressive Psykosers Arvelighedsforhold," *Hospitalstidende* 64 (1921): 152-58; J. C. Smith, "Sterilisation af Åndssvage. Foreløbige Erfaringer på Grundlag af den danske lov af Maj 1934 om Foranstaltninger vedrørende Ånddssvage," *Nordisk Tidsskrift för*

Sinnesslövård 38 (1936): 97-107. See also A. Bruun and J. C. Smith, "Om Sterilisation af Åndssvage i henhold til lov nr. 117 af 16. maj 1934 om Foranstaltningeer vedrørende Åndssvage," *Socialt Tidsskrift* (1939): 369-81.

63. Steincke, *Fremtidens Forsørgelsesvæsen*. Steincke has left an extensive, five-volume biography which only makes the need for a critical biography more acute (K. K. Steincke, *Også en Tilværelse* [Copenhagen: Fremad, 1945-49]). For a bibliography of his considerable literary output, see T. Kjøller-Pedersen, *K. K. Steincke, En Bibliografi*, dissertation (Copenhagen: The Danish Library School, 1977).

64. K. K. Steincke, *Også en Tilværelse: Minder og Meninger* (Copenhagen: Fremad, 1945), 245-46.

65. G. von Hoffman, *Die Rassenhygiene in den Vereignigten Staaten von Nordamerika* (München: J. Lehmann, 1913); R. Larsson, *Biologiske Causerier* (Copenhagen: Gyldendal, 1918).

66. Steincke, *Fremtidens Forsørgelsesvæsen*, 251-52.

67. K. K. Steincke, "Sociallovgivning og Racehygiejne," *Ugeskrift for Læger* 90 (1928): 1138-45.

68. J. Arenholt, "Sædelighedsforbrydelser mod Børn," *Kvinden og Samfundet* 37 (1921): 101-21. See also the debate in the same volume, 34-35, 42-43 (M. B. Westenholz) and 44, 53-54, 60-61 (L. B. Wright).

69. A. Goll, "Sterilisation af Forbrydere," *Nordisk Tidsskrift for Strafferet* 11 (1923): 1-20; G. E. Schrøder, *Ufrugtbargørelse som Led i Moderne Forbryderbehandling, Tilskueren* 39 (1922): 88-112.

70. *Betænkning Angående Sociale Foranstaltninger Overfor Degenerativt Bestemte Personer*, 11-14, 20-23.

71. For the history of the Hardy-Weinberg law, see W. B. Provine, *The Origin of Theoretical Population Genetics* (Chicago: Chicago University Press, 1971). See also R. C. Punnett, "Eliminating Feeblemindedness," *Journal of Heredity* 8 (1917): 464-65.

72. *Betænkning Angående Sociale Foranstaltninger Overfor Degenerativt Bestemte Personer*, 20-23.

73. Ibid., 23-27; H. O. Wildenskov, *Investigation into the Causes of Mental Deficiency* (Copenhagen: Levin og Munksgaard, 1934).

74. *Betænkning Angående Sociale Foranstaltninger Overfor Degenerativt Bestemte Personer*, 28.

75. See Kemp, *Arvehygiejne, Københavns Universitets Årsskrift*, 27, 31-32. For a detailed treatment of the German law, see Bock, *Zwangssterilisation und Nationalsozialismus*; Müller, *Sterilisation und Gesetzgebung bis 1933*; Weindling, *Health, Race and German Politics*; and Weingart et al., *Rasse, Blut und Gene*.

76. V. Rasmussen, *Rigsdagstidende, Folketinget* (1928-29): 3069-76.

77. Rasmussen, *Rigsdagstidende, Folketinget* (1928-29): 3050-94, 4677-88, 4746-77, 5749-55; A. Goll, "Sterilisationsloven af 1. Juni 1929 og dens Resultater," *Politiken* (9-12 June 1933).

78. T. Kemp, "Sterilisation og Racehygiejne," *Politiken* (28 June 1933); K. Sand, "Sterilisation af Syge, Abnorme og Forbrydere," *Politiken* (23 January 1935).

79. Regarding the law of 1934, see *Betænkning om Åndssvageforsorgen, Betænkning nr. 204* (Copenhagen, 1958), 101-12; *Betænkning om Sterilisation og Kastration, Betænkning nr. 353* (Copenhagen, 1964), 19-20, 25, 29. For an unusually blunt statement regarding the application of the law, see R. Marthinsen, *Åndssvaghed og Åndssvageforsorg* (Ribe: Eget Forlag, 1957), 102.

80. A. Bruun and J. C. Smith, "Om Sterilisation af Åndssvage i Henhold til lov nr 117 af 16. maj 1934 om Foranstaltninger Vedrørende Åndssvage," *Socialt Tidsskrift* (1939): 369-81.

81. For a more detailed description of this episode, see Kirkebæk, *Abnormbegrebet i Danmark i 20.erne og 30.erne med Særlig Henblik på Eugeniske Bestræbelser og Særlig i Forhold til Åndssvage*, 144-47. The fact that workers attacked a law enacted by the Social Democratic government was noted, not without malice, by several conservative newspapers.

82. E. Schibbye, *Lov nr 176 af 11 maj 1935 om Adgang til Sterilisation og Kastration* (Copenhagen: J. H. Schultz, 1952); *Betænkning om Sterilisation og Kastration, Betænkning nr. 353*, 112-66.

83. K. Sand, "Den Danske Sterilisationslov af 1. Juni 1929 og dens Resultater, med Overvejelser om Lovens Revision," *Nordisk Tidsskrift for Strafferet* 23 (1935): 31-86. The review appeared with Sand listed as the only author, but it represented the opinion of the whole medico-legal council.

84. Ibid., 78.

85. Ibid.

86. Ibid., 78-79.

87. Ibid., 81.

88. A. Wimmer, *Sindsygdommenes Arvegang og Raceforbedrende Bestræbelser*; K. Hansen, *Arvelighed hos Mennesket* (Nykøbing F.: Eget Forlag, 1929).

89. A. Garbo, *Arvelighed og Socialpolitik* (Copenhagen: P. Haase og Søns Forlag, 1931). The "Zwickauer Gesetzte" was a controversial eugenic proposal forwarded by Gerhard Boeters, the municipal physician of Zwickau, Sachsen, in 1923. See Müller, *Sterilisation und Gesetzgebung bis 1933*, 60-63; and Weindling, *Health, Race and German Politics*.

90. O. Thomsen, *Lærebog om Menneskets Arvelighedsforhold* (Copenhagen: Levin og Munksgaard, 1932); O. Thomsen, *Arvelighedsforhold hos Mennesket*, a series of lectures that were broadcast by Danish Radio (Copenhagen: Levin og Munksgaard, 1930); Ø. Winge et al., *Arv og Race* (Copenhagen: Martin's Forlag, 1934); T. Geiger, *Samfund og Arvelighed* (Copenhagen: Martin's Forlag, 1935).

91. Geiger, esp. 122-79 and 257-78. See also the anonymous review of Geiger's book in *Socialt Tidsskrift* 11 (1935): 121-24.

92. For the changing attitude in Germany under the impact of the world crisis, see Müller, *Sterilisation und Gesetzgebung bis 1933*; and Weindling, *Health, Race and German Politics*. A detailed description of the reaction in the religious communities is given by K. Nowak, *"Euthanasie" und Sterilisierung im "Dritten Reich"* (Göttingen: Vandenhoech und Ruprecht, 1978).

93. For description of the birth control movement in Denmark, see B. Lau, *Børnebegrænsningsbevægelsen i Danmark i 1920erne og 1930erne*, dissertation (Aarhus: Aarhus University, 1972); B. Borgen, *Thit Jensen's Samfundsengagement* (Copenhagen: Vinten, 1976); P. Hertoft, *Det er måske en Galskab* (Copenhagen: Gyldendal, 1985); and J. H. Leunbach, *Racehygiejne* (Copenhagen: Martin's Forlag, 1926). For the polemic between Søren Hansen and Leunbach, see *Ugeskrift for Læger* 87 (1925): 42-43, 64-65, 91-92, 114, 138. Thit Jensen stated her view on birth control and eugenics in T. Jensen, *Frivilligt Moderskab* (Copenhagen: Kria, 1923), a small tract containing a lecture first given in the small provincial town Kolding, 5 November 1923.

94. The history of this eccentric cosmology has been treated in B. Nagel, *Die Welteislehre. Ihre Geschichte und ihre Rolle im "Dritten Reich"* (Stuttgart: Verlag fur Geschichte der Naturwissenschaft und der Technik, 1991).

95. "Den Nordiske Race" was published as a feature in *Det Nye Nord* from 1920-25, but it appeared as an independent periodical in Norway. For a more detailed treatment of Mjøen, see N. Roll-Hansen, "Eugenics before World War II: The Case of Norway," *History and Philosophy of the Life Sciences* 2 (1980): 269-98.

96. See R. Spärck, "Racebegrebet Biologisk Set," in *Arv og Race*, Ø. Winge, et al. (Copenhagen: Martin's Forlag, 1934), 27-36; G. Hatt, "De Menneskelige Racer," in *Arv og Race*, Ø. Winge et al. (Copenhagen: Martin's Forlag, 1934), 37-61; A. Olsen, "Den Jødiske Race," in *Arv og Race*, Ø. Winge et al. (Copenhagen: Martin's Forlag, 1934), 129-43; S. Hansen, "Racerne," *Politiken* (19 June 1933). Paradoxically, Gudmund Hatt wrote in support of Germany during the occupation of Denmark. The fate of "Nordische Gesellschaft" is described in H. J. Lützhoft, *Der Nordische Gedanke in Deutschland 1920-1940* (Stuttgart: Klett, 1971). Virtually the only prominent Dane who was active in this enterprise was Wieth-Knudsen, the economist and anthropologist who had been exiled to Norway (see note 14).

97. G. K. Chesterton, *Eugenics and other Evils* (London: Cassel and Co., 1922).

98. G. Scherz, "Sterilisation og Racehygiejne," *Nordisk Ugeblad for Katolske Kristne* 82 (1933): 38-42; G. Scherz, "Til hvad Gavn er Sterilisation," *Nordisk Ugeblad for Katolske Kristne* 82 (1933): 720-24; Hansen, "Retten og racehygiejnen," 762-71; Steincke, *Fremtidens Forsørgelsesvæsen*, 246-47

99. Scherz, "Til hvad Gavn er Sterilisation."

100. H. Muckermann, *Familien og Folket*, pamphlets 1-5 (Copenhagen: Katolsk Ungdom, 1931).

101. M. Pedersen, "Nogle Betragtninger, særlig Vedrørende Lægers Stilling til Sterilisationsloven," *Ugeskrift for Læger* 91 (1929): 194-95.

102. V. Rasmussen, *Rigsdagstidende, Folketinget* (1934-1935), 5127-31, 5141-43.

103. S. Rifbjerg, *Udviklingshæmmede Børn* (Copenhagen: Levin og Munksgaard, 1935), 194-95.

104. Kemp, *Arvehygiejne, Københavns Universitets Årsskrift*, 27, 31-32. For details of the German sterilization act, see Weindling, *Health, Race and German Politics* and Müller, *Sterilisation und Gesetzgebung bis 1933*.

105. Kemp, "Sterilisation og Racehygiejne"; Goll, "Sterilisationsloven af 1. Juni 1929 og dens Resultater"; Hansen, "Racerne."

106. S. Hansen, "De Tyske Sterilisationslove," *Ugeskrift for Læger* 95 (1933): 912-13.

107. A. Goll, "De Arvesyge og Samfundet," in *Arv og Race*, Ø. Winge et al. (Copenhagen: Martin's Forlag, 1934), 89.

108. H. I. Schou, "Sterilisation af Sindssyge og Abnorme i Tyskland," *Ugeskrift for Læger* 96 (1934): 1248-49.

109. K. K. Steincke, letter, *Ugeskrift for Læger* 96 (1934): 1248-49.

110. T. Kemp, letter, *Ugeskrift for Læger* 95 (1933): 965.

111. J. H. Leunbach, letter, *Ugeskrift for Læger* 95 (1933): 925. Leunbach's advocacy of free sterilization drew strong criticism from Søren Hansen (S. Hansen, letter, *Ugeskrift for Læger* 95 (1933): 964.

112. A. Wimmer, "Moderne Racehygiejne," in *Arv og Race*, Ø. Winge et al. (Copenhagen: Martin's Forlag, 1934), 108-17.

113. A. Garboe, "I Anledning af den Tyske Sterilisationslov," *Socialt Tidsskrift* 9 (1933): 396.

114. H. O. Wildenskov, "Sterilisationslovens Revision," *Socialt Tidsskrift* 10 (1934): 1-13, esp. 5-8.

115. Sand, "Den Danske Sterilisationslov af 1. Juni 1929 og dens Resultater, med Overvejelser om Lovens Revision."

116. See A. Ebbinghaus, H. Kaupen-Haas and K. H. Roth, *Heilen und Vernichten in Mustergau Hamburg. Bevölkerungs und Gesundheitspolitik im Dritten Reich* (Hamburg: Konkret Literatur Verlag, 1984).

117. W. Kopp, "Arvelighed og Racehygiejne i Det Tredie Riges Lovgivning," *Juristen* 19 (1937): 249-60. Compare the views of Schou ("Sterilisation af Sindssyge og Abnorme i Tyskland") and Goll ("De Arvesyge og Samfundet"). This argument was reiterated after the war by several German geneticists. See, for example, H. Nachtsheim, "Das Gesetzt zur Verhütung erbkranken Nachwuchses aus dem Jahre 1933 in heutiger Sicht, Artzliche Mitteilungen," *Deutschen Ärtzteblatt* 33, no. 59 (1962): 1640-44; H. Harmsen, "The German Sterilization Act," *Eugenics Review* 45 (1954): 227-32.

118. The population commission had originally recommended a limited social indication for abortion but was overruled by the Minister of Health and Welfare, K. K. Steincke, who also overruled other recommendations, including the institution of sexual counseling. See Hertoft, *Det er måske en Galskab*; Steincke, *Også en Tilværelse*; and A. Myrdal and G. Myrdal, *Kris i Befolkningsfrågan* (Stockholm: Bonniers, 1934). The effect of this influential book in Denmark and other Scandinavian countries has been described by A. C. Carlson, *Kris i Befolkningsfrågan*, dissertation (Minneapolis: University of Minnesota, 1978).

119. V. Rasmussen, *Rigsdagstidende, Landstinget* (1937-1938), 172-74, 458-85, 786-802, 829-35.

120. T. Kemp, "A Study of the Causes of Prostitution, Especially Concerning Hereditary Factors," in *A Decade of Progressive Eugenics, Scientific Papers of The Third International Congress of Eugenics*, ed. N. Perkins et al., (Baltimore: The

Williams and Wilkins Co., 1934), 255-63; T. Kemp, *Prostitution, An Investigation of Its Causes, Especially with Regard to Hereditary Factors* (Copenhagen: Levin og Munksgaard, 1936).

121. P. Weindling, "The Rockefeller Foundation and German Biomedical Science 1920-1940: From Educational Philanthropy to International Science Policy," in *Science, Politics and the Public Good: Essays in Honour of Margaret Gowing*, ed. N. Rupke (Basingstoke: MacMillan, 1988), 119-40. See also Kevles, *In the Name of Eugenics*, esp. 209-10.

122. "Report to the Rockefeller Foundation of visits to various Institutes, Laboratories, etc. for Human Genetics in Europe July-October 1934, by Tage Kemp," Rockefeller Archives, transfer file 713A.

123. T. Kemp, "Aktuelle Eugeniske Problemer," *Ledetråd ved Folkelig Universitetsforskning*, no. 41 (Copenhagen: Levin og Munksgaard, 1936). T. Kemp, "Den Moderne Arvelighedsforskning," *Nordisk Tidsskrift for Vetenskap, Konst och Industri* (1939): 394-409.

124. Kemp, *Arvehygiejne, Københavns Universitets Årsskrift*; T. Kemp, "The Frequency of Diseases Affected by Heredity in Denmark," *Cold Spring Harbor Symposium in Quantitative Biology* 15 (1952): 129-40.

125. The University Institute provided genetic counseling from 1939. The Heredity Clinic at the University of Michigan was established in 1940 and the Dight Institute in 1941 at the University of Minnesota (Kevles, *In the Name of Eugenics*, 251-54). Of course, Eheberatungsstellen and similar institutions had provided genetic advice even earlier.

126. Kemp, *Arvehygiejne, Københavns Universitets Årsskrift*, 50 table 9.

127. *Betænkning afgivet af det af Arbejds og Socialministeriet nedsatte Udvalg angående den mod Børne og Åndssvageforsorgen offentligt fremførte Kritik* (Copenhagen, 1941); *Betænkning om Åndssvageforsorgens Problemer, betænkning nr. 185* (Copenhagen, 1957); *Betænkning om Åndssvageforsorgen, betænkning nr. 204* (Copenhagen, 1958), 104-11.

128. *Betænkning om Åndssvageforsorgen, betænkning nr. 204*, 105.

129. Ibid., 111.

130. T. Kemp, "Address at the Opening of the First International Congress of Human Genetics," *Acta Genetica at Statistica* 6 (1956-57): xii-xiii.

131. T. Kemp, "Genetic-Hygienic Experiences in Denmark in Recent Years," *The Eugenics Review* 49 (1957): 11-18.

132. *Betænkning om Sterilisation og Kastration, Betænkning nr. 353*, 24, 71-72; *Folketingets Forhandlinger* (1966-1967), 52-55, 925-43.

133. *Betænkning om Sterilisation og Kastration, Betænkning nr. 353*, 29-30; *Folketingets Forhandlinger* (1966-1967), 927 (Ib Thyregod, the Agrarian Party), 941-942 (the Minister of Justice, K. Axel Nielsen, the Social Democrats). For an example of the anxiety concerning the indirect coercion on the mentally retarded, see *Folketingets Forhandlinger* (1966-1967), 932 (Hanne Reintoft, The Socialist People's Party).

134. *Betænkning om Sterilisation og Kastration, Betænkning nr. 353*, 20-21 and table page 19.

135. *Folketingets Forhandlinger* (1966-1967), 932 (Hanne Reintoft, The Socialist People's Party).

Eugenics in Sweden: Efficient Care

Gunnar Broberg and Mattias Tydén

Among all the Nordic countries, Sweden was where eugenics met with its greatest success. This is true both in terms of the early institutionalization of the movement and the eugenic practice as it was manifest in sterilization policies between 1930 and 1960. This relative success is connected with the unusually rapid development of Sweden from a nation with an agrarian economy to an industrialized urban society, hence from a culture dominated by traditional Lutheran Christian values to one dominated by a secularized and modern lifestyle. As this essay aims to show, eugenics in Sweden is linked to both these traditions and also belongs, though in an altered shape, to what has been called "the Swedish model."

This essay begins with the general background of race biology in Sweden. It discusses the development and institutionalization of Swedish eugenics in the first decades of the twentieth century and takes a closer look at the development and application of Swedish laws on sterilization. Finally, we briefly follow the changes in eugenics in the postwar period and conclude with a discussion of the context of the eugenics movement in Sweden.

The Turn of the Century: The Agonies of Modernity

A Swede living at the turn of the century felt the winds of change. Although an American observer stressed "the extraordinarily rapid, tranquil, and successful modernization of Sweden"—and this may have been so—the "tranquillity" should not be exaggerated.[1] This "modernization" involved economic growth, urbanization, political democratization, increased social planning, and an improved standard of living. But it also entailed growing social complexity and diversity, a faster paced "maelstrom of modern life," and a growing sentiment that society had reached a stage where old solutions and old morals no longer applied.[2]

The turn-of-the-century Swede confronted a number of major historical events. The first was emigration: from 1870 to 1914, an estimated one million—or one-sixth of the population—emigrated from Sweden, principally to the United States. Some felt that this was draining the nation of its best young minds. The union between Sweden and Norway—long considered degrading by Norwegians—was broken, after lengthy negotiations, in 1905. Some Swedes wanted to take up arms to round up their wayward brothers, but most simply felt an increasing national impotence. The political and social mobility of the time—the labor movement, the women's rights movement, the temperance movement, the free-church movement—gave rise to further anxiety in conservative quarters. In an atmosphere of weakness and national defeat, the statistician Gustaf Sundbärg sought to capture "the Swedish national character" in the Official Report on Emigration (1911), bearing down on Swedish timidity and insufficient self-esteem while aiming a blow at pushy Denmark. In 1914, influenced by a farmers' rally, King Gustaf V tried in vain to check parliamentarianism and reestablish a secure position for the monarchy with his so-called Courtyard Speech. Sven Hedin, the well-known explorer, attempted to arouse the nation to political participation and military preparedness with his 1914 pamphlet Ett varningsord (A warning)—of which one million copies were printed for a population of less than six million. For Hedin, as for other Swedes—and this had been so since the seventeenth century—Russia was the main enemy. Sweden was the eastern outpost of European civilization, confronting the Asian "heathens" on its border. Historically, its mission was to safeguard European culture and the Lutheran faith. When World War I broke out, Sweden was spared but, as elsewhere, there were hunger riots and fear for the future of the nation.

All these developments pulled at the Swede around the turn of the century. This does not mean that the average Swede considered the real problems the most important ones. Instead, he got caught up in pseudo-phenomena, such as the fear of the consequences for Swedish culture of impending immigration (the foreign workers in Sweden numbered only 1,678 in 1907). It was held that industrialization led to higher costs for society, increasing the number of mentally retarded and mentally ill, and enabling some—the criminals—to profit from this unhealthy development. Living under stress, pressed for time, a growing number of people were said to develop neurasthenia—though this disorder could be viewed as a self-serving invention of an expanding medical profession. But the industrialization of the country also caused a cheapening of ideals as never before. In evaluating the effects of living in a new, industrial society, the starting point was a form of unreflective Lamarckism that assumed that the period's great environmental changes would lead to swift (and most often undesirable) changes in man.

This emphasis on ongoing degeneration was typical of the times. Central to it were medical ideas of degeneration, fleshed out with anthropological cultural philosophy and a full measure of old-fashioned moralism. The antidote to degeneration was to be found in information and hygiene. "The breakthrough of the modern era" in the Nordic countries, from the 1880s to World War I, could be called a new period of enlightenment, characterized, among other things, by broad endeavors in the field of social hygiene.[3]

Among the radical formations of the 1880s was, for example, the student association Verdandi—a name taken from Nordic mythology. It published a widely circulated series of pamphlets dealing with contemporary subjects. Early issues dealt with such topics as "The Decline in the Mortality Rate of Sweden and Its Causes," "The External Diseases of Domestic Animals and Their Treatment," "On the Care of Infants," "How Our Body Protects Itself against Germs," and "Bathing Spells Health." Thus, the population was taught cleanliness in order to be better suited for the requirements of the new society. This opening up of private life for social ends gave society another form of control, but the opposite trend was also there, of course; visits to the bathroom, for example, became an ever more private matter. Propagation and population policies were important areas of instruction, but not the only evidence of this trend. The eugenics movement is only a subdivision of the hygiene movement. Indeed, for many people, the striving for health coupled with a belief in progress became something of a religion. The physician or scientist came to replace the minister as the central figure in the intellectual life of rural communities. In public situations he became the indispensable expert on social questions; he is also the main character in Henrik Ibsen's *En folkefiende* (A public enemy) published in 1882 and in August Strindberg's *I havsbandet* (By the open sea) published in 1890. The various reports on which modern social policies were to be based were largely the result of the work of scientists. Thus the educated middle class gained more influence in society than ever before.

The foremost cultural figure in Sweden at the end of the nineteenth century was Viktor Rydberg, writer and cultural historian. As it happened, his last publication was a long introduction to an 1895 Swedish edition of Benjamin Kidd's *Social Evolution*, entitled "The Downfall of the White Race." Dissenting from Kidd's Darwinian optimism, Rydberg envisioned European culture being overthrown by the Chinese. He predicted that the downfall would come in the very near future and would come about because of moral degeneration, demographic conditions, and the ensuing defects in the population. Rydberg's belief in a swift, negative transformation has clear Lamarckian features, but the cure that he suggests is not initially eugenic or biological; instead, he advocates moral rearmament. With the pathos of a prophet, he really sees no other possible outcome than his own death and the death of his race.[4]

The theme of degeneration reappears in *Sveriges adel* (Swedish nobility), a comprehensive investigation of the Swedish nobility published between 1898 and 1903 by the political scientist and philanthropist Pontus Fahlbeck. The rules of the foundation that he established later to promote inquiries into "that great subject, the decline and fall of peoples, nations, and cultures" are characteristic for his own intellectual profile. The times were evil, in his religiously colored view; yet he sought to do all that he humanly could to turn the tide through research and information. On and off in his work he refers to Adolphe Quételet's *l'homme moyen*, setting against him "not only the superhuman genius but probably also the subhuman born criminal"; as is evident, the ideas of Lombroso had found acceptance. The term "degeneration," so hard to define, is given three meanings: physical degeneration, moral degeneration, and deficient generative power—the latter leading to weak offspring or none, sterility, and finally the end of a lineage. Through statistical, genealogical research, Fahlbeck showed that the "generative power" of the nobility was on the decline. The reason was not only voluntary contraceptive measures— Fahlbeck was opposed to neo-Malthusianism—but also physiological factors hitherto unknown. The fact was that a "reflective" lifestyle, such as that of the nobility, did not further fertility. In addition, by living for themselves and not for the race, they set a dangerous example for the lower classes. Nor would regeneration from the middle class suffice to turn the downward trend. What was needed was a "power of a higher order" which, alone, could make people forgo comforts for the sake of society and the future. "This power is *religion*," Fahlbeck states, "the sense of duty stemming from the cause of all things." He then ends with a neo-Kantian, religiously inspired vision which, with its focus on decline, combines fin de siècle philosophy with social Darwinism.[5]

A voice very different from that of the conservative Fahlbeck was Ellen Key's, the grand old lady of the movement for women's rights in Sweden and an important conveyor of contemporary international opinion. *Barnets århundrade* (The century of the child), published in 1900, appropriately, makes manifest an interest in eugenics, and in *Lifslinjer* (Lines of life), published in 1903, she professes a form of sensual eugenics:

> We should again preserve family history, but not only that written in the old family
> Bibles, with the important dates for birth, marriage, and death; no, that which

takes up also the circumstances which caused birth and death. We should again begin to cast horoscopes, but less by the signs in the sky—though they may regain some of their earlier significance—than by those on earth, and not only by the signs at birth, but long before it. As alchemy became chemistry; astrology, astronomy; such interpretation of signs will probably prepare for what—while waiting for a word with a deeper significance than Galton's *eugenics* and ontogeny—one could call erotoplastics: the principle of love as a consciously creative art instead of a blind, generative power. It would be of immensely greater consequence for mankind if the majority of those women who transform their experiences into half honest and wholly inartistic poems composed completely true family chronicles and entirely honest confessions for the use of science.[6]

Few, however, followed Key's idealistic erotoplastics; with its request for family chronicles and honest confessions, it involved a eugenic research program of sorts, the results of which would have proved fascinating for later historians. Although her writing could be linked to contemporary science, however, as was the case with Rydberg and Fahlbeck, and although Key could be numbered with the adherents of eugenics, her moral and religious arguments carried the most weight.

ANTHROPOLOGY, GENETICS, AND EUGENICS

The idea that there are superior Nordic virtues is common in Swedish tradition and is rooted in the classics and in Viking history and Gothic traditions. It was given a supreme expression in Olof Rudbeck's *Atlantica* (1679). The idea of an especially prominent Nordic "race" is of a later date, however. Linnaeus, of course, in his *Systema naturae* (1735), linked man to a biological concept of race or variation and thus laid the groundwork for physical anthropology.[7] This fact was often recalled during the heyday of race biology in order to stress that research into racial characteristics was a particularly Swedish concern. In that tradition Anders Retzius was to make an important contribution, introducing a cephalic index around 1840, with the ensuing creation of typologies—a method of measurement used internationally in physical anthropology into this century. If we move on a few decades, we find de Gobineau, the race ideologist and French minister to Sweden, in Stockholm; it is not known, however, if his race theories influenced the Swedes more directly. To view man biologically, in accordance with Darwinian or social Darwinian models, was already common; so was anti-Semitism, borrowed mostly from German sources, and theories of the psychology of crime taken over from the Italian school. In addition, as previously mentioned, general pessimistic notions of cultural degeneration were widely spread.

In 1882 the Swedish Society for Anthropology and Geography was established; the physiologist Gustaf Retzius (the son of Anders Retzius) was one of its leading men, along with the explorer Sven Hedin. Following up surveys characteristic of the time the society made arrangements in 1897-98 for a study of the Swedish population. References were made to similar research in Central Europe; it was then pointed out that "[i]n our country, the birthplace of modern anthropology, no such comprehensive investigation has been made." Furthermore, the matter was urgent in view of the marked changes in the population due to migration. The study was carried out, with the greatest efficiency, on some 45,000 recruits and resulted in a handsome volume, *Anthropologia suecica* (1902). An increase in height was recorded; it was also noted that the Swedish race was not quite so Nordic—so "dolicocephal," to use Anders Retzius's term—as one might have believed and hoped. To a later generation the findings appear relatively insignificant, considering the work involved. Accumulating data tended to become an end in itself. *Anthropologia suecica* exposes a science which, while waiting for a tenable theory, contents itself with the collecting of material.

The anthropological tradition in Swedish eugenics should be given some weight, but it was to be eclipsed more and more by the advance of genetics. An institute for plant breeding was established at Svalöf in southern Sweden in 1886 and was then given government grants in 1894. Because of its achievements, the "Svalöf method" became a term used worldwide at the turn of the century. The southern Swedish plant breeding institutes became important for the introduction of Mendelism into Sweden, and at the University of Lund the botanist Bengt Lidforss, specialist on the *Rubus* genus, wrote popular science articles close to his subject, not infrequently with eugenic or even racist features; the latter regrettably, in part because Lidforss must be considered one of Sweden's foremost essayists. At the University of Lund, too, Herman Nilsson-Ehle was trained, a botanist who produced an epochal dissertation on the polymerism of cereal grasses (1910-11) in which he developed an important branch of Mendelian genetics. Nilsson-Ehle was to be awarded a personal chair in genetics, attached to Alnarp, and was influential in the development of Swedish plant breeding throughout his long career. He will appear later as a supporter of the eugenics movement. The impression that Swedish genetics was a concern first and foremost in southern Sweden is strengthened by the fact that good relations had been established with Wilhelm Johannsen in Copenhagen.

It was inevitable, then, that the first Swedish genetics association, the Mendel Society, was formed in Lund (1910). This was early indeed: only two years before, Erwin Baur had established the first genetic journal, *Zeitschrift für induktive Abstammungs- und Vererbungslehre*. (After 1920, the society published its own periodical, *Hereditas*, a forum for the Nordic countries.) Its members were mainly specialists, and Nilsson-Ehle was naturally the central figure. As a matter of fact, the initiative had really come from Robert Larsson, a writer who, although lacking an academic degree, knew the field well and was an important popularizer of new ideas in the areas of genetics and eugenics. His relish for eugenics is apparent from a passage in a letter to the leading Swedish man of the movement, Herman Lundborg: "You are the pathfinder, the pioneer, pointing out possible new routes. You and Ehle (in his field). I am of a more receptive nature." And indeed, race biology and eugenics both appeared on the program of the Mendel Society—when Lundborg was there, for instance (1916), and when Baur visited in 1920 and 1922.

In its early days the eugenic movement liked to favor the notion of a distinct Nordic race and established a connection with both anthropological research and the dawning understanding of hereditary matters. The medical profession especially was to become involved. Among early propagandists, mention should be made of Torsten Thunberg, physiologist and hygienist, who gave an inaugural lecture on "Conditions of Hygiene and Natural Selection" at his installation in Lund (1906); after a glance at population figures, he inexorably moved on to the threat of counterselection in modern society divined by the eugenicists. The anatomist Vilhelm Hultcrantz, one of those involved in the work on *Anthropologia suecica*, expounded on nature's "cruel but beneficial competition" (1907). It was becoming inoperative, he felt; therefore one had to put a stop to "the generating of the unfit, the parasites of society." Such negative eugenic measures should be supplemented with positive ones, however; the law should be followed by the gospel. Subsidies should be given to families with many children as well as to those in the homestead movement— Hultcrantz spoke at the opening of the Uppsala allotment gardens and apparently found pungent eugenic remarks suitable for that idyllic occasion.[8]

In 1909 the Swedish Society for Racial Hygiene (Svenska sällskapet för rashygien) was formed in Stockholm. The majority of its founding members already belonged to the Internationale Gesellschaft für Rassenhygiene, whose Swedish contingent almost equaled the German at the time; a register from 1910 lists 46 Swedes among its 290 members.[9] Thus, it was quite natural for the society to join the German association rather than its rival, the International Eugenic Committee, *in corpore*. Its membership was never large—at no time did it exceed 100—but recruitment took place among highly esteemed academics; Donald MacKenzie's thesis that early eugenic associations functioned as interest groups, promoting the social aspirations of their members, thus finds some support here.[10] The chairman was the zoologist Vilhelm Leche, a Liberal and a Lamarckist; the deputy chairman was Hultcrantz. The founder of Swedish criminology, Olof Kinberg, and Svante Arrhenius, winner of the Nobel Prize for chemistry in 1903, were on the board. Lectures were given and research funded on a small scale. On a few occasions bills were submitted to the society, as when contraception was a topical issue in 1910. The hesitantly positive stance of the board met with little response, however; information on contraceptives remained prohibited in Sweden until 1938. Nor was the society all that successful in influencing public opinion—its greatest achievement was to come in the years after World War I, with a series of popular works—but its mere existence is illustrative for biomedical reform ideas during the first decades of the century.

At about the same time—during the years preceding World War I—the Swedish physician and psychiatrist Herman Lundborg began to preach eugenics as the salvation of the nation. Although he scarcely wanted to reject environmental-type reforms, he stressed, more than others, the principle that "heredity is everything." He shared the widespread worry about what was happening to the country, but at the same time he possessed the zeal of a popular educator and the conviction of a religious enthusiast. Eugenics, and hygienics, had become something of a secularized religion in these circles.

As the main character in Swedish race biology Lundborg deserves a few introductory lines. Shortly before the turn of the century he began an investigation of a hereditary disease in a farming family in southern Sweden, and in 1913, in a sizable work given the somewhat unwieldy title *Medizinisch-biologische Familien-Untersuchungen innerhalb eines 2232-köpfigen Bauerngeschlecht in Schweden*, he was able to show that myoclonus epilepsy was transmitted in accordance with Mendelian recessive laws. In this pioneer work Lundborg made use of a historical-genealogical method and succeeded in isolating the various stages of a disease through laborious archival research. The swift decline of a family was not all that was brought to light, however, but also that of a region, due to unfortunate genetic material and thoughtless intermarrying. The result was at once genetic and sociological. The method will be recognized: it was Dugdale's, in his famous investigation of the Jukes, and also Charles Davenport's, in his strenuous study of pedigrees at the Eugenics Record Office in Cold Spring Harbor.

Clearly Lundborg belonged to Davenport's generation; moreover, he was of a similar temperament, devoid of humor, possessed of a like conviction that eugenics was the only real solution to most of life's problems and, like Davenport, his diligence had its roots in the Protestant work ethic. No one— least of all Lundborg himself—doubted his role as the leader of the Swedish eugenics movement. The following quotation from "The Threat of Degeneration" (1922), an essay on the ever more unfortunate trends in the structure of the Swedish population, will show the preacher in him; an apocalyptic atmosphere is evoked from a position of agrarian romanticism, and then it is time for the eugenic gospel:

> The strong increase of the bottom strata forms the most dangerous part of the whole process, for it is their physical and spiritual deficiencies that are such distinct features in their make-up—the higher strata among the workers are not affected by this judgment, of course. Since the middle class is shriveling up at the same time, and the upper class, which is to be found predominantly in the cities, has but few descendants, it is clear that the population becomes proletarianized and, as a whole, of poorer racial quality than before. *In other words, a host of more or less poorly equipped individuals come into being, and they will soon make their will known, especially in periods of unrest or unemployment.* . . . The racial power of our old farming stock is worth more than gold. It must not be ravaged. We must not only save that precious capital, however, in wise solicitude, but increase it if possible. Of what avail are whole piles of gold, even all the riches in the world, if, for their sake, we head for great disquietude and meet with degeneration in a comparatively short time. It is not easy for an individual to resist all the temptations that are evoked by wealth and luxuries. It is perhaps even more difficult for a whole people to choose a course of self-denial, to do without comfort, to forgo diversions and pleasures and instead live frugally and work hard for the sake of improvement.
>
> Where, then, is salvation to be found, one might ask. Surely the whole of mankind is not doomed to destruction? The answer is: We must pay attention to the genotype to a far greater extent than hitherto; that is, we must work far more than is being done now for the lineage and the race, for good families and healthy children. The individual must learn to see this and make real sacrifices for his descendants, as our forefathers did for us. It is true that modern individualism is not so inclined, but there will surely be a new age, taking a different direction; it has already begun to set in although most people have not noticed it.[11]

THE INSTITUTIONALIZATION OF RACE BIOLOGY

After World War II the various branches of science were being reorganized, in Sweden as in the other Nordic countries.[12] In 1918 Lundborg in his letters discussed plans for a cultural academy, "The Royal Swedish Society for the Study of the People and Culture of Sweden," where race biology was to be strongly represented. The Swedish Society for Racial Hygiene was revived, and in the next few years a successful popular science series was issued, which included contributions on the aims and methods of eugenics, the sterilization issue, modern genetics, and on Lundborg's diseased farming community as a warning to the population of Sweden.

Lundborg was also to edit a more substantial piece of propaganda for the society, *The Swedish Nation*, which was published in English, probably in order to appeal to wealthy American patrons—there was not much to be hoped for from Germany after the war. In 1918 Lundborg organized "an exhibition of racial types," which was to tour Swedish cities and towns that year. The purpose was patriotic and educational in the traditional vein, evoking Swedish history, but there were also links to modern science in the form of tables, photographs of different races, and scientific lectures. Officially it was uniquely successful: "perhaps no exhibition had received so much patronage in our country," read the commentary; "one can say that the Exhibition brought out a real national assembly." The statements suggest that the Swedish public enjoyed listening to race rhetoric. One example that supports this idea, a result of the exhibition, was a beauty contest held in 1921 to "bring to light and define a *Swedish-Germanic racial type*." Lundborg was on the jury, which awarded the prize to a handsome bicycle repairman from the west of Sweden.

In December 1918, Fritiof Lennmalm, professor at the Royal Caroline Institute of Medicine, proposed that a Nobel institute for race biology be established. After the matter had been mulled over, it was rejected by a small majority, officially for formal reasons; according to Lundborg, the rebuff was due to the personal animosity of some of the faculty. Instead a state institute was proposed in the form of a bill introduced in both chambers of the Swedish Parliament in 1921 signed by representatives of all the parties, from the conservatives on the Right to the Social Democrats of the Left. The degree of consensus and the wide support that the bill obtained indicate that lobbying had taken place, ultimately from Lundborg's side. As was standard procedure, a committee was set up to discuss the bill; it was unanimous in recommending the establishment of an institute and also proposed that the bill be submitted to the universities. There, too, it met with enthusiasm.

The debate in Parliament was lively. Those advocating the passage of the bill pointed to the value of preserving the Swedish stock and the possibility that an institute of this kind might prove as useful as the existing ones for plant breeding. Two statements made by the future minister of education and ecclesiastical affairs for the Social Democrats, Arthur Engberg, will show the tenor: "We are lucky to have a race which is as yet fairly unspoiled," he said, "a race which is the bearer of very high and very good qualities." Not surprisingly, therefore, he found it "odd that while we are so very particular about registering the pedigree of our dogs and horses, we are not at all particular when it comes to trying to preserve our own Swedish stock." Deference was shown to the problems within this particular science, and Lundborg was apostrophized as a prominent scientist worthy of support, who had to be kept in the country. The opponents stressed the prevalent financial crisis, which called for cautiousness with regard to long-term commitments. There was no risk that the bill would not be passed, however, and so the first *state* institute for race biology in the world was created.[13] When it opened its doors in Uppsala in 1922, with Lundborg in charge, this was with authority invested by the Swedish people through their elected representatives and ratified by the king. That also lent it status internationally. When the institute found itself in financial difficulties in 1928, Eugen Fischer wrote from Berlin, testifying to its importance and declaring that its organization had inspired the Kaiser Wilhelm Institut für Rassenhygiene.

This breakthrough on a broad front should come as no surprise to anyone who has followed the international history of eugenics. In considering the Swedish debate just after World War I, it is the war that forms the springboard. The Social Democrats, programmatically international, had become ever more national during the war years. Anything that appealed to Swedish values was incontestable to most people and belonged to what could be called a national "superideology." Equally incontestable were references to science as an important factor in the transformation of society and as an agent for moral improvement. Furthermore, the fact that genetics and race biology were new branches of science was to their credit, and so they should be tried. In this manner modernism could be combined with traditionalism in national matters. Then, since calculations showed that race biology would involve only modest costs while it might yield substantial returns, few objections could be raised. Nor, contrary to what was sometimes stated, was the subject particularly difficult to understand; it was fully intelligible to race romantics as well as to mathematically inclined social engineers. The element of popular education in eugenics also had its appeal. Indeed, Nils Hanson, the minister of agriculture, whose statement was seen to carry particular weight, said that research in race biology would be the start of "self-education among our people."

Quite clearly race biology held a comparatively strong position, but it had to gain further credit as a science. Lundborg's interest in modern genetics seems to have cooled in time, but he liked to refer not only to the usefulness of the subject but also to its great complexity and its character of "pure" research. Accordingly, he suggested that a number of geneticists be awarded the 1922 Nobel Prize.[14] Behind his suggestion, quite likely, lay a wish to assert that race biology was a wholly respectable branch of science, worthy of being evaluated in other than coarse economic terms. To act the way he did was of course politic. It was not until 1933, however, that T. H. Morgan was awarded the prize, the first geneticist to be so honored.

By an act of the Parliament, Swedish eugenics had been provided with an institutional base and also with a name and status. This is not to say that the institute was a grand establishment. Its staff consisted of the professor in charge, that is, Lundborg, a statistician, a medical assistant (at one time, Gunnar Dahlberg, who was later to run the institute), an anthropological assistant (most prominent among them, Wilhelm Krauss, a Jewish refugee from Vienna), a genealogist, a woman traveling assistant, and a photographer; all in all seven employees, and a yearly budget of 60,000 Swedish kronor. The institute was run by a board of seven directors appointed by the Swedish government; among them were Lennmalm, Nilsson-Ehle, Hultcrantz, and Lundborg himself, soon to be joined by Nils von Hofsten, a zoologist and geneticist who was to play one of the leading parts when sterilization became a major issue in Sweden. The chairman of the board was the governor of Uppsala county, former Prime Minister Hjalmar Hammarskjöld. Thus, the Institute for Race Biology stood on a solid base and could start its work with considerable self-esteem. All the same it was largely a one-man institute, run almost entirely by Lundborg. In view of its later development, the actual establishment of the Swedish Institute for Race Biology was the highwater mark of the eugenics movement in Sweden.

Its first important task was to make a comprehensive survey of the Swedish population, a counterpart, then, of Retzius's and Fürst's *Anthropologia suecica*. In one year 100,000 Swedes were measured, of whom two-thirds were recruits, 5 percent teacher trainees, 4 percent patients in hospitals or sanatoria, and a fairly large group prisoners. Statistics were collected and photographs taken endlessly, but the investigation was completed within a reasonable period of time. The result was at hand by Christmas 1926, a bulky volume in English entitled *The Racial Character of the Swedish Nation*. It received a great deal of praise: "This is, for the first time, a really definitive anthropological study of a nation," said E. A. Hooton; "[n]o other nation has produced anything that can approach it," asserted P. Popenoe. The work was spread internationally; from as far away as Java there came an order for fifty copies. In 1927, an illustrated popular version was issued in Swedish (*Svensk Raskunskap*), and it sold well—the portrait gallery may, for the voyeur, have held some appeal. The German translation, the *Rassenkunde des schwedischen Volkes,* which the Gustav Fischer Verlag published in 1928, was also, despite considerable cuts, an impressive volume. Here the bicycle repairman who was awarded a prize for his Nordic character appears in the nude, while the illustrations of the Sami people are of middle-aged models. Photography was used in a seductive way in this case, as it often was elsewhere in contemporary physical anthropology. In other respects the findings were similar to those presented in *Anthropologia suecica,* though given in greater detail; there was also a slight upward adjustment of the height of the population.

At the same time, Lundborg continued working on an investigation of the race biology of the Swedish Sami, which he had embarked upon before the war. The area itself is a classic training ground for anthropologists from the Nordic countries, but Lundborg's plans went further than any previous attempt. What he had in mind was nothing less than a complete inventory. For long periods he stayed in Lapland, wholly absorbed in his research, far from the cares of the institute, which ceased to function in his absence. The object was to investigate the consequences of merging one people with another, "while there is still time"—the consequence of "miscegenation," in other words. A wearisome search of public records was begun, covering material from the beginning of the eighteenth century on; at the same time the present generation was being measured during countless visits to Sami teepees and fairs. Besides measurements (taken in accordance with Rudolf Martin's tables) and photographs in profile and *en face,* serological tests were made on a regular basis from the middle of the 1920s on. The investigation was to have been completed by 1930, but the first part of it was not presented until 1935 and the second part in 1942.

Other work, too, at the institute, was concentrated on the problem of miscegenation. Here Lundborg collaborated with S. J. Holmes at Berkeley and Charles Davenport in Cold Spring Harbor, planning to establish institutes for research and propaganda in Central America and Africa. One of the results was Lundborg's annotated bibliography, *Die Rassenmischung beim Menschen* (1931), an erudite but biased work. The quotation with which he ends the bibliography, taken from Fritz Lenz, suggests his involvement: "Wir glauben nicht, dass das der nordischen Rasse drohende Schicksal unabwendbar sei" (We do not believe that the threatening fate of the Nordic race is final).[15] Another result was that Krauss, the institute's anthropologist, was sent to Hawaii in 1934 to study miscegenation there. Writing home, Krauss commented on the excellent collections at Davenport's institute, but felt that the Swedish Institute for Race Biology could well bear comparison—if only one could move into new premises. (This wish is expressed time and again in the annual reports of the institute.)

A high point for the work of the institute was the 1925 Nordic Conference on Race Biology and Anthropology, which was arranged in Uppsala and attracted around forty delegates of some prominence. Similar inter-Nordic arrangements had been under discussion previously, at meetings held for Nordic scientists. It was decided at the conference to form a Nordic association for anthropology, and Norway, with Jon Alfred Mjöen, was given the task of arranging a future conference. None was ever held, however; the feeling of affinity was hardly overwhelming. In fact, there was antagonism both of a personal and of a scientific nature. As his correspondence shows, Lundborg had established good connections especially with his Finno-Swedish colleagues Harry Federley, Jarl Hagelstam, Ossian Schauman, and Kaarlo Hildén, who valued the Swedish example; among his Norwegian contacts J. A. Mjöen was too much of a dilettante and also a competitor when it came to public appeal, and Otto Lous Mohr was hardly a reliable supporter. His contacts with the Danes were sporadic. It was of course essential for him to have Johanssen on his side, but Johanssen wavered in his attitude toward eugenics. Lundborg's relations with the German representatives of the subject were businesslike. They knew his work well, especially his *Familienforschung*, and also needed his support in the hard years after the war. As a member of the International Eugenics Committee, which met in Lund in 1923, he worked for their admission to the commission and refused to attend l'Institut International d'Anthropologie the following year in Paris, since Germany had not been invited. His attitude was typical of the strong pro-German sentiment which was prevalent in academic circles in Sweden from the nineteenth century up to World War II.

An important part of the institute's agenda was public lectures, which were given from 1922 on, numbering ten a year. Here Lundborg could make use of his international connections. In 1923 the future Nazi race ideologist Hans F. Günther had business at the institute in Uppsala and gave a lecture; in 1924 Eugen Fischer, soon to be director of the Berlin Institute for Racial Hygiene as well as rector of the University of Berlin, was there; in 1925 Uppsala was visited by Fritz Lenz of Munich, coauthor, with Ernst Baur and Eugen Fischer, of the German standard work on the subject of eugenics. Hermann Muckermann, Walter Sheidt, Ernst Kretschmer, Egon von Eickstedt, and a host of other Germans found their way to the institute, lecturing on genetics, anthropology, social hygiene, race philosophy, evolution, and plant and animal breeding. Nordic scientists, too, instructed the Uppsala audience which, it was always stated, was large and appreciative—this was the golden era of the public lecture. The talks or readings in the groves of academe and the great notice they attracted were surely important propaganda for the institute.

THE MID-THIRTIES: THE WINDS OF CHANGE

The year 1933 marks a shift in the history of Swedish race biology. The institute reached a crisis point, due to the impending change of director. The affair brought other work almost to a standstill for several years. The board was preparing a new program but its members could not agree with one another or with Lundborg. Partly in reaction to him personally, the press had been cold toward the institute for some time; on several occasions, it was downright hostile. In the prevailing difficult budgetary situation, Parliament cut the sum allocated to the institute year by year, so that the suggested total for 1933 was 30,000 kronor, half of the original amount—which had in itself been totally inadequate. The sum was increased on the initiatives of the ever helpful members of Parliament Alfred Petrén and Nils Wohlin, and several attempts were made to raise money by subscription in order to put the institute on a sound footing; but all such measures were wearing for those whose loyalty had already been put to the test. The developments in Germany and Lundborg's increasingly desperate proposals gave rise to the thought, in some quarters, that the institute should be closed down. The alternative was vigorous regeneration.

The creation of a new program linked to the question of the directorship was a tiresome issue. One part of the discussion centered around whether the person who was to run the institute had to be competent in as many areas as Lundborg was said to be—in psychiatry, statistics, anthropology, and genetics—or if specialization in one area would be sufficient. In 1932 the board insisted that the institute's anthropological study of the Sami be continued to its conclusion, but it also recommended comprehensive medical research into the links between feeblemindedness and certain eye diseases, the inheritance of deaf-mutism, etc. It was pointed out that the institute had long been subordinate to plant and animal breeding institutes, and one way out would be to seek a division into three departments and so gain larger funds; Nilsson-Ehle supported such a change, humbly stating that his own grants were seven times the size of those of the institute in Uppsala, although his research was "immensely less important." Obviously, the board really believed in the institute and was prepared to fight for it.

When the time came to appoint a new head, the board was faithful to Lundborg and his ideas, after all. Chosen for the office but not yet installed was

Torsten Sjögren, who was trained in psychiatry and had worked periodically at the institute. A number of studies in the same vein as Lundborg's—especially his thesis concerning what came to be called Sjögren's syndrome, a juvenile form of amaurotic idiocy and its inheritance—had qualified him for the post. The rival candidate was Gunnar Dahlberg. Trained in medicine, the latter had worked at the institute along with his wife during its first few years, but had later found himself in open opposition to Lundborg. Dahlberg's dissertation, a study of twins, was an important piece of research, too, but directed toward statistical refinement rather than traditional race biology. Politically, Dahlberg stood to the Left, often in a challenging manner. Thus he and Sjögren were two very different candidates; the board was not only choosing a department head, but also deciding the future direction of the institute.

As a consequence, the procedure of consulting a number of experts to have them rank the candidates became a protracted affair. Four general experts were chosen: Harry Federley from Finland and Oluf Thomsen from Denmark, Charles Davenport from the United States, and Ernst Rüdin from Germany. Two specialists were called in: one a statistician and one a psychiatrist. Before the matter had proceeded that far, a number of ballots had been taken at the various universities. In one instance, the medical faculty of the University of Uppsala had disallowed Lundborg's vote. Dahlberg also challenged the fact that Rüdin had been selected as one of the experts: Dahlberg had sided with Karl Saller's eugenic program on several occasions, which had been criticized from the Nazi camp by Rüdin; insidiously, Dahlberg pointed out that Rüdin would risk reprisals if he handed in a positive report. The experts' recommendation was a score of 3-1 for Sjögren—but the ballot taken at the University of Uppsala swung the figures to 10-4 for Dahlberg. The board of the Institute for Race Biology was the more decidedly for Sjögren, marking up 7-1 in his favor, after long deliberations; von Hofsten, for instance, would have preferred a professorship for each of the candidates, thus following up the earlier suggestion that the institute be expanded.

The views of the board should have settled the matter; it took a different turn, however, and Dahlberg was appointed in something of a *deus ex machina* fashion. His political connections proved effective: Gunnar Myrdal, a good friend of his among the Social Democrats, spoke to the minister concerned, and so the question, which had come up as early as 1933, was finally decided in June 1936. Neither of the applicants left the fight unsullied; Dahlberg, for example, worked behind the scenes to quite some extent, against the institute, and his appointment was clearly made on political rather than scientific grounds—the very basis for his accusation against Rüdin. Indeed, the whole affair shows the complexity of eugenics and politics at the time.

Dahlberg proved equal to the task that lay ahead. The distressing business—and Dahlberg estimated that it took five and one-half years—was also a turning point for Swedish eugenics in its older form. It lost its home, for the Institute for Race Biology soon became very different from what it had been under Herman Lundborg, and eugenics also lost its position of authority in the public debate. In German quarters it was held that it had fallen among thieves and become a center for "wiedervölkische Wirken des Marxismus" (the anti-Völkish effects of Marxism).[16]

The change can be demonstrated through a few additional remarks about the representatives of Swedish eugenics who have appeared in the discussion. Among them Herman Lundborg has been pointed to as a member of the old school, convinced of the advantages of the Nordic race, opposed to industrialization and its effects on the energy and morals of the population. In time Lundborg was to subscribe to anti-Semitism, coming to hold, for instance, that the Institute for Race Biology met with opposition because the media were under Jewish control, and profess himself an adherent of Nazism. In 1938 he received an honorary doctorate at Hans F. Günther's University of Heidelberg. Herman Nilsson-Ehle followed the same course, misled by a mind that was at times clouded. He was an active member of the Swedish-German Association, mainly a group of academics, and evidence of the strength of the old cultural connections between the two countries. Although he never wrote extensively about eugenics, he admired Lundborg unreservedly and belongs in the same fold. Their attitudes are almost a coarsening of what has been labeled "mainline eugenics," if by that term we mean the belief in the different worth of different races, the immediate usefulness of eugenic reform, the limited effect of environmental influence, and the decisive role of heredity. In another political quarter we find the Social Democrat Alfred Petrén, who promoted the establishment of the institute and the introduction of sterilization laws. Trained in medicine, he represented a social democracy which emphasized the importance of science in the restructuring of society. Given his age, Petrén, too, belonged to the generation which embraced mainline eugenics.

The zoologist Nils von Hofsten can be placed in this same category, though in a partly contradictory way. A member of the board of the Institute for Race Biology and a lecturer on genetics, he was conversant with the history of the subject. Politically he can be labeled a social liberal, whose radicalism was kindled in the Uppsala of Verdandi, the student association. He was an extreme supporter of positivism, though his belief in science was balanced by a strong interest in literature and in the humanities. The period during which von Hofsten served eugenics—from the 1910s to the 1950s—began long before and ended long after the transitional decade of the 1930s, and yet no clear influence from reform eugenics can be found in his writings, nor can any explicit opposition to traditional eugenics. He took it for granted that comprehensive negative eugenic measures were of value, especially in the case of the mentally retarded. Nils von Hofsten is a key figure, then, who fits into both periods. He was the incorruptible academic expert and the perfect public servant all in one—conscientious, idealistic, and in most instances honorable. The stance he took as rector of the University of Uppsala against the German invasion of Norway is one example of his high morals.

Gunnar Dahlberg belonged more unequivocally to the advocates of the new era. In addition to what has been written earlier, his writings in the areas of social medicine and politics should be mentioned. Foremost is his 1937 *Svensk politisk handbok* (A handbook of Swedish politics), on which he collaborated with Herbert Tingsten, one of the most prominent spokesmen for the Left in the contemporary debate. Dahlberg could be called a Swedish member of the "visible college," made up of Bernal, Haldane, Needham, and Snow, which existed in Cambridge.[17] A quotation from his *Arv och ras* from 1940 (English edition, *Race, Reason and Rubbish*, 1942) shows how he felt that the debate should be conducted:

> It is always more or less uncongenial and somewhat ridiculous to a man of science when matters bearing on his own field are transferred to the plane of party politics, and become the topic of excited controversy among a wider public. To some extent discussion must then descend to a lower level. . . . Time will come when public discussions, such as those we now have about race, will be looked upon as . . . queer. Meantime the problems of human inheritance are important to posterity; and it is natural that we should be interested in them. Scientific men have no claim to rank as a caste with the peculiar privilege of pronouncing judgment on difficult questions.[18]

In spite of everything, then, there was a limit to how far Dahlberg was willing to extend his work outward and "downward"; he did not accept a place on any government commission, for example. There is a strain of the intellectual aristocrat in him, and he ran his institute at least as autocratically as Lundborg. In 1936 he studied similar institutes abroad and then launched a plan which excluded the old anthropological branch altogether. Medical investigations based on hospital records and information in archives were now to be conducted on a statistical basis, and tests on animals were to be used to trace the heritability of tuberculosis, among other things. Dahlberg turned away from the attention paid to diseases that were "of interest only as curiosities" and toward the common diseases of the everyday world. The board was not pleased, but that was the course that was followed.

Thus, given the diffuse nature of the terms, it should be pointed out that the shift from race biology to human genetics occurred long before the Institute for Race Biology was renamed in 1958. The transformation could be described as one in which physical anthropology gave way to genetics and where field studies were replaced to an ever larger degree by experimental laboratory work.

POPULATION POLICIES IN THE 1930S: FROM QUALITY TO QUANTITY

Sweden entered the modern era with vigorous strides. Since the turn of the century an old agrarian nation had become an industrial one, ever more powerful economically. During World War I there had been a severe shortage of supplies, but as a neutral country Sweden had still managed better than other nations. The economic depression at the end of the 1920s left fewer scars than in other parts of the Western world. Though it was hardly viewed in such positive terms at the time, comparatively steady progress had been made. It could be said, perhaps, that the people caught up with the modern era in stages. The theme of degeneration in literature was replaced by a new form of vitalism, linked to the success of the proletarian writers in the 1920s. The advance of social democracy provided fuel for positive visions of the future. The strides made in popular education, such as the many courses arranged by the ABF (the Workers Educational Association) at Brunnsvik, its center for adult education, were important for the promotion of belief in the future and in rationalism which have long been characteristic of the Swedish labor movement.

The year 1930 is generally chosen to signify the start of a new era when the Stockholm Exhibition launched functionalism with its simple, rational design. Its motto was "accept"—accept change, that is, and modernism. In 1928 the Swedish model for the welfare state was labeled "the people's home" by the prime minister, P. A. Hansson, in a famous speech in which he emphasized the need for solidarity between the social classes but also stressed a traditional paternalistic family structure. The Church of Sweden, too, was vitalized, the result, in part, of the inspired leadership of Nathan Söderblom, archbishop and Nobel Peace Prize winner. The Universal Christian Conference on Life and Work arranged by Söderblom in Stockholm and Uppsala in 1925 led to some relaxation throughout the rigid old establishment. So in many ways the scientist and expert contributed substantially to the formation of the country. Söderblom's reputation was probably at its peak at this time. "I know of no country where there has been so close a relation between research and application as in Sweden," wrote one of the officials of the Rockefeller Foundation.[19]

In the mid-1930s the American journalist Marquis Childs published a book on Sweden, in which the country was seen, enthusiastically, to represent "the middle way," combining, on a small scale, great rational solutions with respect for the individual; particular attention was paid to the cooperative movement. But Childs also suggested historical-biological reasons for the successful compromise: "A long, long struggle for existence toughened the Scandinavians," he says, "and always with a land for the most part bleak and harsh." He refers to the Vikings, but also to an ancient tradition of democracy, before he sums up:

> This is hardly to suggest that it is Utopia, or even an approximation of Utopia. But out of an organic growth there has come, or so it appears to-day, a certain wholeness, a certain health, that is rare in the present period. It is a machine civilization; there are proportionately more telephones, more electrical devices, more motor cars in Stockholm than in any other European city; the rural areas are more completely electrified than anywhere else in the world, unless perhaps it be certain cantons in Switzerland. But the machine is not the master. From the past there has been preserved, if only in symbol, the pledge of man's ancient debt to earth and sea; his dependence upon elemental forms of production, the fertility of the soil and the fecundity of animals.[20]

The picture must not be made to appear wholly uniform, however. Childs could have added a few words about the Swedish interest in the rational production of men, or eugenics, or an only slightly concealed xenophobia. In its programs, the Agrarian Party stressed the defense of the Swedish race. The Sami population in the north was often dismissed as exotica for the tourists, while the Gypsies, numbering a modest 600 or so in 1945, were treated as a danger to the Swedish way of life. The group was the subject of an official government report in 1941, which contains plentiful evidence of racist and ethnocentric views. The attitude toward immigrants was often negative in spite of—or due to—the fact that they were so very few. A notorious case was the negative stance taken by the Uppsala Students Union in a statement made in 1939 before the arrival of a small group of Jewish physicians. The students may only have been looking after their own interests, but it is hard to disregard the element of racism that was present; somewhat later, the union at Lund made a similar statement, as did medical students in Stockholm. When it is pointed out that the Nazi parties played so marginal a role in Sweden, it must be remembered that this was only because of their factionalism. Racial hostility as well as pro-German sentiment can easily be documented in Sweden in the 1930s. The former was hardly a guiding principle in the debate on Swedish population policies, however, which began in earnest around the middle of the decade.[21]

Then, for a few years, the declining birthrate was considered a question of vital importance. At the turn of the century the average family had four children; a few decades later, only two. The vision that was conjured up was one of a dying nation. In the 1930s, however, this decline did not strengthen the position of eugenics as it had before; the three decades had weakened it—or translated it from biology into sociology. After economists and statisticians had made their voices heard, Alva and Gunnar Myrdal in 1934 published their *Kris i befolkningsfrågan* (Crisis in the population question), which gave rise to renewed discussion. The reorientation that had occurred was considerable; the interests of women had been moved to the forefront, for instance, in terms of abortion and maternity benefits. In order to educate the public, a vigorous campaign was launched, based on the idea that biological quality was far less scientific a concept than statistical quantity.[22]

The break with the old era and the changing over to "reform eugenics" thus occurred with Dahlberg, who had an ally in Gunnar Myrdal. The latter was wholly oriented to the West. It is true that *Kris i befolkningsfrågan* advocates eugenic measures in terms which—coming from two future Nobel Prize winners—may seem strange to latter-day readers; old eugenic solutions are also recommended (and comprehensive ones at that), even though less importance is attached to them than to other reforms. The Myrdals, however, were not out to protect the "race"; they did not care in the least for Teutonic race mysticism. Invariably they saw the population less as a biological entity than a mathematical or physical quantity. "Race" was a qualitative concept of no use in politics. Clearly, Gunnar Myrdal was influenced by the Uppsala school of philosophy, by what was called "value nihilism" (its international counterpart being "emotivism"), which sorted out emotional and qualitative statements as "unscientific."[23]

Hence Gunnar Myrdal was a primary source of inspiration for the art of social engineering in Sweden, but also, as a consequence, an agent for the removal of biology from the debate in the 1930s.[24] His thoughts on racism would become clearer by and by as Germany continued on its course. From 1938 on he was involved in work on *An American Dilemma* (1944), where he gives a bright picture of the American tradition and where the race problem constitutes a dark anomaly which is hard to explain. It is evident that both Myrdal and Dahlberg regarded the problem of a diminishing population as a social matter rather than a biological one. This philosophy was also the operating principle for the

Swedish Commission on Population (1935-38). Its chairman, Nils Wohlin, was a man of the old school, it is true, but he had to accept that times had changed.

Let us sum up the position of Swedish eugenics around the middle of the 1930s—the time of a change in leadership at the Institute for Race Biology, the first Swedish sterilization law, and the Nazi breakthrough in Germany: Swedish social democracy was stable and embarked on a course of welfare policies. These no longer concerned the working class only, whose basic demands had been met, but a growing middle class, too. New tactical and rhetorical maneuvers were employed, which older Social Democrats at times found hard to accept. A new group of Social Democrats steered society onto the course it has stayed on since then, by and large. The state and the public sector were to be strengthened. This could affect particular individuals adversely; but then, as was generally pointed out, strong centralization was a requisite for freedom of choice, lest the rights of the weak be adversely affected. This way of viewing the matter rendered it possible, paradoxical as it may seem, to both increase the rights of the state vis-à-vis the individual in one context—as in the case of sterilization—and show great solicitude for her in another. Although such a policy may be based on the best of intentions it never quite works, as will become apparent.

EUGENIC LEGISLATION: THE CASE OF STERILIZATION

In Sweden, legislation on sterilization is the prime example of how eugenic theory was transformed into political action. The first Swedish law on sterilization came into force in 1935, and was expanded in 1941. The mentally retarded were sterilized on a large scale up to the early 1950s. However, as we shall see, sociopolitical and economic perspectives also influenced the development of the sterilization program.

Although occasional sterilizations for medical reasons were performed in Sweden at the turn of the century, with one reported as early as 1895,[25] the first sterilization on eugenic grounds took place in 1906. The patient—a severely retarded mother of two—had been sent to a women's clinic in southern Sweden by the local authorities. A second instance on eugenic grounds was recorded by the same physician in 1914, the patient being an epileptic woman.[26] As long as there was no legislation pertaining to sterilization, however, operations performed on other than purely medical grounds were formally illegal. Throughout the 1910s the attitudes toward eugenic sterilization were marked by uncertainty and even skepticism. Thus, although eugenic sterilizations were obviously performed, the debate on eugenic legislation began not with sterilization, but as a discussion on the impediments to marriage.

The topic arose in 1908 as a member of Parliament, Edvard Wavrinsky, introduced two bills seeking to prevent that "infectious and hereditary diseases be transmitted through marriage." Wavrinsky suggested compulsory medical examination before matrimony, as well as a future study to determine the diseases that would make a nullity of marriage possible. The bills did not pass; Parliament's Committee on Civil Law Legislation stressed that the proposal involved an intervention by the state in the personal sphere that could only be justified by "absolutely necessary circumstances, or if it is in accordance with the prevalent opinion." According to the committee, neither of these conditions was at hand.[27]

The following year the principles of race biology and race hygiene were for the first time presented in depth in the Swedish medical journal *Läkartidningen*. In contrast to the Committee on Civil Law, the author, district medical officer A. M. Selling, perceived changing attitudes: "The time of absolute freedom, as proclaimed in theory by the French Revolution, has since long passed, and every infringement on the personal freedom is considered permissible, if in the interest of the public good." Selling forcefully stressed the importance of eugenically based marriage restrictions, as well as economic reforms to facilitate the "marriage and propagation among the physically and mentally, intellectually and morally, better equipped." One may note that the author also referred to the legislation introduced "with youthful courage" by some American states, in particular the Indiana sterilization law of 1907, although it seems that Selling doubted that it would be put into practice.[28]

Vilhelm Hultcrantz showed greater hesitation toward sterilization in a paper on eugenics published in 1911. Although enthusiastically endorsing race hygiene, "the religion of the future," the author limited his recommendations to marriage restrictions and, in cases of insanity and severe alcoholism, to permanent detention. As to sterilization, opinions were divided, according to Hultcrantz: "In our country the time is far from ready for any general legislation in this direction." Even Herman Lundborg shared this view in a report on German eugenics published in *Läkartidningen* in 1912. The question of sterilization had been raised too early, he claimed, and eugenics had to grow much stronger before any compulsory measures could be considered.[29]

Evidently, this was also the conclusion drawn by the various committees that at the same time were preparing a general revision of the Swedish marriage laws. The medical aspects of marriage were discussed in a report by the Medical Faculty of Uppsala University in 1911. According to the faculty, a law on sterilization could not be introduced "without the support of a well-prepared public opinion." In the proposal for changed legislation on marriage, put forward by the parliamentary law-drafting committee in 1913, the question of sterilization was not discussed. Based on the Medical Faculty report, however, the proposal officially introduced race hygiene as a motive for legislation. Thus it was stated that "contemporary race hygiene, eugenics, with growing force demands legislation to protect future generations and in order to maintain and improve the human race."[30] The marriage laws finally instituted in 1915 listed three impediments to marriage aimed at preventing the transmission of hereditary diseases: mental retardation, mental illness, and epilepsy "which is caused predominantly by inner factors."

The attitudes toward eugenic sterilization were gradually becoming more positive. In 1915 *Läkartidningen* published a paper presented to the Lund medical society by a professor of medicine, Elis Essen-Möller. Fourteen sterilizations were described in detail, including the two mentioned earlier performed on eugenic grounds in 1906 and 1914. Referring to the insufficient scientific knowledge on heredity, as well as the attitudes among the public, Essen-Möller did not speak in favor of a sterilization law. Yet, he described sterilization as a more humane alternative than marriage restrictions or institutional care ("it appears to me incomprehensible that sterilization can be designated as brutal").[31]

To cite a final example, one may point to Nils von Hofsten's 500-page work on genetics published in 1919, *Ärftlighetslära*. In the last chapter on race hygiene, von Hofsten stated that it was time for careful eugenic reforms in addition to the 1915 marriage laws. "Segregation" of the mentally deficient could be used more frequently, and in cases of "severe hereditary degeneration" there was no reason to recoil from "such a radical, though at the same time humane, measure as vasectomy." Nils von Hofsten did stress the importance of caution and remarked that the sterilizations carried out in the United States— according to the author more than 620 prior to World War I—reflected attitudes that went far beyond what could be legitimated from the standpoint of eugenic science: "In many cases, even the most radical form of eugenics cannot possibly eradicate an undesirable characteristic, and is far less capable of checking its propagation than anyone who is unfamiliar with the Mendelian laws of inheritance usually imagines."[32]

By the early 1920s the way had been paved for a more outspoken debate on eugenic sterilization. As shown earlier in this chapter, the lobbying effort for race biology and race hygiene had been intensified in Sweden throughout the 1910s. Beginning with the foundation of the Society for Racial Hygiene in 1909, continuing with publications, lectures, and exhibitions, the campaign gained momentum as the State Institute for Race Biology opened in 1922. Yet, while the general principles of race hygiene were enthusiastically embraced, genetics still did not offer any clear guidelines for eugenic sterilization. The proponents of sterilization solved this problem, however, by turning to non-eugenic arguments. Thus, when the issue first came up for discussion in the Swedish Parliament in 1922, emphasis was placed on the social and economic aspects of a sterilization program. From an economic point of view, it was argued, the institutional care of the mentally retarded and mentally ill placed a heavy burden on society. From a social point of view, it was claimed, the mentally retarded—irrespective of the possible "eugenic dangers inherent in their propagation"—were unfit to raise children.

The 1922 bill proposing a law on sterilization was introduced by the psychiatrist Alfred Petrén and signed jointly by Social Democrats, Liberals, and a member of the Agrarian Party. Petrén argued for systematic sterilization of the mentally retarded, although the bill also discussed the possibility of sterilizing epileptics, the mentally ill and, in special cases, rapists and other sexual offenders. There was no question of compulsory measures, however; in Petrén's opinion legislation in this area should be restricted to determining when an operation would be permissible.[33]

By 1922 the eugenic discourse was well-established. The parliamentary committee to which the sterilization bill was referred approved of the various arguments put forward by Petrén, but also started off with a general approval of race hygiene: "To keep the human race in good order, and to improve it, is naturally of considerable interest to the state." Parliament reached a decision to set up a commission to investigate the issue, without putting the question to a vote.[34]

In the following years, however, no political actions to forward a sterilization law were taken, although other activities continued. A booklet discussing eugenic sterilization was published by the Society for Racial Hygiene in 1922, at the same time as Petrén introduced his parliamentary bill. Special reports regarding future legislation on sterilization were delivered by the Institute for Race Biology in 1923, and by the National Board of Health (Medicinalstyrelsen) in 1924. The latter underlined that "sterilization of the insane, the feeble-minded, and epileptics must now be reconsidered in earnest." Eugenics, including the question of sterilization, was given a special section in a comprehensive survey on social questions, *Social handbok*, published by the Society for Social Work (Centralförbundet för socialt arbete) in 1925. In the same year sterilization was discussed by the Swedish Society of Medicine (Läkaresällskapet).[35]

In December 1927 the Swedish government finally set up a Commission on Sterilization consisting of four experts (two professors of medicine, Einar Sjövall and Elis Essen-Möller; a lawyer, Gustaf Lindstedt; and a psychiatrist,

Victor Wigert). The minister for social affairs stressed, however, that the matter was extremely delicate and intricate. One would have to proceed cautiously and define, as narrowly as possible, the groups that were to come under the future law. In a report presented in 1929 the commission, quite unexpectedly, proposed a very restrictive law, limited to voluntary sterilization on genetic grounds. The commission did not consider sterilization on purely social grounds. Society, it was held, was responsible for the upbringing of the children of antisocial individuals, who might grow up to be useful citizens.[36]

Due to the one-sided focus on hereditary diseases and its voluntary principles, the 1929 report met with severe criticism when it was submitted to a number of medical institutes and public organizations. Thus, the proposed law was rejected by the National Board of Health as well as by the National Board of Social Welfare (Socialstyrelsen). Any future law, it was held, should deal first and foremost with involuntary sterilization; indeed, some of the replies advocated compulsory sterilization of specific groups, such as the mentally retarded.[37]

Reviving the issue in 1933, Petrén convinced Parliament to investigate the matter anew. The task was given to Ragnar Bergendal, professor of criminal law, who needed only a few months to prepare a second proposal for a law. With Bergendal's report, the principle of voluntary sterilization was abandoned. His proposal opened the door to sterilization of legally incompetent individuals (i.e., persons considered unable to make a legally valid decision of their own) without their consent. The rights of the individual were explicitly subordinated to the interest of society. Thus it was proposed that sterilization of minors be permitted even if their parents were opposed; sterilization was not to be prevented for "reasons which, from society's point of view, must be considered irrelevant." In some instances, Bergendal stated, it might be better not to inform the patient of what kind of operation he or she was to undergo.[38]

The sterilization bill put before Parliament in 1934 by the Social Democratic government by and large followed Bergendal's report. The government maintained that there would be no question of "compulsory sterilization, properly speaking," since the proposed law did not provide for coercive measures to achieve its object. It was said that "a private interview, suited to their comprehension," could be used to prepare the mentally retarded for the operation; "in most cases that should do to overcome whatever reluctance may have existed initially." Persuading a patient to accept sterilization was thus the method recommended by the government.[39]

The bill was passed by Parliament, and Sweden's first Sterilization Act entered into force on 1 January 1935. Sterilization without the consent of the patient was now permitted in the case of "mental illness, feeble-mindedness, or other mental defects" if the patient had been declared incapable of consenting to the operation (legal incompetence). A prerequisite was that the person who was to be sterilized was "incapable of caring for children" (social indication) or, due to defective genes, would "transmit mental illness or feeble-mindedness" (eugenic indication). Applications for sterilization were to be submitted to the National Board of Health. If the operation concerned a mentally retarded patient, two physicians could decide jointly without consulting the board.[40]

Considering that thirteen years passed before Adolf Petién's 1922 parliamentary bill led to legislation, the hesitation regarding eugenic sterilization should not be underestimated. Why were there doubts about this kind of legislation? First, scientific knowledge did not provide any simple guiding principles for eugenic sterilization. This was noted repeatedly, although the need for race hygiene was usually stressed in general terms at the same time. Thus, when the sterilization law was discussed and prepared in the 1920s, eugenic sterilization was not considered to have an effect on the composition of the Swedish population, mainly because many diseases stem from recessive genes spread among healthy carriers. It was believed that a decrease *might* follow from systematic sterilization only with regard to mental retardation. In this perspective, race hygiene in a "proper sense" was not the motive behind the Swedish sterilization program. Einar Sjövall, a member of the 1927 committee, pointed out in 1929 that a sterilization law would probably lead to disappointment "among those who, tinged with emotion, expect a great and immediate effect on 'racial hygiene.'" Nils von Hofsten, in principle an ardent advocate of sterilization, remarked in 1931: "Sterilization, and negative race hygiene in general, are Sisyphean tasks if one tries to aim at race improvement."[41]

But the reluctance regarding legislation had other grounds as well. It was, for instance, held by some leading physicians that sterilization was a matter for the medical profession alone, not for jurists or politicians. In spite of the formal ban, operations were performed in the 1920s without legal consequences. Thus, a physician in Stockholm reported twenty-seven cases from 1927-29, of which nine concerned mentally retarded patients. A public bureau for assistance to the mentally deranged in Stockholm also referred patients for sterilization in the late 1920s and early 1930s. Included among them were twenty-one mentally retarded, as well as some epileptics and mentally ill. According to the Swedish Society of Medicine and the Caroline Institute of Medicine (Karolinska Institutet), it was questionable if any law on sterilization was needed, since it would limit the rights of physicians to perform such operations.[42]

An important argument was that sterilization could be regarded as an encroachment on personal rights. Yet this was not a salient feature in the contemporary Swedish debate. It is true that the advocates for sterilization throughout the 1910s took it for granted that public opinion was not "prepared" for eugenic legislation. The task, however, was to prepare it. Indeed, severe criticism was delivered occasionally. Thus, Gunnar Hedrén, professor of forensic medicine, published an article in *Läkartidningen* in 1922 objecting to the idea of a sterilization law. With such legislation, he argued, there was a risk that the sense of what was lawful would be stretched successively, "so that, with regard to the right of disposal of the individual, euthanasia, for example, might in time become a lawful measure and perhaps also the taking of life in other instances, whenever it appears desirable for eugenic or other social reasons." Similar arguments were put forth in Parliament in the same year when Carl Lindhagen of the Socialist Party ironically stated: "Why shall we only deprive these persons, of no use to society or even for themselves, the ability of reproduction? Is it not even kinder to take their lives? This kind of dubious reasoning will be the outcome of the methods proposed today." Yet this was a lone voice crying in the wilderness.[43]

STERILIZATION AND SOCIAL REFORMS

During the 1930s support for the sterilization program gained momentum among Swedish politicians. To explain this development one may point to the intense debate on the so-called population crisis in these years, with Sweden recording the lowest birthrate in the world in 1934. Furthermore, eugenics was incorporated into the social policy developed by the Social Democrats from the 1930s on. Let us once more turn to Alva and Gunnar Myrdal, in the vanguard of social engineering, and examine their argument for sterilization.[44]

Indeed, the Myrdals were not racists. On the contrary, their important work on the population crisis, *Kris i befolkningsfrågan*, placed population and family problems in a socioeconomic context, and was, consequently, a plea for social and economic reforms. They evidently regarded eugenics with some suspicion: "The eugenicists, who in part are responsible for the investigation of the qualitative aspects of population questions, have made important contributions in special fields. As to more general guiding principles, their contributions, in part, have been of questionable value."[45]

Still the Myrdals regarded forced sterilization as a part of population policy, and in *Kris i befolkningsfrågan* they advocated "quite ruthless sterilization policies" for the mentally retarded.[46] As technical development and the demand for efficiency proceeded in industrial society, the question of human quality became urgent. Modernization made a small but growing part of the population second-rate, they argued. This "social substratum" was not to be regarded as a separate social group, but rather as a layer of defectives recruited from all social classes. In cases of "eugenically doubtful parentage," society had the right to intervene, not with any aim to improve the race, but for social reasons and for the common interest. As the welfare state developed, Alva Myrdal wrote in 1941, the question of undesirable children would become increasingly important:

> In our day of highly accelerated social reforms the need for sterilization on social grounds gains new momentum. Generous social reforms may facilitate home-making and childbearing more than before among the groups of less desirable as well as more desirable parents. This may not be regretted in itself as the personal happiness of these individuals and the profitable rearing of those of their children already born are not to be neglected. But the fact that community aid is accompanied by increased fertility in some groups hereditarily defective or in other respects deficient and also the fact that infant mortality among the deficient is decreasing demands some corresponding corrective.[47]

Through *Kris i befolkningsfrågan,* and through their work on the Commission on Population—appointed in 1935 with Gunnar Myrdal as a member and Alva Myrdal as a consulting expert—the Myrdals obviously influenced Swedish population policy, although the commission sometimes leaned to the right in a way that Gunnar Myrdal disavowed—"It has a smell of Nazism," he wrote in a 1938 letter discussing the final report of the commission. Clearly, Alva and Gunnar Myrdal spoke about sterilization, and about "desirable parents" and "unfit," in the same manner as most debaters of the time. In matters of eugenics, they based their opinions on contemporary scientists such as Gunnar Dahlberg and Nils von Hofsten. What is worth noting, however, is the way they put sterilization in the context of social reforms. Rejecting traditional race hygiene and anything reminiscent of racism, Alva and Gunnar Myrdal regarded sterilization of the deficient as an inevitable consequence of, as they put it in *Kris i befolkningsfrågan,* "the great sociological process of adjustment" to modern industrial society.

In 1936 the Commission on Population presented a special report on sterilization, the most important preliminary work leading to the 1941 Sterilization Act. First, one may note that the commission did not even find the moral or ethical aspects of eugenic sterilization worth discussing: "The question if sterilization, for other than strictly medical reasons, is justified from a legal or ethical point of view, does not need to be touched upon here." According to the commission, the opinion among the public and authorities had changed dramatically in the past two decades: "Today it is hardly denied by anyone that it is not only justified but also desirable to prevent the procreation of a sick or inferior offspring by means of sterilization."[48]

Second, although rejecting simplistic notions of heredity and race hygiene, the commission stressed the value of eugenics:

> . . . it has earlier been a rather common belief that sterilization among hereditary sick and inferior human beings would result in a strong and rapid improvement of humankind, and erase mental diseases, feeble-mindedness, and other cases of severe inferiority. This belief is not correct. However, this is not to say that sterilization does not have an important effect in this respect. Even an initially insignificant and slow but gradually increased improvement is nonetheless desirable and urgent; in any case a possible deterioration of the human stock can be prevented. . . . Whenever an eugenic sterilization is carried out, however, in the specific case the operation will prevent the birth of sick or inferior children or descendants. Owing to this, sterilization of hereditary sick or inferior human beings is still a justified measure, beneficial to the individual as well as to society.[49]

As to the mentally retarded, the commission expected a "favourable eugenic effect" from sterilization measures, i.e., a reduction in numbers. In most other cases of hereditary diseases and defects, the outcome of sterilization would be less important from a eugenic point of view. On the other hand, the commission emphasized that the *social* aspects of sterilization were vital from a practical point of view. A broadened social indication for sterilization was proposed in order to increase the number of sterilizations where mental retardation, or deficiency of other kinds, were proven not to be hereditary.[50]

To summarize, there were three important elements in the discussion which helped legitimatize sterilization as an acceptable policy during the 1930s. In the first place, the target group for which sterilization was considered was enlarged significantly as social maladjustment became a focus of attention. The Commission on Population considered the sterilization of "certain work-shy individuals, such as prostitutes, vagrants, etc." At the same time the biological importance of sterilization was stressed more forcefully as the debate on population focused on the "qualitative" aspects of the low birth rates. It was frequently held that sterilization would diminish the number of the mentally retarded. Finally, the right of the state to enforce sterilization was no longer questioned. The commission argued that compulsory sterilization in the future might be considered even among the "psychologically inferior, though not formally legally incompetent, with asocial disposition." In its final report in 1938 the commission stressed that social reforms, so far, had to be the central point in population policy, "while genetic research prepares grounds for a perhaps more systematic eugenic policy in the future." Obviously, the commission was ready to consider a much more radical sterilization policy if needed, and if eugenic theory made progress.

When the 1941 Sterilization Act was discussed by the Swedish Parliament, race rhetoric still was quite accepted. Minister of Justice K. G. Westman characterized the proposed law as "an important step in the direction of a purification of the Swedish stock, freeing it from the transmission of genetic material which would produce, in future generations, such individuals as are undesirable among a sound and healthy people." The chairman of the Commission on Population, Nils Wohlin of the Agrarian Party, saw it as a welcome move toward "keeping the Swedish stock sound and vigorous for the future." According to Social Democrat Karl Johan Olsson, the law would be justifiable even if "one or two anti-social individuals who might be 'fit for breeding purposes'" were to be sterilized: "I think it is better to go a little too far," he said, "than to risk bringing unfit and inferior offspring into the world."[51]

Among the members of Parliament there were even those who advocated more radical and coercive legislation than that proposed. A bill signed by thirty-three Social Democrats, seven Agrarians, two Liberals, and one Conservative called for an investigation into "compulsory sterilization of certain anti-social individuals." Four Social Democrats suggested that the law should be amended to allow coercion: once a decision had been made, those who refused to undergo the operation should be brought to the hospital by the police. Discussing the question of compulsion Social Democrat Hildur Nygren remarked: "we must not be so taken up with the idea of freedom and civil rights for each and every person in this generation, that we forget the just demands of the next."[52]

Still, critical voices were also raised. Gustaf Mosesson of the Liberal Party feared that physicians as well as social workers would resign rather than enforce the Sterilization Act. Social Democrat Georg Branting emphasized that social reforms could not be replaced by eugenic measures; the advocates of compulsory sterilization were the victims of a fad. Set Persson of the Communist Party spoke of tendencies which "bear an unpleasant resemblance to that improvement of the race which one seeks to achieve in some totalitarian countries by means of the scalpel." Although this blunt critique led to some discussion on the definition of the social indication in the law, it caused no change in the governmental proposal.[53]

The 1934 Sterilization Act dealt only with sterilizations without consent, performed on individuals classified as legally incompetent. It had been assumed that voluntary sterilization was permissible on medical grounds, or when there were "sound reasons of a eugenic, social, humanitarian, or criminological nature."[54] As a result, in 1935-41 only some 20 percent of the sterilizations were submitted to the National Board of Health for approval. The basic reason for extended legislation was to regulate all sterilization cases by law.

The contents of the sterilization law enacted in 1941 can thus be summarized as follows: The eugenic indication was extended so that, in addition to individuals suffering from mental retardation or mental illness, it also applied to persons suffering from severe physical diseases or defects of a hereditary nature. The social indication was broadened to include "an anti-social way of life," as well as mental illness and mental retardation. Finally, sterilization of women for medical reasons also came under the new law. If prerequisites of eugenic or social sterilization were at hand, the operation could be performed without consent from the patient if he or she, due to mental disturbance, lacked the ability to make a legally valid approval. Only in one respect was the 1941 act more cautious than the preceding law; the possibility for two physicians to decide on sterilization of the mentally retarded, without submitting an application to the National Board of Health, was abolished.[55]

THE IMPLEMENTATION

The Swedish laws on sterilization were introduced at the same time as Denmark, Norway, and Finland enacted similar legislation. When it came to implementation, however, Sweden was far more efficient than its Scandinavian neighbors. Nearly 3,000 people were sterilized while Sweden's first Sterilization Act was in force (1 January 1935-30 June 1941).[56] Regulated by the act of 1941, the number of sterilizations rose significantly during the 1940s, reaching a peak in 1949 when 2,351 operations were reported to the National Board of Health. A slow decline followed in the next decade. From the 1950s to the early 1970s, between 1,500 and 1,900 operations were reported each year. During the whole period that the sterilization laws were in effect (1935-1975), some 63,000 sterilizations were reported. Related to the Swedish population, the number of operations was 0.9 per 10,000 in 1940, 3.3 per 10,000 in 1950, and 2.2 per 10,000 in 1960 (table 1).

Table 1. Reported Sterilizations in Sweden, 1935-1975.

Year	Eugenic indication	Social indication	Medical indication	Total	Percent women
1935	—	—	—	250	94
1936	—	—	—	293	93
1937	—	—	—	410	91
1938	—	—	—	440	93
1939	—	—	—	523	94
1940	—	—	—	581	83
1941	—	—	—	746	69
1942	959	67	135	1,161	63
1943	1,094	52	181	1,327	65
1944	1,437	21	233	1,691	65
1945	1,318	78	351	1,747	73
1946	—	—	—	1,847	—
1947	1,210	65	845	2,120	86
1948	1,188	53	1,023	2,264	87
1949	1,078	44	1,229	2,351	91
1950	858	17	1,473	2,348	94
1951	629	48	1,657	2,334	95
1952	405	73	1,635	2,113	95
1953	330	75	1,434	1,839	96
1954	204	72	1,571	1,847	96
1955	159	76	1,602	1,837	97
1956	172	76	1,520	1,768	97
1957	149	90	1,546	1,785	97
1958	—	—	—	1,786	96
1959	—	—	—	1,849	95
1960	75	120	1,455	1,650	96
1961	62	118	1,619	1,799	96
1962	33	94	1,558	1,685	98
1963	48	96	1,605	1,749	97
1964	34	70	1,655	1,759	98
1965	11	22	1,475	1,508	99
1966	9	26	1,500	1,535	99
1967	1	42	1,465	1,508	99
1968	13	20	1,545	1,578	99
1969	19	58	1,496	1,573	99

Table 1. Reported Sterilizations in Sweden, 1935-1975 (cont.)

Year	Eugenic indication	Social indication	Medical indication	Total	Percent women
1970	20	46	1,797	1,863	99
1971	13	63	1,826	1,902	99
1972	12	45	1,559	1,616	99
1973	17	19	1,328	1,364	99
1974	21	6	1,487	1,514	99
1975	14	3	1,011	1,028	99
1935-1975				62,888	93

Source: *Sveriges Offentliga Statistik: Allmän hälso- och sjukvård* (Stockholm: Statistiska centralbyrån, 1935-1976) [Annual reports on health published by the Swedish Central Bureau of Statistics].]

On what grounds were these operations performed? The social indication for sterilization was used in only a few percent of the cases according to official statistics. In the 1940s and 1950s some 50 to 100 sterilizations were reported each year, but there were never such clear distinctions between social and other grounds as the statistics seem to indicate. As to the mentally retarded, a random sampling shows that frequently both eugenic and social indications were noted in the applications that were submitted to the Board of Health.[57]

The eugenic indication, which was applied primarily to the mentally retarded, was originally considered the most important and was used extensively in the early years of the sterilization program (82 percent of the total number of cases in 1942; 75 percent in 1945). But sterilization on eugenic grounds decreased rapidly during the 1950s; in 1955, 159 eugenic sterilizations were reported, making up less than 10 percent of the total number.

As to sterilization on eugenic grounds, the basis for the evaluation of the Board of Health was the probability, expressed in statistical terms, that a particular disease would be inherited. In simple cases, where the hereditary transmission was well-known, the exact risk could be calculated (as for hemophilia), but more often the board turned to a hypothetical, empirically based index. In 1940 Nils von Hofsten explained the principles of the board in the following manner:

> Our basis is the general statistical probability that a disease, abnormality, or defect (epilepsy, feeble-mindedness, etc.) is hereditary or predominantly hereditary, or,

from a slightly different viewpoint, the probability that it will appear in children or other relatives (the risk of morbidity). Thus, when a case is to be decided (sterilization, abortion, marital capacity), the statistical probability is decisive. That is to say, when the rate is sufficiently high, the burden of proof rests upon the person whose claim it is that, for him or her, the disease or quality . . . has an extrinsic cause so that his or her case is not to be judged by the general statistical risk.[58]

The norm applied was that there were sufficient eugenic grounds for sterilization if the risk of transmitting a disease was assumed to be at least 10 percent. According to this principle, it was held, there were clear eugenic reasons for the sterilization of the mentally retarded and of schizophrenics. For rare recessive defects, such as hereditary deaf-mutism, where the risk of inheritance was assumed to be under 1.5 percent, there were grounds for sterilization only in the case of marriages between kin. For epilepsy the risk of inheritance was estimated between 5 and 8 percent, an uncertain border area. Since epileptics were not allowed to marry, however, and only those who were infertile were exempted from that ban, their applications were usually approved.[59]

The number of sterilizations based on the medical indication, which as noted above applied only to women, rose rapidly at the end of the 1940s. In the 1950s some 80 percent of all operations were carried out for medical reasons. One important purpose of the medical indication was to make it possible for overworked mothers with large families, living in socially distressful situations, to avoid repeated pregnancies by means of sterilization. Thus, the majority of cases were women who were sterilized not due to physical diseases or defects, but because of "weakness." Indeed, the most important change in the postwar application of the 1941 Sterilization Act was the replacement of eugenic sterilizations of the mentally retarded by operations performed on so-called "exhausted mothers" and "weak" women. During the 1950s this category made up one-half of the total cases while in 1945 it stood at only 6 percent.

Since sterilizations on eugenic grounds decreased just as rapidly as the medical ones increased, the total number of cases remained fairly constant from the 1950s on. The first conclusion to be drawn, then, would be that the idea of race hygiene and eugenic sterilization lost some of its attraction during the 1950s. Given the fact that the number of sterilizations of mentally retarded patients decreased rapidly in the postwar period, this is in part correct. The history of Swedish eugenics, however, is marked by continuity rather than by swift changes; eugenic sterilization continued to the late 1960s, albeit on a smaller scale than before. Furthermore, the change from eugenic to medical sterilizations might to some extent have been cosmetic; cases which had previously been referred to as eugenic were now labeled medical.

Let us compare the statistics from the early 1940s with the figures from the late 1950s. From 1942 to 1945 a total of 2,795 women were sterilized due to mental illness or mental retardation. Of these cases 2,733 operations were performed with reference to the eugenic indication, whereas only 62 sterilizations (2 percent) were labeled medical. In the period 1955-1958 1,672 women classified as mentally ill or mentally retarded underwent sterilization. In these four years, however, 1,276 (76 percent) of the operations were performed with reference to the medical indication. Still, this shift in labeling does not alter the overall pattern of a change from sterilization of the mentally deficient to sterilization of "exhausted mothers." Of the total number of medical sterilizations performed from 1955 to 1958 (6,549), the mentally retarded and mentally ill comprised 25 percent, whereas the women labeled "weak" made up 56 percent. The remaining 19 percent suffered from epilepsy, physical diseases, or physical defects.[60]

Let us finally address the issue of sterilization of the mentally retarded, the basic motive for the sterilization program in the 1930s and 1940s. As late as 1947 the National Board of Health stated the following in its "Advices and Directives" on the Sterilization Act:

> Mental retardation holds a special position. Due to its prevalence, its early manifestation, the important role played by heredity, and other circumstances, there is a possibility that, by preventing reproduction, one can effect a significant reduction even within a few generations. This can only be achieved if all feeble-minded persons, or at least the great majority of those who are not confined adequately in institutions, are sterilized, and if this is done before they have children. The importance of this is even more obvious, since the social motives are as strong as the eugenic ones.[61]

A total of 1,113 operations involving mentally retarded patients were performed in the period 1936-1941 under the first Sterilization Act (there are no figures for 1935). In addition, numerous operations were carried out *without* reference to the law, mentally retarded patients having been classified, sometimes erroneously, as legally competent.[62] Thus, approximately half of those sterilized in the years of the first Sterilization Act were mentally retarded.

The criticism leveled at the 1934 Sterilization Act concerned, among other things, the principle that it applied only to those who had been declared permanently legally incompetent. It was held that the "slightly subnormal" would not be sterilized on a sufficiently large scale. Consequently, for a brief time after the introduction of the 1941 act, the number of sterilizations of people classed as mentally retarded rose sharply, so that they formed almost 70 percent of the total number of cases in 1942. After that, however, their share declined steadily. The figures most likely continued to drop in the late 1950s, although we lack clear evidence since statistics showing sterilization on medical indication do not separate mentally retarded from mentally ill from 1954 on (table 2).

Table 2. Reported Sterilizations, 1942-1957, Mentally Retarded and Mentally Ill.

Year	Ment. ret.		Ment. ill		Total number of sterilizations due to mental constitution		
	Eug.	Med.	Eug.	Med.	Numbers	Percent medical	Percent of total
1942	779	0	118	7	904	<1	78
1943	899	0	175	4	1.078	<1	81
1944	1.034	0	305	7	1.346	<1	80
1945	926	1	296	38	1.261	3	72
1946	—	—	—	—	—	—	—
1947	775	0	329	40	1.114	3	54
1948	836	1	256	43	1.136	4	50
1949	680	0	292	41	1.013	4	43
1950	548	1	212	·51	812	7	35
1951	423	1	150	149	723	20	31
1952	277	3	90	248	618	41	30
1953	235	3	75	269	582	47	32
1954	139	?	32	?	474	64	26
1955	113	?	19	?	484	73	26
1956	106	?	36	?	323	56	18
1957	101	?	25	?	511	75	28

Source: *Sveriges Offentliga Statistik: Allmän hälso- och sjukvård* (Stockholm: Statistiska centralbyrån, 1942-1957) [Annual reports on health published by the Swedish Central Bureau of Statistics].

The table can be summarized as follows: Sterilization of the mentally retarded shows a significant decline from the late 1940s on; from the mid-1940s some

300 to 400 sterilizations of the mentally ill are reported annually (although 263 in 1950); among the mentally ill, there is a remarkable shift from eugenic to medical labeling from the early 1950s on; the total number of people sterilized due to their mental constitution declines from 1949 on, both in relative and absolute numbers.

The decrease in numbers might be explained in part by the fact that the most urgent cases of the mentally retarded liable to sterilization—according to physicians, welfare committees, and poor law boards—had already been sterilized during the 1930s and the beginning of the 1940s. In the first period of the new legislation references were made to an "accumulated stock" of the mentally retarded, where sterilization should be effected rapidly. More likely, though, the change reflects a gradually more restrictive attitude toward sterilization among physicians and social-service workers generally, as well as a more cautious stance by the National Board of Health. Such caution is evident in the fact that more attention was paid to the possibility of late maturation among the mentally retarded. In a special circular addressed to institutions for the slightly retarded in 1948, the Board of Health saw fit to stress "the importance of careful consideration" when deciding a case: "In the experience of the Board of Health, there have been cases, and not infrequently, where people who have been sterilized at an early age due to feeble-mindedness have reached a considerably higher or normal mental age after a few years and have been well-adjusted socially."[63]

Even though the Board of Health had become more wary, however, sterilization of the mentally retarded continued, although at a slower rate than before. Thus, in the first six months of 1960, eighty-three applications for sterilization of mentally retarded patients on eugenic or social grounds were approved by the Board of Health. Most of them, fifty-three cases, concerned people in special homes or hospitals. More than half of the applications received were for people under twenty-six years of age; twenty-four of them were between sixteen and nineteen.[64]

COMPULSORY STERILIZATION?

Did the Swedish legislation involve compulsory sterilization? According to the lawmakers it did not. It was maintained that in principle the laws were based on voluntary measures, since those who were legally competent could not be sterilized without their consent, and to force somebody to the operating table was prohibited. The German sterilization law of 1933, with far-reaching possibilities for compulsory sterilization, was not seen as a model for the Swedish sterilization program. Discussing the German legislation briefly in 1936, the Commission on Population stated: "To admit sterilization without consent to the extent of the German law would probably be inconsistent with the Swedish conception of justice."[65] In a debate broadcast on Swedish radio in 1946 Nils von Hofsten strongly condemned German race hygiene, while at the same time defending the Swedish sterilization program: "Our law on sterilization is very different from the one the Germans had. In important aspects its principles are totally the opposite."[66]

It is true that the possibilities of enforcing eugenic sterilization, as well as the far-reaching definitions of "hereditary diseases" (including severe alcoholism), made the Nazi legislation different from the Swedish laws. Yet one should not forget that the original motives for laws on sterilization were the same in Germany and Sweden: to sterilize the mentally retarded. Furthermore, in Sweden as well as in Germany the essence of the sterilization program was to accomplish sterilization whenever such an action was regarded desirable to the common interest, i.e., from the point of view of the state. When von Hofsten got on to the question of coercion, in a 1942 radio talk about the Swedish Sterilization Act, he justified the regulations in the following way:

> Sterilization is such an important operation that the individual should not be allowed to decide the matter for himself. Very many of those who should be sterilized are feeble-minded or mentally ill and are therefore not even able to understand what it is all about, or cannot, at least, judge the reasons. Most of the time they would not want an operation at all; nor would they agree to one. That is why regulations are needed.[67]

In Sweden, however, the authorities advocated persuasion, not force. The Swedish sterilization program contained several procedures by which involuntary sterilization was carried out. The legally incompetent, to begin with, could be subjected to sterilization without their consent according to the 1934 and 1941 laws. How was this category defined? According to instructions circulated by the Board of Health in 1947, a person should be able to understand "the meaning and the consequences" of the operation to be declared legally competent. But: "Such an understanding is not at hand only because he knows that he cannot have a child after a sterilization; it must furthermore be required that he to some extent comprehends the importance of sterilization for himself and for society." As to the mentally retarded, legal incompetence was said to prevail if he or she could be compared intellectually with a person twelve years old or younger.[68]

In cases of resistance the following method was recommended by the Board of Health in 1947:

Thus, if a [legally incompetent] person who, it is felt, should be sterilized is asked in advance and refuses to consent, no attention should be paid to his decision; the documents should be prepared and sent in. If, once sterilization has been approved, he definitely refuses to submit to the operation, it must not be carried out by force, however. Often, it appears, the knowledge that a decision has been taken by the National Board of Health will convince those who were previously reluctant to submit to the operation. As a rule, the best way to treat such patients would seem to be to consider it more or less self-evident that the operation is to be performed once the Board has given permission; should they ask outright, however, it must not be kept from them, of course, that it will not be carried out by force.[69]

There are no statistics showing to what extent people classified as legally incompetent were sterilized in Sweden without their own approval. From 1935 to the end of June 1941 a total of 1,338 sterilizations were carried out in accordance with the 1934 Sterilization Act, which applied only to the legally incompetent. In some 20 percent of these cases, however, the patient signed his own application (table 3). By comparison, 1,615 sterilizations of legally competent persons, performed without reference to the 1934 law, were reported in the same period.

Table 3. Applications for sterilization submitted to the National Board of Health, 1935-1939

Application submitted by	Percent
The patient	21
Parents and guardians	14
Physicians and superintendents of institutions	32
Poor law boards and child welfare committees	32

Source: N. von Hofsten, "Steriliseringar i Sverige 1935-1939, *Nordisk Medicin* 7, no. 34 (1940), 1421. The table is based on a selection of applications (785).

The right to apply for sterilization on behalf of others was broadened in 1941. In addition to parents, guardians, physicians and superintendents of institutions, poor law boards and child welfare committees, the right was now also given to several groups of physicians employed by the state, such as county medical officers. In circular letters sent out by the Board of Health in 1947 it was emphasized to be the *duty* of a physician who was so authorized to work for sterilization. On being informed of a case in which "sterilization would appear to be required from society's point of view," he was to investigate the matter and then, if there was sufficient cause to perform an operation, see to it that an application was sent to the Board of Health.[70]

In time, however, the great bulk of applications came to be signed by the persons actually concerned by the petitions. In 1950 the Board of Health received only 143 applications sent in by others, half of them by superintendents of reform schools and institutions, out of a total of 2,176.[71] One explanation for this shift is to be found in the increased proportion of cases in which legally competent women were sterilized with reference to the medical indication under the 1941 law. At the same time, the "voluntariness" of inmates of asylums and special schools must of course be questioned, although the patients signed their own applications. The Board of Health *recommended* that those who were to be sterilized apply for the operation themselves whenever possible: both "practical and psychological reasons" speak for such a procedure, it was stated in the "Advice and Directives" concerning the Sterilization Act. Whenever a person could be persuaded to sign his own application, his legal incompetence did not have to be proven.[72]

Evidently, a common method was to sterilize the mentally retarded before they left special homes, special schools, or hospitals, on parole or discharge. According to a study published in 1962 some 36 percent (527) of all girls leaving Swedish special schools between 1937 and 1956 were sterilized. The rate rose markedly in the 1940s only to fall sharply in the next decade. In nine out of the twenty-eight schools that were included in the study, almost half or more than half of those who left were sterilized.[73] At times, hospitals and institutions even made sterilization a *condition* for discharge. It is impossible to say how common this procedure was, but according to a statement by officials at the National Board of Social Welfare in 1955: "the application of the [1941] law was earlier so that sterilization in several cases was performed although the operation was later shown to have been unnecessary. By this we have in mind especially cases where sterilization on social indication have been made a condition for discharge from reform schools or other institutions."[74]

Occasionally, the wording in the applications submitted to the Board of Health reveals the methods being used: "[I have] proposed discharge on trial on condition that a sterilization first is carried out. [The patient] has complied with this demand" (a physician signing an application in 1936); "Sterilization approved. Sinnessjuknämnden [the Local Board on Mental Health] stipulates sterilization as a condition for discharge on trial" (1940). A mentally retarded woman who, according to the documents sent in, applied for sterilization herself, later appealed to the Board of Health not to have to undergo the operation: "When I . . . was in hospital in 1942, they kept on at me so as to get me to sign the papers that I don't know if I even read what I signed. . . ." Discussing a woman in her early twenties, in a hospital in 1950, a doctor states: "Even though every method has been used to convince her about the importance of the operation, she stubbornly refused. For this reason there was nothing else to do than to give up the operation."[75]

If, then, inmates of asylums, special schools, etc., were pressured to apply for sterilization, indirect compulsion was also used in other cases. Irrespective of their formal legal competence, certain categories of women were forced to accept sterilization in order to be granted abortion (which will be discussed later), as were certain categories of people in order to be able to marry. As noted earlier, the Swedish marriage laws from 1915 on included impediments to marriage for epileptics if the disease had "a predominantly inner cause," for the mentally retarded, and for the mentally ill. Epileptics could, however, apply for exemption as could the other two categories beginning in 1945, if there was evidence of "an ability to adjust to society."[76]

The principle that came to be applied by the Board of Health in the 1940s was to grant permission to marry on the condition that the applicant underwent sterilization. It is true that such conditional permissions were few in number, yet they reflect the unyielding attitudes as far as eugenics was concerned.[77] In the 1950s, however, there was a clear softening of the board's practice, especially regarding epileptics, and the last time sterilization was stipulated before marriage was in 1962. The shift came after a study by the Swedish geneticist Carl Henry Alström was published in 1950, showing that hereditary epilepsy was considerably less common than previously had been assumed.[78] Yet the prohibition of marriage was not abolished for epileptics until 1968; for those suffering from mental illness or retardation, 1973.[79]

During the 1950s the National Board of Health occasionally received letters which must have caused some discomfort; applications for re-fertilization arrived from people who regretted the operation or could not understand on what grounds they had been sterilized. Thus, a woman sterilized in 1941 at the age of twenty-three, labeled "feeble-minded—probably congenitally" and "sexually highly unreliable," turns to the Board of Health in 1950, when she had been married for five years: "Since I myself did not sign the application for sterilization and really did not know what the whole thing was about, I would like to know now why I was sterilized."[80] A girl of twenty-one, sterilized at the age of fifteen after a few months in a mental hospital in 1944, turns to the Board of Health for information about the operation. She states that her life has been largely spoiled: "It seems incredible to me that the Board of Health, which has been appointed to watch over the safety of the citizens, could allow such an operation of a fifteen-year-old girl, who was also a virgin, and that after only three months of sickness. . . . Since I am perfectly healthy and self-supporting, I feel that the best thing would be if I could be operated on again, so that I could feel like a human being in the future." The board replies that the girl had approved the operation herself ("Your signature is attested by two witnesses"), adding that the likelihood that she would transmit hereditary deficiency had been estimated as "considerable."[81]

And furthermore in 1950: "Help me. How can I help a boy of twenty-five whom I am engaged to, and whom I plan to marry next year? He underwent an operation, so he cannot have children." Reply: "The Board of Health can take no action in the matter of your letter."[82] "I was taken to [mental] hospital March 3, 1948 and released in September. I was sterilized there. . . . Now I wonder if there is any hope for me, won't you help me to have a child. You must help me. Have changed my mind. . . . If you help me you have saved a life. Yours faithfully, N. N." Reply: "No action can be taken."[83]

In spite of the brief replies, the Board of Health obviously was influenced by the letters. An application for re-fertilization in 1960 caused a member of the board to comment to his colleague: "Once again a sad case."[84] The letters showed that the Sterilization Act was applied far too uncritically, and at the Board of Health it was felt that greater care had to be taken. After several decades of committee work at the Board of Health, Nils von Hofsten in 1963 looked back upon the application of the Sterilization Acts and his impression was that the board, "after the first few years, was somewhat more restrictive in granting permission. . . . If that was the case, it was true first of all for very young people and among those mainly the feeble-minded."[85] Considering the lower rates of sterilization among the mentally retarded, and the more cautious position regarding sterilization as condition for marriage or abortion, the general impression is thus one of slowly changing attitudes toward the sterilization program from the mid-1950s on.

WHO BECAME "THE OTHER"? GENDER IN THE IMPLEMENTATION OF THE STERILIZATION LAWS

Sterilization was introduced as a rational and even human—as it was claimed—solution to overcome social and eugenic problems in the interwar period. Today, however, rationality or humanity are hardly the words that come to mind when reading the applications for sterilization, which are kept in the archives of the National Board of Health. Medical certificates are characterized by bureaucratic and scientific thoroughness, extensive case histories according to specific formulas and expert's reports. Yet personal opinions cloaked in scientific terminology were frequent: "the whole family is subnormal," "the sick girl's father seems degenerate," etc. "According to the neighbours her home is a hangout for various riffraff, and she is the great attraction," it was stated in an application from 1935. "Father 'adventurous' and extravagant; mother nervous and hysterical; not said to have a great reputation for honesty" (an application on behalf of a seventeen-year-old, 1946); "Father a vagrant and a loafer, handy with a knife, has a bad reputation and is thought to be an imbecile" (1946).[86] These examples are not unique.

When the right to bear children became an arena for state intervention, hereditary disposition was not the only ground for action by the authorities. Obviously questions of morals and life style were also taken into account as criteria for the judgments; in practice the implementation of the sterilization laws came to focus on persons perceived as different. The topics of eugenics and social control are dealt with elsewhere in this book by Bent Sigurd Hansen, who also notices that although rarely discussed—or observed—in the contemporary debate on the laws and their application, the Scandinavian sterilization laws had a clear bias toward the lower classes.[87]

Another bias concerns gender. There was no rational reason to make women a more important subject for the sterilization policy than men. On the contrary, considering the surgical methods available and the knowledge of heredity at the time, a focus on men would have been logical. First, while sterilization of men was a simple affair, the operation was far more complicated and dangerous when performed on women. The greatest risk occurred when a sterilization was combined with an abortion, a procedure which became frequent in the 1940s.[88] The second reason concerns genetic theory. In the 1940s it was estimated that at least 75 percent of all mental retardation was of a hereditary nature. According to estimates made by Nils von Hofsten in 1944, three genes were particularly important. One of the genes was supposed to be sex-linked and recessive, and mental retardation more prevalent among men than women.[89]

Yet more than 90 percent of the people sterilized in Sweden between 1935 and 1975 were women. In the early 1940s men comprised less than one-third of the cases; from the 1950s on they constituted only a small percent. The increasing number of women reflects the progressively more common sterilization of "exhausted mothers" in the postwar era. As mentioned earlier, the medical indication introduced in the Sterilization Act of 1941 was applicable only to women. Regardless of category, however, the women formed the majority.

For instance, some 65 percent of the cases in the 1940s classed as mentally retarded were women, and in the next decade that figure increased to more than 80 percent.

How can this strong imbalance be explained? The Swedish historian Yvonne Hirdman has stressed the subordinate social position of women. Her analysis of the emerging Swedish welfare state in the 1930s focuses on the utopian visions among leading Social Democratic intellectuals. She underscores their strong belief in the social sciences and rational techniques as important elements in the construction of a "good society," and describes the consequences as private life became instrumentalized. Life was "laid in order," to use her words, by means of social engineering. The rights of women, Hirdman argues, were particularly easy to violate. The "good life" was defined through male standards and norms, and as social reforms such as the sterilization program focused on "the others," women as such became a prime target. The standards for negligence or deviance were more rigid for women than for men.[90]

One could perhaps go one step further, as has been suggested by others, and surmise that the sterilization program reflected the perception—and fear—of female sexuality. Remarks about "hyper-sexuality" and licentiousness, especially among the mentally retarded, were often used as arguments for sterilization, both in official comments on the legislation and in the actual applications for sterilization. The sterilization laws, in this perspective, became a tool to control and regulate the sexuality of women. The laws themselves were not constructed to be applied primarily to women, but male physicians turned them against women, and not against their own sex.[91]

This contrast between intentions and practice is worth noting. In fact, the imbalance between men and women was a cause of concern for the central authorities, as is shown in the comments by the National Social Welfare Board in 1940 which stated that "this paradoxical disproportion" demands "a more satisfactory application of the legislation."[92] Nevertheless, the uneven distribution increased dramatically in the following years. Whether perceived or not, gender bias was present in the legislation. One example of this is the link between sterilization and abortion.

The question of sterilization frequently arose when women came into contact with hospitals and physicians in connection with a pregnancy or an abortion. Applications for sterilization and abortion were usually sent in to the Board of Health at the same time, and it seems likely that physicians or social-service workers whom the applicants encountered sometimes advised or persuaded them to apply for sterilization as well as abortion. It should be repeated that physicians who became aware of cases in which "sterilization would appear to be required from society's point of view" were obligated to investigate the case and apply for sterilization if appropriate.[93]

Thus, a considerable number of sterilizations were combined with an abortion, especially in the latter half of the 1940s and in the 1950s. In the period 1951-55 one woman out of four who had an abortion was also sterilized (in absolute numbers between 1,000 and 1,500 each year). The connection becomes even more apparent if we compare the number of women whose sterilization was combined with an abortion and the total number of women who were sterilized: between 60 and 70 percent of the women who were sterilized in the years 1951-55 underwent the operation in conjunction with an abortion.[94]

Moreover, according to the 1938 Abortion Act, an abortion granted on heredity grounds with the woman as the carrier was to be performed *only* in combination with sterilization—otherwise she might return repeatedly for eugenic abortions, a procedure which the experts involved in formulating the law had deemed "offensive."[95] Thus women applying for an abortion for eugenic reasons had to choose abortion *and* sterilization or no abortion at all. As Nils von Hofsten put it in 1944: ". . . the woman is forced to make a choice: either to give birth to the expected child or have no children at all in the future. That way the seriousness of her intentions and motives is put to a useful test."[96] At least in the 1940s the National Board of Health obviously reacted strongly to cases of abortion without sterilization if a eugenic indication had been cited. It was stressed in 1944 that "[s]terilization must not . . . be omitted on the grounds that the woman refuses to undergo the operation and that it would be better to perform an abortion than no operation at all."[97]

The number of abortions that were conditional on sterilization increased throughout the 1940s, from some 180 per year in 1942 to some 500 in 1949. A great many of them concerned mentally retarded women.[98] Around the mid-1950s the Board of Health stipulated sterilization in 40-50 cases per year, but after that it did so only rarely. The last abortion granted on condition that the patient underwent sterilization was performed in 1964. Hence, between 1941 and 1964 a total of 4,000 women were sterilized in accordance with this stipulation in the Abortion Act. Still, the regulations of the 1938 act were not repealed until 1974 when a new law on abortion came into force.[99]

The most obvious explanation for the predominance of women among the sterilized in Sweden is the change in the implementation of the sterilization law in the postwar period. Even though the imbalance between sexes existed from the beginning, it was at its lowest in the early 1940s when the sterilization program was focused on the mentally retarded (see table 1). As described earlier the development from the mid-1940s is characterized by the shift from eugenic to medical sterilizations, and by the predominance of women sterilized because of "weakness." In part, this change may be explained by a transformed labeling of deviants and outsiders, a change from a eugenic to a sociomedical discourse. Primarily, however, the shift shows that the sterilization law came to be applied to a new category of persons: women living in social distress.

The question may be posed whether certain categories of women in the postwar period began using sterilization as a means of contraception. This, at least, seems to be the explanation given by Nils von Hofsten, who later made the comment that in the 1940s "the knowledge of sterilization as a method to prevent pregnancy soon was spread among exhausted mothers, who were often encouraged by physicians to undergo it." Men, on the other hand, according to von Hofsten, "rarely wish to be sterilized and rather frequently oppose the operation."[100] In part, this assumption is confirmed by a survey of sterilizations performed between 1950 and 1953. The study shows that among the applications approved for men, almost 17 percent were never carried out, either because of resistance or because the applicant simply had changed his mind. Among the women, only 10 percent of the operations were not carried out. If the figures are divided into subcategories, however, a different picture emerges. Among women sterilized without any connection with abortion, resistance was as common as among men: 16.5 percent of the applications did not lead to an operation. When, on the other hand, sterilization was applied for in connection with—but not as a condition for—abortion, the resistance seems to have been at its lowest; or to put it differently: the degree of voluntariness seems to have been high (table 4).

Table 4. Approved applications for sterilization, 1950-1953.

Category	Approvals	No sterilization carried out
Men	470	16.8% (79)
Women	8,364	10% (850)
Sterilization combined with abortion	4,373	6% (266)
Sterilization as condition for abortion	1,254	10.5% (133)
Sterilization without abortion	2,733	16.5 % (451)

Source: N. von Hofsten, *Steriliseringar i Sverige 1941-1953*, Socialmedicinsk tidskrifts skrift-serie 28 (Stockholm: Socialmedicinsk tidskrift, 1963), 41.

What conclusions can be drawn? That the interpretation of sterilization as a means to fulfill eugenic visions, or as a tool for repression of outsiders, reflects only a part of this complex phenomena? That sterilization could *also* be used as an individual relief? In fact, this was the opinion of Elise Ottesen-Jensen, the well-known Swedish-Norwegian sex educator who in the 1930s fought her own campaign against bigotry and ignorance among the moralizing elite in Swedish society. In her view the problem was that the right to be sterilized was restricted—by men in power with no knowledge whatsoever of the lives of ordinary women.[101]

This is not to deny, of course, that the implementation of the sterilization laws was a question of "intervention into women's lives and bodies."[102] Indeed, the dilemma identified by Elise Ottesen-Jensen underscores the fact that the sterilization program was conceived and carried out primarily by men. And since the possibility to use medical sterilization as contraception applied only to women, this opportunity for "relief" clearly cannot be characterized as a gender-neutral solution. It is important to note, however, that gender bias was manifested in different ways at different times and according to different motives underlying the sterilization program. The analysis of the sterilization of the mentally retarded in the 1930s and 1940s must be separated from the analysis of postwar implementation of the sterilization law. To answer the question whether the history of eugenic discourse, in which the debate on sterilization began, could be written as a history of gender-biased beliefs and values—and it probably could—requires a study of its own.

THE PERSISTENCE OF RACISM: THE SWEDISH "TRAVELERS"

Let us change focus from gender to race. We have earlier stressed the transformation from mainline to reform eugenics in the 1930s, according to which old notions of race, and theories about the danger of "miscegenation," were replaced by genetics searching for hereditary diseases. It is important to note, however, that this development of a nonracist "welfare state eugenics," which threw the ballast of race mysticism overboard, first and foremost was an academic affair. Beside those geneticists who came to outline the reform eugenics of the 1930s and 1940s, and beside intellectuals such as Alva and Gunnar Myrdal, others seemingly adhered to the forceful catchwords of early eugenics. The more nuanced view of sterilization which later evolved among specialists was not always noted in the propaganda for eugenic reforms. As we have seen, as late as 1941 leading Swedish politicians characterized sterilization as a means of "purification" of the Swedish stock.

The picture of Swedish "welfare state eugenics" thus seems ambiguous. The racist discourse of the early twentieth century was not completely abandoned in the 1930s. This is obvious by the widespread tendency to regard social misbehavior as a question of genetic inferiority; in short to define social problems as racial problems. Early on, it was a matter of dispute whether alcoholism and vagrancy were hereditary. Still, it was assumed that the "lowest stratum of society," as it was referred to, was at least partly recruited from, as Nils von Hofsten put it in 1933, "genetically inferior individuals [who sank] into it due to their inferior qualities." The roots of antisocial behavior, it was thus claimed, were to be found in personal defects, "inferiority." The National Social Welfare Board stated the argument in the following way in 1939: "experience [lends] ever stronger support to the view that severe alcoholism and other forms of pronounced antisocial behaviour in an orderly community generally arise from an inferiority of some kind inherent in the person in question, and this inferiority often becomes manifest in his offspring as well."[103]

Provided that a segment of the population was doomed to vagrancy and social misbehavior by its hereditary characteristics, the idea that even a certain "race" of social outsiders existed was close at hand. Indeed, this conclusion was drawn as the discussion on antisocial behavior came to focus on the itinerant Swedish group known as "travelers," or *Tattare*. Initially a name for different transient groups, such as the Gypsies, the word *Tattare* in the nineteenth century came to be used exclusively for a domestic group of families living isolated on the fringe of the agrarian society. This equivalent to itinerant groups such as the Irish *Tinkers*, or the German *Gauner*, traveled the Swedish countryside and supported themselves through horse-dealing, small-scale trade, crafts, or, in older times, as hangmen. Although characterized by certain cultural traits and, to some degree, by intermarriage, the *Tattare* hardly constituted an "ethnic group"; rather the travelers were a social outcast formed by continuous exclusion from the majority population. Even though certain *Tattare* families held together for several generations, there were always new members who assimilated into the older groups.[104]

In Swedish folklore the label *Tattare* had a clear-cut meaning. The travelers were supposed to be immoral and idle, and to look "dark" and "southern." At the same time there was a romantic idea of the independent, wayfaring *Tattare* living a life of ease, a character used in novels and on the screen. In the press the travelers were usually associated with alcoholism, violence, and crime as late as in the 1950s. The notion of the *Tattare* as a specific race, or sub-race, was established as the science of race biology was institutionalized at the beginning of the twentieth century. A common view was that the travelers were descended from mixed marriages of Gypsies and the local Swedish population, an opinion held for instance by Herman Lundborg, who added that "it is unfortunately not uncommon that they are proletarians of a very complex heritage, with a bent for criminality."[105]

In the emerging Swedish welfare state the *Tattare* undoubtedly were an anomaly; their irregular lives were considered a severe social problem. In the interwar years the so-called *Tattare* question drew increasing attention from the authorities. A nationwide survey carried out by the Poor Law Commission (Fattigvårdskommittén) in 1922 identified 2,575 individuals as Gypsies, *Tattare*, or "equated with *Tattare*." It is worth noting that while the commission considered sterilization to be a possible future solution in some limited cases of vagrancy, it doubted that eugenic measures could be used to solve the general problems associated with the itinerant groups. Instead the commission recommended education of the *Tattare* and stated that it was crucial for the *attitudes* toward *Tattare* to change.[106]

When a second survey was conducted in 1942 by the National Board of Social Welfare, 7,668 *Tattare* were recorded. The reason for this remarkable increase seems to be that the practice among authorities to label vagrants, or other people living irregular lives, such as *Tattare*, became more common in the interwar period. As has been pointed out in a genealogical study by sociologist Adam Heymowski, the *Tattare* did not constitute a single, coherent group. Beside the "genuine" traveling families, other Swedish *Tattare* "acquired that label not because of their origin but because of their behavior (occupation and criminality), sometimes combined with a certain physical appearance (dark complexion, etc.) and a surname identical with a name borne by a traveler family. The percentage of such cases is probably quite high. The persons involved do not constitute any group or isolate, their only common trait being the *tattare* label applied to them by some authority."[107]

One conclusion to be drawn, then, is that the *Tattare* were more or less created as an out-group as the modernizing industrial state turned its searchlights toward the periphery of society. Moreover, it is striking how the discussion on vagrancy in general, and on the *Tattare* in particular, turned more racist in the same period. Obviously the notion of the alien *Tattare* as a biological reality, and as a biological as well as a social threat, was strengthened between the 1920s and the 1940s. It may seem paradoxical, of course, that Swedish race hygiene shifted toward reform eugenics during the same years. But parallel to the change in scientific genetics, it is possible to notice a persistence, or even a sharpening, of mainline eugenic ideas and concepts; the older notions of races, established by physical anthropology, were still used in the interpretation of the surrounding world. Whether this is to be explained by a widening gap between genetic science and race biology in its popular form, by some degree of influence from Nazi Germany, or simply by the fact that it takes a long time to change human thinking, are questions that remain to be answered.

At the end of the 1930s the National Board of Social Welfare described the *Tattare* as a genetically distinguishable and inferior group of people incapable of social adjustment. In official letters in 1937 and 1940 the board argued for a racial investigation of the group and sterilizations on a regular basis. "Both from a biological and a social point of view they are a burden to Swedish society," the board stated in 1940.[108] Studies published by the educator Manne Ohlander in 1942 and 1943, by the social welfare officer Tor Jacobsson in 1944, and as a dissertation by the linguist Allan Etzler in 1944, also stressed the biological aspects of the *Tattare* question. According to the study by Ohlander, published in Swedish periodicals for pedagogues and psychologists, a mental level below the average was a "racial characteristic" among *Tattare*. On the basis of school records and some intelligence tests, the author claimed that among 117 individuals classified as *Tattare*, 55 percent had an IQ lower than 0.80. Although he admitted that it would prove difficult to generalize the results, Ohlander concluded that "regarded as a race, it's obvious that the *Tattare* are inferior to the Swedish stock. This may probably be concluded from the fact that proportionally more *Tattare* than Swedes are taken into custody into prisons, special homes, treatment units for alcoholics or similar institutions for criminal and negligent individuals." (As Heymowski later commented, Ohlander never considered the possibility that persons belonging to these categories *a priori* were more likely to be stigmatized as *Tattare*.) As to future actions, Ohlander recommended sterilizations "without scruples."[109]

Since their genetic taint was still unproven by more accurate scientific measures, however, the *social* indication for sterilization added to the Sterilization Act of 1941 was regarded as a solution for the *Tattare*. During the debate in Parliament in 1941, the *Tattare* had explicitly been mentioned as a target for the extended Sterilization Act, and according to a statement made by Nils von Hofsten in 1943, the social indication for sterilization introduced in 1941 was without question applicable to the *Tattare*:

> An effective use of the Sterilization Act toward the *Tattare* is no doubt desirable and possible. . . . One step that can be taken immediately, it would appear, is that the National Board of Social Welfare is given the task to direct the attention of certain central and local authorities, at least then each and every poor law board and child welfare committee, to the fact that it is important that measures are introduced to sterilize *Tattare* who, due to mental inferiority or an antisocial way of life alone, are unsuitable for caring for children.[110]

In order to shed new light on the heritage of the *Tattare,* an "anthropometric study" was carried out in 1944 in collaboration with the State Institute for Race Biology. Performed by Gunnar Dahlberg, the investigation, among other things, contained body and head measurements of sixty-six individuals labeled as *Tattare.* Obstacles turned up, however, since, according to Dahlberg, "[s]everal refused and in many cases could only be examined after they had with some difficulty been convinced that it was a purely scientific investigation. . . ." As to the results of the study, Dahlberg concluded:

> From a theoretical point of view, it is interesting that there is a tolerably good agreement between tattare and other Swedes as regards the structure of the body. Nevertheless, tattare seem to constitute a selection of persons with a small brain and so-called asthenic bodily structure with narrow shoulders.
>
> From a practical point of view, it may finally be stated that the investigation has definitively showed it to be impossible objectively to separate out tattare from other Swedish citizens. It cannot be proved by an anthropological investigation that a person is a tattare, and the investigation has not given any support to the assumption that, from a racial point of view, the tattare differs from the rest of the Swedish people. The social problems of the tattare cannot be isolated from the general problems occasioned in our community by the existence of persons leading vagabond and asocial lives.[111]

Dahlberg's study quite obviously demonstrated that eugenic measures were useless to solve the *Tattare* problem. The National Board of Social Welfare also had to concur in this opinion. Yet the case of the Swedish *Tattare* is a good example of the persistence of racial thought. Thus, in 1945 the Board of Social Welfare suggested that the *Tattare* group might consist of two categories, one of which possessed "alien racial traits." Moreover, despite the fact that linguistic and genealogical research during the 1940s and 1950s confirmed the nonracial notion of the *Tattare,* individual scholars continued to describe them as a race of semi-Gypsy origin predisposed to crime and violence. Without doubt, this was also the widespread popular opinion at least up to the 1950s.[112]

Was the discussion of the *Tattare* and their origin purely theoretical, or did it affect the implementation of the sterilization laws? A couple of cases of sterilization, from the 1940s and 1950s, might suggest the latter. In an application for sterilization, made on behalf of a fifteen-year-old girl in 1940—of *Tattare* heritage, according to the child welfare committee—it was stressed that "for the last 25 years the municipality of Holmedal has provided work for the N. family without being able to say that its members have contributed in the least to society. . . . It is safe to say that to sterilize this person would be an act of mercy, for herself, for society, and perhaps most of all for the offspring she will surely bring into the world if an operation is not performed."

In the medical report that accompanied the application, the girl's alleged origin was the central point. She was said to "appear dull," but at the same time she is characterized as attentive and aware of her spatial and temporal situation; her memory and mental processes were said to be accurate, and testing showed a mental age of 13.9 years. "However, the patient appears far more retarded than this figure indicates," the physician stated. "In view of the fact that the applicant is of a *Tattare* family, where it has been hard to accept a regular life in society for generations, and in view of her feeble-mindedness, I feel that I should approve the application for sterilization." The Board of Health authorized the operation.[113]

The cited case from 1940 is hardly typical. Nevertheless, due to the heavy stigma, in other cases, being categorized as a *Tattare* was a contributing, though not sufficient, reason for sterilization. In these cases the applications reflect the general stereotypes attached to the group: "Dark, typical *Tattare* in looks. . . . Typical *Tattare* mentality: evasive, untruthful, and coward" (application for a seventeen-year-old girl, 1943); "of *Tattare* stock, with generations of pronounced antisocial behavior . . . has the friendly, polite manner of *Tattare*, with a goodly measure of ingratiation. Cheerful. Plenty of self-pity. . . ." (1942); "A blonde of *Tattare* extraction, well aware of the importance of the [intelligence] test in relation to the application for sterilization. Tense and quite nervous facing the test situation but tries to make her inadequate answers sound knowledgeable by means of a ready tongue and a great many words. Movements uncoordinated, speaks vulgarly and nasally in a nonchalant tone. . . . Suggested step: Her extremely glib attitude in combination with her previous antisocial life motivate sterilization, in spite of an IQ of 73. Apparently she has none of the qualities required for motherhood and the responsibility it entails" (a twenty-one-year-old woman for whom the poor law board sent in an application, 1950). In this last case no operation was performed since the woman refused.[114]

According to a case from the late 1950s, *Tattare* was still a relevant conception: when a woman in her late twenties, reportedly suffering from "social and moral incapacity," applied for an abortion in 1957, there was some discussion as to whether sterilization should be stipulated before an abortion was granted. There may have existed "a certain eugenic taint," according to the minutes of the Board of Health; the woman was born to unknown parents, but "her father is said to have been of *Tattare* or Gypsy family, which may be confirmed by her exotic appearance."[115] The following year Torsten Romanus, the Board of

Health adviser on questions of sterilization, makes the ambiguous comment to the minutes that the theory of the genetic inferiority of the *Tattare* "so far, at least, has no solid scientific support." It was not out of the question, then, according to Romanus, that such support would appear in the future.[116]

Statistics do not show how many *Tattare* were sterilized in Sweden. As a group the *Tattare* were never subjected to sterilization on a regular basis, even if this was frequently suggested in the debate. And yet the "*Tattare* question" disappeared in the postwar period; "the travellers as a group are doomed to disappear in the near future," predicted Adam Heymowski in his 1969 study.[117] On one hand, the welfare state obviously had no room for the itinerant way of life; on the other hand, the folklore contributing to the categorization of *Tattare* slowly vanished. And although old concepts evidently survived longer than might be expected, race biology as such lost ground. When eugenics no longer provided solutions to social problems, the concept of *Tattare* disappeared as individuals earlier labeled as travelers were incorporated into the postwar welfare reform program. The case of the *Tattare*, then, first and foremost, shows how race biology created its own reality.

POSTWAR TRANSFORMATIONS: FROM EUGENICS TO MEDICAL GENETICS

In the 1950s and 1960s the ideas that had sustained the old type of eugenics gradually faded from the scientific debate in Sweden. The general view changed too, even though arguments based on race were to be found in schoolbooks, for example, into the 1950s at least.[118] In the course of time, words such as "race," "racial hygiene," "*Tattare*," "Lapp," "Negro," "genetically deficient," and "inferior" lost currency except as historical concepts, placed within quotation marks. In their place paraphrases came to be used, and are being used, which has led to something of a semantic shift, rendering the former meaning invisible, but perhaps not completely gone. An important factor in this change was the Statement on Race issued by UNESCO in 1950: in this statement the biological concept of race was dismissed, not only because it was compromised but also because it was unscientific. Instead the sociological term "ethnic group" was launched. Two Swedish specialists—Gunnar Dahlberg and Gunnar Myrdal—were involved, and both were well-qualified for the work.[119] Indeed, Dahlberg had focused on the vagueness of the concept of race in a number of articles in the 1940s. In Sweden, official repudiation of the race concept followed the UNESCO statement; thus Verdandi, the same radical student association that had advocated eugenics in accordance with a more Darwinian model at the turn of the century, arranged a roundtable conference on race in 1953, and also published the proceedings from the meeting. The example shows the change that had taken place within a leading academic group, from a pronounced biological view toward sociological notions.[120]

Ever more rarely, then, was man discussed as a biological entity. Traditional Darwinism reached its peak around the turn of the century, and eugenics was well established a few decades later; after that, however, the public debate made surprisingly few references to a biological world view.[121] Neither ethology nor sociobiology attracted much attention from anyone other than specialists. Consequently it is hard to make comprehensive statements about the attitude of Swedish geneticists toward the reductionist tendencies in modern biology or the recent inroads made by biology into sociology.

The research conducted at the Institute for Race Biology under Gunnar Dahlberg in the postwar years did not attract attention as before. The subjects that were handled were mainly sociomedical and medical: the inheritance of TB and cancer and less spectacular afflictions such as anemia, defective metabolism, and eczema. Increasingly mathematical, eugenics became a field for the specialist. Jan Arvid Böök, who succeeded Dahlberg in 1956, was trained in Lund and clearly drawn to mainline eugenics, as he had shown during the war. Before his appointment he published a manifesto in support of Dahlberg's program, however, emphasizing the need to revise the taxonomy of various diseases by means of genetic analysis and also to investigate the relationship between pathological genes and biochemical processes. As a final point he gave prominence to the study of the distribution of genetic diseases in different segments of the population and their relation to various demographic features— part of the stock-in-trade of the old type of race biology; however, this was actually the only point derived from it. At the same time, in 1956, the institute changed its name to the Department of Medical Genetics.[122]

Thus eugenics in the 1950s eliminated the old notions of anthropology and compromised race mysticism. The great threat was no longer degeneration or "biological erosion" but the effects of radioactive fallout; to deal with the new problem, international cooperation and up-to-date genetic research were advocated. In practice, however, Böök's own work came to be linked to Lundborg's studies of isolates. Their genealogical-statistical methods have remained a vigorous branch of eugenic research. All in all, genetics was to expand considerably in Sweden during the 1960s and 1970s. As the number of known hereditary diseases increased (from 412 in 1958 to some 2,300 in 1975), scientists and physicians paid greater attention to medical genetics. Units similar to the Department of Medical Genetics in Uppsala were established in Stockholm in 1970 and in Lund in 1975.[123]

The trend toward continuity rather than a complete break with the past is evident if we look at the various editions of a textbook by Arne Müntzing, *Ärftlighetsforskning* (1953, 1960, 1964, 1971, 1977; the English translation, published in 1961, bears the title *Genetic Research: A Survey of Methods and Main Results*). Throughout, Müntzing, who was professor of genetics at Lund University, showed great respect for "genetic hygiene" (renamed "eugenics" in 1971, "medical genetics" in 1977). Thus, 80 percent of the patients in mental hospitals in Sweden (some 45,000 in the 1953 edition) were said to suffer from hereditary illness—good grounds, all by itself, for Swedish sterilization policies. A study by H. O. Åkesson was cited (in 1964) to show that only 27 percent of the children of mentally retarded mothers were normal. All in all, 3 percent of the total population were of such low intelligence that they could not lead a normal life. Müntzing emphasized the cost this entails and advocated that such dangerous inheritance be registered in accordance with Tage Kemp's Danish model. It is interesting that he suggested that the change that took place in the reasons given for sterilization, from "genetic" to "medical," were, to some extent, nominal.[124]

Finally, let us mention criminology, a science halfway between research and concrete social questions. Olof Kinberg, the most prominent criminologist in the first half of the twentieth century, believed strongly in eugenics. When the sterilization issue was being discussed, sexual psychopaths had been grouped, from the very start, with those who would come under the new law; whether the grounds were to be social or eugenic was a matter of opinion. For Kinberg, however, it went without saying that eugenics could also reduce criminality in the long run. In 1942, with one of his students, Gunnar Inghe, he published a broad investigation of the problem of incest in Sweden, offering glimpses of wretched social environments. Steps should be taken to eliminate those, of course, but Kinberg and Inghe also advocated a more radical sterilization policy than that in existence; they pointed out that 3 percent of those involved suffered from oligophrenia, for example. Inghe and Kinberg were hardliners, but they were not alone. Thus, in 1944 a law on castration was introduced, a law that could hardly have been instituted in the period between the wars, and one which demonstrates Kinberg's influence; it belongs in the severe climate of the war years, along with the Sterilization Act of 1941 and the Vagrancy Commission of 1942. The law on castration was applied less with each passing year, however (43 cases in 1944; 36 in 1945; 11 in 1946). The decrease could have been the result of a diminishing need for the measure, but it could also have been due to a change in attitudes.[125] In the field of criminology itself, such a change was gradual, manifest only in the 1960s with the appearance of the sociologist Gustaf Jonsson, whose launching of the term "the social heritage" had a tremendous impact on the Swedish discussion of biological determinism in the 1950s and 1960s.[126]

ABANDONING EUGENIC STERILIZATION

The change in the application of the Sterilization Act of 1941 has already been mentioned. During the 1950s sterilization on eugenic grounds gradually decreased, as did sterilization of the mentally retarded. An important question is whether the eugenic principles were relinquished eventually because of new scientific findings or for some other reason. Sweden's most important contribution in this field probably was C. H. Alström's 1950 study on epilepsy, in which the heritability of the disease was toned down. From available statistics it would appear that Alström's findings had an almost immediate effect on actual practice. It was some twenty years later, however, that they led to a proposal for new legislation.

Apparently, old beliefs in eugenics changed slowly, allowing the Swedish sterilization program to continue into the 1950s and 1960s, whether justified by medical, social, or genetic reasons. Moreover, sterilizations no longer drew much public attention. The lack of discussion was a result of several developments: the invasion of the specialists; the fact that laws had already been instituted; the conventional view that "one doesn't talk about things like that"; and Sweden having a fairly clear conscience for not having been involved in the atrocities of World War II. Looked upon as a question for the specialist, sterilization of the mentally retarded continued, although to a lesser extent than before, causing little or no reaction. These were measures where the authority had been transferred from the central level to the one where physicians, social workers, experts, and institutions had the power of decision and where public control consequently was limited.

At a political level, however, it is possible to discover a changing attitude toward sterilization in the 1950s and 1960s, most likely connected to an altered view of the relations between state and individual. The national perspective became less prominent in the debate on population policies, where the discussion moved from the general level to the specific, to that of the individual. (It is significant, in this context, that the term "population policies" was discredited after World War II; it was replaced by "family policies" in the 1950s.)[127] Arguing that sterilization was a "significant mutilation" whose effects on mental health could be serious, Parliament stressed the need for caution, stating, in 1955, that the operation should be resorted to only when other means of implementing social policies were likely to prove ineffective. A few years later, in 1960, Social Democrat Olof Palme noted in Parliament that "the theories at the back of the eugenic indication [for sterilization] would appear somewhat questionable." He added that "society should avoid intervening by means of compulsion in such very personal matters."[128]

Thus, sterilization came to be looked upon as a personal right, rather than a tool for population policy. There are several reasons for that change. Society at large was being transformed, and a number of factors led to a higher degree of individualization at the expense of both class consciousness and belief in established authorities. One was the rapid economic growth in Sweden; almost everybody benefited from it, and the rising standard of living enabled greater individual freedom and autonomy. Another factor was that Swedish welfare programs placed considerable emphasis on the independence of the individual; this was true in such areas as housing, social assistance, and the family. Yet another element was the rise in the general level of education, which meant greater political involvement on the part of the individual, enabling him to make himself heard in the public debate or to deal with state officials.[129] (As a matter of fact, the interaction between individuals and institutions became increasingly informal from the 1960s on.) Finally, a weakening of the older, traditional forms of social control worked in the same direction, giving room for individualization.

All these developments, some longstanding but accentuated in the postwar period, must have undermined the foundations for a large-scale sterilization program of the coercive type. At the same time new techniques, such as the intrauterine contraceptive device and the contraceptive pill, probably contributed to making sterilization an outdated method. Furthermore, there were growing doubts as to the effectiveness and scientific justifiability of eugenic sterilization. The change is evident, for example, in Müntzing's summary of what is otherwise an enthusiastic plea for sterilization: the measure can "only influence and improve the average genetic make-up of a population to a very small degree," he states. Instead the idea is to "prevent or ease human suffering" in particular cases. The phrase appears for the first time in the 1964 edition of Müntzing's book.

It was not until 1967, however, that the National Board of Health admitted that the policy of sterilizing mentally retarded patients had been implemented because of a somewhat exaggerated belief in the importance of heredity: "a gradual shift in the etiology of feeble-mindedness [has] brought about the realization that other factors than genes can be influential." At the same time, it was said, sterilization of the mentally retarded was most often legitimate on social grounds.[130] The situation was not reconsidered in earnest until the early

1970s when Karl Grunewald, a National Board of Health official, leveled sharp criticism at the sterilization of mentally retarded patients. A number of case studies were published, obviously showing that the mentally retarded were sterilized on questionable grounds.[131] The 1941 Sterilization Act was replaced in 1975, when all sterilizations without the consent of the person concerned were prohibited. Thus all forms of involuntary sterilization came to an end in Sweden, and since that date only voluntary operations take place, mostly as a means of family planning.

EUGENICS, STERILIZATION, AND THE SWEDISH MODEL: SUMMARY

The eugenics movement made rapid headway in Sweden at the beginning of the twentieth century. Eugenics became institutionalized at an early date and racial hygiene was put into practice in the Sterilization Acts of 1934 and 1941. As far as eugenic sterilization was concerned, Sweden actually held a leading position, Germany excepted, a fact somewhat unflattering for Swedish twentieth-century history. What, then, were the characteristics of Swedish eugenics, and how may its spectacular breakthrough and position be explained?

First of all it must be stressed that racial hygiene never was a German-Swedish specialty—although in both countries there flourished a dubious obsession with the so-called "Nordic race." In the early twentieth century eugenics was established in countries such as the United States, Great Britain, and the Soviet Union. Furthermore, and as shown elsewhere in this book, sterilization laws similar to those in Sweden were passed throughout Scandinavia during the 1930s. As to the Swedish sterilization program, the United States, rather than Germany, served as a model.

Nevertheless, it may be appropriate to speak of a form of "welfare state eugenics" in Sweden which, because of its progressive character and freedom from race mysticism, differs in part from that in other countries. A central feature in the policies developed in the 1930s by the Social Democrats was the combination of social welfare and efficiency. The idea was that *preventive* social measures, such as equal education and health care, made for rational use of "human resources."[132] It is plain to see that applied race biology, too, could be incorporated into this political idea. It was a widely held view in the 1930s that eugenics, and not least a large scale sterilization program, could yield considerable economic gains for the state. The systematic sterilization of the mentally retarded would reduce the cost of institutional care, special schools, and poor relief. Indeed, in the Swedish Parliament, the Social Democrats were among those who advocated sterilization the most vigorously.

Sterilization was only one component in a comprehensive Swedish program concerned with population questions. The program was governed in part, but not wholly, by eugenic principles. The "population crisis" of the 1930s steered the debate to the question of quality versus quantity. The extensive emigration in the previous decades, the threatening immigration of people who, it was said, belonged to "inferior racial groups," and the extremely low birthrate caused particular worry. The marriage laws introduced early in the century provide clear evidence that eugenic ideas had taken root even then. The 1940s legislation on abortion was intended to preclude reproduction among the genetically least suitable, as were the laws on sterilization. Maternity benefits (1937) and the government child allowance (1948), on the other hand, were reforms aimed at increasing the birthrate of the population at large.

It was not difficult, then, to find room for eugenics in the restructuring of Swedish society that was taking place in the 1930s and 1940s. The resources of the state were mobilized to build the new *folkhem* ("the people's home," the metaphor used from the 1920s on), modernity was an honored term, and race biology a modern and untried science. Hygiene was another key concept, and eugenics—racial hygiene—only one side of the passion for cleanliness and health. The ambition to clear away what was old, dirty, and diseased could range from a commitment to physical hygiene to an aspiration to create, by means of a eugenic program, a sound and healthy people free from defective genes.[133]

Without doubt, the eugenics movement was a complex phenomenon, politically as well as scientifically. The Swedish example shows clearly that eugenics was not the exclusive domain of a right-wing ideology. As we have seen, Social Democrats, Agrarians, and Conservatives all took an interest in eugenics at an early stage. From a scientific point of view, the shift from mainline (or, perhaps better, "traditional") to reform eugenics during the 1930s should be stressed. Physical anthropology and racial mysticism were replaced by genetics. Less inspired by biology (social Darwinism), eugenics turned to mathematics, statistics, and physics (social engineering). Gunnar Dahlberg represents the new era as director of the Institute for Race Biology from 1936 on, as do the writings on population policy by Alva and Gunnar Myrdal. By the same token, sterilization was to a lesser extent regarded as a means for "race improvement," but as a measure applicable to *individual cases* of genetic (or social) deficiency. On the whole, it is important to stress the social aspects of the Swedish sterilization program, but this transformation was far from absolute. The old notions of race were indeed tenacious, as is shown by the conception of the Swedish *Tattare*.

As to the question of the connection between the professional profile of a natural scientist and his attitude toward politics and social conditions, there is no simple answer. Herman Lundborg, as we have seen, became a supporter of the Third Reich, which would seem to harmonize with his scientific pursuits. Herman Nilsson-Ehle apparently took a similar course. Gunnar Dahlberg's research, too, clearly accords with his position as a Social Democrat. We must not take such consistency for granted, however. Olof Kinberg's Liberal leanings and his work as a criminologist seem truly discordant.

Nils von Hofsten, in some respects the epitome of Swedish eugenics, is interesting from several points of view. Indeed, von Hofsten was no fanatic in the matter of race; as rector of the University of Uppsala, and as a cultural figure keen to do battle, he was to repudiate Nazism in the war years. His long involvement in the sterilization issue, where he worked as a consultant with the diligence of a civil servant, demonstrated his great conviction and showed his motives were not all political: he strongly believed in the importance of science and the expert in organizing society. That belief he never abandoned. To an unusually high degree, von Hofsten represents a Swedish alliance between academic research and public responsibility.

The application of sterilization laws appears to have been particularly consistent and determined in Sweden. From the 1930s and well into the 1950s there were considerably more sterilizations in Sweden than in Norway, Denmark, or Finland, both in absolute numbers and in relation to population. When it came to putting the eugenic ideas into practice, then, this was done with customary Swedish thoroughness: an efficient bureaucratic organization was available; extensive forms were filled in before each sterilization; experts on genetics stood by in debatable cases; in the field, there were energetic physicians and social workers.

From a medical point of view, the sterilization question was new and exciting, and the great interest that the medical profession took in the matter is an important factor when it comes to explaining the development in Sweden. The 1930s saw the emergence of somatic methods in the treatment of mental illness. Electric shock treatment and insulin shock were two of the therapeutic methods used most frequently in the period. Given the assumption that mental disorders were related to organic defects, it was tempting to look for simple and practical forms of treatment. Referring to the statistically calculated risk of transmission, the advocates of sterilization held that it was a concrete step which had an immediate effect. Thus, the sterilization program was seen as a technical solution to medical, social, and economic problems. What was humane and efficient was combined, it was said; the inhuman and costly institutions of older times no longer had a function to fill, but were to be replaced by quick and painless operations.

The historical perspective shows a different picture, however, far removed from that clinical vision: what we see is the blurred use of authoritarian measures and anonymous violence. The treatment of the mentally retarded and the socially maladjusted was removed from public view and carried out without interference. The fact that physicians came on the scene did not mean that the attitudes toward these groups had changed. If efficiency and rationality were keywords in the discourse, the implementation of the sterilization program shows other driving forces as well. First, the right to bear children became a moral question to a high degree. Clearly, what was labeled asocial and inferior behavior was instead *different* behavior, as the discussion of the *Tattare* reveals. Second, the question of gender must be central to an understanding of how the sterilization program was carried out. The argument put forward by feminist researchers that the sterilization program reflected male norms, and that male physicians used sterilization as a tool against women, seems plausible. Again, the question of who was different is a central point.

The Swedish debate on sterilization focused on the advantages for the state, and the national interest united the separate political groups. The individual was either useful or useless, a resource or an encumbrance, a being of full worth or, in the parlance of the day, inferior. The idea that people should have the right to decide about their own bodies was regarded in 1936 by the Commission on Population as "an extremely individualistic view."[134] Postwar developments, however, caused a fundamental shift in thought from the national level to that of the individual: sterilization became—and has remained—a personal matter. Population policies were replaced by family policies, and sterilization, instead of being looked upon as a state instrument, became an individual right. The process reached its final stage with the 1974 Sterilization Act. It is possible, of course, that the change, at least in its first phase, was primarily a change in rhetoric. The question is to what extent the talk of sterilization as "an individual right" reflects a real change in outlook with regard to eugenics and population policies; or, to put it differently, how tenacious the old notions are.

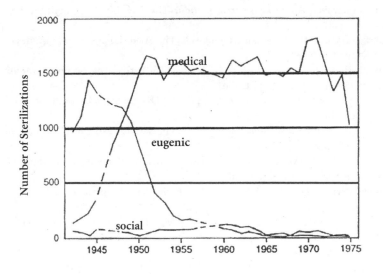

FIGURE 1. REPORTED STERILIZATIONS IN SWEDEN, 1942-1974, AND INDICATIONS

Source: *Sveriges Offentliga Statistik: Allmän Hälso- och sjukvård* (Stockholm: Statistiska centralbyrån, 1935-1976) [Official Statistics of Sweden: Health]. Note: no information available for 1946 and 1958-59.

One has to consider Sweden's historical situation when discussing continuity. The fact that the country stood apart from World War II meant that the eugenic features of its population policies were not automatically re-examined after the war, as was the case in Germany. Nor was there anything to impede continuity with regard to individuals—physicians and specialists—or institutions. Furthermore, throughout the twentieth century Sweden has been characterized by continuity, consensus, and cautious change. Consider the following characteristics: a development free from open social conflict; basic agreement about the concept of the welfare state; the growth of the public sector; a stable power structure. All of these factors either contributed directly, or at least did not hinder continuity with regard to the values that were behind Sweden's population policies and attitudes toward eugenics, or the way in which they were put into practice.

ABBREVIATIONS IN NOTES

AKM Riksdagstrycket, *Andra kammaren: motion* [The Swedish Parliament, Second Chamber bill]

AKP Riksdagstrycket, *Andra kammarens protokoll* [The Swedish Parliament, Minutes of the Second Chamber]

ALU Riksdagstrycket, *Andra lagutskottet* [The Swedish Parliament, Second Standing Committee on Civil Law Legislation]

FKM Riksdagstrycket, *Första kammaren: motion* [The Swedish Parliament, First Chamber bill]

FKP Riksdagstrycket, *Första kammarens protokoll* [The Swedish Parliament, Minutes of the First Chamber]

FLU Riksdagstrycket, *Första lagutskottet* [The Swedish Parliament, First Standing Committee on Civil Law Legislation]

LU Riksdagstrycket, *Lagutskottet* [The Swedish Parliament, Committee on Civil Law Legislation]

MA Riksarkivet, *Medicinalstyrelsens arkiv,* Rättspsykiatriska nämnden [The National Archives of Sweden (Stockholm), Archives of the National Board of Health, Board of Forensic Psychiatry]

P Riksdagstrycket, *Proposition* [The Swedish Parliament, Government bill]

SA *Socialstyrelsens arkiv,* Socialpsykiatriska nämnden [Archives of the National Board of Social Welfare (Stockholm), Board of Social Psychiatry]

NOTES

1. Quoted in S. Sörlin, *Framtidslandet: Debatten om Norrland och naturresurserna* (Umeå: Carlsson, 1988), 15.
2. M. Berman, *All That Is Solid Melts into Air: The Experience of Modernity* (London: Allen Lane, 1982).
3. D. Pick, *Faces of Degeneration: A European Disorder c. 1848-c. 1918* (Cambridge: Cambridge University Press, 1989).
4. G. Broberg, "Lamarckismen i Sverige," *Lychnos. Lärdomshistoriska samfundets årsbok 1988* (Uppsala: Almqvist & Wiksell International, 1988).
5. P. Fahlbeck, *Sveriges Adel* (Stockholm: Gleerup, 1898), 1:438-48.
6. E. Key, *Lifslinjer* (Stockholm: Bonnier, 1903), 1:129.
7. G. Broberg, "Linnaeus As an Anthropologist," in *Linnaeus: The Man and His Work,* ed. T. Frängsmyr (Berkeley: University of California Press, 1983).
8. T. Thunberg, *De hygieniska förhållandena och det naturliga urvalet,* Vår tids livsfrågor 43 (Uppsala: Appelberg, 1906); J. V. Hultcrantz, according to *Upsala Nya Tidning,* 28 May 1907.
9. According to a circular letter published by the Deutsche Gesellschaft für Rassenhygiene, 1910.
10. D. MacKenzie, "Eugenics in Britain," *Social Studies of Science* 6 (1976).

11. H. Lundborg, *Degenerationsfaran och riktlinjer för dess förebyggande*, Svenska Sällskapets för Rashygien Skriftserie 9 (Stockholm: P.A. Norstedt & Söners, 1922), 21-22, 24-25.

12. The following section is based on G. Broberg, "Rasbiologiska institutet—tillkomståren," in *Kunskapens trädgårdar*, ed. G. Broberg et al. (Stockholm: Atlantis, 1988), where further references are given.

13. AKP 1921 no. 42, 48-66.

14. His proposal comprised four different constellations: De Vries, Correns, and Tschermak—who rediscovered Mendel's work; Johannsen and Bateson—who introduced the paired concepts genotype/phenotype, and the term genetics; Morgan and his school—who renewed laboratory research; and Nilsson-Ehle and Baur—who were prominent in the area of genetics and plant breeding.

15. H. Lundborg, *Die Rassenmischung beim Menschen* (The Hague: Martinius Nijhoff, 1931), 170.

16. W. K., "Professor Herman Lundborg," *Die Sonne. Monatsschrift für Nordische Weltanschauung und Völkische Lebensgestaltung* 15, no. 7-8 (1938): 177.

17. G. Worskey, *The Visible College* (London: Verso, 1985).

18. G. Dahlberg, *Race, Reason and Rubbish* (London: George Allen & Unwin Ltd., 1942), 15-16.

19. T. B. Kittredge, according to W. A. Jackson, "The Making of a Social Science Classic: Gunnar Myrdal's *An American Dilemma*," *Perspectives in American History*, New Series vol. 2 (1985): 234. See also D. W. Southern, *Gunnar Myrdal and Black-White Relations: The Use and Abuse of "An American Dilemma" 1944-1969* (Baton Rouge: Louisiana State University Press, 1987); G. Myrdal, *Historien om "An American Dilemma"* (Stockholm: SNS förlag, 1987); M. Curti, "Sweden in the American Social Mind of the 1930s," in *The Immigration of Ideas: Studies in the North Atlantic Community: Essays Presented to O. Fritiof Ander*, ed. J. I. Dowie and J. T. Tredway (Rock Island, Illinois: Augustana Historical Society, 1968).

20. M. Childs, *Sweden: The Middle Way* (New Haven: Yale University Press, 1936), xiv-xv.

21. On Nazism in Sweden, see U. Lindström, *Fascism in Scandinavia 1920-1940* (Stockholm: Almqvist & Wiksell International, 1985); H. Lööw, *Hakkorset och Wasakärven: En studie av nationalsocialismen i Sverige 1924-1950* (Göteborg: Avhandlingar från Historiska Institutionen i Göteborg, 1990). On refugee policy and attitudes toward immigrants, see T. Hammar, *Sverige åt svenskarna: Invandringspolitik, utlänningskontroll och asylrätt 1900-1932* (Stockholm: Caslon Press, 1964); H. Lindberg, *Svensk flyktingpolitik under internationellt tryck 1936-1941* (Stockholm: Allmänna förlaget, 1973). For a survey of the history of the Swedish Jews during the 1930s and 1940s, see S. Koblik, *The Stones Cry Out: Sweden's Response to the Persecution of the Jews 1933-1945* (New York: Holocaust Library, 1988).

22. On Swedish population policy in the 1930s, see A. Hatje, *Befolkningsfrågan och välfärden: Debatten om familjepolitik och nativitetsökning under 1930- och 1940-talen* (Stockholm: Allmänna förlaget, 1974); A. Kälvemark, *More Children of Better*

Quality? Aspects of Swedish Population Policy in the 1930's, Studia Historica Upsaliensia 115 (Uppsala: Almqvist & Wiksell International, 1980); A. Ohlander, "The Invisible Child? The Struggle over Social Democratic Family Policy," in *Creating Social Democracy: A Century of the Social Democratic Labor Party in Sweden*, ed. K. Misgeld, K. Molin, and K. Åmark (University Park: The Pennsylvania State University Press, 1992); A. Carlson, *The Swedish Experiment in Family Politics: The Myrdals and the Interwar Population Crisis* (New Brunswick: Transaction, 1990).

23. S. Kjällström, *Den gode nihilisten: Axel Hägerström och striderna kring upp-salafilosofin* (Kristianstad: Rabén & Sjögren, 1986).

24. On social engineering in Sweden in the 1930s and 1940s, see Y. Hirdman, *Att lägga livet tillrätta: Studier i svensk folkhemspolitik* (Stockholm: Carlssons, 1989).

25. L. Öberg, *Barnmorskan och läkaren. Kompetens och Konflikt i Svensk förlossin-ingsvården 1870-1895* (Stockholm: Ordfront, 1996).

26. E. Essen-Möller, "Bidrag till frågan om steriliseringens berättigande ur medicinsk och rashygienisk synpunkt," *Allm. svenska läkartidningen* 12, no. 1 (1915); E. Sjövall, "Diskussionen om det svenska förslaget till steriliseringslag," *Nordisk med-icinsk tidskrift* 2, no. 25 (1930).

27. AKM 1908 no. 2 and no. 31; LU 1908 report no. 9.

28. A. M. Selling, "Rasbiologi och rashygien: Några grundlinjer," *Allmänna svenska läkartidningen* 7, no. 6-7 (1909).

29. J. V. Hultcrantz, "Någa ord om rashygien (eugenik)," *Social tidskrift* 11, no. 7-8 (1911): 297-98; Herman Lundborg, "Rashygieniska sträfvanden i utlandet," *Allmänna svenska läkartidningen* 9, no. 30 (1912): 643.

30. Lagberedningens, *Lagberedningens förslag till revision av Giftermålsbalken och vissa delar av ärvdabalken*, vol. 1 (Stockholm: P.A. Norstedt & Söners, 1913) [The law-drafting committees proposal for changed legislation on marriage, including the report by the Medical Faculty of Uppsala University], 131, 596.

31. Essen-Möller, "Bidrag till frågan om steriliseringens berättigande ur medicinsk och rashygienisk synpunkt."

32. N. von Hofsten, *Ärftlighetslära* (Stockholm: P.A. Norstedt & Söners förlag, 1919), 494.

33. FKM 1922 no. 38.

34. ALU 1922 report no. 24, 12.

35. E. Essen-Möller, *Sterilisationsfrågan*, Svenska sällskapets för rashygien skriftserie 10 (Stockholm: P.A. Norstedt & Söners, 1922); G. H. von Koch, ed., *Social handbok: Översikt av offentligt och enskilt samhällsarbete i Sverige* (Stockholm: Centralförbundet för socialt arbete, 1925); Svenska läkaresällskapet, *Förhandlingar vid Svenska läkaresällskapets sammankomst år 1925* (Stockholm: Svenska läkaresäll-skapet, 1925), 97-121 (in which the report from the Board of Health is cited).

36. Socialdepartementet, *Betänkande med förslag till steriliseringslag*, Statens Offentliga Utredningar no. 1929/14 (Stockholm: Socialdepartementet, 1929).

37. Justitiedepartementet, *Förslag till lag om sterilisering av vissa sinnessjuka, sinnesslöa eller av annan rubbning av själsverksamheten lidande personer*, Statens Offentliga

Utredningar no. 1933/22 (Stockholm: Justitiedepartementet, 1933), 30-63; state-ment by the Board of Health published in *Svenska Läkartidningen* 28, no. 45-48 (1931); statement by the National Board of Social Welfare published in *Sociala Meddelanden,* no. 12 (1931).

38. FKM 1933 no. 188; Justitiedepartementet, *Förslag till lag om sterilisering av vissa sinnessjuka, sinnesslöa eller av annan rubbning av själsverksamheten lidande per-soner.*

39. P 1934 no. 103, 28.

40. Kungl. Maj:t, *Lag om sterilisering av vissa sinnessjuka, sinnesslöa eller andra som lida av rubbad själsverksamhet,* Svensk författningssamling no. 1934/171 [Sterilization Act of 1934] (Stockholm: P.A. Norstedt & Söners förlag, 1934).

41. E. Sjövall, "Steriliseringsfrågans läge i Sverige," *Nordisk medicinsk tidskrift* 1, no. 19 (1929): 300; N. von Hofsten, *Ärftlighetslärans grunder,* vol. 2 (Stockholm: Albert Bonniers förlag, 1931), 369.

42. Sjövall, "Diskussionen om det svenska förslaget till steriliseringslag"; H. Forssner, "Sterilisationsproblemet i Skandinavien med några reflexioner av en praktiker," *Nordisk medicinsk tidskrift* 2, no. 11 (1930); H. Sjögren, "Erfarenheter inom ett poliklinikklientel beträffande sterilisering," in *Nionde nordiska mötet i Stockholm 1936 för undervisning och vård av blinda, dövstumma, epileptiker, sinnesslöa och av talrubbningar lidande* (Stockholm: O. Eklund, 1938), 503-9.

43. G. Hedrén, "Några reflektioner med anledning av den vid innevarande riksdag väckta motionen om utredning rörande sterilisering av sinnesslöa m.fl.," *Svenska läkartidningen* 19, no. 14 (1922): 276; C. Lindhagen in FKP 1922 no. 42, 46.

44. See especially A. Myrdal and G. Myrdal, *Kris i befolkningsfrågan,* 4th ed. (Stockholm: Albert Bonniers förlag, 1935), 245-66. Cf. Carlson, *The Swedish Experiment in Family Politics,* esp. 81-95.

45. Myrdal and Myrdal, *Kris i befolkningsfrågan,* 17.

46. Ibid., 263.

47. A. Myrdal, *Nation and Family: The Swedish Experiment in Democratic Family and Population Policy* (Cambridge: M.I.T. Press, 1968 [1941]), 215.

48. Befolingskommissionen, *Betänkande angående sterilisering,* Statens Offentliga Utredningar no. 1936/46 (Stockholm: Socialdepartementet, 1936), 8-9, 58.

49. Ibid., 14-15.

50. Ibid., 14-17.

51. AKP 1941 no. 25, 48 (Westman); FKP 1941 no. 24, 28 (Wohlin), no. 24, 33 (Olsson).

52. FKM 1941 no. 105 and AKM 1941 no. 144 (same wording); AKM 1941 no. 37; AKP 1941 no. 25, 44.

53. FKP 1941 no. 24, 47 (Branting); AKP 1941 no. 25, 51-52 (Mosesson); AKP 1941 no. 25, 55 (Persson).

54. P 1934 no. 103, 23.

55. Kungl. Maj:t, *Lag om sterilisering,* Svensk författningssamling no. 1941/282 [Sterilization Act of 1941] (Stockholm: P.A. Norstedt & Söners förlag, 1941).

56. If not otherwise stated, all the statistics presented in the following are based on annual reports published by the Swedish Central Bureau of Statistics: Statistiska centralbyrån, *Sveriges Offentliga Statistik: Allmän Hälso- och sjukvård* (Stockholm: Statistiska centralbyrån, 1935-1976) [Official Statistics of Sweden: Health]. It should be noted that the figures refer to the number of *reported* sterilizations for a particular year, not the factual number of operations performed.

57. The data on the implementation of the Swedish sterilization laws, presented in this article, are based on documents in the Archives of the National Board of Health and the National Board of Social Welfare (both in Stockholm). Methodology and results of our study are presented in detail in G. Broberg & M. Tydén, *Oönskade i folkhemmet: Rashygien och sterilisering i Sverige* (Stockholm: Gidlunds Bokförlag, 1991).

58. Minutes, 6 October 1940, MA vol. AI, 11.

59. Medicinalstyrelsen, *Råd och anvisningar rörande tillämpning av 1941 års steriliser-ingslag och abortlagen,* Meddelanden från Kungl. Medicinalstyrelsen 93 (Stockholm: Medicinalstyrelsen, 1947), 5; N. von Hofsten, *Steriliseringar i Sverige 1941-1953,* Socialmedicinsk tidskrifts skriftserie 28 (Stockholm: Socialmedicinsk tidskrift, 1963), 47.

60. The significant shift from eugenic to medical labeling is partly explained by the fact that the two clusters include eugenical sterilization of the mentally retarded, a category which decreased dramatically in the 1950s. This group must be included in the comparison, however, since the statistics showing medical sterilization in the late 1950s do not separate the mentally retarded from the mentally ill. Nevertheless, if the mentally retarded women are excluded from the 1942-1945 cluster, the pattern remains; only 8 percent of a total number of 750 women classed as mentally ill were sterilized on medical grounds in this period.

61. Medicinalstyrelsen, *Råd och anvisningar rörande tillämpning av 1941 års steriliser-ingslag och abortlagen,* 5.

62. N. von Hofsten puts the figure at 226 for the years 1935-1939. See N. von Hofsten, "Steriliseringar i Sverige 1935-1939," *Nordisk medicin* 7, no. 34 (1940).

63. Medicinalstyrelsen, "Kungl. Medicinalstyrelsens cirkulärskrivelse till föreståndare och läkare vid vårdanstalter för bildbara sinnesslöa" [unpublished circular], Typescript, 1948, Stockholm, Archives of the National Board of Social Welfare.

64. Card index of sterilizations, 1960, SA vols. DIII, 5-6; Applications for sterilization, 1 January to 30 June 1960, SA vols. EI, 303-13. On the mentally retarded in Sweden, see M. Söder, *Anstalter för utvecklingsstörda: En historisk sociologisk beskrivning av utvecklingen* (Stockholm: Ala, 1979), vols. 1-2.

65. Befolingskommissionen, *Betänkande angående sterilisering,* 22.

66. N. von Hofsten, et al., "Falska analogier: Ett radiosamtal om vetenskapens popu-larisering i Uppsalastudion," Typescript, 7 March 1946, Uppsala University Archives, Files of N. von Hofsten, vol. 504:E1.

67. N. von Hofsten, "De arvshygieniska verkningarna av sterilisering," Typescript, 1 April 1942, Uppsala University Archives, Files of N. von Hofsten, vol. 504:G2.

68. Medicinalstyrelsen, *Råd och anvisningar rörande tillämpning av 1941 års steriliseringslag och abortlagen*, 3-4.
69. Ibid., 14.
70. *Kungl. Maj:ts kungörelse med tillämpningsföreskrifter till lagen den 18 maj 1934 (nr 171)*, Svensk författningssamling no. 1934/521 (Stockholm: P.A. Norstedt & Söners förlag, 1934); *Kungl. Maj:ts kungörelse med tillämpningsföreskrifter till lagen den 23 maj 1941 (nr 282)*, Svensk författningssamling no. 1941/387 (Stockholm: P.A. Norstedt & Söners förlag, 1941); Medicinalstyrelsen, *Råd och anvisningar rörande tillämpning av 1941 års steriliseringslag och abortlagen*, 6.
71. Diaries on applications for sterilization, 1950, SA vols. EIc, 5-6. With reference to documents on the Swedish sterilization program in the Social Welfare History Archives, University of Minnesota, Philip R. Reilly writes that among the sterilizations performed in Sweden 1948-49 "about half" were involuntary—a statement not confirmed by documents kept at the Swedish National Board of Social Welfare. P. R. Reilly, *The Surgical Solution: A History of Involuntary Sterilization in the United States* (Baltimore: The Johns Hopkins University Press, 1991), 109, 177.
72. Medicinalstyrelsen, *Råd och anvisningar rörande tillämpning av 1941 års steriliseringslag och abortlagen*, 9.
73. K. Grunewald, "Graviditet och sterilisering hos svenska särskoleflickor under åren 1937-1956," *Psykisk utvecklingshämning* no. 1-2 (1960). The Board of Health stated in 1950: "If there seem to be reasons for sterilization, it is of course natural that this is taken into consideration before parole" (Minutes, 19 April 1950, SA vol. A, 2).
74. Cited in FLU 1955 report no. 23, 14. Further comments on persuasion in H. Forssman, "Sterilisering och befolkningspolitik," *Socialmedicinsk tidskrift* 35, no. 4 (1958): 136; von Hofsten, *Steriliseringar i Sverige 1941-1953*, 21.
75. Applications for sterilization, 1936, 1940, 1942, MA vols. EIb, 2, 9, 18; Applications for sterilization, 1950, SA vol. EI, 61.
76. Outlines and minutes on marriage cases, 21 September 1949, SA vol. BII, 1.
77. To give some examples: On 1 July 1948, the right to grant exemptions from the prohibitions of marriage was transferred from the government to the Board of Health. In the second half of that year, the Board issued thirty-three marriage licenses; in nine cases sterilization was stipulated. In 1950, the same stipulation was made for ten of the forty-four cases that came before the board (Outlines and minutes on marriage cases, 1948-1951, SA vols. BII, 1-2). Cf. Justitiedepartementet, *Medicinska äktenskapshinder*, Statens Offentliga Utredningar no. 1960/21 (Stockholm: Justitiedepartementet, 1960).
78. Seen in relation to the total number of sterilizations, those that were occasioned by epilepsy were few. In the period of the first Sterilization Act, there were probably some thirty sterilizations per year, most of which were voluntary and hence not subject to the control of the Board of Health. In the 1940s there was a slight increase; the greatest number reported for epileptics was in 1944 (ninety cases, eighty-eight of which were eugenically indicated). Around the middle of the 1950s some twenty-five to thirty-five epileptics were sterilized per year. See von Hofsten,

"Steriliseringar i Sverige 1935-1939" and Statistiska centralbyrån, *Sveriges Offentliga Statistik.*

79. On sterilization as condition for marriage: C. H. Alström, *A Study of Epilepsy in Its Clinical, Social and Genetic Aspects,* Acta Psychiatrica et Neurologica Supplementum 63 (Copenhagen: Munksgaard, 1950); Outlines and minutes on marriage cases, 19 August 1955, 13 May 1960, SA vol. BII, 4, BII, 7; Justitiedepartementet, *Medicinska äktenskapshinder,* including an appendix, "Äktenskapsärenden i Medicinalstyrelsen," by N. von Hofsten; T. Romanus, "Verkningar av det i abortlagen uppställda steriliseringsvillkoret," enclosure to Minutes, 8 December 1967, SA vol. A, 16.

80. Reports on sterilization, 1941, MA vol. EIc, 14; Applications for sterilization, 1950, SA vol. EI, 63.

81. Applications for sterilization, 1944, MA vol. EIb, 76; Applications for sterilization, 1950, SA vol. EI, 76.

82. Applications for sterilization, 1950, SA vol. EI, 81.

83. Applications for sterilization, 1950, SA vol. EI, 83.

84. Note enclosed to Applications for sterilization, 1960, SA vol. EI, 313.

85. Von Hofsten, *Steriliseringar i Sverige 1941-1953,* 53. Cf. Minutes, 2 September 1955, SA vol. A, 3.

86. Applications for sterilization, 1935, MA vol. EIb, 1; Applications for sterilization, 1946, MA vols. EIb, 100-1.

87. See Bent Sigurd Hansen, "Something Rotten in the State of Denmark," in this volume.

88. The mortality rate for women was 3 per 1,000 operations in the 1940s, but lower in later years (von Hofsten, *Steriliseringar i Sverige 1941-1953,* 42-44.) The imbalance in death rates was noticed already in the 1940s (see von Hofsten, "Steriliseringar i Sverige 1935-1939," 1429-30).

89. N. von Hofsten, "De arvsbiologiska verkningarna av sterilisering," *Nordisk medicin* 21, no. 1 (1944): 179-80.

90. Hirdman, *Att lägga livet tillrätta,* esp. 229-34.

91. This argument is emphasized by Li Bennich-Björkman and Jeanne Freiburg in comments on earlier versions of our work on Swedish sterilization policy (L. Bennich-Björkman, "Så tuktas en argbigga: Den svenska steriliseringspolitiken," *Kvinnovetenskaplig tidskrift* no. 2 [1992]; J. Freiburg, "Counting Bodies: The Politics of Reproduction in the Swedish Welfare State," *Scandinavian Studies* 65, no. 2 [1993]). On eugenics and gender, see also N. L. Stepan, *"The Hour of Eugenics": Race, Gender, and Nation in Latin America* (Ithaca & London: Cornell University Press, 1991).

92. "Förslag till lag om arbetsfostran m.m. Socialstyrelsens utlåtande," *Sociala Meddelanden,* no. 10B (1940): 806-7.

93. Minutes, 12 February 1954, SA vol. A, 3. Cf. von Hofsten, *Steriliseringar i Sverige 1941-1953,* 34.

94. In addition to Statistiska centralbyrån, *Sveriges Offentliga Statistik,* see von Hofsten, *Steriliseringar i Sverige 1941-1953,* 33-37.

95. Justitiedepartementet, *Betänkande med förslag till lagstiftning om abrytande av havandeskap*, Statens Offentliga Utredningar no. 1935/15 (Stockholm: Justitiedepartementet, 1935), 120-21.

96. Minutes, 31 January 1944, MA vol. AI, 15.

97. Minutes, 31 January 1944, MA vols. AI, 15. Cf. Minutes, 8 December 1943, 16 February 1944 and 23 March 1944, MA vol. AI, 14-15. The "important stipulation" was stressed in the "Advice and Directives" of the Board of Health concerning abortions, as well (Medicinalstyrelsen, *Råd och anvisningar rörande tillämpning av steriliserings- och abortlagarna*, Meddelanden från Kungl. Medicinalstyrelsen 84 [Stockholm: Medicinalstyrelsen, 1939], 6; Medicinalstyrelsen, *Råd och anvisningar rörande tillämpning av 1941 års steriliseringslag och abortlagen*, 17).

98. In the period 1950-53, some 65 percent of those women whose abortions were conditional upon sterilization were mentally retarded, some 17 percent "psychopaths," and some 11 percent mentally ill, according to a study by von Hofsten (von Hofsten, *Steriliseringar i Sverige 1941-1953*, 37).

99. Statistiska centralbyrån, *Sveriges Offentliga Statistik*. In the statistics these conditional cases were labeled, not very clearly, "Sterilizations in connection with an abortion." It is apparent, however, from what is stated elsewhere in the official statistics and from a comparison with the figures compiled by von Hofsten himself, that these were abortions where sterilization had been stipulated.

100. N. von Hofsten, "Steriliseringarna och aborterna," in *Medicinalväsendet i Sverige 1813-1862*, ed. W. Kock (Stockholm: Nordiska bokhandeln, 1963), 515, 517.

101. On Elise Ottesen-Jensen, see M. Södling, "Svenska kyrkan och trettiotalets befolkningsfråga," Typescript, 1993, Department of Theology, Uppsala University, 105.

102. Freiburg, "Counting Bodies," 232.

103. N. von Hofsten, *Steriliseringsfrågan ur rasbiologisk synpunkt*, Svenska föreningens för psykisk hälsovårds småskrifter 5 (Stockholm: Albert Bonniers förlag, 1933), 48; The National Social Welfare Board cited in P 1941 no. 13, 16.

104. On the Swedish *Tattare*, see A. Heymowski, *Swedish "Travellers" and Their Ancestry*, Studia Sociologica Upsaliensia 5 (Uppsala: Almqvist & Wiksell, 1969); I. Svanberg, ed., *I samhällets utkanter: Om "Tattare" i Sverige*, Uppsala Multiethnic Papers 11 (Uppsala: Centre for Multiethnic Research, 1987); M. Tydén and I. Svanberg, "I nationalismens bakvatten: Hur svensken blev svensk och invandraren främling," in *Bryta, bygga bo: Svensk historia underifrån*, ed. G. Broberg, U. Wikander, and K. Åmark (Stockholm: Ordfronts förlag, 1994).

105. H. Lundborg, *Rasbiologi och rashygien*, 2nd ed. (Stockholm: P.A. Norstedt & Söners, 1922), 161.

106. Fattigvårdslagstiftningskommittén, *Förslag till lag om lösdrivares behandling*, Statens Offentliga Utredningar no. 1923/2 (Stockholm: Socialdepartementet, 1923), 342. Sterilization was, however, recommended by some local police districts from which the Commission received statements.

107. Heymowski, *Swedish "Travellers,"* 109.

108. "Förslag till lag om arbetsfostran m.m. Socialstyrelsens utlåtande," *Sociala Meddelanden,* no. 10B (1940): 807.

109. M. Ohlander, "Zigenare, Tattare och hjälpskolan," *Hjälpskolan. Organ för nordiskt hjälpskoleförbund* 21 (1943): 79-80, 82; M. Ohlander, "Begåvningsförhållanden hos Tattare," *Tidskrift för Psykologi och pedagogik* 1, no. 2 (1942): 109, 113; Heymowski, *Swedish "Travellers,"* 27.

110. FLU 1943 report no. 41, 22 [supplement by von Hofsten].

111. G. Dahlberg, "Anthropometry of "Tattare," a Special Group of Vagabonds in Sweden," *Uppsala Läkareförenings Förhandlingar,* New Series 50 (1944): 72, 79.

112. "Tattarnas antal och levnadsförhållanden," *Sociala Meddelanden,* no. 5 (1945): 379. On the racial notion of *Tattare,* see for instance A. Etzler, "Om tattarnas härstamning," *Sociala Meddelanden,* no. 1 (1957) and B. Lundman's critical review of Heymowski's, "Swedish 'Travellers' and Their Ancestry," *Svenska landsmål och svenskt folkliv* 93 (1970): 122-24.

113. Applications for sterilization, 1940, MA vol. EIb, 9.

114. Applications for sterilization, 1942, MA vol. EIb, 18; Applications for sterilization, 1943, MA vol. EIb, 35; Applications for sterilization, 1950, SA vol. EI, 61.

115. Minutes, 22 February 1957, SA vol. A, 4.

116. Minutes, 30 May 1958, SA vol. A, 4.

117. Heymowski, *Swedish "Travellers,"* 112.

118. L. Olsson, *Kulturkunskap i förändring: Kultursynen i svenska geografiböcker 1870-1985* (Malmö: Liber, 1986), 112-20.

119. A. Montagu, *Statement on Race: An Annotated Elaboration and Exposition of the Four Statements on Race issued by the United Nations Educational, Scientific and Cultural Organizations,* 3rd ed. (London: Oxford University Press, 1972). The choice of a third Swede is baffling, however. It fell on "Professor Joseph Sköld, Stockholm University," who, it was said, was unable to attend due to sickness. The person referred to is the linguist [Jo]Hannes Sköld, active in Lund, who died in 1930.

120. *Bordssamtal i rasfrågan,* Verdandis skriftserie 3 (Uppsala: Verdandi, 1955).

121. There are exceptions, of course. In the recent period, mention could be made of Björn Kurtén, the Finland-Swedish paleontologist; Bengt Hubendick, the marine biologist; Björn Afzelius, the cytologist; and Marianne Rasmusson, the geneticist; in addition there are a great many popular works in translation (by Julian Huxley, Desmond Morris, and by critics such as Stephen Jay Gould).

122. J. A. Böök, "Medicinsk genetik," *Nordisk medicin* no. 56 (1956): 1087.

123. J. Lindsten, et al., *Klinisk genetik* (Stockholm: Socialstyrelsen, 1976).

124. A. Müntzing, *Ärftlighetsforskning* (Stockholm: LTs förlag, 1953); A. Müntzing, *Ärftlighetsforskning,* 2nd ed. (Stockholm: LTs förlag, 1960); A. Müntzing, *Ärftlighetsforskning,* 3rd ed. (Stockholm: LTs förlag, 1964); A. Müntzing, *Ärftlighetsforskning,* 4th ed. (Stockholm: LTs förlag, 1971); A. Müntzing, *Ärftlighetsforskning,* 5th ed. (Stockholm: LTs förlag, 1977).

125. O. Kinberg, G. Inghe, and S. Reimer, *Incestproblemet i Sverige* (Stockholm: Natur & Kultur, 1943). Cf. R. Qvarsell, *Utan vett och vilja: Om synen på brottslighet och*

sinnessjukdom (Stockholm: Carlsson, 1993). There were other voices, however: when the Swedish Society of Medicine discussed the matter in 1933, Bror Gadelius and Bernhard Jacobowsky, leading representatives of the psychiatric profession, for example, pointed out that many character defects which appeared constitutional were in fact caused by temporary environmental factors.

126. See G. Jonsson's dissertation, *Delinquent Boys: Their Parents and Grandparents*, Acta Psychiatrica Scandinavica Suppl. 195 (Copenhagen: Munksgaard, 1967).

127. As noted in Ohlander, "The Invisible Child," 255.

128. FLU 1955 report no. 23, 18-20; FKP 1960 no. 13, 27.

129. Cf. O. Petersson, A. Westholm, and G. Blomberg, *Medborgarnas makt* (Stockholm: Carlssons, 1989), 325-80.

130. Minutes, 8 December 1967, SA vol. A, 16.

131. K. Grunewald, "Kritisk granskning av ansökningar om sterilisering av mentalt defekta," *Läkartidningen* 67, no. 44 (1970); K. Grunewald, "Indikationerna för sterilisering av psykiskt utvecklingsstörda måste ändras," *Läkartidningen* 67, no. 44 (1970).

132. For an analysis of the Social Democrats' welfare program, see K. Misgeld, K. Molin, and K. Åmark, eds., *Creating Social Democracy: A Century of the Social Democratic Labor Party in Sweden* (University Park: The Pennsylvania State University Press, 1992).

133. On hygienism in Sweden in the early twentieth century, see E. Palmblad, *Medicinen som samhällslära* (Göteborg: Daidalos, 1990); K. Johannisson, "Folkhälsa: Det svenska projektet från 1900 fram till 2:a världskriget," *Lychnos. Årsbok för idéhistoria och vetenskapshistoria* (Uppsala: Swedish Science Press, 1991).

134. Befolingskommissionen, *Betänkande angående sterilisering*, 46.

Norwegian Eugenics: Sterilization as Social Reform

Nils Roll-Hansen

Introduction: A Classical Liberal Versus an Instrumental View of Science

Much of the recent historiography of eugenics is built on an instrumental interpretation of science. Science is seen as a tool by which society achieves its economic and social aims, while its role in the cultural and political activities which form these aims is neglected. Efficiency and not truth becomes the purpose of science. This conception of science as an expression of "instrumental reason" which aims to "rationalize" social activity was developed in particular by German philosophers and social scientists around the beginning of the twentieth century. Max Weber's ideal of a "value-free" and means-oriented science and a deep distinction between science and politics expressed a fundamental change taking place in the view of science. Though he was himself a transition figure who was ambivalent toward a full-blown instrumental view, his writings have been a constant source of inspiration for such interpretations. Since the 1960s and the "student revolution," these ideas, which were partly shared and anticipated by logical empiricism and pragmatism, have also made a great impact on the theory of science in the Anglo-American world.

In this instrumental view, science, and natural science in particular, tends to be seen as a separate domain of human activity concerned with efficient ways of manipulating natural and social phenomena and neutral to the values of our "Lebenswelt"—the world we live in. The theoretical conceptions developed by science are interpreted as constructs of human imagination with no descriptive relation to the real world. They may be useful for manipulating our experiences but give no deeper insight and understanding of the world. The instrumental view of scientific knowledge was coupled to an emotive or voluntarist view of ethics which emphasized the impossibility of drawing normative conclusions from descriptive premises. It was impossible to derive "ought" from "is," as David Hume had claimed. Neither of these views won full acceptance. The theory of biological evolution is one obvious example of

151

how science continued to influence the goals and norms of our social behavior. Together, the instrumental interpretation of scientific theory and the insistence on a fundamental break between our ideas about what is and what ought to be drive us toward a picture of science as an esoteric and magical activity which mysteriously produces powerful technology.

This instrumental Weberian view of science was absorbed and popularized, for example, by the neo-Marxist Frankfurt School of Sociology in the 1930s and 1940s. The dangers of technocracy and uncontrolled technological development were stressed. A pessimistic picture of a world gradually succumbing to a disastrous dictatorship of experts was drawn. It was in many ways the dystopia mirroring the socialist utopia of this period. The faint hope of these pessimistic critics of modern civilization was that catastrophe could be blocked by asserting the primacy of politics and achieving control of technological development through democracy.

An alternative to the instrumental view of science is to consider it as fundamentally a cultural activity aiming to gain knowledge of the world. According to this view, science is a main source of our understanding of the human condition and a main factor in forming the specific values and aims of our social activities, including politics. It is not merely a means to achieve aims that have other sources. In this classical liberal view, science is an extension of our ordinary knowledge. It describes the world we live in, and its legitimization is fundamentally dependent upon this link to our "Lebenswelt." By denying or neglecting the role of science in the formation of social and political values and goals, instrumentalism undermines this side of science and may easily have the effect of strengthening the threats of technology that it pretends to combat. By severing the links to common sense, science becomes less comprehensible, less usable as a guide, and more difficult to control.

The imprint of the instrumental conception of science is found, for instance, in the sociology of knowledge approach taken by Peter Weingart, et al., in their account of eugenics in Germany, *Rasse, Blut und Gene* (1988). In an earlier paper I pointed out how the instrumental conception of science leads to a confusion of science with politics in Weingart's account of German eugenics.[1] When links to the common sense picture of the world are severed, the political implications become arbitrary and the enlightening role of scientific knowledge is lost. Sheila Weiss's study of Wilhelm Schallmayer and his legacy emphasizes the instrumental perspective even in the title, *Race Hygiene and Rational Management of National Efficiency*. Benno Müller-Hill describes the generally smooth cooperation of the German scientific community with the Nazi government on population and race policies,[2] and he attributes this to the inherent amoral or "value-free" nature of science. Salvation can only come from adding something that is foreign to the scientific tradition, namely, human moral values. "It is the plight of scientists to become schizophrenic," sighs Müller-Hill.[3]

A broader and more differentiated perspective on the social role of eugenics, emphasizing the cultural, normative, and political effects of accumulating knowledge and not only the instrumental connection, is found, for example, in Kenneth Ludmerer's book on genetics and society in America (1972) and in Daniel Kevles's book on eugenics in America and England (1985). Garland Allen's complaints about the laissez-faire attitude and withdrawal of geneticists from public debates in the period between the world wars also imply a basic belief in the enlightening role of science.[4] With pertinent reservations with respect to uncertainty and lack of knowledge, scientists have an obligation to tell the public in a clear way what is true and legitimate knowledge on controversial issues.[5]

The interpretation of science as instrumental and "value-free" fits quite well with the attitudes and practices of a number of leading German geneticists during the Nazi period. For instance, Eugene Fischer, Fritz Lenz, and Otmar von Verschuer were highly adaptable to the ideology of the political system that took over in 1933. They used the rhetoric of the instrumental and ethically neutral, "amoral," view of science to justify their actions and detach themselves from possible moral blame. At the same time they also cultivated a normative role for biological visions of an ideal human being. The latter often implied a narrow kind of scientific perspective which, under the given circumstances, reinforced Nazi ideology.

But there were also exceptions to this disgraceful submission of science to current politics in the Germany of the 1930s. Hermann Muckermann, one of the main pioneers of the Kaiser Wilhelm Institute for Anthropology, Human Genetics and Eugenics, and the director of one of its divisions, was promptly discharged from his post after the Nazi takeover. He was a Catholic priest as well as a scientist. He supported a moderate eugenics program. But he also had a commitment to social responsibility and specific human values that were incompatible with the demands of the Nazi government on the institute.[6]

The question of the adequacy of the instrumental view of science in accounting for the development of eugenics in Norway is the underlying concern of this essay. Central themes are the views and the behavior of scientific experts. We will look at their views of the social role of science and the responsibility of the scientist and at the way they used scientific insight to argue for or against specific social policies. Most of them were what we can call Social Democrats in a broad sense. Irrespective of whether they supported the

Norwegian Labor Party, the Liberals (Venstre) or the Conservatives (Höyre), they were committed to the construction of a social welfare state. The moderate version of eugenics which they adhered to was an integral part of programs for social reform.

The population question caused much concern in the 1920s and 1930s, in Norway as in other Nordic countries. There was a widespread feeling that concurrent with a halt in population growth was an increase in the number of the mentally disabled, insane, and other groups with low social capabilities. This social degeneration was generally conceived as genetically determined and a result of the accumulation of poor hereditary material.[7] The established way of preventing the procreation of "inferior" social groups was institutionalization. Sterilization was proposed as a means that would be more humane by not restricting any other aspects of behavior than procreation. It was also argued that sterilization was more effective in this respect than restrictions on marriage or confinement in institutions. Furthermore, sterilization would save money by making possible the release of many institutional inmates. But in spite of these arguments, sterilization was not introduced in Norway during the early phase of eugenics—mainline eugenics—when racism and rather simplistic views of inheritance were predominant. In Norway, as in the other Nordic countries, sterilization laws with eugenics as an important aim were introduced only in the 1930s. This main achievement of the Norwegian eugenics movement came at a time when British and American eugenics had entered a period of decline and waning influence.[8]

How is the timing of the introduction of eugenic sterilization in Norway to be explained? What made it possible for a procedure that was not acceptable in the first decades of the century, and which was again rejected by the 1960s, to be introduced by law in the 1930s? Here we will discuss some factors that were influential in this development. First, there was the progressing secularization of social life with a gradual undermining of traditional Christian ethical norms. This made sterilization easier to accept. Second was a rising belief in scientifically based social planning which may have culminated in the period between 1930 and 1960. This belief provided support for eugenic sterilization. One factor that worked against eugenic sterilization was the growing insight into human genetics. Throughout the period in question this growth in scientific knowledge was largely disappointing to eugenic enthusiasts. Biological and medical research contradicted the idea of a genetically caused degeneration of the population and showed that many of the proposed eugenic measures would have less effect than had originally been hoped. A second factor that gradually undermined eugenic programs was an ideology of individualism, a growing emphasis on individual rights against the interests of the state or collective. The frightening experience with Nazi population policies in the period from 1933 to 1945 enhanced the reactions against eugenic thinking in general.

The enlightening and educating role of science is a central topic of this discussion. Even in the case of eugenics, where science was deeply involved in the formation and execution of activities which we strongly condemn, it was also the source of the reliable knowledge and insight necessary for an effective criticism and rejection of Nazi policies. The historiography that depicts the evils of eugenics under Nazism appeals not only to our general ethical norms but also to true science as opposed to the faulty science on which Nazi eugenics was based.

This account will try to present evidence for the enlightening role of science. What impact did results from research and critical scientific discussion have on the formation of policy goals and norms of behavior? Was such a role discernible and important, or was science merely an instrument in the hands of political forces? And what was the temporal scope for this guiding and critical role of science? Were the results comprehended, accepted, and used as soon as they were published, or did it take decades before they were sufficiently widely understood and integrated into public thinking to have much effect? This study aims to draw attention to the "enlightening" aspect of science as a counterweight to the instrumental interpretations currently popular in science studies.

THE BEGINNING OF NORWEGIAN EUGENICS

Public interest in eugenics, or race hygiene as it was usually called, reached a high point in the years before World War I. At this time two main proponents were the pharmacist Jon Alfred Mjöen and the psychiatrist Ragnar Vogt. Another psychiatrist, Johan Scharffenberg, who was to become a main propagandist for the 1934 Sterilization Law, was also active. And the young medical doctor and biologist Otto Lous Mohr made a brash entry in 1915 through his sharp criticism of Mjöen's approach to eugenics.[9]

Jon Alfred Hansen Mjöen (1860-1939) studied abroad for many years after obtaining his pharmaceutical degree in Norway in 1881. His interest in race hygiene was stimulated and developed in Germany where he became acquainted with Alfred Ploetz in 1897. In 1901 he was elected a member of the Norwegian Academy of Science on the basis of work in organic chemistry. In 1906 he founded a private research institute for eugenics, Vinderen Biological Laboratory, which never developed into a scientific institution of any importance, however.

In May 1908 Mjöen spoke before the Medical Society in Oslo on "Race Biology and Hygiene of Reproduction."[10] The meeting was organized by the later general secretary of the Norwegian Medical Association, Jörgen Berner.[11] It marked the beginning of Mjöen's activity as a propagandist for eugenic reforms in Norway. The message was that the threat of genetic and social degeneration demanded a change in social policy. So far, all attention had been concentrated on the environment and biological inheritance had been neglected. Mjöen presented the first version of what later came to be known as "The Norwegian Program for Race Hygiene." Like other contemporary eugenic programs it distinguished three forms—negative, positive, and prophylactic race hygiene.

Mjöen's first, and probably his most remarkable, success in Norwegian politics was the introduction of a progressive system of taxation of alcoholic drinks according to their alcohol content. Earlier taxation had been based on the price of the raw materials used. Mjöen argued that it should be based on the character of the product, i.e., its alcohol content. His main argument was built on the harmful effects of alcohol, in particular the effect on biological heredity. Of a four-man commission named by the ministry of the interior, Mjöen was alone in maintaining that alcohol damaged biological heredity. But his system for the classification and taxation of beer was included in the law that was unanimously passed by Parliament in 1912,[12] and is still part of Norwegian daily life.

Ragnar Vogt (1870-1943) was the founder of modern psychiatry in Norway. He was elected a member of the Norwegian Academy of Science in 1913, and in 1915 he became the first Norwegian professor of psychiatry. He shared the common belief of the period that mental illness was strongly determined by biological heredity. Apparently the belief in heredity as a main cause of mental illness reached a high point toward the end of the nineteenth century. In 1857, according to the classification of new patients at Norway's main mental hospital, Gaustad, the most important cause was masturbation, with fifty-three cases. The second most frequent cause was drunkenness and intoxication, with thirty-five cases, and in third place was hereditary inclination, with twenty-one. In 1892 the relative importance of environmental (social) and hereditary (biological) causation was reversed; there were 263 cases attributed to hereditary inclination and only four to masturbation.[13] Most likely this move from a moralizing social explanation to a hereditary biological one helped the patients to liberate themselves from authoritarian oppression in their local communities. It was a change that strengthened the rights of the individual relative to those of authorities representing society.

Investigating the heritability of manic-depressive mental illness, Vogt concluded that it was not a dominant trait in the Mendelian sense, but perhaps a recessive trait: "Most of the children of our patients appear to have escaped the pathological inheritance, which is in good harmony with a theory of recessiveness." In his conclusions from this investigation, Vogt also emphasized that the manic-depressive condition did not cause either "idiocy, epilepsy, alcoholism, or paranoia" in the offspring.[14] He was, in other words, critical of the then-popular view that there was a common hereditary basis for a broad spectrum of mental illness, mental retardation, asocial behavior, and moral depravity.

In his studies of human genetics, Vogt had an earlier local tradition to draw on. In the 1880s and 1890s the Norwegian physician Wilhelm Uckerman had studied the dependence of deaf-mutism on consanguineous marriage and found consanguinity to be four times more frequent among the parents of deaf-mutes than of normal children. Uckerman did not want legislation to forbid consanguineous marriage, but he hoped this information would influence behavior and that better communication would break the isolation of small communities and reduce the frequency of such marriages.[15]

Vogt's critical attitude toward many popular prejudices about biological heredity was also evident in his lecture to the Norwegian Students Association (Det Norske Studentersamfund) in October 1912. Here he maintained that there was no firm evidence to show that the use of alcohol affected biological inheritance. He also pointed out that the eugenic benefit from sterilization of conditions caused by recessive inheritance was small. The frequency would decrease only marginally even after many generations.[16] In contrast to Mjöen he kept abreast of contemporary research in human genetics. When Mjöen lectured on eugenics to the Academy of Sciences in February 1914, Vogt stood up and explained the nature of recessive traits. And he maintained that the "socially most important hereditary diseases, like deaf-muteness, feeblemindedness and mental illness" were, most likely, recessive.[17]

However, Vogt was in no way free from the common prejudices of his time. Apparently he did not even think of questioning the biological basis of his own racism and antifeminism. In a book on genetics and race hygiene, Vogt took it for granted that blacks were biologically inferior to whites, in particular to Nordics, and that women were made for the tasks of the home and procreation.[18]

Vogt's attitudes strikingly illustrate the limitations which science can never hope to escape. Its dependence on the common world view of its times can only be severed to a limited degree. But the difficulty in launching fundamental and wide-ranging criticism of current world views does not imply that scientific criticism cannot be of great importance. As already indicated, Vogt was also a sober scientist who warned against alarmist attitudes and hysterical reactions. With respect to the degeneration of the race that was so widely feared, Vogt maintained that there was so far a complete lack of evidence for such a phenomenon. He was, however, worried that the tendency among the upper classes to have few children could cause a lowering of average hereditary quality in coming generations.

Neither Mjöen nor Vogt wanted to introduce sterilization at this stage except on a voluntary basis. Mjöen did not want to antagonize public opinion. Vogt wrote that one should not use harsher means than were necessary. Only if contraception or prohibition of marriage did not work should sterilization or even confinement be considered.[19]

Johan Scharffenberg (1869-1965) visited the famous hygiene exhibition in Dresden in 1911 and wrote an article in the daily newspaper of the Norwegian Labor Party. Socialists, he declared, had to understand that not only was an improvement in environmental conditions necessary but also a "purification of the hereditary material itself through rational human breeding." He added that some American states already had laws that made it possible "to sterilize the most inferior individuals (feebleminded, vagabonds etc.), from whom there is reason to expect offspring that will be a burden to society."[20] Scharffenberg was a staunch individualist with a critical scientific spirit. His unorthodox views and untiring polemics had considerable impact on Norwegian public debate throughout his long life. Most famous, perhaps, are his candid attacks on Hitler and Nazism both before and during the German occupation of Norway, 1940-45. A series of newspaper articles in 1933, warning that Hitler was "a psychopath of the prophetic type—on the verge of insanity," resulted in considerable German diplomatic pressure on the Norwegian government to stop him.[21]

THE ATTACK ON MJÖEN

Mjöen was successful in attracting public attention abroad as well as at home. He was a prominent participant at the First International Congress of Eugenics in London in 1912 and became a member of the Permanent International Committee for Eugenics which was elected at this congress, with Leonard Darwin as chairman.[22] Norwegian medical and biological experts were beginning to worry about the impact that Mjöen might have on research and legislation. He was an active member of the Liberal Party which formed the government from 1913 to 1920. At the national convention of the party in June 1914, Mjöen lectured on "the question of making race- and folk-diseases a state responsibility." In the ensuing debate the minister of justice said that he agreed with many of Mjöen's views on eugenics and that he had "very radical plans" for a revision of the penal code.[23]

When in late 1914 Mjöen published a popular book on race hygiene, the young medical doctor Otto Lous Mohr attacked him in a newspaper review. Mohr (1886-1967) had received his medical degree in 1912 and studied cytology abroad during the year 1913-14. The essence of his criticism was that Mjöen was a dilettante in medicine and biology, that he obscured important issues, and misled the public by spreading unrealistic hopes about the effectiveness of the proposed eugenic measures. Mohr was not against eugenics in general and he did not react to the racist tendencies in Mjöen's book. On the contrary, he pointed to the book by Vogt as a sound and scientifically reliable alternative to Mjöen.[24]

Kristine Bonnevie was the first female professor in Norway and a specialist on cytology and genetics. She joined the attack on Mjöen, stressing that her criticism was not directed at the principles of eugenics that Mjöen advocated, but at the uncritical and misleading way in which he presented them. For instance, he pretended that by preventing the lowest race elements from procreating, society would, within one or two generations, save large sums of money on social institutions, police, the judicial system, support for the unemployed, etc. It was irresponsible to make such promises without presenting proof for one's claims, wrote Bonnevie. When Mjöen tried to defend some of his proposals in a reply, she was unwilling to continue the debate. Mjöen's book had already "for too long occupied the attention of the public."[25]

Mjöen's supporters, who were laypeople and not experts in medicine or biology, also believed in enlightenment through science. They objected to the smugness and arrogance of his scientific critics. One lawyer protested the insulting treatment that Mjöen had received and maintained that he had at least made an effort to bring knowledge to the public, in contrast to the purely academic activities of people such as Mohr.[26] This brought a sharp reply from Kristian Schreiner, a professor of anatomy and a prominent physical anthropologist, entitled "A Word on Science and Dilettantism." People such as Mjöen did not understand that the young science of eugenics was not yet ripe for application in practical politics, wrote Schreiner. As long as there appeared to be no danger that "the matter would be politicized," Mjöen's warm enthusiasm had been disarming. But his international appearance as an expert on eugenics had made "the few experts that we have in this area" react. Schreiner attacked with indignation the lack of respect for science upon which Mjöen's defense seemed to be based. Mjöen appeared to believe that "social interests and political activity" provided a sufficient platform for a leading role in scientific matters and that it "exempts the person from factual criticism."[27] In other words, Schreiner could not accept Mjöen's attempt to bypass the scrutiny of scientific experts by addressing himself directly to the public.

In April 1916 Parliament decided to establish an institute for genetics. The proposal aimed to exclude Mjöen, to secure a sound scientific basis for research, and to avoid dilettantism. Eugenics was a main argument for the new institute. Knowledge about human genetics was expected to have important applications to social policy in the future. This was emphasized by the four authors of the proposal,[28] in the statement of the executive committee of the university ("Det Akademiske Collegium"), and in the parliamentary debate. Though some parliamentarians were skeptical of the high hopes for practical application expressed in the proposal, there was a clear majority in its favor. The minister of health and welfare explained that it was important to start work right away when there was a well-qualified person ready to begin, namely Kristine Bonnevie.[29]

At the meeting of Scandinavian natural scientists ("Det 16. Skandinaviske Naturforskermötet") in July 1916, Kristine Bonnevie gave an introductory lecture to a discussion of "Human Genetics, Aims and Means of Research." She pointed to the isolated, small populations in remote Norwegian valleys as particularly interesting material for genealogical studies, a source that was quickly disappearing with new and better communications. An extensive survey of such populations was being organized by the newly established Institute of Genetics at the University of Kristiania (Oslo).[30] In fact, Bonnevie had for some years been investigating a variety of human anomalies such as harelip, hemophilia, polydactyli, and dwarfism.[31]

Thus Mjöen was ostracized from the good society of medical and biological experts on genetics and his attempt to obtain state support for his eugenic research was stopped. But the establishment of the first university Institute of Genetics in Scandinavia demonstrates the importance of eugenics for the early institutionalization of genetics. A main purpose of Bonnevie's institute was to gain insight into human genetics as a guide to eugenic policies.

This early controversy also illustrates how eugenics in Norway, as in other countries, was closely integrated with a general progressive movement for social reforms. The details of Mjöen's Norwegian program included allowances for mothers, and fights against alcohol, narcotics (such as tobacco), and environmental poisons (such as lead). There was at this time a strong tendency to explain social phenomena in biological terms. This was not peculiar to the scientific community but part of a generally held world view.

To interpret the attack on Mjöen in the spring of 1915 merely as a defense of the professional interests of the experts would be to discard the expressed motives of the actors and attribute to them a false consciousness. No doubt one effect was that the access and influence of an outsider, Mjöen, was curtailed. But in accordance with the classical liberal ideal of science the experts conceived themselves to be acting in the public interest. They would have scorned any suggestion that they were merely furthering their own private interests. It was in the interest of the public to prevent Mjöen's eugenic proposals from being realized, as well as to stop him from obtaining state funding for his research and educational work. The experts argued that Mjöen's advice was scientifically unsound and that it would therefore be futile or dangerous to follow. In hindsight it is difficult to disagree with this judgment.

The role of the scientific experts in the controversy over Mjöen's book in 1915 and the establishment of the Institute for Genetics in 1916 illustrate the active political engagement of many Norwegian scientists in this period. Together with scientific knowledge, the experts drew on both political ideals and ethical norms in forming their judgments on social policy. And these views were highly respected and influential among the general public. This central political role of the experts was based on a common view of science and its social role. It was the task of science to help clarify the political aims as well as the consequences of different choices of action. From the beginning of the discussions about eugenic policies in Norway, this guiding and critical role of science was central. It was taken for granted by all participants in the debate about eugenics. For Mjöen and his supporters the necessity of eugenics sprang from scientific knowledge. The main argument of the opponents was that the knowledge was not yet sufficiently clear and certain and that the time for implementation had not yet come. The instrumental aspect of science was peripheral in these debates. But it was present, for instance, in the discussions about the effectiveness of certain means in attaining specific ends.

BIRTH CONTROL AND WOMEN'S LIBERATION

While eugenics was never more than a minor issue in Norwegian general politics, birth control and associated problems of family planning were major issues during the first decades of the century. A main figure in the birth control movement was Katti Anker Möller.[32] An important part of her program was the establishment of birth control clinics ("mödrehygienekontorer") to provide information on child care, contraception, sexual hygiene, etc. The first such public clinic was established in Oslo in 1924. Möller also campaigned to abolish the law that made abortion a crime. In a lecture on "The Liberation of Motherhood," in January 1915 (a few months before Mohr's attack on Mjöen), she argued that the fetus should be considered a part of the woman's body and under her jurisdiction. This was, at the time, a very radical view, and Möller's concluding words, *"we love motherhood, we want it to prosper, but in full freedom and under our own responsibility,"* did not prevent a deluge of protests. She was bitterly attacked even by some of her collaborators in the women's rights movement.[33]

In June 1914 Otto Lous Mohr married Katti Anker Möller's daughter, Tove, who was to become a medical doctor and continue her mother's work for birth control and sexual education. Otto Lous Mohr also became deeply involved in this campaign. Among other things he played an active part in the introduction of sexual instruction in Norwegian schools.

Katti Anker Möller's participation in the London eugenics congress in 1912 was disappointing from her feminist point of view. Mjöen introduced her to the German eugenicist Alfred Ploetz, whose views on women she found appalling.[34] Ploetz, in his lecture to the congress, attacked neo-Malthusianism,[35] and generally looked upon women as "birth-machines for the state," according to Möller.[36] Mjöen, in his 1914 book on race hygiene, also attacked neo-Malthusianism and women's liberation. In Mjöen's view these movements would reinforce the trend toward degeneration through a predominant decrease in reproduction by the most valuable elements in the population.[37] He counted women's emancipation among the major dissolving forces in society because it distracted women from their essential role in reproduction.[38] Mjöen wanted biological enlightenment but emphasized that his aim was not to provide "sexual instruction in the schools."[39] Such education was, in his view, part of a dangerous cultural radicalism.

As in other countries the questions of birth control and sexual instruction were serious sources of division within the eugenics movement. Mjöen and his wing of the Norwegian eugenics movement continued to be strongly opposed to the radical approach in family politics. The experts' wing of the movement generally had a positive attitude, though Vogt, for example, no doubt retained some of his early antifeminist attitude.[40] Katti Möller's campaign was inspired by an ideology that emphasized the rights of the individual. Mjöen's views on eugenics and women's liberation were grounded in the traditional rights of the collective to regulate the life of the individual and demand subordination to its interests.

THE THREAT OF ALCOHOL AND THE ETHICS OF RISK-TAKING

The struggle for temperance or complete abolition of alcohol was perhaps the most pervasive and powerful popular movement in Norway in the late nineteenth and early twentieth century. As already mentioned, Mjöen was engaged in alcohol research before World War I. The social misery produced by alcoholism was evident and Mjöen shared the widely held view that a main cause was the damaging effect of alcohol on the hereditary material. If true, this hypothesis could give eugenics a powerful ally. However, scientific research failed to confirm it.

Mohr, in contradiction to Mjöen, gave the comforting assurance that drinking alcohol did not damage the hereditary material. There was no scientific basis for the common belief that children conceived under the influence of alcohol tended to be inferior, he argued: "The sins of the parents are not inherited by the children in the form of a reduction in the value of hereditary potential."[41]

Mjöen condemned this lenient attitude toward alcohol as an irresponsible handling of scientific results by a "spectacle-wise" academic. Mohr was guilty of neglecting the risk involved by the uncertainty of the results, argued Mjöen. He admitted that no effects on the hereditary material had been proven. But the lack of scientific proof in no way justified the lack of action. "We have every reason to believe that alcohol is a much more serious enemy for the family, the people and the race than one has so far considered it to be!"[42]

The argument of unacceptable risk was often used by Mjöen to justify eugenic measures. The risk incurred by not acting was so serious that it was morally irresponsible not to take immediate action even on the basis of quite uncertain knowledge. He also justified steps against race crossing with the same kind of argument. He admitted uncertainty about the detrimental effects and agreed that more knowledge must be sought, but in such a situation it was safest to say, "*Until we have acquired sufficient knowledge be careful!*"[43]

HUMAN GENETICS AND EUGENICS IN THE 1920S AND 1930S

The Norwegian eugenics movement continued to be divided along the lines of the 1915 debate. The medical and biological experts organized themselves into the Norwegian Genetics Society ("Arvelighetsforeningen"), whose leading members were Mohr, Vogt, Bonnevie, and Scharffenberg. Mjöen was excluded from the good society. In addition to his small and dilettante group of researchers at the Vinderen Biological Laboratory, Mjöen organized "The Consultative Eugenics Committee of Norway," which included men of prominent public standing. Nordal Wille, professor of botany at the University of Kristiania (Oslo) and one of the central figures in Norwegian science at the time, was chairman until his death in 1924. From 1920 to 1931 Mjöen intermittently published a journal titled *Den Nordiske Rase* (The Nordic Race),[44] and he continued to be an active member of the international eugenics committee.

At the Second International Congress of Eugenics in New York in 1921, Mjöen was greeted by Henry Fairfield Osborne, president of the congress, as a "leader in the vigorous movement of race hygiene in Scandinavia."[45] Mjöen's lecture on the detrimental effects of race crossing received considerable publicity in the local American press. His empirical bases were experiments with rabbits and investigations of individuals born of the crossing between Lapps and Norwegians. He showed pictures of "disharmonic" rabbits with one hanging and one upright ear and of "half-breeds" that he believed appeared clearly inferior when contrasted with Nordic heroes such as Fridtjof Nansen or Charles Lindberg.[46] But Mjöen's investigation of human race crosses remained, to a large extent, at the anecdotal stage. He did not make serious efforts to provide a representative survey or to correct for differing social circumstances. His lecture nevertheless became the starting point for a discussion of the harmfulness of race crossing among American geneticists.[47]

Kristine Bonnevie lectured at the New York eugenics congress on the inheritance of fingerprints.[48] The inheritance and development of the papillary patterns of human fingertips was to remain a central part of Bonnevie's research interests for the next two decades. Her work in human genetics attracted considerable international interest, and she participated in writing and editing the big *Handbuch der Erbbiologie des Menschen* published in Berlin in 1939-1940.

However, the optimistic hopes for significant applications of human genetics, which characterized the founding of the Institute for Genetics at the University of Kristiania (Oslo) in 1916, were soon much subdued. There is little explicit discussion of eugenics in the publications of Bonnevie after 1920, though her fundamental attitude was obviously still positive. Presumably her view was that when a more thorough knowledge of human heredity had been attained, eugenic policies would become a natural thing. She saw mental retardation and other kinds of psychic abnormality as having a large hereditary component and thought that a correlation between such traits and certain types of fingerprints could be demonstrated.[49]

In the early 1930s inheritance and development of finger and palm patterns were main research topics in Otmar von Verschuer's group at the Kaiser

Wilhelm Institute for Anthropology, Human Genetics and Eugenics in Berlin. The work of Bonnevie formed part of their scientific basis.[50] Her pupil, Thordar Quelprud (born 1901), worked at the Kaiser Wilhelm Institute with Verschuer and others from 1931 to 1934. Quelprud's specialty in this period was ear forms. The idea of using these easily observable traits as markers for more important but not so easily observable traits, for instance, psychical properties, was the same as in Bonnevie's work.[51] After his return to Norway, Quelprud conducted a large study of Huntington's chorea. He went back to Berlin for a short period of study in 1938-39.

In 1927 the American geneticist, Charles Davenport, made an attempt to recruit Bonnevie as a member of the Commission of the International Federation of Eugenic Organizations. Davenport wrote to Bonnevie that if he was to succeed Leonard Darwin as head of this organization, he would want more "scientific persons" to participate actively in its work.[52] But Bonnevie was reluctant. She did not want to enter as an individual, and the "competent organizations" in Norway wanted more information on the "positive plans and purposes of the Commission" before they were willing to appoint a representative. Under present circumstances "our organizations are not very much in favor of going in as members of the Commission," she replied.[53] The Norwegian biological and medical experts were apparently reluctant to join an organization in which Mjöen was a prominent participant and views similar to his were influential.

Bonnevie's prudent approach to eugenics is exemplified in a brief popular article on "Heredity in Man" published in 1931, which describes various genetic malformations and diseases. In conclusion she confirms a moderate eugenic program: We must study human heredity because it is important for our understanding of social and individual behavior. Through "education and social reforms" we must protect "good and valuable inheritance" and provide it with proper conditions for development. At the same time we must try to "limit the spread, or at least check the development of less valuable genes."[54] Again, it seems clear that Bonnevie was more concerned with the enlightening than with the instrumental role of science. As a scientist she was primarily concerned with setting the right aims by producing as correct a picture of the real situation as possible. That science is a source of technical means would follow as a matter of course when, some time in the future, it was able to provide a valid and comprehensive description of the material structures and causal relationships of biological inheritance.

By the early 1920s Otto Lous Mohr had acquired much more knowledge of genetics and developed a much more critical view of eugenics than he held in

1914. He had worked with Thomas Hunt Morgan in New York for a year, 1918-19, and had become familiar with the most recent advances in chromosome research. It is likely that the growing doubts of Morgan and other leading American geneticists concerning the eugenics movement made an impression on the young Mohr.[55] Likewise, his interest in social questions, stimulated by his wife and mother-in-law, probably contributed to his critical attitudes. By the 1920s Mohr was both a first-rate geneticist and an active advocate of birth control and other feminist and radical social causes. His interest in social reforms no doubt increased his sense of the scientific weaknesses of mainline eugenics.

Internationally Mohr counted as one of the founders of medical genetics.[56] After his year with Morgan at Columbia University, Mohr worked on deficiency mutations in Drosophila for a number of years. Later he made important contributions to the study of lethal and sublethal mutations in cattle and in man.[57] At the 1932 International Congress of Genetics Mohr was elected chairman of the committee responsible for the next congress. He thus became strongly involved in the politics surrounding the planning and subsequent cancellation of the international congress planned for Moscow in 1937. This close contact with the events in the Soviet Union in the 1930s reinforced his moral stance on the autonomy of science relative to politics. The unwillingness of the Soviet government to include human genetics in the program was a main reason for moving the congress to Edinburgh.

In a popular book on genetics published in 1923, Mohr briefly discussed what this science had to say on the subject of man. He rejected negative as well as positive eugenics as practicable policies for the time being and pointed out the conservative implications of many of the proposed measures. In the present situation, he emphasized, it is much more important to improve the conditions under which children are raised than to try to improve their biological inheritance. Regarding the threat of degeneration, he saw no scientific evidence that the European race was degenerating genetically.[58] In general, Mohr maintained that our knowledge of the genetic factors that determine human physical and spiritual health was still quite insufficient for the formulation of a sensible eugenics program.[59] The popular analogy with plant and animal breeding was misleading, he argued. Not only would it be unacceptable politically and ethically to apply the same methods to humans, but it was also unlikely that any agreement could be reached on what properties to breed for.[60]

Mohr sharply criticized the doctrine that race crossings may be harmful. He gave a quotation from T. H. Morgan to support his view on this question:

The possibility that a certain mixed line may be more valuable than either of the pure lines from which it originated, is sufficient to make us wary of the popular doctrine about so-called racial purity. Whatever advantages certain pure human races might have from a political, religious or military point of view, this must not make us blind to the biological advantages of certain mixtures.[61]

Again we see that Mohr's general objection to the eugenic proposals was that they were scientifically ill-founded. In some cases there was good evidence that the consequences would be contrary to the claims; in others the evidence for positive effects was simply lacking. Mohr was not opposed to eugenics on principle. His social perspective was in many ways deeply biological, as can be seen in his programmatic article on human breeding under culture ("Menneskeavlen under kultur"). Here he saw overpopulation as the main cause of "housing shortage, unemployment and permanent unrest on the labour market."[62]

Mjöen and Mohr represented opposite poles in the Norwegian eugenics debate from 1915 until Mjöen's death in 1939. Mjöen was the enthusiastic representative of popular and national sentiments and Mohr was the critical scientist supporting a radical program for social reform. Repeatedly, Mohr's appeals to scientific knowledge and critical method clashed with scientifically superficial but popular views supported by Mjöen.

Mohr's message was that the improvement of the environment was by far the most important immediate task. But the environmental factors that he mentioned were to a large extent biological: hygiene, nutrition, proper physical exercise. A similar biological view of society was found in most liberal and left-wing social thinking of this period. A representative example is Gunnar and Alva Myrdal's book, *Krisen i befolkningsspörsmålet* (Crisis in the population question), which was published in a Norwegian translation in 1936.[63]

Social Radicalism Versus Rural Romanticism

As we have seen, the rejection of the popular eugenics movement by established medical and biological experts was a rejection of what was seen as excesses and unscientific attitudes and not a rejection of the basic ideas of eugenics. What Bonnevie, Vogt, Mohr, and the others primarily objected to was the premature and unscientific application of genetics to man. That society could and should be improved by applying sound scientific knowledge, including human genetics, they did not doubt. They had a strong belief in the progress of science and its positive effects on social progress.

The people in Mjöen's camp were much more skeptical of modern technology and the general cultural effects of a mechanistic natural science. Their biological perspective was of a more romantic and holistic character. They saw modern industrial society with its urban culture and associated materialistic view of life as a major threat against a happy future for humanity. It was typical that humanistic idealists such as Christen Collin, professor of literature, and Alfred Eriksen, clergyman and for a period parliamentary leader of the Labor Party, joined Mjöen's Consultative Eugenics Committee of Norway.

In the 1920s and 1930s the scientific expertise tended toward a policy of more or less radical social reforms while Mjöen's group was conservative. In both groups we find reservations against the introduction of sterilization as a eugenic measure—reservations which were considerably weakened by the early 1930s.

In addition to the traditional moral scruples among the scientific experts, there was a growing doubt about the efficiency of eugenic measures. Other important ideological factors were ideals about the free development of the individual which gradually increased in influence, especially among intellectuals. New norms of behavior, promoting a free upbringing and sexual liberation, made a breakthrough in the 1930s, effectively propagated by enthusiastic "cultural radicals." This development served, on the one hand, to weaken the system of traditional moral norms that was a hindrance to the introduction of sterilization, but on the other hand, it strengthened the ideology of individualism which was later to become a main factor in the abolition of eugenic sterilization.

Doubts about the moral acceptability of sterilization were important in Mjöen's group. In addition to a respect for traditional Christian ethics there was a reaction against the new individualistic moral ideas of the cultural radicals—a worry that the existing moral order would be broken down. Abortion was a particularly hot issue. Cultural radical and progressive social reformers such as the Mohrs were in favor of a liberalization of the practice while conservatives such as Mjöen resisted. Wilhelm Reich became a focus in this cultural conflict during his stay in Norway between 1934 and 1939.[64] Characteristically, the cultural radicals and the liberal experts were in favor of the free right of an individual to be sterilized on demand, while the more conservative group around Mjöen was mostly against this. The latter was interested mainly in eugenic sterilization and saw it as a concern of the collective and not as a place for the expression of individual rights.

Mjöen's group worried about the neo-Malthusianism aspect of sterilization—that it would reduce the total number of babies. This was one reason for opposing the right to sterilization on personal demand. The fear of depopulation was strong in the 1930s and Mjöen's conservative type of eugenics drew support from this sentiment.

Historians seem to agree on a general decline of eugenics in the English-speaking world after the 1920s, but G. R. Searle also notes that there was a revival of eugenics in Britain in the 1930s. According to Searle, an important factor in this new popularity of eugenics was the support of liberal or left-wing social reformers such as C. P. Blacker, J. S. Huxley, and J. B. S. Haldane, who were opposed to the conservative social views typical of the older generation of eugenicists. In particular they objected to racist and antifeminist elements in eugenic thinking. They also emphasized the need to take into account the newest results of scientific research and maintained that many of the older eugenic proposals were scientifically untenable. Searle calls these liberal and left-wing supporters of eugenics "reform eugenicists."[65]

Daniel Kevles has used the distinction between the old, conservative "mainline eugenics" and the new "reform eugenics" as a means of periodization: mainline eugenics dominated up to the 1920s and reform eugenics took over in the early 1930s.[66] This periodization points to an important historical change which can also be discerned in Norway, and I will therefore use the terms in approximately the same sense as Kevles. But it is also clear in the Norwegian case that this distinction does not quite correspond to the two camps in the debate over eugenics. The split between Mjöen and the experts which took place in 1915 was certainly a reaction against conservative social politics as well as a lack of scientific knowledge. On the other hand, some of the people in the anti-Mjöen camp, e.g., Vogt and Scharffenberg, continued to support views that can be characterized as mainline rather than reform eugenics well into the 1930s.

TOWARD A STERILIZATION LAW

The introduction of sterilization, both for the purpose of race hygiene and as a treatment for habitual sex criminals, became a hotly debated issue in the 1920s. An important source of inspiration for this debate was the intensification of sterilization practices in California in the years just after World War I.

In Norway the question of sterilization was treated in the first report of a government commission for revision of the penal code published in 1927.[67] This commission was set up by the Ministry of Justice in 1922. The chairman was Jon Skeie, professor of law, and among the nine members were Ragnar Vogt and Tove Mohr, as well as a third medical doctor, Ingeborg Aas.

In an appendix to the first report, Aas argued strongly in favor of sterilization, castration, and vasectomy, as a means of protection against sexual criminals. In many cases such operations would also mean a cure and a relief from abnormal tendencies, she argued. Sterilization and castration could also save much money for the state by making it possible to pacify violent persons and thus set them free from asylum or prison. She saw a close connection between the penal and the race hygienic applications since the latter very often concerned persons who had come into conflict with the law and had been imprisoned. According to Aas, public opinion had been much shaken by the sexual crimes in immediately preceding years and was likely to accept relatively harsh laws.

Vogt, in another appendix, took a negative view of the efficiency of sterilization as a way of treating sexual criminals. Vasectomy had very little effect on sexual behavior and was therefore quite useless in this connection. Castration had quite uncertain and usually small effects if the person had already reached sexual maturity. For race hygienic purposes, on the other hand, vasectomy was the right operation and castration both unnecessary and ethically unacceptable. Vogt emphasized that race hygiene as such was outside the domain of the penal code, but added that penal law should not unnecessarily hinder a carefully monitored introduction of race hygiene.

The commission produced a thorough discussion of eugenics against an international background. A separate appendix to the report contains a summary of Harry Laughlin's survey, *Eugenical Sterilization in the United States.* The commission concluded that sterilization could not be recommended either as punishment or as a means of security against habitual sex criminals. But it announced a future report recommending voluntary sterilization to be clearly entitled by law. Race hygienic sterilization was apparently less topical in Norway than in Sweden, Denmark, and Finland. Aas wrote in her appendix that as far as she knew such operations had not been carried out in Norway. Yet when the day came, she continued, it was important that there be a clear legal basis.

The commission for revision of the penal code continued to work on the question of sterilization and presented a proposal for a new law in January 1932; however, there were also other initiatives that prepared the way for the sterilization law that was passed in 1934.

Proposals for a Law

Mjöen's Norwegian Consultative Eugenics Committee sent a proposal to the Ministry of Justice in August 1931. It was a description of the principles that the committee thought ought to form the basis of a law and not a concrete proposal for a law text. Mjöen's committee was little more than a paper organization with a letterhead, but its public influence should not be underestimated. Its effect as a pressure group consisting of prominent citizens may have been considerable, and it did at least give Mjöen's activities some legitimacy. According to the letterhead of 1931 the committee then had eight members. Mjöen was the chairman and Wilhelm Keilhau, later professor of economics at the University of Oslo, was the secretary. The other members were: Jörgen Berner, general secretary of the Norwegian Medical Association; Halfdan Bryn, medical doctor and president of the Royal Academy of Science in Trondheim; Alf Guldberg, professor of mathematics; Klaus Hansen, professor of medicine; Fridtjof Mjöen, doctor of medicine (and the son of Jon Alfred Mjöen); and Harald Nöregaard, barrister of the high court.

Mjöen's committee proposed that in order to prevent psychically abnormal persons from procreating at the existent rate, one should introduce compulsory segregation and voluntary sterilization. As a means of segregation, work camps in the countryside were recommended. Persons who were not dangerous to society in other ways could regain freedom by undergoing voluntary sterilization. The statement of the committee emphasized that the situation was now so serious that society could no longer remain passive. To wait for genetic research to definitively clarify the laws of inheritance for all psychic defects was not acceptable.[68] Again Mjöen appealed to what has more recently been termed "the precautionary principle"—that with uncertain knowledge and possibility of great risk, it is best to be careful and err on the safe side.

In January 1932 the proposal for a sterilization law formulated by the commission for revision of the penal code was published. This proposal followed up the earlier intention to provide a legal framework for voluntary sterilization. With respect to sexual criminals, the commission wanted to make it possible for prisoners to choose to undergo castration in their own interest, that is, to regain freedom. Another major conclusion was that sterilization ought to be permitted on the request of the person involved or with the agreement of a person's guardian for purposes other than prevention of sexual crimes. Under this heading were included eugenic and social reasons. Sterilization on medical grounds was already covered by existing law. In order to make eugenic and social sterilizations legal a special law on sterilization was needed. Though eugenic motives were not explicitly mentioned in the law text and were given relatively little attention in the report of the commission, it is clear that eugenics was an important motive for passing the law.

According to the second paragraph in the proposal, any person over twenty-one years of age could be sterilized at his or her own request given a "respectable reason" ("respektabel grunn"). This key phrase was introduced by Ragnar Vogt[69] and indicated a moral limitation on the right of the individual to decide her or his own sterilization. For instance, sterilization merely for means of contraception was not considered a "respectable reason" at this time. It only became so in the postwar period. The third paragraph of the proposal stated: "Persons who are insane or are mentally defective can be subjected to sexual surgery at the request of a guardian, when there is reason to assume that the person will not be able to provide for the needs of self or offspring, or that a mental disease or grave physical defect will be passed on to the offspring, or that because of abnormal sexual instinct he is likely to commit sexual crimes." This passage was included with insignificant change in the law that was passed two years later.

The 1934 Sterilization Law thus provided for sterilization motivated by a consideration for the direct offspring, either on social indications, because the parent was unfit to take care of the child, or on genetic indications, because there was a likelihood that a hereditary disease would be passed on to the child. There were two passages expressing special protection for the rights of the individual. One said that an insane person should not be sterilized if there was hope of a cure or substantial improvement in the condition. Another said that a mentally disabled person could not be sterilized against his own wish or consent if he had reached or could be expected to reach the mental level of a nine-year-old.

During the same month, January 1932, Johan Scharffenberg published his own law proposal in the daily newspaper of the Labor Party.[70] The main differences from the proposal of the commission on penal law were that Scharffenberg explicitly mentioned eugenic reasons in the text of the law, and he was less strict in demanding the agreement of the guardian in the case of minors or other persons without full legal rights. There was, in other words, a stronger element of coercion in Scharffenberg's proposal. He also emphasized that he considered this to be only the first step in the direction of a full-blown eugenic social program. He expected more radical measures to be demanded in the future, "when the public has understood that human breeding must be made as *efficient* ('*rasjonell*') as plant and animal breeding." But one had to proceed gradually. According to Scharffenberg, both his own proposal and that of the commission for revision of the penal code were more radical than the few laws that had so far been passed in Europe, i.e., in Denmark and a few Swiss cantons.[71]

The Consultative Eugenics Committee also formulated a draft for a sterilization law. In a statement written in August 1933 for the medical faculty of the university at the request of the Ministry of Justice, Ragnar Vogt compared this proposal with that of his own commission and the newly introduced German law, "Gesetz zur Verhütung erbkranken Nachwuchses." He emphasized that Mjöen's proposal, like the German law, was based on a principle of compulsory ("tvungen") sterilization in contrast to the voluntary ("frivillig") sterilization that his commission had proposed.

As long as the initiative, or at least a right to veto, rested with the person concerned or a guardian, Vogt thought that sterilization was essentially voluntary and that there was little danger of misuse of the law. According to Mjöen's proposal, an initiative for sterilization could be taken by the heads of mental hospitals or other similar institutions, and the guardian could not veto but only appeal to an expert committee. The proposal did not say what should be done in the case where the person to be sterilized resisted. In Vogt's opinion, Mjöen's proposal was in this respect halfhearted, in contrast to the German law which explicitly stated that "direct force" could be used if necessary. Vogt also characterized Mjöen's proposal as a "class law" since it made it possible for rich people to evade sterilization by letting themselves be privately hospitalized. Essentially the same points were made in a shorter report by Otto Lous Mohr.[72]

THE BROAD CONSENSUS ON STERILIZATION

Characteristic of Norway, as well as the other Nordic countries, was the broad support for a mild form of eugenics. There was hardly any opposition in principle to the Sterilization Law of 1934. It was a moderate law, however, moderate also compared to the views of many of its supporters.

From the late 1920s onward, Scharffenberg was very active in campaigning for a sterilization law. In 1932 he published a popular book on genetics which was strongly pro-eugenics. This book of 1932 bore greater similarity to Vogt's book of 1914 than to Mohr's work of 1923. Scharffenberg ascribed an important role to genetic factors as causes of mental illness and retardation as well as various types of social misbehavior from vagrancy to theft and other kinds of crime. He had worked in mental hospitals and was for many years physician at the state penitentiary in Oslo. But Scharffenberg also declared that he stood clearly on the side of those geneticists who worked "strictly scientifically." He regretted the many false or unsubstantiated claims and the many "impracticable or psychologically and ethically unacceptable proposals" that had been made in the name of eugenics since the days of Plato.[73]

Scharffenberg criticized some aspects of the German law of 1933. A main objection was that it did not permit sterilization on social grounds but only for eugenic or purely medical indications. In Scharffenberg's judgment this one-sided concern with biological heredity was the major weakness of the law.

Under the German law, if mental retardation did not have a genetic cause, the person could not be sterilized, but Scharffenberg felt that the mentally retarded were never fit to raise children. He also found the list of conditions that the law considered to be hereditary too inclusive. Alcoholism, for instance, is usually caused by environment and not by heredity, he maintained. Still he considered the law to be an interesting experiment, the effects of which ought to be followed with attention, "provided it is applied with reason."[74]

The Sterilization Law of 1934 was also acceptable to left-wing Socialists such as Karl Evang, a young medical doctor and prominent Socialist intellectual. The staunch individualist and uncompromising moralist Scharffenberg was one of his idols, and as a student he was an assistant to Otto Lous Mohr for a short time. Later Evang was to serve as a very powerful and influential director of the public health service in Norway, from 1938 to 1972, minus the years of German occupation (1940-45). He was a colorful and charismatic person and an ardent spokesman for a scientifically based and centrally planned social welfare state.[75]

In his 1934 book on race politics and reaction (*Rasepolitikk og Reaksjon*), Evang violently attacked Nazi racism but accepted the Norwegian sterilization law with only minor objections. The idea of limiting the number of carriers of poor genetic material is rational and has always been supported by socialism, he wrote, and he maintained, though the socialist is well aware of the negative role that eugenics plays in a capitalist society, he is also aware of the important positive role that eugenics can play in a rationally planned socialist society.[76] Evang was less of a biological determinist than Scharffenberg. Like Mohr he emphasized the importance of the environment. He did, however, support a eugenic policy under Socialist auspices, provided it was based on sound science. This was a common view among intellectuals belonging to the political Left.

Even from the church there was little if any public criticism. The feeling was that this was a moderate law which could not be resisted. Pastor Ingvald B. Carlsen, leader of a mission for vagrants (Omstreifermisjonen), published an article, "Modern Eugenics and the Christian View of Life," in the main Christian journal for general political and cultural questions. He found that the proposed law "signified a *radical* break" with earlier Christian norms for social work. So far, according to Carlsen, Christian ethics had seen the miserable individuals in society—the feebleminded, insane, morally defective, etc.—solely as objects of Christian spiritual care and mercy. Now it was demanded that one should help prevent such individuals from being born. The traditional objection of Christians was that life is sacred—man should not interfere with the work of God. Still, Carlsen found the proposed law acceptable considering how much suffering it would help prevent. To interfere in favor of existing life against life which did not yet exist must be permissible, he argued. And degeneration was a real threat, it was "absolutely necessary to do something," thought Carlsen.[77]

The fear of degeneration was still strong and widespread in the early 1930s and appears to have been a major motivating force in the passage of the 1934 Sterilization Law. The economic and social crises, with high and persistent unemployment, created an atmosphere where such ideas thrived. Mohr, Vogt, Bonnevie, and other experts on human genetics had repeatedly emphasized that there was no tenable scientific justification for the claim that such degeneration had taken place or was presently occurring. This did not prevent most people from feeling that there was a strong threat, and that it was "necessary to do something" to avert it. Apparently the experts held what we would consider to be relatively moderate and sober views on eugenic sterilization compared to general public opinion. There was also a divergence of opinion among the experts, for instance, between Mohr and Scharffenberg. Mohr's daughter reported persistent and loud discussions between the two of them in her father's study during the 1930s.[78]

PASSING THE LAW

In Parliament, too, the fear of degeneration was felt, and the need to act was strongly expressed and met with little objection.[79] The spokesman for the law proposition was a representative from the Farmers Party (Bondepartiet), Erling Björnson. He was a strong nationalist, the son of the Norwegian national poet Björnstjerne Björnson, and became a member of the Norwegian Nazi Party after the German occupation in 1940. Being a farmer himself, Björnson compared the management of a country's population to the management of livestock on a farm. Personally he would have liked a more radical law in the direction of compulsory sterilization, similar to the one that had recently been passed in Germany.

Björnson made a special point of expressing gratitude to the men and women who had prepared the Norwegian people so that "the law today is sure to pass." He had in mind particularly the Norwegian Consultative Committee for Eugenics and "its untiring leader Dr. Alfred Mjöen, who through the passing of this law will receive the recognition in our country that he has long ago gained abroad." Björnson did not mention any of the medical or biological experts such as Vogt, Aas, or Scharffenberg.

Only one voice opposed the law in Parliament. This was the single representative of the Social Rights Party (Samfundspartiet). He found the law to be a dangerous attack on the rights of the individual. It is not biology but social conditions that create criminals, he argued, and only by changing social conditions can crime be reduced. The law completely neglected the results reached by modern psychology, and in particular by psychoanalysis. He found this to be "one of the most dangerous law proposals that have ever come to light in this country." A parliamentarian of the Labor Party, Judge Carl Bonnevie, found this criticism highly exaggerated: of course the rights of the individual should be respected, but they had to be weighed against the interests of society. This law sprang from "a more profound view of the interests of society as well as responsibility for future generations."[80]

After a brief debate the law was passed with one dissenting vote.

LATER CHANGES IN LAW AND PRACTICE

The law of 1934 remained in force until 1977, with a minor change taking place in 1961. The main point of the 1961 change was to emphasize the rights of the individual. The consent of a guardian, or corresponding authority, was to be sufficient only "if the person is incapable of deciding on the operation." In the 1977 law the initiative was placed even more firmly with the person to be sterilized or somebody with a close personal relationship to that person. Another major change in the 1977 law was that voluntary sterilization of persons over twenty-five years of age and with full legal rights became a private issue between the patient and his doctor. The official application was no longer necessary in such cases.

In spite of the clear shift from collective to individual interests, there is a great deal of continuity in the Norwegian laws on sterilization. The law of 1977, like the one of 1934, makes it legal to sterilize persons of certain categories even if they have no wish to be sterilized. At present, as in 1934, a person can be sterilized on the initiative of a guardian if there is "considerable danger" that children will inherit a "serious illness or deformation," or if the person is incapable of providing properly for children. In other words, there is still a genetic and a social justification for such sterilization. But as already stressed, the conditions for taking an initiative for such an operation are more narrowly circumscribed now than in 1934, emphasizing that sterilization should be as voluntary as possible.

The legal status of the person to be sterilized and the source of initiative divides sterilizations according to the 1934 law into three categories: (1) sterilization on the application of the person concerned (those with full legal rights); (2) sterilization on the application of the person with the consent of a guardian; and (3) sterilization on the application of a guardian or corresponding authority (for those incapable of applying).[81] (fig.1) If we take categories 2 and 3 to be representative of eugenic sterilization, we see a gradual increase in the 1930s to a high level in the 1940s and a decrease in the 1950s. The statistics also show a dramatic increase in sterilizations on the application of the person concerned after 1945. The latter rise reflects the gradual introduction of sterilization as a means of contraception and has nothing to do with eugenics.

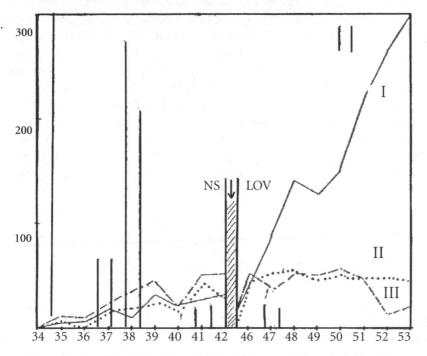

Figure 1. Sterilizations Granted for Women, 1934-1953, Applicants

- - - - - Applications submitted by the patient (for persons with full legal rights)
············· Applications submitted by the patient with consent of a guardian or corresponding authority
— · — · — Applications submitted by guardian or corresponding authority (for persons incapable of applying)

Source: K. Evang, *Sterilisering etter lov av 1. juni 1934 om adgang til sterilisering m.v.* (Sarpsborg: F. Verding, 1955).

The statistics of the four Nordic countries are not easy to compare due to different categorization and differing degrees of completeness in the available material. For instance the Norwegian law, and the corresponding statistics, do not include sterilizations on medical indications.[82] Sweden has, by far, the best statistics for the period in question, the 1930s to 1950s. In Sweden the number of sterilizations of the mentally retarded rose rapidly from about 200 per year in the late 1930s to a peak of about. 1,000 in 1944 and then declined to about 100 by 1955. As already indicated the trend was similar in Norway though the number relative to the population of the country was considerably smaller. There was a gradual rise in sterilizations of the mentally retarded and the mentally ill in the first eight years from 1934 to 1942. In the 1930s the average annual number of sterilizations in Norway, under the 1934 law, was around seventy-five, two-thirds of which belonged to categories 2 and 3. For the feebleminded there was an average of eighty-seven sterilizations per year in the period 1945 to 1954, according to Evang.[83] In the years after World War II the number in this category fell slowly for women and more rapidly for men.[84] In the period 1965 to 1973 the average number was twenty.

The total annual number of sterilizations in Norway had, by 1975, grown to 4,582 while the number in categories 2 and 3 was 32. The vast majority of sterilizations were thus carried out on persons with full legal rights on their own application. A main reason for the introduction of the 1977 law was to simplify the procedure for the large majority of sterilizations which were then considered unproblematic.

Table 1. Sterilizations in Norway, 1934-1976, Granted Applications.

Period	Number of Sterilizations	Percent Women	Annual Average
1 June 1934-31 December 1942	653	83	76
1 January 1943-8 May 1945 (Nazi law)	487	84	207
9 May 1945-30 June 1954	2,569	91	283
1 July 1954-1965	8,005	93	696
1966-1976	29,177	62	2,652
1934-1976	40,891	ca 75	951

Source: K. Evang, *Sterilisering etter lov av 1. juni 1934 om adgang til sterilisering m.v.* (Sarpsborg: F. Varding, 1955), 13; The Norwegian Parliament, Government Bill 1976/1977 no 46, "Om lov om sterilisering m.v.," 16.

Note: No figures for 1 July-31 December 1959. Sterilizations on medical indications are not included. Higher figures during the Nazi law, some 280 annually, are estimated by Gogstad (A. Chr. Gogstad, *Helse og Hakekors. Helsetjeneste og helse under okkupasjonsstyret i Norge, 1940-45* [Bergen: Alma Mater Forlag, 1991], 209.

Table 2. Sterilizations, 1945-1954, Mentally Retarded, Mentally Ill,
Epileptics, and Others, Granted Applications.

Category	Numbers	Percent of Total
Mentally Retarded	782	30
Mentally Ill*	184	7
Epileptics	44	2
Others	1,559	61
Total	*2,569*	*100*

*Includes the category "formerly mentally ill."
Source: K. Evang, *Sterilisering etter lov av 1. juni 1934 om adgang til sterilisering m.v.*
(Sarpsborg: F. Varding, 1955), 13, 39.
Note: Sterilizations on medical indications are not included.

EUGENICS DURING THE GERMAN OCCUPATION 1940-1945

In June 1942 the puppet regime of Vidkunn Quisling substituted for the 1934 law a new law "for the protection of the race" ("Lov til vern om folkeætten").[85] The commission that prepared the law was headed by the Nazi director of the health service, H. Thoralf Østrem, who had supplanted Evang. Among its members were Klaus Hansen, professor of medicine at the University of Oslo, who had been a member of Mjöen's Eugenics Committee, and Gunnar Hiorth, associate professor of genetics at the Agricultural College of Norway. Hiorth was the genetic expert for the Nazi commission.

In accordance with Nazi ideology and German political pressure this new sterilization law emphasized biological inheritance at the cost of environmental factors and social considerations, extended the range of conditions for sterilization, and gave guidelines for coercion and even the use of physical force. Generally it weakened the protection of individual rights. It has been pointed out that during the German occupation there was a change in the whole legal perspective from an individualist standpoint to one in which the individual was subordinated to the interests of "the people." The initiative for sterilization was then in the hands of any medical doctor, or head of a prison, school, hospital, etc., where the person lived. The guardian had no veto any more, and the law allowed use of force.[86]

In 1942 Thordar Quelprud was made associate professor and head of a new Institute for Biological Heredity (Arvebiologisk Institutt) created at the University of Oslo by the Nazi government. This institute was set up as an alternative to the Institute for Genetics established under the leadership of Kristine

Bonnevie in 1916. Mohr had taken over the leadership of this institute in 1938 and a modernization of the laboratory supported by the Rockefeller Foundation had just been finished when the Germans invaded Norway in April 1940. Mohr was arrested in 1941, forbidden to live in Oslo when subsequently released, and removed from his professorship in 1943.[87] Quelprud's scientific and pedagogical qualifications for the job were not in doubt. He had been warmly recommended for a position as associate professor in genetics by Kristine Bonnevie in 1938. During the war years Quelprud, in addition to his university teaching, gave special courses on genetics and anthropology for Nazi cadres.[88]

According to Evang (1955), there was a sharp increase in the number of sterilizations under the Nazi law. During the years 1938 to 1941 the average annual number was a little below 100 while in 1944 it rose to about 200. While the total number of sterilizations allowed was 663 for the 8.5 years from 1 June 1934 to 31 December 1942, the number for the 2.5 years of the Nazi law, 1 January 1943 to 8 May 1945, was 487.[89] But the actual increase in eugenic sterilization was even sharper than Evang acknowledged. According to a recent study, the average annual number of sterilizations under the Nazi law rose to around 280.[90]

It is thus clear that even in an invaded and occupied country such as Norway there was no strong and unanimous reaction of scientific experts against the views on biological inheritance propagated by the Nazi movement. A significant part of the Norwegian genetic expertise was willing to cooperate with the Nazi authorities in carrying out their population policy. The Nazi government was able to boost eugenic sterilization in spite of a widespread and growing general resistance to its regime. In the early period of the occupation there was considerable resistance among Norwegian Nazi officials against a radical sterilization law on a German model, but this resistance weakened as the war went on. Apparently, there was also little or no sabotage of the law by Norwegian doctors.[91]

EUGENICS AFTER WORLD WAR II

The experience with Nazi population policies had little immediate impact on the practice of sterilization in Norway after the Second World War. There was no immediate and strong change in the attitude of the proponents of a moderate eugenic sterilization program. Vogt's successor in the main chair in psychiatry wrote in the autumn of 1945 that the law of 1934 needed revision; the sterilization of the mentally ill and retarded ought to be used much more than it had been so far—"It is better to prevent than to treat."[92]

According to Evang's statistics the sterilization of legally incompetent persons reached a plateau in the late 1930s and only started to drop around 1950. The rise in the number of such sterilizations under the Nazi law in the period 1943-45 appears as a sharp outgrowth on an otherwise smooth curve of rise and fall. But no doubt the Nazi experience made the moderate eugenicists think more critically about the feasibility and, in particular, the desirability of systematic programs to improve human heredity. The experience was constantly present in postwar discussions of eugenics. And even if it did not change the mind of old eugenicists very much, it was probably quite important in forming the opinion of the new generation.

As head of the public health service, Evang acknowledged in 1955 the deterrent effect of Nazi practice on eugenic sterilization in general: the "embarrassing intermezzo of the lackey service of science to Hitler necessarily must have scared many people." But he commented, hopefully there has now been time "to work this off and discuss the problems on an objective basis."[93]

In a popular article of 1948 Kristine Bonnevie had no doubts about the importance of biological inheritance for differences in social behavior. She even suggested that racial differences in cultural ability may have a genetic basis. Yet she avoided any explicit mention of eugenics. She emphasized that the progress of human society is a cultural phenomenon, and remarked that with respect to the progressive (biological) evolution of man himself "there is nothing we can do."[94]

In 1951 the eighty-two year-old Scharffenberg lectured to the Genetics Society (Arvelighetsforeningen) on genetics and eugenics, warning against excesses:

> . . . many eugenists sustain a fanciful hope of being able to *improve the human race* according to the principles of plant and animal breeding, and they overestimate the influence of *heredity* compared to *environment*. They therefore often neglect social reform work.[95]

But Scharffenberg still supported the right of society to sterilize the mentally retarded, emphasizing their inability to care for offspring as the main reason for sterilization. His old belief in biological inheritance as an important factor in much social misbehavior was dampened but not abandoned. His view was that genetics "should soberly point out that *the aim of eugenics is utopian*, but nevertheless it must support the use of *sterilization* under expert control."[96]

Evang was among those who continued to argue for eugenic sterilization of the feebleminded. In the 1955 paper on sterilization, to which we have already referred a number of times, he held that sterilization could have a significant effect on the future number of the mentally retarded. In support of his view Evang referred to the analysis of the Swedish biologist Nils von Hofsten who was an advisor to the Swedish government on sterilization questions. Evang referred in particular to two papers by von Hofsten published in 1944 and 1951.

Von Hofsten's 1944 paper described the theoretical genetic basis of the 1941 Swedish sterilization law. Von Hofsten did not believe in the simple Mendelian inheritance of mental retardation through one recessive gene. He suggested the interaction of two to three genes, one of which was dominant. The effect of sterilization on such assumptions could be quite significant—not much less than for one recessive gene, he claimed.[97] On the assumption that "75% of all feeblemindedness is hereditary," von Hofsten calculated that the going rate of sterilization might produce a reduction of the mentally retarded in the Swedish population from 1 percent to 0.7 percent, or by about 19,000 in two generations. Such a reduction implied a substantial decrease in social and economic costs, and could by no means be called "practically insignificant," he argued.[98]

In his 1951 paper von Hofsten presented a more systematic analysis of the effect that selection would have on different genetic combinations under various conditions. He presented the same models as in 1944, together with some new ones, but he was less optimistic with respect to the social benefits of sterilization. To "avoid misunderstanding," he wrote, "I have never shared the belief, once widely spread, that an important improvement of the 'race' is possible by means of sterilization."[99]

Evang in 1955 claimed that Norway had "not at any time" been affected by the excessive optimism concerning the results of eugenic sterilization that had been felt "in certain other countries." It was, on the contrary, a "somewhat *too strong pessimism*" that had been prevalent, he contended, on the basis of von Hofsten's analysis. Evang was a little more moderate in his assumptions than von Hofsten was in 1944, however. For instance, Evang wrote that "most authors assume that 40-60% of existing feeblemindedness is caused by biological heredity";[100] von Hofsten in 1944 based his calculations on 75 percent inheritance.

In his belief in the moderate usefulness of eugenic sterilization, Evang had support from leading Norwegian psychiatrists. Vogt, Scharffenberg, and Langfeldt have already been mentioned. Ørnulf Ødegård, like Evang, was an active member of the Society of Socialist Physicians and held similar views.[101]

In 1957 Tage Kemp, head of the Institute for Human Genetics at the University of Copenhagen, also argued for eugenic sterilization of the mentally retarded. But unlike von Hofsten in 1944 or Evang in 1955, he did not assign any particular percentage or model of inheritance and thus gave no estimate of the expected reduction in the number of mentally retarded.[102]

It has been argued that the growth of knowledge in human genetics failed for a surprisingly long time to undermine the simple theory that mental retardation depended on one recessive Mendelian gene.[103] My account confirms that belief in a strong genetic determination of mental retardation prevailed among influential human geneticists and psychiatrists in the Nordic countries until well after the Second World War. But this did not mean that they believed in determination by one recessive gene.

Concluding Remarks

The science of genetics as a source of enlightenment for social and political action has been the focus of this study. I have tried to show that for the experts that were participating in the Norwegian public debate and in the decision making on eugenics, science was primarily a source of general understanding of the nature and implications of the eugenics proposal. The medical instruments and methods used in carrying out eugenic policies, during the period which we are considering, were rather simple and did not depend much on advanced genetic research.

The main role of science was to help form a picture of the situation with its possible threats and its options for action. In a democratic society the basis for social policy is, of course, the picture of the situation generally accepted by public opinion. What science can do is to gradually modify this picture. It can to some degree correct prejudice on specific questions. But this function presupposes trust. The respect of the general public for the scientific experts depends on the belief that science, in spite of its fallibility, has the power to correct our picture of the world. This enlightening function of science depends, in turn, on a subtle balance between trust and skepticism. Too easy acceptance of hypothetical statements from scientists can lead to pernicious superstitions. It seems that the Norwegian genetic experts were generally quite well aware of the incompleteness and uncertainty of their knowledge. It was, in fact, one of their main arguments against far-reaching eugenic programs, such as the proposals of Mjöen, that the knowledge upon which they were based was too uncertain and incomplete.

This essay has demonstrated how the scientific experts were prominent participants both in the public debate that set the political agenda and in the further decision making process. They were highly influential in forming the 1934 law and the whole framework for the practice of sterilization in Norway. Because they possessed the technical competence, they also had a large share in developing the practical procedures and instruments and in executing the program of sterilization. The point is that this "instrumental" role was carried out within a framework originally set, and later gradually modified, through a process of scientifically informed public debate. The role of the scientific experts in this latter process is often superficially treated in the recent historiography of eugenics. Strongly hereditarian views among the general public on mental retardation, mental illness, and various kinds of social misbehavior are taken to be the result and therefore also the responsibility of genetic science.[105] Upon closer scrutiny the popular hereditarian views turn out to have other sources as well and to depend in large measure on simplistic popularizations which were sharply criticized by scientific experts.

Many historians of eugenics do not make enough effort to distinguish valid knowledge and legitimate expertise from what merely poses as such. Mjöen, for instance, was a popularizer with a general scientific status and considerable public charisma. But he was not a reliable expert on genetics. This lack of attention to the precise content of science and thus to its limitations can easily lead to exaggerated views of its influence and importance, analogously to the fanciful "scientific" beliefs on degeneration, race crossings, environmental poisons, etc. held by Mjöen and other popular proponents of eugenics. It is true that some geneticists did support quite radical eugenic measures and that most geneticists of the 1930s and 1940s were in favor of a moderate eugenic policy. It is furthermore true that some geneticists did not protest but let their expertise and scientific authority be exploited by the Nazi eugenics programs. But it is also true that some of the most effective criticism of current eugenic proposals in Norway came from geneticists.

This account has described eugenics as a program for social policy, or rather as a set of several more or less conflicting programs. These programs were built on knowledge about the existing situation as well as on values and aims that one wanted to realize in the future. In the case of eugenics, knowledge concerning human heredity played a central role, and the major source of new knowledge in this field was genetic science, in particular human genetics. The question of whether or not eugenics was "pseudoscientific" then becomes a question of what was sound knowledge about human genetics.

That eugenic policies were in part based on claims without a sound scientific basis is hardly disputed. Dubious claims were made even by persons with high scientific standings, such as the German geneticists Otto von Verschuer, Eugen Fischer, and Fritz Lenz.[106] In general it is unlikely that these unsound claims may in the future become scientifically well-founded. To this extent there is quite general agreement among geneticists as well as historical scholars of science that a fund of knowledge about human genetics exists which has a validity transcending particular times and circumstances. There is in this sense a difference between "good" and "bad" science, or "science" and "pseudo-science," if one wants to use those terms. Clearly, eugenics cannot be generally dismissed as a "pseudoscience."[107] But this is not because the distinctions between correct (true) and incorrect (false) or between well-supported (rational) and unsupported (irrational) claims to scientific knowledge are not important. Eugenics was a set of programs for social policy, and these programs were built partly on sound scientific claims and partly on claims which were unsound, judging by the state of genetic science at the time. In other words, eugenics was in part pseudoscientific and in part scientifically sound.

In contrast to my analysis in terms of an enlightenment project, eugenics has often been interpreted as a movement for the rationalization of human behavior in the service of the state. This view has been especially developed in historical studies of German eugenics.

According to Peter Weingart, the history of eugenics and human genetics is "one continuous process of rationalization." He reads the story of eugenics as "the process of ultimate rationalization—namely, that of human reproduction." Weingart's model of rationalization is built on a conception of science with notable relativist elements. He makes little effort to distinguish hypotheses from well-established facts. Scientists "are the first to instill their prejudices and biases into" the theory of human genetics. In his social, contextual analysis, the truth or falsity of scientific claims have subordinate importance. He considers beliefs, "labeled as scientific knowledge," as "the chief resource of power and legitimacy for the expert community."[108] A skeptical and relativist view of scientific knowledge makes an instrumental interpretation of science natural. It becomes difficult to distinguish the cognitive content of science from its actual effects in the short run.

Sheila Weiss claims to have revealed "the logic of German eugenics" through an analysis of Wilhelm Schallmayer's work. The rationale and aim of German racial hygiene was "technocratic and managerial rationality."[109] Eugenics embodied the idea that national power "was a product of the rational management of *population*." This logic led to Nazi population policies ending in the holocaust of World War II.[110] But even if this logic of management is the framework of her account she also gives room to other and more humane purposes, such as health and well-being. One may also ask if economics is not more relevant as a source of inspiration for managerial efficiency than eugenics and genetics.

The preceding account of Norwegian eugenics does not fit well with the instrumental or pragmatic view, of science inherent in the accounts of Weingart and Weiss. In their view science is primarily considered as a means to obtain social ends. Science is important because it "works," not because it tells us what the world is like. This essay has tried to show that the instrumental picture of science and its social role is seriously incomplete in the case of eugenics. What Weingart and Weiss see as the contribution of science to social policy, besides instruments, is a general logic of managerial efficiency. The role of genetic knowledge in forming political aims is neglected.

According to the classical liberal view of science, typically held by the actors in my account, science also has an instrumental side. However, this technical usefulness is not the core of science. Knowledge is the core, and usefulness follows from having knowledge. Knowledge of the nature of things and of their causal connections is an important source of new and more efficient technology. But that is by no means always the case with knowledge about the world. Often it provides understanding of the likely course of events without the possibility of significantly interfering with the process. Astronomy is a classic example. In such cases the understanding of causal connections can nevertheless influence behavior, through adaptation to natural and social circumstances by the formation of norms and goals. This is, for instance, a main effect of modern ecological science. It was also the main social role of human genetics during the first half of the twentieth century.

At the beginning of this discussion, the question was posed as to why the sterilization law in Norway, and in the other Scandinavian countries, was introduced at such a late stage in the development of the international eugenics movement. This movement had, by the 1930s, entered a phase of moderation and decline, at least in the English-speaking world. Most American sterilization laws, for example, were introduced well before 1930. It was suggested that allegiance to traditional Christian moral norms had been the main obstacle at an earlier stage and also that some of the positive driving forces were still relatively weak.

It is striking how the introduction of sterilization laws in Europe in the 1930s was a phenomenon of Protestant countries. Under liberal democratic political conditions such laws were introduced only in countries where the Lutheran denomination was dominant, namely Denmark, Norway, Sweden, Finland, Iceland, and Estonia. Germany has a northern Lutheran part and a southern part dominated by Catholics. Here the sterilization law was introduced only after the Nazis had taken over. In some other countries with strong Protestant traditions sterilization laws were up for serious consideration but rejected, as, for instance in England, Holland, and Czechoslovakia.

It is also remarkable how the Norwegian sterilization law was passed with hardly any opposition in Parliament. It was what can be called a consensus law, or with another metaphor: the least common denominator of public opinion. Everybody tended to think in eugenic categories, but a law proposal also had to be toned down to satisfy the smoldering moral doubts in large parts of the population. The law was considered by the eugenics enthusiasts as merely a first cautious step.

In countries with a vigorous opposition, such as Holland and England, the idea of a sterilization law was quietly dropped. Pressing such laws through against a vocal minority was more or less impossible. In a liberal democratic society one needs a high degree of consensus to act in such morally sensitive matters. It seems a likely guess that if a liberal democratic regime had continued in Germany after 1933, no sterilization law would have been introduced.

By the 1930s cultural and social modernization was well-advanced in the northern Lutheran countries of Europe. Norway, Sweden, and Denmark were culturally and socially more homogeneous than most other European countries. It was the start of an era of Labor Party rule. These countries were developing a social welfare state based on planning and science.[111] Secularization, and a program of social planning combined with a lack of vociferous opposition, made the North European sterilization laws possible at just this time. If we ask why such laws came so much earlier in the United States, part of the answer could be that the state there had been secularized and separated from the church long before. Opposition to immigration was another very important factor in the growth of eugenics in the United States in the early twentieth century.

In the Norwegian debate on the sterilization law the church was remarkably quiet. The church felt uncomfortable with the proposal. But as we saw in the argument of Pastor Ingvald B. Carlsen, it was also hard to reject a minimal eugenics program. In terms of the prevention of suffering, the balance seemed so obviously positive. It also appears significant that the sterilization law was introduced at the same time as more liberal views on abortion, sexual education, and other things related to procreation were taking hold. The influence of the traditional moral norms that hindered sterilization had become much weaker around 1930.

Yet as the law was being introduced and applied, its scientific rationale was gradually being undermined. Both the threat of degeneration and the practical possibilities of organizing a positive or negative eugenics program were turning out to be much less than believed by enthusiasts such as Mjöen and Scharffenberg. This advance in the knowledge of human heredity was already important in the 1930s, as is seen in the arguments of Otto Lous Mohr. But much of the new insight was still quite uncertain. Contradictory hypotheses, which gave legitimization to eugenic sterilization, continued to have scientific plausibility. We see this in the arguments of von Hofsten and Kemp as late as the 1950s. One new piece of knowledge with considerable impact was presumably the discovery, at the end of the 1950s, that Down's syndrome was caused by the presence of an extra chromosome in the cells.[112] With this kind of mechanism many of the old considerations concerning the inheritability of mental retardation lost their relevance. More generally, psychiatry and psychology in the late 1950s experienced an international wave of interest in environmental factors at the cost of biological inheritance.[113]

Eugenics, including sterilization, was part of the comprehensive program for social reform aiming toward the welfare state. Karl Evang was one of the main ideologists and architects of the Norwegian welfare state. The scientizing of politics and the responsibility of the state for the welfare of the individual were core principles in Evang's ideology.[114] His long-lasting support for eugenic sterilization demonstrates the integration of eugenics into a general program for the welfare state.

From early on, the ideology of central and large-scale social planning was opposed by an ideology of individual freedom. A centralized system was seen as a threat to the right of the individual to live a life according to his or her own aims and values. Sterilization was a sensitive and ambiguous theme in this respect.

Important ideological changes in the status of individual rights are also indicated by studies of Norwegian legal history. It has been claimed that by the 1930s the balance between society and individual in Norway was shifting in favor of society. The law was becoming a means for general social benefit rather than a protection for individual rights and interests. By the 1970s this development had been reversed.[115] One expression of the reaction against growing state power in the postwar period was the introduction of the "ombudsman" system in the 1960s.[116]

In summary, this account of the rise and fall of eugenic sterilization in Norway can be framed by two hypotheses: (1) by around 1930 secularization had gone far enough to remove earlier moral obstacles, and sterilization was introduced as a part of the general program for a social welfare state; (2) by the 1950s the biological vision of eugenics had been seriously eroded by new scientific knowledge, and the ideological balance between collectivism and individualism had become unfavorable to nonvoluntary sterilization. Thus the period from the 1930s to the 1950s appears as a "window" where eugenic sterilization was possible. This general interpretation also implies that the main role of medical and biological science, and especially genetics, was to inform the public about the social implications of adopting or rejecting different eugenic policies rather than to produce instruments and justifications of politically and ideologically determined aims. This enlightening role can be expressed by a contrafactual claim: If degeneration had turned out to be as serious and rapid as was imagined by the mainline race hygienists, then eugenic measures such as sterilization would have continued to thrive in the decades after World War II. If human biology had turned out to be different, different social policies would have been in demand.

NOTES

1. N. Roll-Hansen, "Eugenic Sterilization—A Preliminary Comparison of the Scandinavian Experience to that of Germany," *Genome* 31 (1989): 890-95.
2. B. Müller-Hill, *Tödliche Wissenschaft. Die Aussonderung von Juden, Zigeunern und Geisteskranken 1933-1945* (Hamburg: Rowohlt, 1984); B. Müller-Hill, "Genetics after Auschwitz," *Holocaust and Genocide Studies* 2 (1987): 3-20.
3. Müller-Hill, "Genetics after Auschwitz," 17.
4. G. Allen, "Geneticists, Eugenics and Class Struggle," *Genetics* 79 (1975): 36-37.
5. G. Allen, "Genetics, Eugenics and Society: Internalists and Externalists in Contemporary History of Science," *Social Studies of Science* 6 (1976): 105-22.
6. H. Ebert, "Hermann Muckermann. Profil eines Theologen, Widerstandskämpfers und Hochschullehrers der Technischen Universität Berlin," *Humanismus und Technik* 20, no. 1 (1976): 29-40.
7. For examples of the strongly hereditarian attitudes among leading medical doctors in Norway in the 1930s, see A.-L. Seip, "Politikkens vitenskapeliggjøring. Debatten om sosialpolitikk i 1930-årene," *Nytt Norsk Tidsskrift* 6 (1989): 210-25.
8. G. R. Searle describes a revival of the British eugenics movement in the 1930s, with sterilization as a main cause ("Eugenics and Politics in Britain in the 1930s," *Annals of Science* 36 [1979]: 159-69). But its influence was limited; no serious attempt to pass a sterilization law materialized. See also K. M. Ludmerer, *Genetics and American Society: A Historical Appraisal* (Baltimore: The Johns Hopkins University Press, 1972); D. Kevles, *In the Name of Eugenics* (New York: Alfred A. Knopf, 1985); G. Allen, "The Eugenics Record Office at Cold Spring Harbour, 1910-1940: An Essay in Institutional History," *Osiris* 2 (1986): 225-64.
9. A more detailed account of the early Norwegian eugenics debate is found in N. Roll-Hansen, "Eugenics before World War II: The Case of Norway," *History and Philosophy of the Life Sciences* 2 (1980): 269-98 and N. Roll-Hansen, "Den norske debatten om rasehygiene," *Historisk Tidsskrift* (1980): 259-83.
10. J. A. Mjöen, *Rasehygiene,* 2nd ed. (Oslo: Jacob Dybwad, 1938), 270. This is a very different book from the 1914 edition.
11. J. A. Mjöen, "Det nordiske program for rasehygiene. Fremgangsmåter for en socialbiologisk befolkningspolitikk. Et förste skritt," *Vor Verden,* no. 5 (1931): 181.

12. *Stortingsforhandlinger* 1910, vol. 3a, Ot. prp. no. 7, "om utfœrdigelse av en lov om tilvirkning av öl m. v." No date. The law was passed 12 July 1912.

13. Ørnulf Ødegård, *Arv og Miljö i Psykiatrien* (Oslo: Aschehough, 1952), 46.

14. R. Vogt, "Om arvelighet ved manisk-melankolsk sindsygdom," *Tidsskrift for Den Norske Lægeforening* 30 (1910): 463.

15. V. K. Uckerman, *De Dövstumme i Norge* (Kristiania: A. Cammuermeyer, 1896).

16. R. Vogt, "Racehygiene," *Naturen* 37 (1913): 65-80.

17. J. A. Mjöen, "Rasehygiene," *Forhandlinger* (Proceedings) Det Norske Videnskabsakademi i Kristiania, 1914, 4-5.

18. R. Vogt, *Arvelighetslære og Racehygiene* (Kristiania: A. Cammermeyer, 1914).

19. R. Vogt, *Arvelighetslære og Racehygiene*, 100-l.

20. J. Scharffenberg, "Hygieneuufstillingen i Dresden," *Social-Demokraten* (25 October 1911).

21. N. J. Lavik, *Makt og galskap* (Oslo: Pax, 1990).

22. Other members of the Permanent International Committee for Eugenics were: Sören Hansen, police surgeon in Copenhagen; Lucien March, director of general statistics in France; Raymond Pearl, American geneticist; Yves Delage, French biologist and historian of science; and Vernon Kellogg, American zoologist. A photograph of the committee elected in London is reproduced in J. A. Mjöen, *Racehygiene* (Kristiania: Jacob Dybwad, 1914).

23. For more details, see Roll-Hansen "Eugenics before World War II: The Case of Norway" and N. Roll-Hansen, "Den norske debatten om rasehygiene."

24. O. L. Mohr, "Dr. philos. Mjöen og hans racehygiene," *Aftenposten* (7 March 1915): 2-3.

25. K. Bonnevie, "Om racehygiene og om dr. Alfred Mjöens nye bok," *Tidens Tegn* (24 March 1915): 6-9; J. A. Mjöen, "Segregation av lavvæ rdige raceelementer. Svar til professor i zoologi Bonnevie," *Tidens Tegn* (23 April 1915): 9-10; K. Bonnevie, "Dr. Mjöens racehygiene for siste gang," *Tidens Tegn* (24 April 1915): 2.

26. T. Wyller, "Kand. med. Mohr og dr. Mjöen," *Norske Intelligenssedler* (31 March 1915): 4. Mohr did not yet have a doctoral degree.

27. K. E. Schreiner, "Et ord om videnskap og dilettantisme," *Norske Intelligenssedler* (8 April 1915): 5-6.

28. The authors were K. Bonnevie, R. Vogt, H. H. Gran (professor of botany), and E. Poulsson (professor of medicine).

29. *Stortingsforhandlinger* 1916, vol. 1a, st. prp. no. 7, hovedpost V, 61-64, "Institut for arvelighetsforskning"; *Stortingsforhandlinger* 1916, vol. 6a, Inds. s. XXI, 12; *Stortingsforhandlinger* 1916, vol. 7a, Forhandlinger i Stortinget (3 April 1916), 618-22.

30. K. Bonnevie, "Indledning til diskussion om arvelighet hos mennesker; forskningens maal og midler," *Det 16. skandinaviske naturforskermöte 1916* (1916): 857-64.

31. K. Bonnevie, "Arvelighetsundersökelser i Norge (Forelöpig meddelelse)," *Norsk Magasin for Lægevidenskaben* 13 (1915): 1177-1222.

32. See T. Mohr, *Katti Anker Möller—en banebryter* (Oslo: Tiden, 1968).

33. Ibid., 99-134.

34. Katti Anker Möller, notebook from the 1912 Eugenics Congress in London, University Library, Oslo, manuscript collection.

35. Neo-Malthusians recommended contraception and family planning in order to improve the social standard of the lower classes.

36. T. Mohr, *Katti Anker Möller—en banebryter*, 93-94.

37. Mjöen, *Racehygiene* (1914), 149-57.

38. Ibid., 209-12.

39. Ibid., 195.

40. See, for example, R. Vogt, "Svar til professor Mohr," *Tidsskrift for den Norske Lægeforening*, no. 10 (1935): 577-79.

41. O. L. Mohr, *Arvelærens Grundtræk* (Kristiania: Olaf Norlis Forlag, 1923), 75.

42. J. A. Mjöen, "Alkohol som racegift," *Tirfing*, nos. 1-2 (1927): 8.

43. J. A. Mjöen, "Harmonic and Disharmonic Racecrossings," *Eugenics in Race and State*, vol. 2, scientific papers of the Second International Congress of Eugenics, New York, 22-28 September 1921 (Baltimore: Williams & Wilkins Co., 1923), 61.

44. "Den Nordiske Rase" was published in Copenhagen as part of *Det Nye Nord* (*The New North*).

45. H. F. Osborne, "Address of Welcome," *Eugenics, Genetics and the Family*, vol. 1, scientific papers of the Second International Congress of Eugenics, New York, 22-28 September 1921 (Baltimore: Williams & Wilkins Co., 1923), 1-4.

46. Mjöen "Harmonic and Disharmonic Racecrossings."

47. W. B. Provine, "Geneticists and the Biology of Race Crossing," *Science* 182 (1973): 790-96.

48. K. Bonnevie, "Main Results of a Statistical Investigation of Finger Prints from 25,518 Individuals," *Eugenics, Genetics and the Family*, vol. 1, scientific papers of the Second International Congress of Eugenics, New York, 22-28 September 1921 (Baltimore: Williams & Wilkins Co., 1923), 198-211.

49. K. Bonnevie, "Papillarmuster und psychische Eigenschaften," *Hereditas* 8 (1927): 180-92.

50. See, for example, G. Geipel, *Anleitung zur erbbiologischen Beurteilung der Finger- und Handleisten* (München: J. F. Lehmanns Verlag, 1935).

51. See, for example, T. Quelprud, "Zur Erblichkeit des Darwinschen Höckerchens," *Zeitschrift für Morphologie und Anthropologie* 34 (1934): 343-63.

52. Letter from C. B. Davenport to K. Bonnevie, 19 March 1927, Davenport Collection, American Philosophical Society Library, Philadelphia.

53. Letter from K. Bonnevie to C. B. Davenport, 19 March 1927, Davenport Collection, American Philosophical Society Library, Philadelphia.

54. K. Bonnevie, "Arv hos menneskene," *Folkehelseforeningens tidsskrift* 11, no. 7 (1931): 9.

55. See, for example, G. Allen, "Genetics, Eugenics and Society: Internalists and Externalists in Contemporary History of Science," *Social Studies of Science* 6 (1976): 116.

56. See, for example, A. M. Dalcq, "Notice sur la vie et l'œvre de M. O.-L. Mohr. Correspondant étranger," *Académie royale de médecine de Belgique* 7 (1967): 691-98.

57. See, for example, G. H. Waaler, "Professor, Dr. med. Otto Lous Mohr, vitenskaps-mannen," *Det Norske Videnskaps-Akademi i Oslo, Årbok 1967* (Oslo: Universitetsforlaget, 1968), 1-23.

58. Mohr, *Arvelærens Grundtræk,* 62.

59. Ibid., 67.

60. Mohr, "Menneskeavlen under kultur," *Samtiden* 37 (1926): 22-48.

61. Mohr, *Arvelærens Grundtræk,* 64. Retranslated by the author from Norwegian into English.

62. O. L. Mohr, "Menneskeavlen under kultur," 30.

63. A. Myrdal and G. Myrdal, *Krisen i befolkningsspörsmålet* (Oslo: Tiden, 1936).

64. L. Longum, *Drömmen om det frie menneske. Norsk kulturradikalisme og mel-lomkrigstidens radikale treklöver, Hoel—Krogh—Øverland* (Oslo: Universitetsforlaget, 1986).

65. Searle, "Eugenics and Politics in Britain in the 1930s," 163ff.

66. Kevles, *In the Name of Eugenics,* 164ff.

67. Ministry of Justice, *Innstilling fra den av Justisdepartementet 11. mai 1922 opp-nevnte komite til revisjon av straffeloven. Förste del.* (Oslo: O. F. Arnesen, 1923.)

68. Letter from Mjöen and Keilhau to the Ministry of Justice, 19 August 1931, with an enclosed statement, "Forestilling i anledning sterilisasjon og segregasjon av for-brytere og andre helt lavverdige individer," Archive, Ministry of Justice.

69. R. Ingebrigtsen, "Sterilisasjon etter lov av 1. VI. 1934 om adgang til sterilisasjon m.v.," *Nordisk Medicin* 54 (1955): 1835ff.

70. J. Scharffenberg, "Forslag til sterilisasjonslov for Norge," *Arbeiderbladet* (30 January 1932): 2-3.

71. J. Scharffenberg, "En tysk sterilisasjonslov," *Arbeiderbladet* (1 September 1933): 3, 8.

72. Report from Ragnar Vogt to the Medical Faculty of the University of Oslo, 23 August 1933, 19pp., Ministry of Justice; Statement by O. L. Mohr, no date, Ministry of Justice.

73. Scharffenberg, *Hovedpunkterne i Arvelaren,* (Olso: Der Norse Arbeider-partis Forlag, 1932),109.

74. Scharffenberg, "En tysk sterilisasjonslov," 3, 8.

75. For a general account of Karl Evang and his professional medical regime in the health service, see T. Nordby, *Karl Evang* (Oslo: Aschehoug, 1989).

76. K. Evang, *Rasepolitikk og reaksjon* (Oslo: Fram Forlag, 1934), 130-31.

77. I. B. Carlsen, "Moderne slektshygiene og kristen livsoppfatning," *Kirke og Kultur,* no. 7, (1933): 401-14.

78. Author's conversation with Tove Pihl, June 1980.

79. *Stortingsforhandlinger 1934,* vol. 8, "Lov om sterilisering" (8 May 1934), 157-62.

80. Samfundspartiet had a single representative in Parliament during part of the 1930s. The party wanted a fundamental reform of the economic system to reach a more just society. One idea was to abolish money in favor of "social credit."

81. I am here following Evang's (1955) classifications.

82. K. Evang, *Sterilisering etter lov av 1. juni 1934 om adgang til sterilisering m.v.* (Sarpsborg: F. Verding, 1955), 14.

83. Ibid., 40.

84. Ibid., 48.

85. See studies by H. S. Aasen, *Rasehygiene og menneskeverd. Nasjonalsosialismens steriliseringslov av juli 1942*, no. 4 (Oslo: Institutt for offentlig retts skriftserie, 1989); and A. Chr. Gogstad, *Helse og Hakekors. Helsetjeneste og helse under okkupasjonsstyret i Norge, 1940-45* (Bergen: Alma Mater Forlag, 1991).

86. Aasen, *Rasehygiene og menneskeverd*, 43-55.

87. See *Universitet i Oslo, 1911-1961*, vol. 1, (Oslo: Universitetsforlaget, 1961), 634-35.

88. Quelprud became a member of the Norwegian Nazi party "Nasjonal Samling" (National unity) in 1933 or 1934, but resigned in 1936 because of the biological ideas propagated in the newspaper of the party. He joined the party again toward the end of 1941, and resigned finally in September 1944. Soon after that he closed down his institute. Quelprud's professional activity during the war years was concentrated on research and teaching (Thordar Quelprud folder in "Landssvikarkivet," Norwegian National Archives, Oslo).

89. Evang, *Sterilisering etter lov av 1. juni 1934 om adgang til sterilisering m.v.*, 13. I have not been able to verify to what categories those sterilized under the Nazi Law belonged. But since the law did not even provide for sterilization on the application of the person to be sterilized it seems quite clear that the proportion sterilized on purely eugenic grounds and under more or less strong forms of coercion was higher than earlier.

90. Gogstad, *Helse og Hakekors*, 209.

91. Ibid., 195-215.

92. G. Langfeldt, "Psykiatriske arbeidsoppgaver i etterkrigstiden," *Tidsskrift for den Norske Lægeforening* 65 (1945): 307-10.

93. Evang, *Sterilisering etter lov av 1. juni 193*, 43.

94. K. Bonnevie, "Slekt, individ og samfund," *Norsk Slektshistorisk Tidsskrift* 11 (1948): 244.

95. J. Scharffenberg, "Genetikk, arvelære og eugenikk," lecture to Arvelighetsforeningen, 22 March 1951, manuscript collection, University Library, Oslo, 25.

96. Ibid., 40.

97. N. von Hofsten, "De arvsbiologiska verkningarna av sterilisering," *Hygiea. Medicinsk Tidskrift utgiven av Svenska Läkaresällskapet* 106, no. 5 (1944): 179.

98. Ibid., 179-80.

99. N. von Hofsten, "The genetic effect of negative selection in man," *Hereditas* 37 (1951): 157.

100. Evang, *Sterilisering etter lov av 1. juni 1934*, 37.

101. Ødegård, *Arv og Miljö i Psykiatrien*.

102. T. Kemp, "Genetic-Hygienic Experiences in Denmark in Recent Years," *The Eugenics Review* 44 (1957): 16-17.

103. D. Barker, "The Biology of Stupidity: Genetics, Eugenics and Mental Deficiency in the Inter-War Years," *British Journal for the History of Science* 22 (1989): 347-75.

104. N. Roll-Hansen, "Geneticists and the Eugenics Movement in Scandinavia," *British Journal for the History of Science* 22 (1989): 345.

105. See, for example, G. Allen, "Geneticists, Eugenics and Class Struggle," *Genetics* 79 (1975): 29-45; K. Roth, "Schöner neuer Mensch," in *Der Griff nach der Bevölkerung*, ed. H. Kaupen-Haas (Nordlingen: Delphi Politik, 1986), 11-63; S. Weiss, *Race Hygiene & National Efficiency: The Eugenics of Wilhelm Schallmayer* (Berkeley: University of California Press, 1987); and P. Weingart, J. Kroll, and K. Bayertz, *Rasse, Blut und Gene* (Frankfurt: Suhrkamp, 1988).

106. See, for example, the review by H. J. Muller of the famous textbook on *Human Heredity* by Erwin Baur, Eugen Fischer and Fritz Lenz (English translation 1931). Muller praises the first part of the book but finds the second part full of scientific fallacies due to racist prejudices. As Fischer and Lenz "venture into psychology, anthropology, history and sociology . . . we soon find them acting as mouthpieces for the crassest kind of popular prejudice. Throwing overboard their previously admitted principle that environment as well as heredity is of immense importance in the development of human characteristics, particularly those of a mental nature, they readily accept all the superficially apparent differences between human groups as indicative of corresponding genetic distinctions" H. J. Muller, *Studies in Genetics: The Selected Papers of H. J. Muller* (Bloomington: Indiana University Press, 1962).

107. M. B. Adams, "Toward a Comparative History of Eugenics," in *The Wellborn Science: Eugenics in Germany, France, Brazil, and Russia,* ed. M. B. Adams (Oxford: Oxford University Press, 1990), 220.

108. P. Weingart, "The Rationalization of Sexual Behavior: The Institutionalization of Eugenic Thought in Germany," *Journal of the History of Biology* 20 (1987): 160.

109. S. Weiss, "Wilhelm Schallmayer and the Logic of German Eugenics," *Iris* 77 (1986): 34.

110. S. Weiss, "The Race Hygiene Movement in Germany," *Osiris* 3 (1987): 195, 236.

111. The ideological symbiosis between science and the welfare state is now attracting much attention from scholars. For example, Lennart Olausson at the Center for Science Studies at the University of Göteborg is studying the interaction between social science and educational policies in Sweden.

112. Kevles, *In the Name of Eugenics*, 244ff.

113. Author's conversation with Einar Kringlen, 11 June 1992.

114. Nordby, *Karl Evang*.

115. See, for example, R. Slagstad, "Prövingsretten i det norske system," *Nytt Norsk Tidsskrift* 6 (1989): 349-50.

116. An ombudsman is a civil official to whom one can appeal administrative decisions and address other grievances concerning public administration.

From Race Hygiene to Sterilization: The Eugenics Movement in Finland

Marjatta Hietala

Introduction

Finland passed sterilization legislation in 1935 as part of a general Nordic movement, following Denmark (1929) and Norway (1934), with a Swedish sterilization law also coming into effect in 1935. Why was Finland willing to adopt such a eugenic legislative program?

Finland's position is particularly interesting for two reasons: there was an influential Swedish-speaking minority in the country which considerably influenced the development of eugenic thinking; and the country did not gain its independence until 1917 and was still in the process of building national confidence in the 1930s.

From 1809 to 1917 Finland was an autonomous Grand Duchy of the Russian Empire. During this time, the period of autonomy, its administration was a legacy from pre-1809 Swedish rule, and the Swedish-speaking minority (in 1900 12.9 percent) continued to hold most influential positions in administration, industry, and commerce. The majority of schools in the country were Swedish-speaking. Even though the position of the Finnish-speaking population was gradually gaining strength, actual struggles over language, for example about using Finnish in university teaching, did not begin to appear on a major scale until the 1920s.

The Finnish speakers wished to gain improved access to the upper echelons of power and were committed to the creation of a new national culture with its own independent identity. In general, Finnish society in the nineteenth century has been described as strongly conservative in outlook and marked by a deep division between the educated classes and peasantry, a division reflected in wide differences in levels of education, learning, and social attitudes. On the other hand, due to the work of the church, literacy was at a high level, education was generally accepted as a means of upward social mobility and, as elsewhere in the Nordic countries, huge popular movements with educational and instructional aims sprang up. During the closing years of the autonomous period the attitude toward the Russians changed from previous loyalty to deep antipathy, caused by the oppressive measures instituted by the Russians.[1]

In 1918 the newly independent Finland experienced a civil war, based on ideological differences between socialists and nonsocialists (the Reds and the Whites), the impact of which continued throughout the 1920s and 1930s, for it left Finnish society divided into two hostile camps. The role of the labor movement became a minor one. Yet a number of new laws were enacted at the beginning of the 1920s that dealt with compulsory education, prohibition, freedom of religion, military service, and land reforms that allowed leasehold farmers to purchase the land they worked. Elementary schools spread into rural areas and the number of secondary schools grew substantially. In the realm of higher education Helsinki University was joined by two new universities, the Swedish language Åbo Akademi in Turku, founded in 1919, and the Finnish language Turun Yliopisto in Turku, founded a year later. Åbo Akademi became the only Swedish language university outside Sweden and it had an important role for Swedish speakers in the 1920s.

In the political climate of Finland rural peasant values were the cornerstone of Finnish identity, and rural society was the ideal model for the whole of Finnish society. From the very first years of independence the Agrarian League came to occupy a virtually continuous place in government. No significant social reforms covering the industrial sector were introduced; agrarian-inspired nationalists concentrated solely on domestic values. Many Conservatives preferred to concentrate on highlighting Finland's role as a bastion and outpost of the West pitted against the East. In this they drew on the anti-Russian sentiment and sense of ethnic superiority which had increased during the nineteenth century, particularly among the Swedish-speaking intelligentsia, and which were now adapted to the cause of anti-Bolshevism.

The various attempts made to underline a sense of Finnish identity to complement national independence, and stress the importance of the Finnish language as an ideal medium for expressing that identity, were linked to the feelings of self-confidence which had emerged from gaining independence. It was argued that only a linguistically homogeneous people, one speaking the same national language, could really be assumed to find a strong sense of national purpose while bilingualism in any form spelled dangerous compromise. The emergence of these ideas led many Swedish speakers to conclude that the position of the Swedish-language minority was increasingly threatened.[2]

The Finnish nationalists were interested in other Finno-Ugrian peoples such as the Estonians and Hungarians, while the Swedish-speaking Finns endeavored to develop their links with Scandinavia. At the political level, cooperation with the Finnish-speaking Right and Center was not easy for the Swedish People's Party, although this party was needed in governments for the nonsocialist parties to maintain a parliamentary majority. Many Swedish-speaking Finns also felt some apprehension toward Finnish Socialists. According to the Swedish speakers, the only way to help Finland was to forge closer links with Scandinavia and to safeguard Scandinavian constitutional and political values and the wider Western cultural inheritance. This eagerness to strengthen the ties with Sweden was increased by all the evidence that Sweden had experienced a profound social change.

At the individual level the fight for the Swedish language was not always considered essential. Finnish identity was most important. Consequently, many Swedish-speaking families changed their family names to Finnish ones and/or sent their children to Finnish-speaking schools. Thus, behind a genuine Finnish family name there could be found a long Swedish-speaking tradition. But some of the most eager groups to maintain the links with the Swedish-speaking culture were the Swedish-speaking students.[3]

The struggle between the Swedish-speaking and the Finnish-speaking Finns can be seen not only as a language struggle between the majority and the minority, but also as a struggle for the maintenance of the Swedish-speaking elite in Finland where the position of the Finnish-speakers appeared to be gaining strength. This struggle also manifested itself in the attitudes about, and the willingness to apply, eugenic ways of thinking.

For it was indeed the question of the standing of the two languages that formed the key to the spread of eugenics in Finland. While the English eugenics movement showed a strong tendency toward class consciousness, maintaining the social standing of the upper and middle classes, and the German eugenics movement was driven by anxiety about the decrease in the German population and falling birthrates,[4] the Swedish-speaking minority in Finland eagerly embraced racial hygienic principles in the campaign to improve the stock of Swedish speakers. But the Finnish-speaking population also took some interest in racial hygiene.

AIMS OF THE STUDY

This study will try to explain the birth and development of racial hygienic thinking and propaganda in Finland. I will examine the differences between the two linguistic groups concerning the adoption of eugenic ideas. This approach is inductive. I will analyze those factors which lay behind the laws and systematically analyze articles, speeches, and discussions in the press as well as discussions in the professional journals for medical practitioners, social workers, educators, and lawyers. I will explore whether there were any political connections with the Finnish Right, particularly in the 1930s.

What was the role of the German example at that time? What happened during World War II? How did the Finns adapt other people's models in drawing up their own sterilization laws?

In recent years there has been much discussion of professionalism and specialization. At the turn of the century, especially in medicine, innovation, progress, and scientific advance came to be valued highly. Experts became important in the task of changing society.[5] In Finland, reliance upon the printed text was strong because of its centralized administration model and because of the monolithic Lutheran state religion. People trusted experts and professionals. Training and trained people enjoyed high esteem and one of the most valued groups was the medico-legal experts.

In addition, the dimension "individual—community" had a special importance in relation to the issue of sterilization, for the political philosophy of Finland during its struggle for independence was based on the tenets of J. V. Snellman, a Hegelian philosopher. According to his teaching, the individual should always make himself subservient to the interests of the community.

In light of my former research,[6] I will consider sterilization in Finland from the standpoint of the spread of innovations. Finnish researchers did not develop the idea of sterilization but adopted it from other sources, applying innovations and ideas worked out elsewhere. This approach can also be used as the theoretical point of departure, if necessary, and it influenced the selection of research material and the method of observation.

Innovations were seized upon first by those intermediaries who have been described by terms such as "opinion leaders," "pioneers," and "pathbreakers." As a result of their own experiences, they had knowledge of the innovation itself and faith in it. They considered it so worthwhile that they wanted to convince others of its value. Yet it may also be that the role of actual "convincer" fell to somebody else.

Numerous questions will be explored here, such as who brought racial hygiene to Finland and from which sources. Who were the opinion leaders in Finland on this issue—among the Swedish-speaking population and among the Finnish speakers? What was the motivational background of these opinion leaders? To what professional groups did they belong? How had these experts from different professions become involved in eugenics? In what form did they introduce the ideas of racial hygiene and what effect did these have on public opinion? How were they able to convince the Finnish people to the extent that in 1934 only fourteen members out of a Parliament of 200 voted against the Sterilization Act?

THE QUESTION OF THE RACIAL ORIGINS OF THE FINNS

Since the eighteenth century Finns have aroused interest among anthropologists and linguists because of their language. The Finnish language belongs to the Finno-Ugric group of languages, which are spoken by only twenty-three million people even today.

In the circles of physical anthropometry and craniometry many different opinions were presented concerning the Finns. According to the established differences among European peoples classifications in the nineteenth century, Finns were considered "inferior" people. At first they were classified as brachycephalous and Mongols; later, however, the concept of an East Baltic race arose as a compromise. In the 1920s the German Hans F. K. Günther began to employ the term "East Baltic," but as an "Aryan" himself he saw the East Baltic and, indeed, all eastern peoples in negative terms.

The Swedish-speaking part of the population of the country, however, was considered to belong to the more noble Nordic race. Pro-Swedish elements even claimed that Finnish speakers could not be expected to maintain the Swedish speakers' cultural standards.

In an independent Finland the Finnish Academy of Science launched an extensive anthropological research project in 1924, under the leadership of Yrjö Kajava. A great number of medical students worked on this project which was financed by an annual state grant, and research was carried out among the populations of the various provinces as well as among the Lapps and the Swedish-speaking population in Finland. The results of measuring some 15,000 people were published by the academy in printed form which made a tremendous amount of information about the somatic characteristics of the Finns available for the first time, providing a wealth of material for native and foreign racial research. This reflected the interest in the racial qualities of the Finnish people, typical of the early days of an independent Finland, but it was also connected with the racial theoretical research interests of that period.[7]

In the 1920s the features of the East Baltic race were first identified with those of the Finnish-speaking people. But as research progressed, it was discovered that some characteristics of that race were present also among the Swedish-speaking population and that over the years these two races, the East Baltic and the Nordic, had been mixed with each other. In his 1940 article,

"Antropologi och demografi," Harry Federley (who will be discussed later) suggested that the Nordic element was more dominant among the Swedish-speaking Finns. The purest form of the Nordic type could be found in the Åland Islands. The East Baltic race, whose status as an independent race was disputed among anthropologists, differed from the Nordic one mainly because of its lower height, its more square facial features, and the shape of the nose, which was observed to be often broad and slightly snub. The skin was fair but florid, and the chin was not prominent as that of the Nordic race. In the 1930s and 1940s, scientists such as Federley no longer classified the psychological characteristics of these two races, noting merely the existence of these physical differences. By implication, however, there emerged differences in the level of cultural development which manifested themselves in the state of general health and hygienic conditions; this was supported by statistics which demonstrated that, for example, infant mortality was lowest in the areas of the oldest culture, that is, in southwestern and southern Finland. The further east and north one went, the higher the rate of infant mortality.[8]

By the 1930s and 1940s Finnish speakers reacted with considerable equanimity to these race classifications.[9] But during the civil war in 1918, opinions in Finland about such supposed differences between the two races were inflamed. The victory of the Whites was interpreted in Swedish-speaking circles as a victory for Western culture while the Reds were associated with Mongols.[10]

The notion of Finns as Mongols remained, for example, in Swedish encyclopedias well into the 1950s,[11] even though the belief in the Mongol origin of the Finnish speakers began to be refuted systematically in the early years of Finnish independence. One of the most obvious public methods was the organization of beauty contests, the first of which occurred in 1919 followed by another in 1926, with the judging in both cases depending entirely on photographs. The aim was to discover an enduring ideal of womanhood as an expression of Finnishness. In this way the outside world's image of the Finnish race was meant to be rectified and a better image marketed, for the Finns themselves felt that their country, so recently independent, had to provide the world with a more truly representative picture of its inhabitants.

The goal of the beauty contests was to dispel the prejudices which appeared, for example, in foreign literature, suggesting that the Finns were an ugly people. Independent Finland also needed its national symbols to increase its own feeling of solidarity. The winners of the beauty competitions were to become the representatives of a racially pure Finnish womanhood in the eyes of the rest of the world. Even serious artists, including Wäinö Aaltonen, the sculptor, are now believed to have been trying to create in their work a new female image which differed from the prevailing stereotype of Mongol-like Finns. It was a real triumph for Finland when Ester Toivonen was declared Europe's most beautiful woman in 1934. This victory in the Miss Europe competition played · a real part in reinforcing a positive Finnish identity.[12]

The athletic triumphs of Finns also served the same purpose. Finland became world famous in 1912 by winning nine gold medals at the Stockholm Olympics, thereby taking its place among leading athletic nations, a place it continued to occupy for a number of decades. The greatest hero was Hannes Kolehmainen, winner of the 5,000-meter and 10,000-meter events and the marathon, who was said to have "run Finland on to the world map." Far and away the most famous runner, however, was Paavo Nurmi, who won nine gold medals and three silver medals in the Olympics between 1920 and 1928. At the Paris Olympics alone he won five gold medals, two of them on the same day.[13] During his career Paavo Nurmi also set thirty-one outdoor track world records. Onni Okkonen, the art historian and Nurmi's contemporary, wrote the following regarding a statue of Paavo Nurmi: "Paavo Nurmi is the symbol of the Finnish athletic ideal. This statue embodies forever the racial type of a quiet, determined and untiring character who steadfastly reaches his goal in life."[14]

THE ROLE OF EXPERTS

In spite of its northern geographical location, Finland was not isolated from developments elsewhere in Europe. During the period of autonomy its intelligentsia maintained intensive contacts with Central Europe, and at the end of the nineteenth century Finnish doctors and engineers studied for long periods in German universities. German was widely spoken by Finnish engineers and technical researchers.

The medical faculty of Helsinki University, Finland's only university before the 1920s, had strong ties with the German-speaking world. As late as 1935 a total of forty-six out of sixty medical textbooks used in this facility were written in German.[15]

In addition, both Swedish-speaking and Finnish-speaking doctors and scientists had their own personal networks of links with foreign colleagues. Partly as a result of growing nationalism, it was in the interest of the autonomous state to expand professional education. An increase in the number of high-level personnel well-grounded in science and technology would help to build Finland into a truly modern state. Like their counterparts in Germany, members of the Finnish government believed that scientific achievement was a necessary ingredient in building up the *Kulturstaat*. Medical experts in particular had a key role to play in developing the health, welfare, and hygiene of the nation.

On the basis of the traveling reports of Finnish surgeons, one can calculate that about two-thirds of all their trips were made to German universities. At the turn of the century Finnish doctors often participated in courses there on hygiene, psychiatry, tuberculosis, gynecology, and pediatrics.[16] They were also in the habit of touring extensively in Europe to attend congresses which in turn gave rise to subsequent reports, some of which were very detailed, in one case reaching a length of 600 pages.[17] Finnish doctors were aware of the main trends in medicine and related studies, partly through observations of their own and partly through professional journals. Finnish tradition demanded an intensive following of international developments, a custom which provided one of the most important foundations for the country's subsequent independence.

In contrast with these strong ties with the German university world, which continued well into the 1930s, links with British and French academic circles were weak until the mid-1930s.[18] Thus, in addition to the German links, the other major channel for the spreading of new ideas was the keen following of Nordic developments. Due to linguistic and other cultural contacts the Swedish-speaking Finns had worked in close contact with the other Nordic countries, and especially with Swedish experts. At its best this can be observed in the activities of the Svenska Litteratursällskapet and the Samfundet Folkhälsan i Svenska Finland. On the emotional-cultural level, the close connection among Swedish speakers was recognized and both Ossian Schauman and Harry Federley employed the terms "*Vårt svenska folk*" (our Swedish people) or "*Den svenska stammen*" (the Swedish tribe) to link Swedish-speaking people in Finland with those in Sweden.[19]

From its earliest days the Nordic countries were closely involved in the international eugenics movement.[20] The Nordic race, which was much admired, was also one of the topics at the International Congress of Eugenics held in New York in 1921. The Third Congress of Eugenics was attended by the Finnish professor Harry Federley, whose membership was proposed by Herman Lundborg.[21] Federley had been involved in the eugenics movement for some years, and as early as 1911 he had been approved as a member in the Internationale und Deutsche Gesellschaft für Rassenhygiene in Germany.[22]

THE FIRST EXPRESSIONS OF EUGENICS IN FINLAND, 1890-1920

At the turn of the century, when Mendel's laws were discovered, biology in Finland still followed, in part, a strongly Linnaean tradition, but Darwinism was emerging as the new leading force in natural science. There was relatively little experimental biology and this probably caused the delay in the acceptance of Mendelism. The first detailed presentation of Mendel's rule and its relation to the newest theories of heredity was by T. H. Järvi. At that time the first popular presentation of Darwinism in Finnish also appeared.

The majority of supporters of the eugenics movement were followers of Mendel and attempted to discover those combinations of inclinations which, in certain circumstances, would lead to the development of antisocial characteristics. Special attention was paid to the role of heredity in the development of epilepsy, mild retardation, and of alcoholism.[23] The first signs of the emergence of eugenic thinking in Finland date back to 1908 when Robert Ehrström gave a lecture on the spread of neuroses in the period 1890-1907. He was convinced of the hereditary nature of the condition and believed that it was influenced by endogenic factors. According to Ehrström there were fewer cases of neurotic stomach conditions in the Swedish-speaking areas of Finland. His discourse provoked a lively discussion which included, for example, mention of the sparsity of population in the Finnish-speaking areas and its possible effect on mental health.[24] At this time eugenic ideas were still of greater interest to Swedish speakers than to Finnish-speaking people.

It was, however, only some years later, after the publication of the reports of the Congress of Family Research in Giessen in 1912 and the Eugenics Conference held in London, that expressions of racial differences from the medical point of view arose again. In the same year Georg von Wendt wrote a book, "Våra plikter mot kommande släktled. Några grunddrag ur den allmänna rashygienen" (Our duty to the future generations. Some principles of general eugenics), in which he joined battle with "racially harmful" elements.[25] This work was translated into Finnish the same year and it was published in the *Ajankysymyksiä* series. In his foreword von Wendt stated that "The aim of this booklet is to be an inspirer. Even if as a result of it only one single degenerate individual fewer is born to suffer and to spread suffering to future generations, then the book will have fulfilled its given task."[26]

On 7 March 1912 the Ekonomiska Samfundet i Finland gathered to hear a lecture by Professor Albert Palmberg on the social and national consequences of the current birthrate and rates of infant mortality. In line with the spirit of the times he also discussed eugenic measures even though the main emphasis of his talk was on efforts to lower infant mortality. Palmberg held the opinion that "It would be fortunate for society if reproduction by idiots, alcoholics and other degenerate people could be prevented."[27] Like colleagues in other countries at the beginning of the century, Palmberg, who had devoted his whole life to the battle against epidemic diseases and the improvement of hygiene, saw the mentally ill, alcoholics, and people with deviant behavior as "degenerate."

In 1913 Finns were given the opportunity to hear a lecture by the Swedish eugenicist Herman Lundborg, then a docent of psychiatry, on trends in eugenics, in connection with which he presented a report on his genealogical research projects.[28]

In the article "Rashygienen en samhällsplikt" (Eugenics a social duty), published in the *Hufvudstadsbladet* on 11 January 1913, strong emphasis was placed on the degeneration then apparent among civilized nations. For example, in France, as first nation in Europe, the birthrate had fallen below the mortality rates. "When this trend coincides with the degeneration of the people the situation is more alarming. This is proved by the decrease in numbers of men fit for military service, the inability of mothers to breastfeed their babies and the increase in alcoholism and venereal diseases."[29]

The article appealed to the intelligentsia of Helsinki, asking them to take a serious view of eugenics and not to consider it merely an "elegant epidemic," for "what do all our cultural achievements mean if they vanish with us and if our heirs are no longer capable of maintaining our standards because of their physical and psychological weaknesses?"

The idea of sterilization was discussed publicly at the 6th Nordic Conference on the Welfare of the Handicapped in Helsinki in 1912. On that occasion the Danish professor Keller, director of the Bregninge Institute for Idiots, suggested using sterilization in the care of criminals and "morons." At the same meeting Dr. Albert Björkman, then the medical superintendent of the Pitkäniemi Central Institution, suggested the adoption of sterilization "for preventing the ever increasing incidence of mental illnesses, feeblemindedness and mental degeneracy." According to him this measure should be applied to common criminals, sexual criminals, "idiots," genuine epileptics, those long-term mentally ill people who had been discharged from an institution and, finally, to alcoholics who had been treated in institutions at least twice. The director of the Perttula Reformatory, Edwin Hedman, had reached the same conclusions. According to him society should be allowed the right and power to prevent the continuation of a degenerate line and he considered sterilization as one effective measure.[30]

Both Albert Björkman and Edvin Hedman were accustomed to following the international debate. Hedman had also actively participated in Nordic congresses on the treatment of mental illness and Björkman had studied theoretical psychiatry extensively in Germany, Switzerland, France, Great Britain, and Sweden.[31]

At a meeting of the Turku Medical Association on 25 October 1913, Dr. Stråhle suggested that modern eugenics should be included in the topics for debate at the general symposium of medical practitioners to be held later that same year. It was considered important to disseminate information on the reasons for degeneration and possible preventive measures.[32] At their next meeting the association decided to propose the incorporation of the theme into the agenda.[33] This symposium of the Finnish Medical Association debated the issue in 1913 and supported the idea, though it felt unable to take any initiative over the foundation of an association for racial biology.[34]

Kalle Väänänen, a teacher of natural sciences, published the first popular, extensive commentary by a Finnish speaker on the need for eugenics— "Periytyminen ja ihmissuvun jalostaminen" (Heredity and the cultivation of the human race by breeding), which came out in 1916. The book was based on a lecture series given at the Helsinki Workers Institute in the previous year. As his sources Väänänen used "Heredity in relation to Eugenics" by Charles B. Davenport; "Parenthood and Raceculture" by Caleb W. Saleeby; "Fortpflanzung, Vererbung, Rassenhygiene" by Max von Gruber and Ernst Rüdin; "Vererbung und Auslese im Lebenslauf der Völker" by Wilhelm Schallmayer, and "Rasbiologi och rashygien" by Herman Lundborg.

Väänänen began by discussing the influence of Darwin's *Origin of the Species*, then introduced the Mendelian laws, discussed the breeding of plants and animals, and moved to a discussion of human beings in the light of genetics. He explored physical qualities, the heredity of mental abilities, illnesses, malformations, criminality, and alcoholism, and outlined the parasite families of the human race, marriages inside the family, degeneration and the movement for racial improvement. On these points he sought support from Galton and outlined the genealogical research of Davenport. Väänänen adopted a clear view in support of negative racial improvement: "It is wrong, and even criminal, to allow such people who have those hereditary qualities harmful to the race, to produce children. For the only way to eliminate these deficiencies is to prevent reproduction by such people." Equally "harmful to the race" and to society were hereditary diseases such as idiocy, epilepsy, venereal diseases, deaf-mutism, as well as criminality and alcoholism.[35] As a solution he suggested two measures: lifelong isolation, either in prison or in hospital, and sterilization. Väänänen encouraged the use of these methods simultaneously according to circumstances, emphasizing the good results achieved in Switzerland and in the United States by the use of sterilization. He also appealed to the general public not to accept the marriage of physically or mentally disabled people. On the other hand he rejected the very idea that poor and rich people form two different types of human beings. Like many earlier developers of eugenics,[36] Väänänen also took a stand for an improvement in the conditions of the working class. In line with the spirit of the time—and of Lundborg—Väänänen valued conditions in the countryside much more highly than those in the towns. He wanted to prevent migration to the towns by young country people. Similarly, all physically and mentally healthy and strong individuals should be bound more closely to their own land.[37] Finally, Väänänen suggested that an award should be given to all families with more than four or five children, proposing that a tax should be levied on those with only one or two children.

All this may demonstrate the variety of levels at which the movement for racial improvement was perceived in Finland in the 1910s. It meant "faith in the future of a healthy, strong and happy human race and work in those terms for future generations."[38] The qualitative improvement of the people was referred to in several ways, for example, in connection with organizing gymnastics and athletic societies and the temperance movement.[39] Taavetti Laitinen wrote a "table of commandments" for instruction material called "Alcoholism and heredity," which was distributed by the Valistus Association. It may not have been mere coincidence that in the first issue of the *Valkonauha*, a Christian magazine for women concerned with questions of morals and published by Suomen Valkonauhaliitto, the first page was allocated to an article by L. Leidenius, "A little about eugenics."[40] (Later on, the same association fought against moral corruption, for example, by attacking film programs and demanding censorship.)

The picture that emerges in Finland during the 1910s shows that the most active supporters of eugenics and sterilization were the chief medical officers of the mental asylums, the directors of reformatories, and those responsible for child welfare, although some representatives of the temperance movement, such as Taavetti Laitinen, were also involved.

RACIAL CAMPAIGN AMONG SWEDISH-SPEAKING PEOPLE IN THE 1920S

Samfundet Folkhälsan i Svenska Finland

In an independent Finland the eugenics movement received its first support from the Swedish-speaking doctors and population. The key figure was Harry Federley and the key association, the Samfundet Folkhälsan i Svenska Finland (Association of public health in Swedish-speaking Finland). This association, which is described as a "Eugenic Society" in Davenport's papers, was established in 1921 to promote public health in Swedish-speaking Finland. Yet eugenic work had already been adopted by its forerunner, the Florinska Kommissionen, which had promoted scientific research on the mental and physical health of the Swedish-speaking minority as well as on the circumstances affecting it.

The Samfundet Folkhälsan i Svenska Finland embarked on a battle to maintain the number and quality of the Swedish-speaking part of the Finnish population. This group felt that its opponents were not only the "blind forces of nature" but also the "primitive nationalism" favored, it believed, by the Finnish-speaking part of the population. The supporters of the association consequently adopted the catch phrase, "Det får ej finnas dåliga svenskar i detta land" (There must be no bad Swedish men and women in this country).[41]

Following Finnish independence the relative status of the Swedish-speaking part of the population declined. The 1920s were characterized by attempts to entrench earlier positions, and the fear of a deterioration in the share and quality of the Swedish-speaking part of the population stimulated ideas of racial hygiene and involved comparisons with the Finnish speakers.

In his article, "Eugenic work in Swedish Finland," the first chairman of the Samfundet Folkhälsan i Svenska Finland, Professor Ossian Schauman, claimed:

Finland is inhabited by two different races{not races, people}, the Finnish and the Swedish. The population of Swedish origin amounts at present to 370,000 souls, thus constituting only 11.5 per cent of the whole population. About 10 per cent of the Swedes are spread in small colonies among the Finnish population, while 90 per cent inhabit certain stretches of land along the coast and a major part of the archipelago. The whole area of Swedish settlements amounts to 15,000 square kilometres or to 4.5 per cent of the whole surface of Finland.

Schauman made his case as follows: "The Swedish culture is of a considerably older date than the Finnish. Only 50 or 60 years ago government officials were still mostly recruited from the ranks of the Swedish population. Lately, thanks to intense Finnish propaganda, an ever increasing number of Finnish schools have been founded and the Finnish educated classes are steadily increasing in number." The battle for maintaining the privileges of this minority in an independent Finland involved the publishing of studies of the Swedish-speaking part of the population, the provision of statistics on the distribution of schooling and training places, and information on the location of the

Swedish-speaking population in the various provinces of the country. Already in 1921 it had been noted that at the University of Helsinki there were 2,602 Finnish-speaking students and only 666 Swedish-speaking students. Similarly it was pointed out that the university which used only Swedish in its teaching, Åbo Akademi, had taken in only 140 students.[42] The Swedish speakers wanted especially to maintain their position in the towns. It was claimed that in 1930 the percentage of Swedish speakers living in towns was 35.4 percent whereas only 16.4 percent of the Finnish-speaking population were townspeople. It was part of their case that the Swedish-speaking population wished to live in towns and formed an important part of the upper class. This was supported by educational statistics which showed that, in 1930, the proportion of the Swedish-speaking population with more than elementary education was 16.1 percent compared to 5.3 percent for Finnish-speaking people.[43] With the same keen interest the Swedish speakers also monitored the development of birthrates in various parts of Finland. In general it was observed that the birthrate was decreasing in the southern provinces and was increasing steadily toward the eastern areas.

Both Ossian Schauman, first chairman of the association, and Harry Federley, its secretary, had close contacts with Lundborg and Rasbiologiska Institutet. Like his Nordic colleagues, Ossian Schauman was also interested in the temperance movement. The Samfundet had its own publication and a number of branches, for example, in Espoo and Kirkkonummi. Eugenic instruction had been pioneered, however, by the Florinska Kommissionen of Svenska Litteratursällskapet i Finland (the Swedish Literature Society in Finland), which had begun this work among the Swedish-speaking part of the Finnish population in 1912.

In 1911 the Swedish Literature Society received a donation from Miss Jenny Florin, which was used to establish the Pehr Ulrik Florin Foundation and, on 13 January 1912, the Florinska Kommissionen of the Swedish Literature Society. Later donations facilitated practical measures by the institution. Thus, for example, funds donated by the Captain Bertel Paulig Foundation were used for special awards for mothers from 1919 onward. A donation by the heirs of Wilhelm Schauman, counselor of mining, facilitated the carrying out of a special information campaign in hygiene and the Samfundet Folkhälsan i Svenska Finland was able to establish two new sections, one for research and the other for practical hygiene. During the 1920s much emphasis was placed in particular on the activities of the latter section.[44]

In practice the Samfundet at first adopted a policy of positive eugenics. As early as the 1920s this commission established a total of eighteen district nurses' posts in the country. The district nurses were to work in the Swedish-speaking areas and one of their main tasks was to instruct the population on the significance of eugenics in matters related to personal, domestic, and school hygiene. The further training of the Folkhälsan district nurses included lectures on eugenics.[45] Special attention was paid to temperance work and campaigning against tuberculosis. The association also distributed some 60,000 posters, "Our Ten Commandments," which encouraged the Swedish-speaking population of Finland to display a sense of responsibility and racial awareness. By means of courses and practical advice, expectant mothers were to be instructed in rational childcare and nursing as well as in general hygiene. Lessons on health care were arranged in elementary schools, pupils were examined, and homes visited.[46]

Particular emphasis was placed on the impact of hereditary factors, not only on the individual but also on the whole of the population and its future development. A special advisory clinic for hereditary matters was established in Helsinki. Eugenic propaganda (*rashygienisk* propaganda) was considered to be especially important and at the same time a difficult topic to teach. In Finland the teaching of eugenics was thought to be more successful in the countryside than in the towns. After all, country people were by definition dealing with animals! On the other hand, it was discovered that eugenic theories were unappealing to educated people with a background in the humanities.·

AWARDS FOR MOTHERS

More efficient than instructional programs in promoting eugenics were the awards to mothers already introduced by the Florinska Kommissionen. According to the rules of Samfundet Folkhälsan i Svenska Finland, in order to qualify for an award, the mother had to belong to "the Swedish tribe," she and her husband had to be from healthy Swedish parents, and they had to have at least four children between four and seventeen years old who were mentally and physically healthy, well-groomed, and full of vitality. In the course of eight years, from 1920 to 1928, a total of 601 mothers were indeed awarded a special diploma and 211 mothers received a monetary reward.[47] Table 1 shows the regional distribution of awards from 1920-25.

Table 1. Awards for Women

Province	Year	Applications	Awarded by Diploma	Awarded by Diploma and Monetary Reward
Turku	1920	115	16	11 (500 FMK)
Uusimaa	1921	379	139	48 (500 FMK)
Ostrobothnia	1922	385	231	47 (500 FMK)
Åland Islands	1923	—	86*	—
Turku	1925	83	42	28 (800 FMK)
Total		962	514	134

Source: Harry Federley, "Belöningar för berömlig modersgärning," *Barn och Ungdom. Nordisk socialpedagogisk tidskrift* (1926): 5-6.
* Some of these also received money.

In several of his articles Harry Federley maintained that the basic idea behind the awards to mothers was eugenic, expressing this particularly clearly, for example, in the piece he wrote for the *Archiv für Rassen- und Gesellschaftsbiologie.*[48] It was made clear that the Samfundet wanted to offer encouragement only to the best of the Swedish-speaking families in Finland, those who had able people to give to the fatherland. It was emphasized that the association was not concerned with helping poor or large families but that its aim was to give encouragement to the best in their attempts to move forward. Such people were a great asset. The social status of the award winner was not a relevant factor but only her biological and social capacity (*duglighet*).

Federley admitted, however, that "it is not possible to follow all regulations to the letter for it would require an anthropological study to be done beforehand. It is in any case obvious that because the East Baltic and Nordic races have lived next to each other for hundreds of years this must have resulted in racial mixtures which are now difficult to trace." Therefore, "belonging to the Swedish tribe" indicated merely that the Swedish-speaking Finns had linguistic and cultural rather than racial ties.[49]

The condition in the regulations that the parents should be members of healthy families was intended to open people's eyes to just how important the choice of the right spouse actually was. The best patrimony a child could acquire was a good genotype. The stipulation of a minimum of four children was directly aimed at promoting the survival of the Swedish-speaking parts of the population in as large a number as possible. Clerical families who had produced many of the great men in the Nordic countries were mentioned as a reference group.[50]

Federley spoke of a eugenic awakening. For him the well-being of a country was dependent on the nature of its population. "Nothing can be achieved if its genotype is bad" and "Those people have a great responsibility who amid their well-being do not think about tomorrow but only of this moment—when it is a question of the future of the nation." It was more important to take care of the quality and health of the future generations than to look after the sick, feebleminded, and immoral people.[51]

The emergence among the Swedish speakers of a strong eugenics movement is partly explained by the close connections that the leaders of the movement still had with the other Nordic countries. Already, for linguistic reasons, the Scandinavians formed a reference group. In earlier research papers the rise and influence of the Swedish nationalist movement in the 1920s have also been emphasized, as well as the nationalism especially evident among university students.[52]

In his article, "Det sjunkande födelsetalet ett varningstecken" (The decreasing population, a warning sign), for example, Federley presented a table which showed that there was an alarming decrease in the birthrate among Swedish-speakers and especially among their upper social classes. The decrease in the birthrate was greater in the Swedish-speaking areas than in areas where Finnish was mainly spoken. What was lost in quantity needed to be compensated for by improved quality.[53]

Positive eugenics enjoyed extensive support among the Swedish-speaking part of the population. "A people with a strong sense of race survive better in the fight for existence," claimed Lars Ringbom, who even employed the concept of "a racial instinct" (rasinstinkt). The eugenic way of thinking gave support in this struggle for existence. Eugenics was considered a cultural trend which would save the nation, or part of it, from degeneration. Ringbom was in favor of marriage guidance and family planning services as well as the segregation of mentally retarded or "degenerate" people in labor camps (työsiirtola). In the early 1920s the time was not considered ripe for the establishment of a system of compulsory sterilization.[54] In 1923 Federley reported on the new marriage legislation in Sweden which prohibited the marriages of those suffering from venereal diseases or epilepsy, and he also welcomed a motion on sterilization presented to the Swedish Parliament. The most important thing was the awakening of the population to a eugenic way of thinking.[55]

This promotion of eugenics on the part of the Samfundet Folkhälsan i Svenska Finland belongs, at this stage, to so-called positive eugenics, and its propaganda work can be compared with that of the Eugenic Society in London.

Harry Federley: Pioneer in the Swedish-speaking Eugenics Movement

The most important Finnish representative of the eugenic way of thinking was Swedish-speaking Harry Federley (1879-1951), secretary of the Samfundet Folkhälsan i Svenska Finland. Born in Viipuri in 1879, he had from an early age become familiar in his own home with Swedish-Finnish cultural traditions and displayed a keen interest in the arts and sciences. In 1896 he enrolled in the University of Helsinki, joined the Swedish section of the Uusimaa Student Nation, and began to study his chosen subject, biology. His first publication dealt with botany. Later on he diverged into zoology, particularly lepidopterology, and published his dissertation on butterflies in 1907. By then he already had some notion of the significance of chromosomes in heredity, an idea which he had come across when researching the relationship of chromosomes in the bastards of butterfly genera. His extensive treatise on the chromosomal relationships in these species' hybrids, entitled "Das Verhalten der Chromosomen bei der Spermatogenese Pygaera anachoreta, curtula and pigra sowie einiger ihrer Bastarde," appeared in 1913. This classic study was published in the leading genetics journal of the time, *Zeitschrift für induktive Abstammungs- und Vererbungslehre*, and its importance was soon realized wherever genetics were studied.

Federley's research findings created great interest in the world of science. Such men as the Danish geneticist Johannsen wrote of "the brilliant research work" of Federley and in 1912 he was invited to become secretary of the Finnish Academy of Sciences. In 1909 he had already been appointed reader in zoology but exchanged this post in 1915 for the readership in genetics, which had been introduced as a new discipline into Helsinki University's curriculum, and held the chair of genetics from 1923. The research of the department focused on chromosomes. Federley continued his studies of lepidopteran cytogenetics but he was also active in other areas of genetics including the role of heredity in human welfare.[56]

Federley maintained close contacts with a great number of scientists, Swedish and German in particular. Corresponding with hundreds of them, he had to make 300 offprints of his articles. Between 1916 and 1919 Federley stayed in Stockholm with the support of a Rosenberg traveling grant and from September 1929 to January 1930 he worked in Berlin in the laboratories of Professor Richard Goldschmidt in the Kaiser Wilhelm Institut. The wide

Nordic contacts Federley had made manifested themselves when he was invited to be a member of the Academy of Science in Stockholm, Oslo, and Copenhagen. In the field of eugenics he made a notable career as secretary of the Samfundet Folkhälsan i Svenska Finland and as its chairman from 1937 on.

Harry Federley also became a popularizer of eugenic ideas and genetics, and being a staunch believer in popular education, he was not only a member of the board of the Finnish Red Cross but also got involved in the work of such organizations as the Svenska Folkskolans Vänner (Friends of Swedish elementary schools) and the Delegationen för Svenska Literaturens Främjande (Delegation for promoting Swedish literature).

Federley was most anxious about the current state and future of the Swedish-speaking part of the population, and the ideas he put forward were the same as those of his European colleagues, such as his friend Herman Lundborg. As has been noted earlier, he did not approve of the sharp decrease in the birthrate, especially among the upper social classes. Federley was also concerned over degeneration in general. Environmental factors were secondary when compared to hereditary characteristics. If one concentrated only on improving environmental circumstances, no permanent improvement would be achieved. One would only be able to make an impact in each particular generation while the choosing of parents would be most important for future generations.[57] Like Herman Lundborg he also believed that the risk from hereditary conditions was greater in cities. Federley thought that a healthier population stock existed in the countryside, but according to him this healthy rural population was no longer sufficient to revitalize the urban population because the resources of the countryside had been exhausted. Particularly alarming, in his opinion, was the fact that the poorer strata of the population had the largest families.

As early as 1926 Federley suggested that because marriage counseling and propaganda had proven ineffective, special segregation or sterilization measures should be considered for those with an "inferior" genetic inheritance. As a member of the state committee on sterilization he returned to these issues in 1927.

In his article, "Degenerations faran och dess avvärjande sterilisation" (Risk of degeneration and its removal by sterilization), in the same year, Federley debated whether the notion of sterilization was alien to the Western concept of justice. Nevertheless, he believed that only with a law allowing compulsory sterilization could real results be achieved. Such a measure alone could have a positive impact in the fight against degeneration.[58]

Federley keenly followed developments in the United States, Sweden, Norway, and Denmark, and he was interested in the institutes of eugenics and the research carried out in them. He also corresponded with the leading Scandinavian representatives of the eugenics movement, such as Herman Lundborg and Jon Alfred Mjöen, who were the central contact figures in the Nordic countries. He corresponded extensively with the Norwegian Otto Lous Mohr, mainly on genetics research, and similarly with Charles Davenport in the United States.[59] After World War II Mohr especially seems to have confided in Federley when criticizing the representatives of the German eugenics movement.

In Federley's international communications eugenics played only a small part. Thus the correspondence with Alfred Ploetz, for example, dealt almost entirely with the concerns of lepidopterists, and in the correspondence with Fritz Lenz eugenics was mentioned only on three occasions—when Lenz is recommending to Federley the book "Die biologischen Grundlagen der Rasenhygiene" by Siemens,[60] when he mentions the popularity of a book by Baur Fischer and Lenz on which he asks Federley to comment, and when he invites Federley to contribute to a festschrift in honor of Alfred Ploetz.[61] In a 1924 letter to Federley, Fritz Lenz expressed his reservations about the activities of both Lundborg and Mjöen, but at the same time he seemed to believe the movement for racial hygiene (die rassenhygienische Bewegung) was becoming more scientific.[62]

Federley also visited the Eugenics Institute in Uppsala, Sweden, where Herman Lundborg was director, and gave lectures on such issues as criminality and the study of twins. Like Mjöen and Lundborg, he focused his attention on alcoholism and criminality.

As his leitmotif Federley maintained that it was not the external circumstances of a nation but the inner vitality which decided its future development: A healthy people full of vitality cannot be destroyed by violent catastrophes or plagues, but will survive however bad the external circumstances may be. Therefore, all possible defects harmful to the human race and influencing heredity should be eradicated.[63]

Harry Federley was a serious scientist. He was also a good lecturer who attracted handsome audiences, considering the small total of students at Helsinki University in the 1920s and 1930s. Thus his lectures on general genetics were followed by eight to twenty-three students and his first lecture course on human genetics drew an audience of forty-two.[64]

During the 1920s and 1930s, any interest in eugenics among the medical profession was slight and thus little public criticism emerged with respect to the eugenic writings which he published frequently in the late 1920s and the first half of the following decade. At the beginning of the 1930s, Federley had to refute prejudices related to eugenics as a method of promoting the advance of one certain race, but it was only during the preparation of the Sterilization Act and after the enactment of this law that his ideas met some opposition. Among Finnish scientists Federley maintained close contacts with those studying criminality, such as Veli Verkko, professor of criminology, statisticians such as Ernst Lindelöf, and psychologists such as Arvo Lehtovaara.[65]

In the 1940s, when Federley was chairman of the Samfundet Folkhälsan i Svenska Finland, the activities of this association expanded. With the aid of a bequest from Ossian Schauman, an Institute for Research on Heredity was established in connection with an institute for training children's nurses, also founded by the association. According to Federley, this new institute would strengthen the links with Scandinavia.[66]

To summarize, eugenic ideas first gained support from the Swedish-speaking Finns in the 1910s, for from that point on, such ideas fitted well into a campaign, steadily gaining in momentum, which aimed at maintaining Swedishness in Finland.[67] In 1923, in his article "Rashygieniska syften och mål" (Racial hygienic aims and objectives), Lars Ringbom reproached the Finnish-speaking part of the population for their indifference toward eugenic questions. According to him, Finnish speakers were interested only in the numbers of the population and not in its quality. He also claimed that the Finnish speakers' "racial sense" was in contrast to that of the Swedish speakers. Ringbom felt that the conflicts over language were about to damage the future of the whole nation.[68]

One may speculate on the reasons for this reluctance on the part of the Finnish speaking part of the population to adopt eugenic ideas. One explanation may be that the Finnish-speakers were, at that time, much engaged in the establishment of a national identity and in refuting the racial prejudices shown toward Finnish people at the international level.

EUGENIC THINKING AMONG FINNISH SPEAKERS IN THE 1920S

People in Finland followed intently the establishment of the Institute of Racial Biology in Sweden; for example, an article on this event was included in *Suomen lääkäriseuran julkaisuja* published by the Finnish Medical Association in 1921.[69] In the same year, on 31 July, *Helsingin Sanomat* featured an introductory article, "Concerning Eugenics," which described various kinds of eugenic measures in different countries. The author of this article considered the theme topical because the Swedish Parliament had recently decided to establish the first national institution for racial research and mentioned that there had been voices in Finland demanding legislative action to prevent racial degeneration.[70]

The next year a fascinating exchange of opinions was published in the humorous column of the Finnish-speaking journalist Tiitus (pseudonym) concerning the racial purity of Swedish people, or what one businessman in Sweden thought about himself and about others. Tiitus gave a summary of an article published in the Swedish daily *Dagens Nyheter*, which disapproved of mixed marriages contracted by Swedes, especially with Germans, on the grounds that in northern Germany there existed a racial mixture of Slavs, Celts, and Jews![71]

In the 1920s the term "eugenics" began to appear from time to time in Finnish public discussion. For example, during the debate on the prohibition of women's night work in 1927-28, an article was published in *Helsingin Sanomat* with the headline, "The issue of the prohibition of women's night work in industry. Sooner or later this eugenic measure must be undertaken." Behind these sentiments one can discern opinions expressed in Lundborg's writings about industry. At that time there was an assumption that night work was unsuitable for women for eugenic reasons. According to some eugenicists, factory work was bound to lead to debauchery and hedonism. In addition to the new set of values appearing in factories, it was feared that this work would have adverse effects on motherhood.[72]

In the same year eugenic writings appeared in connection with the civil servants' salary question. On 7 September 1928 Vilho Annala, professor of economics, wrote an article with the headline, "The present payment of civil servants and the degeneration of the race," suggesting the consequences to which the planned reduction of civil servants' salaries might lead. The author claimed that civil servants were the elite of the nation. They included the most mentally alert, industrious and decent people who had been able to put their children through secondary schools and universities. Their children would then in due course become civil servants. According to him it was sad that civil servants' families would have to remain small for economic reasons. "Who can guarantee that those unborn because of circumstances would not have included some Snellmans, Kivis and Nobel-prize winners? For it has to be remembered that for the Finnish-speaking element of the population an opportunity has arisen, for the first time in its history, to build up a noteworthy intellectual culture over two successive generations."[73]

THE QUESTION OF STERILIZATION

At the joint meeting of the Finnish Association of Lawyers and the Finnish Medical Association Duodecim in April 1921, Professor Allan Serlachius suggested that persons congenitally retarded should be prevented from reproducing.

He would not, however, wish these measures to be applied to other groups of people. At a public meeting on the welfare of "morons," held in Helsinki in June 1925, the director of the Department of Child Welfare, Baron Adolf von Bonsdorff, introduced a debate on their welfare in Finland. In his speech he also paid some attention to sterilization as a means of combating mental retardation, defending the idea of making sterilization legal by reforming the relevant acts. He opined that even if the mentally retarded could not be eliminated by making them artificially infertile, given that most of them had had healthy parents, the effort should still be made to prevent them from bringing children into the world. Von Bonsdorff suggested that the government should appoint a committee to investigate whether it would be desirable for an Act to be passed in Finland allowing the sterilization of "idiots" and epileptics for social and humane reasons, and that if such a need were recognized a committee should produce proposals for such a law. The suggestions by the introductory speaker were unanimously endorsed by other participants in the meeting.

In 1925 the Medical Association of Turku also discussed sterilization and Dr. Albert Björkman delivered the introductory address. He suggested that there were a great number of mentally ill, retarded, and psychologically "degenerate" individuals among the people of Finland. According to him, this state of affairs was the underlying reason for financial losses, a number of social problems, moral deterioration, crimes, etc., which could not but have a harmful effect on the future development of the nation. He took a stand for both sterilization and segregation as well as institutionalization. The latter, he estimated, would eventually become so expensive for society that any system of isolation in institutions should be complemented with a sterilization program for such persons "for whom it would be desirable, provided it were applied with due consideration." Björkman also included epileptics in the group in question.[74]

By this time a considerable body of opinion had also come to favor the use of sterilization in Finland. In his article "Social reforms which aim to improve racial health," published in the *Sosiaalinen Aikakauskirja*, Federley attempted to encourage the emergence of pro-sterilization attitudes by pointing out that because researchers in genetics had been able to gather extensive genealogical material, for example about psychological deficiencies, it was possible, on the basis of this data, to predict with considerable probability and in some cases with full certainty, how the genes peculiar to these conditions would be inherited. Appealing to his readers, Federley drew attention to a motion already submitted to Parliament which would give doctors the right to sterilize mental patients, "idiots," epileptics, and those sentenced for sexual offenses.[75]

In the 1920s the British Eugenic Society carried out an investigation into the measures of sterilization under preparation in different countries. From its findings it can be concluded that the Nordic countries, the United States, and Switzerland were well ahead of the others. In Indiana, a sterilization act had already passed in 1907, and in the Nordic countries the planning of such a law had reached quite an advanced stage by the 1920s.[76]

On 15 April 1926 the Finnish government appointed a committee to prepare a thorough report on whether a law should be enacted in Finland to facilitate the sterilization of the mentally retarded, the mentally ill, and epileptics, on social and humane grounds. Counselor of Justice Walter Andersin was made chairman and the members were the chief medical officer of the Nickby Lunatic Asylum, Counselor of Medicine Edvard Johan Horelli; an assistant lecturer in the department of surgery at the Helsinki General Hospital, Dr. Arne Johannes Palmén; and the extraordinary professor of genetics, Federley. The first secretary of the committee was a justice of the court of appeal, Lauri Woipio, who was followed, after his death, by Vilho Ebeling, another lawyer. The committee prepared a survey of legislation concerning the mentally retarded, mentally ill, and epileptic in the United States, the Nordic countries, and certain other parts of Europe. It gathered statistical data on these groups in Finland and in the course of its work the committee also invited expert opinion on the necessity of sterilization from the chief medical officers of the lunatic asylums and institutes for the mentally retarded. Those participating included not only Finnish speakers and Swedish speakers but also those of the latter group who had Finnified their family names. All of them supported the main thrust of the committee's proposals for legislation provided that the act adopted the principle of voluntary application. An exception was Aatos Lehtonen, medical officer at the Lunatic Asylum of Turku Prison. In his view antisocial psychopaths should be sterilized without their own consent.[77] On the other hand, the chief medical officer of Pitkäniemi Central Institution, Väinö Mäkelä, took a very critical stand against some of the arguments for the proposed bill. According to him, there was not enough research to prove the hereditary element of schizophrenia, for example, and he proposed that more funds be allocated to genealogical research on topics such as psychosis and epilepsy.[78]

The committee report was completed on 4 May 1929 and it supported the enactment of an act of sterilization.[79] Sterilization should be carried out only with the consent of the patient himself, however, or, if he was not legally competent, with the consent of his guardian. It should be restricted to the mentally retarded, to those with mental illness or epilepsy, and to the congenitally deaf and dumb. On the other hand, criminality, alcoholism, and such behavior as the misuse of drugs should not in themselves be arguments for sterilization, nor should venereal diseases. In addition to the racial, hygienic, and social aims, human advantages were also mentioned. For example, someone who might otherwise need to be confined to an institution could be discharged after sterilization.

In the explanatory memorandum of the report, written by Federley, developments with regard to sterilization in different countries were described, as were the causes of racial degeneration. Among these were included mental illness, mentally retarded, and epilepsy as well as a predisposition to tuberculosis. According to the committee, a strong racial degeneration was taking place in the Western civilized world due to the decrease in the birthrate among the upper classes; while the proportionate share of the most able part of the population was decreasing, the share of the "inferior" part was increasing.

The explanatory memorandum continued, "It hardly needs to be said that human genetic inheritances are different in value. Idiots are nothing but a burden to society and cannot work in any way for its benefit, while the mentally handicapped and criminals can in certain circumstances even endanger society's existence and the development of its wealth. Thus caring for the progress of mankind remains the task of the gifted and diligent. Among the various races and nations these different groups are not, however, represented in equal proportions. In general talented individuals do not emerge as readily among the Negroid races as among the white races, while, on the other hand the percentage incidence of mental illnesses and feeblemindedness is much smaller among the black races."

The committee also collected Finnish material. It estimated that the number of mentally ill was some 14,000, the mentally retarded 10,000, and epileptics 3,000. It also collected information on these same groups under the care of the Ministry of Social Affairs. The committee inquired how many out of these groups were inclined to have sexual intercourse and how many were therefore kept in hospital, old people's homes, or under supervision within a private family. Above all, the members of the committee paid attention to women, inquiring how many of those belonging to the aforementioned groups had illegitimate children, how many of such children there were and how many of them had shown symptoms of mental illness. Replies were received from 529 rural and urban communes, the total population of which was 2,977,413 (the population of Finland at that time was 3,558,000).

The committee envisaged two types of measures for checking undesirable developments. Positive action would involve persuading the "best individuals" to stop limiting the number of their children while negative measures would be aimed at preventing births to "inferior individuals."

The committee's report is of interest for two reasons. It conveyed, with expertly chosen examples, the latest knowledge on medical conditions assumed to be congenital, as well as their incidence in Finland. Its expertise proved convincing to the medical profession, many members of which had prior knowledge of eugenics derived from congresses and foreign travel. Federley also received support from Nordic colleagues.[80]

The detailed descriptions of degenerate families contained in the report, and the accounts of the mentally retarded being looked after by local authorities convinced public opinion of the need for sterilization. Following are some examples of the case studies collected by the committee in which sterilization was held to be justified for genetic reasons. These were important because they were used in the effort to put pressure on local authorities as they made decisions. In all, twenty cases were described of which eleven were women and nine were men. These included not only housemaids but also people who lacked any occupation or any proper trade (the widow of a laborer, for example, as well as an unskilled worker, a man born out of wedlock, a tinker, the ward of a local authority, the daughter of a butcher, an elderly woman, etc.). It is significant that these examples do not include representatives of any of the professions or higher occupations—this was also the case in the mid-1930s, even though Finnish advocates of sterilization had emphasized that any application of the Sterilization Act did not involve considerations of social class or financial background.

S. R. imbecile, twenty-seven-year-old daughter of a butcher; peaceful, could be nursed in freedom at home were it not for her eagerness for sexual intercourse; therefore recently she had been cared for in a district lunatic asylum; at home, gave birth to an illegitimate child.

H. F. imbecile, twenty-one-year-old illegitimate man; as a child ill-mannered and violent, had been nursed for six years in the Perttula Reformatory for Idiots, currently totally calm and docile; had particularly strong sexuality and, to satisfy it, had also practised bestiality.

E. S. imbecile, thirty-year-old housemaid, calm, fit to work, had had seven illegitimate children of whom five were conceived by her mentally ill father; one of the children was an idiot, two were dead and the rest so young that their mental condition could not yet be estimated.

J. M. imbecile woman without occupation, mother had been of dubious reputation and odd, the patient had six children all of them idiots and maintained by the local authorities.

N. N. middle-aged insane man, who believed he would be cured of his illness if he were allowed to have sexual intercourse with a virgin or a pregnant woman.

M. L. elderly epileptic woman with three illegitimate daughters, the eldest of whom had one and the youngest, three illegitimate children, both of whom were again pregnant at the time of reporting.[81]

These cases were frequently quoted in speeches and in the press. They were the main instrument used in the justification of sterilization and in all the attempts to convince the public of the need for such measures.

The press reported extensively on the information collected in the committee report, according to which some 25-30 percent of the mentally ill, mentally retarded, and epileptic in Finland were maintained by poor relief. Moreover, it was claimed that the incompleteness of the data available possibly obscured higher numbers and the costs associated with them.[82]

Subsequently, advisory opinions were solicited from the National Board of Health, the National Board of Prison Administration, provincial governors, the director of the Perttula Institute for Feebleminded, the Inspectors of Poor Relief, and the Association for Mental Health. All these groups were already actively involved in the issue of sterilization. With the exception of the governor of the Åland Islands, all those invited to provide an opinion adopted a positive stance toward the idea of enacting a law on sterilization. The governor of the Åland Islands, however, advocated a suspension of the sterilization debate until adequate information could be gleaned from the application of sterilization laws in other countries.[83]

The committee's report was much more cautious in its tone than the subsequent 1935 Sterilization Act; therefore, we must examine the factors that contributed to the harshness of that act.

THE PUBLIC DISCUSSION OF STERILIZATION 1929-1935

The committee report was carefully noted in the most important newspapers, including the right-wing *Uusi Suomi*, the Agrarian *Ilkka*, the Liberal *Helsingin Sanomat*, and the left-wing *Sosialisti*. All gave the news the same headline, "Statutory sterilization will not be supported. Person's own proposal or that of the guardian must be required," and no extensive debate materialized in the pages of the major dailies though in the *Työläis- ja talonpoikaisnaisten lehti* some attempt was made to provoke public discussion on the related issue of abortion.[84]

The committee report did, however, cause discussion in other arenas. Einar Böök, an expert on social and working class issues, suggested in *Huoltaja-lehti*, the organ of municipal social welfare and private charity work, that the report of the Sterilization Committee dealt only with one group of measures for preventing the degeneration of the nation. He also raised the issue of the need for further special institutions, particularly for the mentally retarded. Many of those in need of care were either wrongly placed in old people's homes or became a burden on the poor relief and could not receive proper nursing or training.[85]

The report of the Sterilization Committee was also discussed in a number of professional journals. In most of the articles deep concern was expressed about the increase in the number of the insane and those with "inferior" genotypes. Greater emphasis than ever before was placed on how expensive the care of the adults alone would be for the country.

A member of the committee, Edvard Johan Horelli, wrote a two-part article on sterilization in *Vankeinhoitolehti* in which he suggested that in 1927 the city of Helsinki had incurred an expense of eleven million marks caring for the insane, the mentally retarded, and the epileptic. He supported sterilization and the provision of care in a closed institution, along with a ban on marriage, because even in wealthier countries it had not been possible, for reasons of cost, to put into effect a full policy of institutional care.[86] He emphasized that the precondition for eugenic sterilization should be that the condition of a mentally ill person was the result of hereditary factors. Horelli was also ready to admit that the basis of criminality was an inferior combination of genes, which made individuals unable to adapt themselves to the social order.[87] Another member of the committee, Arne Johannes Palmén, then the editor of the professional medical journal, *Duodecim,* also wrote about the report in his journal observing that race hygiene research was about to leave the realm of theory and become a practical concern of everyday life.[88]

During this same period, attempts to establish sterilization laws in Denmark, Sweden, and Norway were followed closely in Finland. The Danish legislation forbidding the marriage of the mentally retarded was considered an exemplary model,[89] and Danish proposals for a sterilization act were set out in the *Vankeinhoitolehti,*[90] while the Swedish Sterilization Committee Report, referring to the *Sociala Meddelanden* publication, was introduced in *Sosiaalinen aikakauskirja.*[91] The committee reports for Finland and Sweden were similar in nature. In both, a stand was taken on the principle that the legislation should be based on voluntary action, i.e., the consent of the patient or his guardian should be required and the measure should not be carried out before the individual in question had reached marrying age. Thus in 1929 both the Finnish and Swedish approaches still differed from the American view according to which "a person living in an orderly society must in many respects resign himself to restrictions of freedom if they are necessary for society as a whole."[92] Most of the press articles described in a colorful style the kind of cases that placed a burden on poor relief.

FEAR OF AN INCREASE IN THE MENTALLY RETARDED

The report of the Sterilization Committee did not lead to the immediate publication of a bill, though the matter was under preparation first at the Ministry of Social Affairs and subsequently at the Ministry of the Interior. Nevertheless, at the end of the 1920s, a number of groups continued to take an interest in the organization of care for the mentally retarded.

Certainly during the Depression poor relief was becoming more and more of a burden on the local authorities. In 1928 the Board of the Sielunterveysseura (the Association for Mental Health) submitted a petition demanding an inquiry into conditions in Finnish workhouses. A year later the director of the Perttula Reformatory sent two memoranda to the Ministry of Social Affairs proposing the expansion of that reformatory and the appointment of a special committee to investigate the organization for the welfare of "idiots." In the same year, 1929, Suomen apukouluyhdistys (the Finnish Association for Schools for Retarded Children) submitted a petition to the Finnish government pleading for the appointment by the state authorities of a committee to make an overall survey of care for the disabled. A similar memorandum was also submitted, again in the same year, by Kenraali Mannerheimin lastensuojeluliitto (General Mannerheim's Child Welfare League) suggesting that the government should appoint a committee to investigate issues related to the mentally retarded and asocial children of compulsory school age. In spite of support from the Ministry of Education, however, such a committee was never appointed. Nevertheless, in 1932, Einar Böök, the head of the department in the Ministry of Social Affairs, again made the suggestion that the government should appoint a committee of experts to discuss the welfare of the mentally retarded in the widest sense.[93]

Sielunterveysseuran aikakauslehti was the journal of the Mental Health Association, established in 1919. One of its main concerns was to spread knowledge of socio-hygienic work, so far the most neglected area.[94] From 1931 until 1933 *Sielunterveysseuran aikakauslehti* included articles on eugenics in every issue. The first in the series was the text of a talk on society and the mentally handicapped given by the director of Perttula Reformatory, Reidar Hedman, at the spring meeting of the Mental Health Association.[95] In it he opposed philanthropy, citing the psychiatrist Emil Kraepelin. Like many others he employed as the basis for his estimates of the current situation the calculations of the British Mental Deficiency Committee, according to which the total of the mentally retarded was thousands of the total British population.

Like many of his professional colleagues Reidar Hedman believed in the all-importance of intelligence tests. He thus continued the hard line laid down in 1906 by his father Edvin L. Hedman. The son, too, was of the opinion that it was a fallacy to think that the mentally disabled could be educated. Like his father he considered mental deficiency an incurable illness and wanted to move away from caring for the results of degeneration to the elimination of its cause. Indirectly, Hedman adopted a stand in favor of the sterilization of the inmates of reformatories before their discharge. Hedman based this opinion on research by Fritz Lenz and on the efficient German system of isolating mentally retarded people so that they could not contribute to the increase in population, and, like the Danish Christian Keller, Hedman also linked criminality with mental deficiency. Hedman proposed further measures aimed at preventing the birth of mentally retarded individuals.

Finally, Hedman, at the end of his discourse, touched on sterilization and expressed his new view that as many of the mentally retarded as possible, including those sterilized, should be given an opportunity to receive education, schooling, vocational training, and other necessary relief and care.

When Hedman gave a lecture in Helsinki in 1931 on the theme "Society and the Mentally Deficient," a lively discussion followed and the majority of the audience took a more optimistic stance. It was pointed out, for example, that even if it were not possible to increase intelligence, such characteristics as diligence and good will could help the mentally deficient to manage their lives.[96]

In its last issue for 1931 the *Sielunterveysseuran aikakauslehti* published a comment by the medical doctor S. E. Donner on the report of the Sterilization Committee,[97] and every issue in 1932 discussed eugenics at some point. The first of these contained an article by Ilmari Kalpa, another doctor, in which he discussed preventive measures to be taken against hereditary forms of mental illness,[98] as well as a second article by Hedman on "Mental Health and Public Health."[99] In this second article he suggested that much more attention had been paid to physical health than to mental health.

Kalpa's article was based on a talk given at the 50th Anniversary of the Finnish Medical Association, Duodecim, and suggested that a sterilization act was needed to complement the Marriage Law, even though the latter treated mental illness, epilepsy, and idiocy as barriers to marriage.

Toward the end of 1932 the journal published the texts of two German lectures, one by Professor Ernst Rüdin on the significance of the achievements of psychiatric genetic biology for practical eugenics[100] and the other by Professor Rainer Fetscher on marriage guidance and sexual hygiene.[101] Eugenics was also featured as a topic in a month-long extracurricular theoretical course for trainee psychiatric nurses in 1933. The initiative for arranging this came from the psychiatric nurses themselves and the course took place at the Helsinki College for Nursing. The program included thirty-five hours on race biology and eugenics, psychiatry, neuroses, and mental hygiene along with discussions of mental treatment and welfare.[102]

Among the members of the Sterilization Committee it was Federley and Arne Johannes Palmén who wrote most actively about the dangers of racial degeneration and the necessity of sterilization (vasectomy and salpingectomy). They also strongly opposed the idea of using sterilization as a form of punishment. Palmén emphasized that in some special cases, where the sick person had a particularly strong or misguided sexual drive, castration should also be considered.[103]

At the beginning of 1934 the debate clearly expanded beyond the mentally retarded and mentally ill, and new groups became the subject of debate even though the former groups—estimated to be growing ever larger—remained the center of interest. The press continually published reports on the increase in welfare costs and in 1933 the newspaper *Uusi Suomi* set up an expert inquiry on whether the sterilization of individuals by legal action was desirable or not. Again Federley was one of the respondents, emphasizing the humane purpose of sterilization and making a clear distinction between it and castration. He also tried to rectify the "generally" prevailing opinion that children would also inherit their parent's personal qualities though emphasizing that no doctor could cure inherited inclinations.[104]

In 1934 *Huoltaja*, the professional journal covering municipal poor relief, suggested that Finnish welfare personnel unanimously agreed about the need for an act on sterilization.[105]

PREVENTION OF CRIMINALITY: ATTITUDES GAIN MOMENTUM

At the beginning of the 1930s the debate widened to include crime and its prevention. On the occasion of Crime Prevention Week, 7-13 January 1934, special attention was paid to the links between criminality and racial health and most of the lectures dealt with eugenics. The lectures were considered important enough to be given in Helsinki's House of Estates, in the former Hall of the Nobility, and there was full attendance.

Drawing particular attention was a lecture by Federley in which he emphasized that criminality depended in the first place on genotype and only secondarily on circumstances which could only strengthen or weaken inherited inclinations. Federley based his opinions on the latest research with twins. According to him, "research with twins had strengthened the hand of researchers in genetics in a way they could hardly have imagined." After convincing his audience that both mental illness and retardation were hereditary, Federley proceeded to discuss the work of Johannes Lange, psychiatrist who worked in Munich.

Federley preached that environmental factors were secondary when compared with genetic factors. By attempting to influence environmental factors one could never improve breeding significantly. For crime prevention it was therefore necessary for society to control the reproductive capability of weak individuals.[106] Other lecturers such as the Belgian professor A. Ley and the Swede Olof Kinberg also dealt with the ability of medical science to assist in the prevention of crime.[107]

Some practical aspects of racial health were also given attention. Federley himself provided illustrations of some operative methods for preventing reproduction, presented the findings of the Sterilization Committee on the mentally retarded, mentally ill, and epileptics, and emphasized the need for the speedy adoption of a sterilization act.[108]

The lawyer Brynolf Honkasalo, for his part, discussed the biological, criminal-political, and social reasons for supporting the demand for the adoption of sterilization.[109] As examples of the fertility of mentally retarded mothers, Honkasalo cited the figure of six children per family in Rostock (referring to the studies by Reiter and Osthoff) and presented the figures for Berlin (by Cassel) and Munich (by Prokein) where the mentally retarded had on average three children per couple whereas the average was 1.87 in the case of normal parents.

The future could hardly be bright if the calculations of the German professor Fetscher or the Swedish professor Kinberg became a reality. Honkasalo also extrapolated figures for Finland, when presenting examples collected by the Sterilization Committee. Honkasalo took his stand on compulsory sterilization, placing the interests of society before those of the individual.

During Crime Prevention Week it was also possible to hear a lecture on the trends and causes of crimes of violence in Finland by Professor Veli Verkko, a renowned researcher into criminality who attempted to explain the exceptionally high incidence of capital crimes in Finland in terms of the national character and the soul of the nation.

Yet another speaker was Paavo Mustala, inspector of the Prison Administration. He drew attention to regional differences and opined that the great majority of criminals came from the "socially and medically weak, 'loose' part of the population." He also claimed that unemployment and the use of alcohol had considerably encouraged criminality in recent years.[110] The matron of the Helsinki School of Nursing, Karin Neuman-Rahn, introduced a softer, more sensitive approach describing the varied advisory and welfare services provided in other countries for the mentally ill and those with criminal proclivities. She hoped that similar programs could be launched in Finland.[111]

Dr. Väinö Mäkelä, who had already expressed his doubts about the efficacy of such laws when the Sterilization Committee Report was still topical, again presented his reservations and worries concerning their application. Mäkelä reminded his audience that the hereditary nature of mental illnesses was a very complicated matter.[112]

Mäkelä's opinions may, indeed, have had an effect on the way the Sterilization Act was applied because he was elected as the member representing geneticists on the scientific board of the National Board of Health from 1935 to 1937. In 1936 he presented comments on the sterilization and castration legislation of Finland, the other Nordic countries, and Germany to a meeting of Finnish medical practitioners, and a year later he had an article published in the *Archiv für Rassen- und Gesellschaftsbiologie journal.*[113]

It was reported that in the discussion which followed the lectures the quick enactment of sterilization legislation was generally supported. It is worth noting that the structure of these lectures was very similar. They presented the results of the most recent research in the Nordic countries and in Germany—research and statistics from Germany were greatly trusted by the Finnish people. Many of the speakers and participants in the debate had made at least one or more journeys to Germany, and had even studied there for lengthy periods and personally knew the authors of these studies. In addition, case studies displaying the life histories of the insane, mentally retarded, and criminal individuals could not but have an effect. The examples presented by the Sterilization Committee stuck in people's minds and gave rise to an increasingly strong concern over the rocketing growth in criminality.

It appears that by 1934 the professionals concerned with the welfare of the mentally ill and retarded, as well as those responsible for municipal poor relief had been abundantly informed about the act on sterilization and warned about the degeneration of the racial quality of the nation. Those working in the prisons had received detailed descriptions of "degenerate" families and the work of the Sterilization Committee. The development of positive attitudes toward compulsory sterilization was most probably also helped by the statements of the director general of the National Board of Health, Hannes Ryömä, advocating the establishment of compulsory sterilization for "idiots," "imbeciles," and the "feebleminded." In the course of the year 1934, demands for a sterilization act emerged from many quarters against the background of the passage of similar acts in Denmark, Sweden, Norway, and Germany, while the debate on the sterilization legislation also led to a discussion of birth control and abortion.

There were, however, objections to the sterilization legislation and these were made in two main arenas—in Parliament itself during the discussion of the bill and in the press. Toward the end of 1934, *Tulenkantajat*, the organ of progressive writers, published the comments on the issue of two socialist medical practitioners, both of whom condemned the idea of compulsory sterilization.[114]

The Social Democratic journal *Soihtu* reported a discussion of sterilization by the Hungarian doctor Ferenc Jahn in an article, "Fascism and social policy" which appeared in the *Journal of the Federation of Socialist Medical Practitioners*. The editors of *Soihtu* believed that "the great majority of those in need of society's protection are those made to feel inferior by their social standing. . . . It is not sterilization but better economic conditions and a more all-embracing social policy that would raise those in these lower social strata to the level of appreciated human beings."[115]

Women as Promoters of Eugenics

While the proposed legislation was still under discussion, Kyllikki Pohjola, a Conservative Member of Parliament (MP), wrote an article on the bill for *Suomen Nainen*, the journal of the Conservative Women's Association. The message of Pohjola is evident from the title of the article "Sterilization Bill," where she emphasizes that a society must have the right to prevent the birth of sick people and that sterilization will bring relief for many social problems.[116]

The official crime statistics indicated that between 1927 and 1930 the incidence of sexual abuse of children had increased by 70 percent, and in 1933 the Morality Committee of the Finnish Women's National Federation submitted a petition to the Ministry of Justice pleading that the government should undertake urgent measures to protect minors and young people from sexual crimes. The petition also conveyed the view that women should be appointed as jurors in the rural district courts and pressed for more women constables to whom all police actions concerning girls could be referred.[117]

Women MPs of the Right, and especially the deputy from the extreme-Right IKL, Hilja Riipinen, were willing to incorporate into the law the sterilization of those who had molested minors and corrupted children. Hilja Riipinen's petitionary motion for the adoption of castration in order to protect children and young people from sexual crimes was passed by Parliament in the 1934 session. It also confirmed the proposal to increase the number of women police.[118] During the parliamentary debate in 1935 on the contents of the Sterilization Act, Riipinen called this law the Child Protection Act for, according to her, it would not only protect living children but also the children of the future.

The organ of the Social Democratic Working Women's Federation, *Toveritar*, had also adopted a positive attitude toward sterilization, drawing its evidence from the United States, Germany, and Sweden, where the sterilization laws had already made good progress. Human breeding was compared with that of animals.[119]

This positive attitude of women toward sterilization had clearly been strengthened by recent information concerning the number of sexual crimes. The *Naisen ääni* (Woman's voice), which represented the right-wing women's movement, keenly followed the debate on the sterilization legislation of the 1930s, and its demands even included castration. Once the Sterilization Act had been passed the journal was satisfied that at least some action had been taken for child welfare. Not surprisingly, it also approved the allowance of castration, under a special decree, in cases of convicted child molesters.[120]

Dr. Rakel Jalas was one of those already actively advocating sterilization at the beginning of the 1930s in *Huoltaja*. From 1929 to 1937 Jalas worked as the medical officer in the Ministry of Social Affairs and as the assistant inspector of poor relief. As a member of *Huoltaja*'s editorial staff she had a readily available forum for expressing her opinions. She also took an active part in the work of the Mental Health Association (Sielunterveysseura) and was on the Board of Turva, a home for inebriates. Dr. Jalas served as the vice-chair and later the chair of the Morality Committee of the Finnish Women's National Federation, and it was through this channel that she forwarded her demand for the introduction of castration. Like many other doctors Jalas had made study tours in the Nordic countries and in Germany and Austria.

The leitmotif of Rakel Jalas was, "It is not welfare work as such, but preventive welfare which helps the progress of our society. We should not so much help the poor man as prevent him from becoming poor."[121] Once the Sterilization Act had been passed she widely publicized birthrates among the various social classes and aimed at drawing public attention to measures promoting population growth, such as family allowances, maternity care, the possibility of young people's marrying early, organizing of efficient health care, and providing early sex education.

As for the position of women Jalas was rather conservative and did not, for example, support women's careers for, according to her, working outside the home would lead to a decrease in fertility and would thus be an adverse trend.[122] Her basic ideology was social-Darwinian: no longer does society free itself from weak individuals by the method of natural selection, the instinct which commands the weaker to give way to the stronger, and so in order to survive, society must resort to multifarious other measures and mainly to those which aim at preventing the birth of weak individuals.[123]

THE STERILIZATION BILL OF 1935

Early in the 1930s the burden of municipal poor relief was felt to be so heavy that any measure seemed justified that would bring some alleviation, and the mentally retarded, who were often cared for in old people's homes, formed a natural target as this issue gained increasing attention. Throughout the 1920s the burden of poor relief had been increasing. In 1923, 2.95 percent of the population received permanent or casual relief, but by 1932 the total of those receiving relief had increased to 6.18 percent of the whole population. Since the recipients of relief usually had families, it was calculated that by 1932 the total number of people actually receiving relief was 350,861 or 9.4 percent of the whole population. This was proportionally equivalent to the figures for 1880![124]

It is not surprising, therefore, that the Sterilization Bill had an easy passage at the beginning of the 1930s. Many parallel trends were having an effect simultaneously: the increase in welfare costs, the increase in the number of "unfit" individuals, and the increase in crime. All these were to be read from the statistics on which Finns had learned to rely. Similarly, descriptions of the unfortunate fates of basically "inferior" people, the latest research of scientists, as well as examples from foreign countries, all influenced the decision makers.

During the passage of the government's bill on sterilization, extensive arguments were presented, which basically followed the views already expressed in the 1929 committee report.[125] In the end the Sterilization Act was passed— albeit after hectic debate—with the final vote showing an overwhelming majority in favor. Only fourteen members out of 200 voted against the bill, though the opponents of the Sterilization Act considered it a "Class Act" or one against the law of nature. This was in the parliamentary session of 1934, following a debate in which much use was made of extensive surveys of foreign developments. The Economy Committee of the Parliament considered it important to enact a law on the basis of which deficient and criminal elements in society could be made incapable of reproduction. In this connection it was maintained that the desired results could not depend on voluntary methods and therefore sterilization should be made compulsory. In borderline cases it should be left to the officials' discretion whether the measure was necessary when taking into account the interests of society and a common sense of justice. The committee proposed also that sterilization should be carried out free of charge.[126] The most debated issue in Parliament was the question of whether sterilization should be compulsory. The chairman of the Economy Committee, Professor Reinikainen, a Social Democrat, emphasized that "idiots" and mentally ill people could not undertake voluntary action in this important matter.[127] The representative of the extreme Right Patriotic People's Movement, Professor Sundstrom (later Salmiala), demanded, in the name of a healthy society, the compulsory sterilization of criminals with unnatural sexual instincts who were considered dangerous to other people. He was supported by other MPs of the movement, such as Eino Tuomivaara and Hilja Riipinen.

The minister of the interior, Puhakka, considered the spirit of the bill permissive and not binding.[128] Some other MPs, such as Social Democrat Wiik, believed that the bill was putting poor people in an unequal position compared with more wealthy groups. This aspect was the most debated point in the parliamentary discussions. A more exact phraseology to be used in connection with the application of the law was therefore demanded from various quarters "in order to make sure that the act would not be misused."[129]

After the bill had been passed in the Grand Committee of Parliament its first section was amended to include a clause applying the act also to epileptics if there was a good reason to assume that this disability would be inherited by any future children. Many MPs felt that progress in the application of the Sterilization Act should be cautious and, on the basis of foreign information, they were prepared to exclude epileptics from the bill.[130] Since 1757, as a legacy from Swedish law, epilepsy had been an impediment to marriage in Finland. In the 1929 Marriage Act the statutory impediments also included mental illness and idiocy. People suffering from epilepsy, a venereal disease at a contagious stage, or deafness and mutism required the permission of the president of Finland to marry. For those supporting the sterilization of epileptics, however, this latter regulation was not sufficiently effective. Some MPs of the Left were prepared to reject the Sterilization Act entirely because of their concern for the injustice that might ensue; others as noted above, considered it a class-motivated act. Some also opposed the act because it demonstrated an anti-Christian view of the world.[131]

Professor Matti Väinö, who held a chair in anatomy, was one who opposed the preparation of the act. In the course of the debate he cited many examples of famous men who would never have been born if such an act had been in operation, and similar arguments were used by other opponents of the act.

Lassila was also concerned about the dangers inherent in sterilization operations, claiming that in Germany 2,800 people had died as a result of them. For this reason Federley, wishing to acquire correct information, wrote to his friend Lenz who expressed his admiration that Federley had undertaken to fight the opponents of the sterilization laws. He claimed that the figures presented by Lassila (5 percent) were exaggerated and that the real mortality figure, which mainly involved sterilized women, was only 3 per every 1,000 sterilization cases and was actually decreasing. Lenz agreed with Lassila's other point, however, that the hereditary nature of schizophrenia remained unproved, and claimed that sterilization in Germany had been carried out mainly on the mentally retarded whose illness certainly was hereditary.[132]

TURNING THE IDEA OF STERILIZATION INTO REALITY

The Sterilization Act, which became effective on 13 June 1935, was first discussed in the press by the director general of the National Board of Health, Hannes Ryömä, in the *Huoltaja* and by Dr. Arne J. Johannes Palmén in the *Sosiaalinen Aikakauskirja*.[133] The latter article was also quoted in the *Suomen Poliisilehti*, a journal for policemen.[134]

The Sterilization Act also allowed the voluntary sterilization of legally competent persons if there was a justified fear that, when married, they would produce "inferior" children or if, because of their abnormal sexual drive, they would be a danger to those surrounding them. The act actually went further than the committee had proposed six years earlier by adopting the policy of compulsory sterilization. It decreed that "idiots" (with a mental age less than six), "imbeciles" (with a mental age of six to fourteen), and the insane (e.g., those suffering from schizophrenia or manic-depression) could be made incapable of reproduction on two grounds: first, if there was reason to assume that their disability could be transmitted to the next generation, or second, if it was probable that their children would not be cared for because of such disability. The capacity to reproduce would also be removed from those persons who had been proven, by a non-appealable judgment, guilty of a crime or an attempted crime demonstrating an unnatural sexual drive either in terms of its strength or its direction.

The Sterilization Act and the subsequent statute stipulated that an application for sterilization had to be made in writing to the National Board of Health. An initiative could be taken by the director of a mental hospital or other similar institution and in other cases by the municipal board of health. If the person concerned was in a penal establishment the right to initiate the application was vested in the director of that institution, and similar rights were enjoyed in the countryside by the bailiff or district police superintendent and in the towns by the public prosecutor or the police inspector. In the complementary statute to the act, it was further stipulated that the sterilization application should be processed by the National Board of Health, which was to investigate each case separately and satisfy itself that the measure was necessary. The person for whom sterilization was proposed, as well as his or her spouse or guardian, was also given the opportunity to express an opinion on the case. Sterilization itself could be carried out by using salpingectomy, vasectomy, or castration, and had to be done in a hospital approved by the National Board of Health.

Regarding children still under age it was the duty of the school inspectors to provide information on such cases so that these children could be freed from compulsory education. It was left to the municipal boards of health to investigate the possible need for sterilization.[135]

The major difference between this Finnish act and the Swedish one was that the latter covered a wider range of cases, for it referred also to persons who could be assumed, with good reason, to be unable to care for their children because of mental illness, mental retardation, or other mental disturbance. Nevertheless, the involuntary nature of sterilization under the 1935 Finnish act meant that it was a more far-reaching measure. On the other hand, a decision by the National Board of Health in Finland was required for any operation whereas the decision of two doctors was at first sufficient in Sweden. In Denmark the power of decision-making was vested in the Ministry of Justice.

Interestingly enough, in contrast to their reaction to the committee report, the press now paid little attention to the compulsory nature of the new act. The newspaper of the Social Democratic Party, *Suomen Sosiaalidemokraatti*, and the press of both the Center and Agrarian parties simply reported that the act had become law.[136]

From the very beginning the new Sterilization Act was criticized as being too harsh. Yet many people felt that the act was likely to prove ineffective because it could not prevent callous, shocking "acts of violence caused by the sexual drive" and in 1943 a committee, under the leadership of Brynolf Honkasalo, met to suggest possible amendments. One indicator of the "inefficiency" of the act was the fact that by 1943 only 500 people had been sterilized even though the total number of mentally disabled who could be the object of such sterilization was 15,500 and of these the number of actual "idiots" was over 4,000. In the face of these statistics and citing experience gained by Turunen in Germany, the committee proposed that the act should be enforced more efficiently. In order to reduce sexual crimes castration was proposed and the issue of abortion also arose.[137]

The workings of the Finnish Sterilization Act have been discussed in detail by C. A. Borgström, who wrote his master's thesis under the supervision of Federley himself and was a member of the committee on sterilization. He wrote his doctoral dissertation on the implementation of the act, discussing those sterilizations performed by permission of the Finnish National Board of Health.[138] (table 2) Borgström took a hard-line approach to the application of the sterilization laws.

As early as the beginning of the 1930s Federley had arranged contacts for Borgström with leading members of the German eugenics movement and, when Borgström wrote an article for the *Archiv für Rassen- und Gesellschaftsbiologie*, it was Federley who persuaded Lenz and Rüdin to accept it.[139] Borgström's dissertation of 1955 contains an extensive comparison of the application of the laws enacted in the various Nordic countries during the 1930s.

Table 2. Amount of Sterilizations with Permission of the Finnish Board of Health, 1935-1955

Year	Total	percent of those women
1935-36	54	85.2
1936-37	102	76.5
1937-38	121	81.0
1938-39	112	72.3
1939-40	32	65.6
1940-41	37	78.4
1941-42	27	74.1
1942-43	24	91.7
1943-44	42	88.7
1944-45	37	83.8
1945-46	67	89.6
1946-47	84	91.7
1947-48	73	89.0
1948-49	82	85.4

Table 2. Amount of Sterilizations with Permission of the Finnish Board
of Health, 1935-1955 (cont.)

Year	Total	percent of those women
1949-50	102	86.3
1950-51	189	92.1
1951-52	136	94.1
1952-53	162	87.0
1953-54	201	86.1
1954-55	224	86.2

Source: C. A. Borgström, *Tillämpningen av lagen om sterilisering i Finland 13.6.1935-30.6.1955 kastreringarna obeaktade*, Bidrag till kännedom av Finlands Natur och Folk 103 (Helsingfors: Finska Vetenskapssocieteten, 1958), 50.

The total number of people sterilized between 1935 and 1955, with the permission of the Finnish Board of Health, was only 1,908, of whom 276 were men. During that period the National Board of Health considered 2,286 sterilization cases. In 199 cases it declined the petition for an order to sterilize or the request for sterilization, while in 2,087 cases the decision was in the affirmative. Within this latter group the actual operation was performed in 1,908 cases but not in the remaining 179. On average 95.4 persons were sterilized annually. Of the 1,908 subjects who were sterilized, 1,461 had been ordered to undergo the operation, while 447 (23.4 percent) had requested it themselves. Both orders and permissions increased in number after World War II.

Of those sterilized, 58.6 percent were mentally retarded, 14.5 percent were schizophrenics, 9 percent were epileptics, and 5.1 percent were psychopaths. Among those who successfully requested permission for sterilization the epileptics formed the largest group, followed by psychopaths, schizophrenics, and the mentally retarded in that order.[140] The total number of feebleminded without any other abnormal mental condition was 1,119. The indication for sterilization was eugenic in origin in 61.1 percent of the ordered cases and in 67.8 percent of personal applications.

How did the implementation of the law differ among the Finnish-speaking and the Swedish-speaking communities? In those with a purely Finnish-speaking population the number of individuals sterilized per 100,000 was 28.0 and in communities with a largely Swedish-speaking population the corresponding figure was 15.5. In Åland the local authorities did not bring forward a single petition for sterilization, which was not surprising given the negative comments of the governor of that province. According to Borgström, "It seems reasonable to infer that the Swedish-speaking population in Finland is much less inclined than the Finnish-speaking population to adopt such a measure as sterilization." It remains an open question whether Swedish-speaking medical officers working in Finnish-speaking regions were more efficient than those who could use their native tongue with the patients.

The petition to sterilize was brought by communal boards of health in 54.1 percent of cases, by medical directors of mental hospitals in 25.0 percent, by social boards in 12.4 percent, and by rural commune medical officers, directors of mental institutions, or others in 8.5 percent of cases.[141] Of sterilized people 77 percent were from rural communes, 18.7 percent from towns, and 4.3 percent from urban districts (market towns). In 250 of the 548 communities local authorities did not make a single sterilization petition; 10 or more applications had been made in 12 communities.

The majority of both sterilization applications and of actual operations concerned women (1,632); the number of men amounted to only 14.5 percent of the total of 1,908. There was an assumption that women had an exceptionally strong sexual drive, which was deduced from the number of their illegitimate children. It was also made clear that women's sterilization involved moral arguments. Of all the sterilized women with neuropsychiatric disturbances, a total of 200, or 12.7 percent, were already pregnant when action was taken.

Borgström calculated that the total of 1,908 sterilized at that time already had 3,247 children of whom 2,900 had survived; of those 366 were mentally retarded. He also estimated that the sterilization of those under twenty-six years of age had prevented the birth of some 575 children. Borgström suggested that the annual target for sterilization should be set at 700.[142] The Finnish results revealed the overwhelming majority of the sterilized to be women; these results are parallel to those of international investigations.[143]

From the sterilization applications sent to the National Board of Health, it emerges that small, poor communes were the first to take advantage of the Sterilization Act, a fact ignored by Borgström in his study. Behind these applications there was often a real anxiety about the financial ability of the commune to sustain the mentally retarded as well as apprehension at the increasing growth of their families.

The report of the communal medical officer often tells the tale of an unhappy childhood and of the misfortunes encountered subsequently.

Case A: An Inmate of an Old People's Home

Heredity: Parents nervous, no mental illness; inclined to steal and to sell alcohol
    illegally
Interrelationship of the parents: Not related to each other
Damaged at birth: No
Physical, especially head, injury: None
Periods: Regular
Pregnancies: 2 births; no miscarriages
Misuse of alcohol and narcotics: None
Ability/special talents: Backward
Sexual drive: Strong
First years: Cared for at home when child, passed two forms of the elementary
    school; worked as a servant and spent the last four years at the old people's
    home
When examined: 8 xii 1935
Physical examination: Physically fit
Psychiatric examination: Behavior, posture, movements normal; mood, sensitive,
    gets easily angry; aware of the time and place; weak judgment

In his final comment the doctor stated: "Because XX has a strong sexual
drive and has brought into this world two physically and mentally disabled
children and because she herself wishes to be sterilized I support her application for it on the basis of the 2nd section of the Sterilization Act."

Case B: A Twenty-Eight-Year-Old Woman of an Almshouse

Another case was a twenty-eight-year-old woman from a family of nineteen
members. She had to go to the almshouse after giving birth to an illegitimate
child because her sister no longer wished to give her a home. Her father had
been killed by the Reds during the civil war and her mother had died. The doctor observed that the patient had weak judgment and erotic inclinations.
"Because the sexual drive is very heightened her thoughts appear often to cir-
culate round these matters," and recommended her to be sterilized.

These and similar documents are painful to read, for the individuals
involved were fully at the mercy of society. The most disturbing, perhaps, were
the objective tests used for evaluating the mental development of the subjects.
These tests contained many factual questions to which those with a limited or
nonexistent education were unable to find a correct answer. Thus, one inmate
was questioned about who was ruling Finland and when he said that it was

God the answer was considered a wrong one. Similarly, they had to explain in these tests the message of various proverbs.[144]

POSITIVE EUGENICS AMONG FINNISH SPEAKERS DURING THE 1930S

In addition to the Sterilization Act, which can be classified as a measure of negative eugenics, ideas of positive eugenics were also developing. Anxiety among Finnish-speaking Finns about the decrease in the population became an important topic in the 1930s, when the question was much discussed in the press and many statisticians and social scientists participated in the debate. Gunnar and Alva Myrdal's books were often referred to in Finland. Parliament received many political motions which both drew attention to the problems brought about by the population decrease and touched on the eugenics movement. In 1937 a special committee was established to examine issues related to population. These matters became especially topical after the outbreak of the Winter War in 1939.[145]

Discussing the latest population problems in 1940 Armas Nieminen, senior lecturer and later professor in social policy, spoke of the disadvantages caused by decreasing birthrates. He argued that history had proved that stagnation in the increase of population was a symptom of the weakening of the political importance of a nation and that any decrease in the population was always linked to the degeneration that leads to the destruction of a nation.[146]

The task of improving the Finnish-speakers' quality and quantity belonged to the program of Väestöliitto (the Population and Family Welfare Federation), founded in 1941. The objectives set out for this new organization were to disseminate information concerning population policy and to promote positive attitudes toward family life. The federation also pioneered a genetic instruction service. It was expected to pursue a population policy which aimed at providing greater social security.[147]

Although the tasks of the federation centered on measures for the promotion of quantitative population growth, the qualitative aspect and eugenics were already being touched upon during the establishment phase of the organization. "The aim of the Federation is to disseminate information on the importance of both the size of the population and its quality not only for the survival of the nation but also for its material and intellectual progress." In conjunction with Helsinki University's Institute of Genetics, Väestöliitto established a clinic for genetic consultation.

In Finland the qualitative aspect of the population question was linked with the question of the vitality of the nation. During the war years some isolated public remarks attracted attention not only in relation to the numerical growth of the population but also to its quality.[148] The ingredients for a healthy nation emerged clearly from the discussion of population politics; these ingredients were to be found in the countryside, and in line with the practice in other Nordic countries, eugenic propaganda in Finland was linked to the fight against industrialization and urbanization.

At the level of regional policy this meant continuing the task started in the 1930s of settling the most remote parts of the country, such as Lapland. After the war thousands of small holdings and war veteran settlements were created in these backwoods. The joint program of the Agrarian and Center parties, in particular, included the decentralization of government offices and institutions as well as the improvement of operational prerequisites for light industries and handicrafts in the countryside. The trend toward urbanization had to be slowed down because it was supposed to have a negative impact on the quality of the people.

THE 1950 STERILIZATION, CASTRATION, AND ABORTION ACTS

After World War II a general feeling of rootlessness was increasingly evident. Public opinion, however, had not become more tolerant or permissive. On the contrary, the increase in sexual and violent crimes had a strong impact on public attitudes and there emerged demands for stronger measures such as castration for sexual offenders. In principle the 1935 act had allowed such castration and it had been applied in fifty-four cases.[149]

The justification for the acts on sterilization and castration was the claim that "Society must be able, even by force, to prevent any act of reproduction which might produce individuals who are not only totally incapable of leading a normal social life but are also bound to increase the burden society has to bear in caring and providing for such people."[150]

The 1950 Sterilization Act stipulated that sterilization could be carried out on eugenic, social, or general medical grounds. If medical reasons were cited the operation could be executed on the decision of a consultant and a surgeon nominated by the National Board of Health. In other cases the decision was vested in the board itself. In cases of emergency abortion, a qualified doctor could, in certain circumstances, make a personal decision on sterilization.[151]

The fact that sterilizations could be made for medical reasons with the authority of two physicians increased the yearly number of sterilizations (see table 3). On the basis of the statistics of the Finnish National Board of Health it is possible to analyze different categories for sterilizations with the permission of the board. Typical of the application of this act, sterilizations were usually carried out on women on medical grounds. The proportion of male sterilizations remained between 1 and 2 percent.[152]

Table 3. Sterilizations in Finland, 1951-1970.

Year	Total	Medical reasons[*]	Eugenic reasons[**]	% of total	Social reasons[**]	% of total
1951	780	569[***]				
1952	1009	777[***]				
1953	1061	813[***]				
1954	1068	733[***]				
1955	1236	1014[***]				
1956	1582	1582	362	22	23	1
1957	1727	1727	372	22	21	1
1958	2206	1767	413	19	26	1
1959	2596	1921	436	17	239	9
1960	3197	2362	514	16	321	10
1961	3193	2353	463	15	377	12
1962	3388	2612	411	12	365	11
1963	3511	2729	380	11	402	11
1964	3297	2676	216	7	405	12
1965	3206	2713	237	7	258	8
1966	3543	3012	271	8	260	7
1967	4022	3521	269	7	232	8
1968	4294	3817	218	5	259	6
1969	5437	4983	298	5	156	3
1970[****]	5727	2385	141	5	101	3
total	56080	44066	5001		3445	

Source: *Public Health and Medical Care*, The Official Statistics of Finland XI, 1950-1970.

   *   Either based on a consensus decision of two doctors or on the evidence of somatic disease or defect as agreed by a statement of the National Board of Health.

  **   Statement of the National Board of Health.

 *** With authorization of two doctors.

**** 1.1.-31.5. Based on sterilization law of 1950; 1.6.-31.12. Based on new sterilization law of 1970.

As table 3 makes clear, the annual number of sterilizations carried out in Finland in the period 1951-1970 was ten times the number during the most active period of sterilizations in the 1930s. From 1951-1970 approximately 70-

75 percent of all sterilizations were made with the authorization of two doctors; most of these were in conjunction with interruption of a pregnancy. In 1970 the number of sterilizations decreased and the number of abortions increased. The new law on abortion, which became effective in 1970, widened the range of possibilities; some believe that abortions were used as a contraceptive device. The last years of the 1960s can also be described as a period of general sexual liberation.

While sterilizations on eugenic indications reached their peak in 1958 (19 percent of all sterilizations) and then steadily decreased toward the end of the 1960s, social grounds were employed most often in 1961 and 1964 (12 percent of all sterilizations).

In the explanatory memorandum for the Castration Act, it was emphasized that such measures had been carried out far too rarely and that the reform aimed at making the application of the law more efficient. Indeed, the spirit of this act was considered to be similar to that of the 1935 sterilization legislation.

In the 1950 Castration Act it was stipulated that castration could be carried out as an act of criminal policy and on humanitarian grounds. In relation to compulsory castration it was stated that "A person, who has been found guilty of . . . a [sexual] crime or of an attempted crime, and who, because of their sexual drive, is dangerous to another person can be castrated without their own agreement." The same applied to people even in institutional care who were dangerous because of their sexual drive, or were mentally retarded or permanently mentally ill. A castration proposal for a person in institutional care was made by the principal of that particular institution and in other cases by the local police superintendent. As to certain sexual offenders the issue had always to be submitted for the decision of the National Board of Health.[153]

The Castration Act met with strong opposition. The opponents laid great emphasis on the apparent anomaly that just as the death penalty was being abolished such a measure of compulsory castration was to be adopted in Finland. Critics like Professor Bruno Salmiala, who was mentioned earlier, drew attention to the unwelcome publicity the act was attracting abroad.[154] The most criticized point, however, was the stipulation that a decision on castration could be reached without hearing the person concerned. This was considered quite a sensitive matter though in some cases one could appeal to the Supreme Court. Because of the strong criticism directed toward the Castration Act this measure was hardly applied. In the period 1951-1968 a total of 2,777 applications were made but the operation was carried out in only ninety cases—and all ninety occurred during the early part of the period, between

1951 and 1958. After 1958 no castrations were performed, because attitudes had changed (see table 4).[155]

Table 4. Castrations, 1951-1968.

Year	Petitions for castration (Total)	Total	Decisions made on castration Rejected	Carried out
1951	126	26	15	11
1952	184	38	18	20
1953	168	51	29	21
1954	179	50	29	18
1955	132	24	7	14
1956	133	7	3	3
1957	152	5	3	2
1958	147	1	—	1
1959	143	—	—	—
1960	154	1	—	—
1961	202	—	—	—
1962	211	—	—	—
1963	152	—	—	—
1964	114	—	—	—
1965	128	—	—	—
1966	164	—	—	—
1967	165	—	—	—
1968	123	—	—	—
Total	2,777	203	104	90

Source: Raimo Lahti, *Vuoden 1970 abortti-, sterilisaatio- ja kastraatio-lainsäädäntö*, Helsinki 1970, 88.

Finally, according to the 1950 Abortion Act, abortion could be allowed on medical, social, criminal, and eugenic grounds.

THE 1970 STERILIZATION, CASTRATION, AND ABORTION LEGISLATION

In the face of changing public attitudes, reform of the 1950 legislation was demanded. In the 1960s Finland experienced profound changes in its industrial structure, and urbanization and migration from the countryside had a strong impact on public opinion at many levels.

A firm impetus was given to such a reform by a number of joint Nordic motions. As early as 1954 a motion had been presented for a standardization of the legislation. The plan failed, however, when the Norwegian abortion law was enacted in 1960. The matter became topical again when a committee was appointed in Sweden to revise its abortion law and in 1966 Denmark, Sweden, and Finland submitted a members' motion on such subjects at the Nordic level. Thus the reformed Finnish act of 1970 resembles closely the relevant Danish act.[156]

The 1970 act no longer recognized compulsory sterilization or castration. According to the explanatory memorandum, compulsory measures were be avoided unless they could be considered unconditionally required by society. Anybody under the age of eighteen was not be sterilized at all. The special permission of a guardian or trustee was needed for sterilizations of mentally ill or retarded persons. Furthermore, this could only happen under very special circumstances.

Sterilization could be carried out at the request of the person concerned, if there were good reasons to believe that:

(1) his/her children would be mentally retarded and that they would suffer from or develop a serious illness or physical disability;

(2) because of his/her illness or disturbed mind or because of some other circumstance there would be a serious impediment to his/her ability to take care of the children;

(3) when, considering the lifestyle and other circumstances of the person and his/her family, the birth and care of children would be a considerable burden;

(4) his/her possibilities of employing any other forms of birth control would be exceptionally difficult.

Similarly, a woman could be sterilized, at her own request, if her life or health would be endangered because of pregnancy, or due to her own physical deficiency or weakness.

The rules governing sterilization were revised to such an extent that the possibility of carrying out the operation in conjunction with an abortion was restricted even further. The criteria to be applied under item 4 were used on occasion to emphasize the preferential use of contraceptive methods.[157]

In the 1970 Abortion Act great emphasis was placed on mental hygienic, social, and psychological factors when deciding on a possible abortion. Moreover, much attention was paid to the great number of illegal abortions. According to the Abortion Act, abortion was possible if the continuation of pregnancy or delivery would endanger the woman's life or health because of illness, physical deficiency, or weakness; if giving birth to and caring for a baby would be likely to prove a considerable burden, taking into account the lifestyle and other circumstances of the woman and her family; if the illness or disturbed mental state of either of the parents or any other comparable factor would seriously limit their ability to take care of the child. Abortion was further permitted if the mother was under seventeen or over forty years of age or if she already had four children.[158]

This act reflects the breakdown in traditional values that occurred in Finland during the 1960s and 1970s as a result of changes in the industrial structure, urbanization, and modernization.

CONCLUSION

In Finland, as in other countries, the eugenic way of thinking was linked, both among the Finnish and Swedish speakers, with anxieties about the decreasing population and its qualitative deterioration. The biological sciences seemed to offer solutions to social problems. The medical experts contributed a great deal to the modernization of the nation. In the face of such challenges, why did people turn to the latest research displaying evidence on heredity as a factor in mental illness, epilepsy, alcoholism and, later, also in criminality?

I have endeavored to examine the source material within the context of the spread of innovations, for the Finnish developers of racial hygiene did not usually produce new information in support of eugenics but applied the already existing results of foreign research to Finnish circumstances. Nor was the racial hygienic way of thinking linked with any particular political movement in Finland. The information that inspired it came from many sources and was provided at many different levels in forms ranging from scientific research reports (Federley) to popular presentations (Väänänen).

A key issue in the spread of eugenics in Finland was the esteem that professional experts such as medical doctors enjoyed in Finnish society. People were accustomed to relying on expert opinions. This echoes the conclusions of Paul Weindling concerning Germany.[159] Nor did the majority of people have any opportunity to dispute "scientific" results even if they entertained some doubts about their effects. This state of affairs was aided by the fact that the majority of medical practitioners in Finland, including the head of the National Board of Health, were pro-sterilization. There was, therefore, hardly any public debate on these issues at all.

No special eugenics institute in the style of the Swedish Institute for Eugenic Research was ever established in Finland, nor were there special organizations or periodicals, even though those most actively involved in the work of the Samfundet Folkhälsan i Svenska Finland did have plans for such ventures.

Finland's Swedish-speaking minority, one of the most prominent members of which at that time was a professor of genetics, Harry Federley, felt their own position to be particularly threatened and had begun to be more concerned than ever before about the quality of their community. In a first attempt to tackle such issues, this minority adopted such measures of positive eugenics as awards to mothers, giving relevant instruction both in schools and among adults, and the special training of key groups such as district nurses.

Continuing such a policy of concentrating on positive eugenics, information was disseminated in Finland through numerous Swedish-language magazines and journals, which dwelt especially on the risks of alcoholism and the importance of choosing a suitable spouse. Perhaps as a result, once the Sterilization Act became law, relatively few applications for sterilization were received from communes with a Swedish-speaking population even though Harry Federley himself was, from the mid-1920s, a supporter of sterilization, and one of the most active and influential figures during the process of drafting the legislation. Due to his wide network of foreign contacts he was able to convey the latest research results which he then popularized for a wide variety of audiences. In the 1930s Federley in particular placed great faith in the results of research on twins.

Finnish scientists had learned the principles of a solid positivistic scholarly approach from the German cultural sphere. In Finland as in the United States social workers saw sterilization legislation as a means of reducing the numbers of the "unfit" elements in the population. During the Depression small communes in particular became aware of the economic burden laid upon them by the care of the mentally retarded, the mentally ill, and epileptics. The arguments and predictions of Federley, lawyers, and a number of medical officers in mental institutions and prisons, concerning the increase in the "inferior" elements of the population helped to convince the social workers of the local authorities and others of the need for such legislation. Moreover, examples drawn from the United States and the other Nordic countries as well as German models had an indirect influence on public opinion. Consequently, in 1934 the Sterilization Act was placed on the statute book with almost unanimous support; of the fourteen out of 200 members of Parliament who voted against it, all were drawn from the extreme Left.

To summarize, measures of positive eugenics were carried out by Swedish-speaking Finns beginning early in the century. The more categorical negative measures such as the Sterilization Law did not gain wide support until the 1930s and then mainly among Finnish speakers, including not only the supporters of the Agrarian Party but also supporters of the Social Democrats and the Conservatives.

During the 1930s, however, under the influence of the Swedish economist Gunnar Myrdal, a more extensive debate also began among the Finnish-speaking community, touching not merely on population policies but also on possible positive eugenic measures, such as aiding the choice of a suitable spouse. The establishment of Väestöliitto was a prime example of this. Väestöliitto adopted a program of aid for large families and established an advisory service on issues connected with heredity. In order to promote a healthy increase in population the organization encouraged urban families to have four, and country families six, children.

Between 1935 and 1955 a total of 1,908 people were sterilized in Finland with the permission of the National Board of Health, the great majority being women with only 276 men undergoing the operation. In all, the National Board of Health received 2,286 sterilization applications, concentrated most heavily in the closing years of the 1930s. The Finnish-speaking communes put forward proportionately more applications than the Swedish-speaking ones with Swedish speakers apparently placing greater trust in the positive methods of racial hygiene. During the period 1935-55, 61 percent of all sterilizations were eugenic. After the enactment of the new Sterilization Act in 1950 medical grounds increasingly became the basis for sterilization decisions. It was possible to perform sterilizations with the authorization of two doctors. This increased the number of sterilizations by 100 to 120 percent per year. The total number of sterilizations between 1951 and 1970 was 56,075, approximately 99 percent of which were performed on women.

During the war the value placed on each individual was exceptionally high and the number of sterilizations decreased. Nevertheless, in the 1940s the opinion was often expressed that the aims of the 1935 act were too modest, and articles were published in the press calling for more rigorous measures to fight criminality. In particular there was a call for the castration of sexual criminals. The 1950 Sterilization Act and Castration Act were compiled in the same spirit as the 1935 Sterilization Act and compulsory sterilization and castration were to be abolished only by the act of 1970 which also provided wider opportunities for abortion. The enactment of this law is connected with the change in values and norms in Nordic society and especially in Finland, which experienced a profound change in its industrial structure in the 1960s: the countryside became empty while the cities grew.

From the standpoint of the spread of innovations this study suggests that Finland adopted the use of sterilization in the same way as it adopted and applied other international innovations at that time. Behind the gaining of her independence lay a solid body of cultural activity. European and other international developments had been followed keenly, and attempts were made to apply these developments efficiently in a Finnish context, often without any adequate questioning of the reliability of the new information.

In general the intermediary in the transmission of new information was typically some high-ranking civil servant who had personally shared the experience of the relevant processes in various countries and who, moreover, had maintained personal contacts with foreign experts. Often this intermediary also had the role of convincer, influencing decision-makers by methods which seem highly efficient even by present-day standards. On the one hand, he would present the newest research results and statistics and, on the other, appeal to his audience's emotions by presenting individual case studies of, in this instance, "degenerate" or sick people, accounts that often included negative forecasts about the future as well.

In Finland pragmatism governed both the search for and the application of this new information. A scholarly analogy of what occurred would be that too often applied research was unsupported by basic research. In addition, the latest research findings appeared to support the notion that the nation's existence could be safeguarded by breeding its people more insightfully. This seemed only a small step further than the earlier prevalent belief that the same goal could be achieved by education and the application of new innovations.

Finnish thinking in the field of race hygiene, which led to the enactment of the sterilization law, does not appear to have had any conscious links with any particular ideology. Nevertheless, it may well be that the values and world view of the intermediaries were similar to those that prevailed among their colleagues in Europe and especially in Germany, where many of them had previously studied.

The nearest analogy to the Finns' eagerness to employ sterilization can be found in their ready acceptance of the Prohibition Act in 1919, which was one of the first significant actions by the Parliament of the newly independent Finland. Both of these laws were passed without any significant opposition. (Interestingly enough, it was the Swedish People's Party which was the strongest adversary of the prohibition legislation.) Both of these acts had a similar objective: the strengthening of the new nation's existence. In the case of prohibition a reference group was found in the United States, which demonstrates that, in spite of the cultural bond with Germany, innovations were adopted from any country where they could be found as long as they were in accord with the Finnish people's own needs. There are many examples of such Finnish pragmatism in exploring and adopting innovations.

Concentration on the adoption of the innovations of others saves the resources of a small country and accelerates her progress. This certainly happened in Finland. The negative side of the matter, however, is that innovations can be too readily adopted on unexamined or even false grounds. This was, indeed, what happened with both the Sterilization Act and earlier in the matter of prohibition. Not surprisingly, therefore, the Prohibition Act was eventually rescinded by a referendum in 1931, even though it still had quite widespread popular support, especially in the countryside. The abolition of compulsory sterilization had to wait until the 1970s, when society had adopted a new, more liberal set of values and when the modern welfare system was able to cope with the most difficult cases.

NOTES

1. J. Paasivirta, *Finland and Europe: The Early Years of Independence 1917-1939* (Helsinki: Finnish Historical Association, 1988), 14-15.
2. Ibid., 242-43, 322. On prohibition, see J. Kallenautio, "Kieltolaki ja sen kumoaminen puoluepoliittisena ongelmana," *Alkoholitutkimussäätiön Julkaisuja*, no. 31 (1979).
3. Paasivirta, *Finland and Europe*, 324-25, 333.
4. See, for example, K. Pearson, "On the Relationship of Intelligence on Size and Shape of Head and to Other Physical and Mental Characters," *Biometrika* (1906): 105-46; S. Wiseman, ed., *Intelligence and Ability: Selected Readings* (Harmondsworth: Penguin Books, 1967), 1-13; D. A. MacKenzie, *Statistics in Britain 1865-1930: The Social Construction of Scientific Knowledge* (Edinburgh: Edinburgh University Press, 1981). About attitudes of the middle class, see M. Freeden, "Eugenics and Progressive Thought: A Study in Ideological Affinity," *The Historical Journal* 22, no. 3 (1979): 645-71.
5. On professionalism in medicine, see G. E. Markowitz and D. Rosner, "Doctors in Crisis: Medical Education and Medical Reform during the Progressive Era 1895-1915," in *Health Care in America: Essays in Social History*, ed. S. Reverby and D. Rosner (Philadelphia: Temple University Press, 1979); Ronald L. Numbers, "The Fall and Rise of the American Medical Profession," in *Sickness and Health in America: Readings in the History of Medicine and Public Health*, ed. J. W. Leavitt and R. L. Numbers (Madison: University of Wisconsin Press, 1985).
6. M. Hietala, *Services and Urbanization at the Turn of the Century: The Diffusion of Innovations*, Studia Historica 23 (Helsinki: Finnish Historical Society, 1987); H. Saarinen, "Studien und Bildungsreisen von Finnen nach Berlin 1809-1914," in *Miscellanea*, Studia 33, ed. A. Tammisto, K. Mustakallio and H. Saarinen (Helsinki: Finnish Historical Society, 1989), 203-48.

7. A. Kemiläinen, "Mongoleista eurooppalaisiksi 1900-luvun rotuteorioissa," in *Mongoleja vai Germaaneja? Rotuteorioiden suomalaiset,* Historiallinen Arkisto 86, ed. A. Kemiläinen, M. Hietala, and P. Suvanto (Helsinki: Finnish Historical Society, 1985), 295-389.

8. H. Federley, *Antropologi och demografi: Den svenska folkstammen i Finland* (Helsingfors: Nordiska Förlags AB, 1940).

9. V. Tallgren, "Rotuopesita roduntutkimukseen Suomen 'älymystön' aikakauslehdistössä (Arvi Grotenfeltin, Tor Karstenin ja Kaarlo Hildenin käsityksiä)," in *Mongoleja vai Germaaneja? Rotuteorioiden suomalaiset,* Historiallinen Arkisto 86, ed. A. Kemiläinen, M. Hietala, and P. Suvanto (Helsinki: Finnish Historical Society, 1985), 351-405.

10. P. Kalevi Hämäläinen, "Suomenruotsalaisten rotukäsityksiä vallankumouksen ja kansalaissodan aikoina," in *Mongoleja vai Germaaneja? Rotuteorioiden suomalaiset,* Historiallinen Arkisto 86, ed. A. Kemiläinen, M. Hietala, and P. Suvanto (Helsinki: Finnish Historical Society, 1985), 407-20.

11. T. Aro, "Suomalaisten rotu saksalaisissa ja pohjoismaalaisissa tietosanakirjoissa," in *Mongoleja vai Germaaneja? Rotuteorioiden suomalaiset,* Historiallinen Arkisto 86, ed. A. Kemiläinen, M. Hietala, and P. Suvanto (Helsinki: Finnish Historical Society, 1985), 195-247.

12. M. Hietala, "Suomalaisen naistyypin etsiminen," in *Mongoleja vai Germaaneja? Rotuteorioiden suomalaiset,* Historiallinen Arkisto 86, ed. A. Kemiläinen, M. Hietala, and P. Suvanto (Helsinki: Finnish Historical Society, 1985), 431-46.

13. Paasivirta, *Finland and Europe,* 342-52.

14. O. Okkonen, *Väinö Aaltonen 1915-1925: Tutkielma* (Helsinki: Otava, 1925), 51.

15. T. Mäkinen, "Yhdysvaltojen ja Suomen välisten tieteellisten kontaktien kehitys 1917-1970," unpublished master's thesis, Department of History, University of Turku, 1980, 32; P. Weindling, *Health, Race and German Politics: Between National Unification and Nazism, 1870-1945* (Cambridge: Cambridge University Press, 1989), 2-4, 15-25.

16. Lääkintöhallitus, Matkakertomukset 1896-1925, The National Archives of Finland [National Board of Health, Travel Reports, 1896-1925]; M. Hietala, "Berlin und andere Grossstädte als Vorbild für die Selbstverwaltungen von Helsinki und Stockholm um die Jahrhundertwende," in *Blicke auf die deutsche Metropole,* ed. G. Brunn and J. Reulecke (Essen: Reimar Hobbing, 1989), 201-24.

17. See M. Hietala, "The Diffusion of Innovations: Some Examples of Finnish Civil Servants' Professional Tours in Europe," *Scandinavian Journal of History* 8, no. 1 (1983): 23-36; M. Hietala, "Innovaatioiden ja kansainvälistymisen vuosikymmenet," in *Tietoa, taitoa, asiantuntemusta: Helsinki eurooppalaisessa kehityksessä 1875-1917,* vol. 1, Historiallinen Arkisto 99:1/Helsingin kaupungin tietokeskuksen tutkimuksia 1992:5:1 (Helsinki: Finnish Historical Society/Helsingin kaupungin tietokeskus, 1992).

The Finnish district surgeon Konrad Relander wrote a 600-page report when he visited water works, sewage plants, slaughterhouses, disinfection institutes and hygiene institutes in cities all around the Europe in 1895-1896 (K. Relander, "Kertomus hygieniseltä opintomatkalta Eurooppaan 1894-1895," Lääkintöhallitus, Matkakertomukset 1894-1895, The National Archives of Finland [National Board of Health, Travel Reports, 1894-1895].

18. Paasivirta, *Finland and Europe*, 335-41.

19. J. Hagelstam, *Minnestal över Ossian Schauman vid Samfundets årsmöte den 30 mars 1922* (Helsingfors: Skrifter utgivna af Samfundet Folkhälsan i Svenska Finland, 1922), 8-13; H. Federley, *Antropologi och demografi: Den svenska folkstammen* (Helsingfors: Nordiska Förlags AB, 1940).

20. Scandinavians responded to racial hygiene with the greatest enthusiasm. Ernst Rüdin recruited from Norway and Sweden thirty-three members to the Deutsche Gesellschaft für Rassenhygiene in 1907 and 1909 (See Weindling, *Health, Race and German Politics*, 150).

21. In 1932 the U.S. Executive Committee of the Eugenics Research Association nominated Federley to represent Finland on an Advisory Board of the Eugenical News. In 1920 Federley was invited as a representative member of Finland in the International Federation of Eugenic Organizations.

22. Alfred Ploetz to Harry Federley, 31 August 1928, and Harry H. Laughlin to Harry Federley, 16 January 1934 and 23 May 1934, Papers of Harry Federley, Helsinki University Library; Weindling, *Health, Race and German Politics*, 150.

23. P. Portin and A. Saura, *The Impact of Mendel's Work on the Development of Genetics in Finland*, Folia Mendeliana 20, Supplementum ad Acta Musei Moravie Scientiae Naturales LXX (Brno: Moravske Musei Moravie, 1985), 41-45.

24. R. Ehrström, "Är rasdifferensen af betydelse för frekvensen af de funktionella neuroserna i landet," in *Finska Läkaresällskapets Handlingar* (Helsingfors: Finska Läkaresällskapet, 1908), 527-37.

25. G. von Wendt, *Våra plikter mot kommande släktled. Några grunddrag ur den allmänna rashygien* (Borgå: Söderström & CO Förlagsaktiebolag, 1912).

26. G. von Wendt, *Tehtävämme tulevia sukupolvia kohtaan: Eräitä yleisen rotuhygienian peruspiirteitä*, Ajankysymyksiä 2 (Porvoo: Werner Söderström OY, 1912).

27. A. Palmberg, "Nativitetens och barndödlighetens speciala och nationella betydelse," in *Ekonomiska Samfundet i Finland: Föredrag och Förhandlingar*, vol. 7 (Helsingfors: Ekonomiska samfundet, 1912). Palmberg's book on public health, *Allmän hälsovårdslära* (Borgå: Werner Söderström OY, 1889), was translated into English, Spanish, and French.

28. "Rashygienen: Socialpoliticens vapenbröder," *Nya Pressen*, 18 January 1913.

29. "Rashygienen en samhällsplikt," *Hufvudstadsbladet*, 11 January 1913.

30. A. Björkman, "Förekomsten av sinneslöhet i Finland och några därav föranledde reflexioner," in *Sjätte nordiska mötet för abnormsaken i Helsingfors 24-27, juli 1912* (Helsingfors: Helsingin Uusi kirjapaino-osakeyntiö, 1915), 308-30; paper presented by Dr. I. Kalpa, medical superintendent of Pitkäniemi hospital, at a conference of Finnish welfare workers in Vaasa on 27 July 1934, *Huoltaja*, no. 16 (1934): 325-31.

31. Albert Björkman visited institutions for mental health in Berlin, Heidelberg, Basel, Neuchatel, Geneva, Lausanne, Bern, Münsingen, Zürich, Baden, Strassburg,

Bonn, Düsseldorf, Dortmund, Bielefeld, Bremen, Köpenhamn, London, Paris, Leipzig, Lund, Kristinehamn, Stockholm (Lääkintöhallitus, Matkakertomukset, 1896-1925, The National Archives of Finland [National Board of Health, Travel Reports]).

32. "Från våra läkareföreningar i landsorten: Utdrag ur Åbo Läkareförenings protokoll den 25 Oktober 1913," *Finska Läkaresällskapets handlingar* 56, (Helsingfors: Finska Läkaresällskapet, 1913).

33. "Från våra läkareföreningar i landsorten: Utdrag ur Åbo Läkareförenings protokoll den 7 December 1913," *Finska Läkaresällskapets handlingar* 56 (Helsingfors: Finska Läkaresällskapet, 1913).

34. A. Wallgren, "Finska Läkaresällskapets allmänna möte i Åbo den 19 och 20 September 1913," *Finska Läkaresällskapets handlingar* 57 (Helsingfors: Finska Läkaresällskapet, 1913).

35. K. Väänänen, *Periytyminen ja ihmissuvun jalostaminen* (Helsinki: Otava, 1916), 137.

36. See, for example, D. Paul, "Eugenics and the Left," *Journal of the History of Ideas* (1984): 567-90.

37. Väänänen, *Periytyminen ja ihmissuvun jalostaminen*, 140-47.

38. Ibid., 150.

39. H. Federley, "Rashygien: Föredrag hållet vid Nordiskt förbundet för kvinnogymnastik kongress i Ekenäs den 25 Juli 1924," *F.F.F. Svenskt förbund för fysisk fostran för Finlands kvinnor* (1924): 139-53; A. Halila, *Suomen naisvoimistelu ja urheiluseurat vuoteen 1915: Suomenkielisten miesvoimistelu-ja urheiluseurojen synnystä, perustajien yhteiskunnallisesta koostumuksesta ja emäseuroista*, Historiallisia tutkimuksia 53 (Helsinki: Finnish Historical Society, 1959), 12-20.

40. L. Leidenius, "Vähän rotuhygieniasta," *Valkonauha: Suomen naisten kristillinen siveellisyys- ja raittiuslehti*, no. 1 (1916).

41. H. Federley, "Det sjunkande födelsetalet: Ett varningstecken," *Församlingsbladet*, no. 7 (1924).

42. O. Schauman, *Eugenic Work in Swedish Finland: The Swedish Nation in World and Picture* (Stockholm: Hasse W. Tullberg Co., 1921), 3.

43. H. Federley, *Antropologi och demografi: Den svenska folkstammen* (Helsingfors: Nordiska Förlags AB, 1940).

44. J. Hagelstam, *Minnestal över Ossian Schauman vid Samfundets årsmöte den 30 mars 1922* (Helsingfors: Skrifter utgivna af Samfundet Folkhälsan i Svenska Finland, 1922). Herman Lundborg was the first correspondent member of Samfundet folkhälsan i Svenska Finland (see H. Federley, *Berättelse över Samfundets verksamhet under år 1921-1922* [Helsingfors: Skrifter utgivna af Samfundet Folkhälsan i Svenska Finland, 1922]).

45. H. Federley, "Rassenhygienische Propaganda-arbeit unter der schwedischen Bevölkerung Finlands," *Archiv für Rassen- und Gesellschaftsbiologie* 24 (1930): 326-33; H. Federley, *Folkhälsan i Svenska Finland: ärftlighetens betydelse för folkhälsan* (Helsingfors: Svenska Litteratursällskapet i Finland, 1920), 9-30; "Program för

Samfundets Folkhälsan i Svenska Finland teoretiska kompletteringskurser 1927" [program for a training course], The Institute of Genetics, Papers of Harry Federley, Helsinki University; G. Wellin, *Folkhälsan i Svenska Finland: Om barnens vård* (Helsingfors: Svenska Litteratursällskapet i Finland, 1920), 31-47; "Våra svenska hälsosystrar," *Svenska Pressen*, 10 January 1931.

46. H. Federley, "Samfundet Folkhälsan 1921-1931," in *Samfundet Folkhälsan i Finland: Berättelse avgiven av Samfundets sekreterare Federlay* (Helsingfors: Samfundet Folkhälsan, 1932), 10-19.

47. H. Federley, "Belöningar för berömlig modersgärning," *Barn och Ungdom. Nordisk socialpedagogisk tidskrift* (1926): 1-7.

48. H. Federley, "Rassenhygienische Propaganda-arbeit unter der schwedischen Bevölkerung Finlands," *Archiv für Rassen- und Gesellschaftsbiologie* 24 (1930): 326-33.

49. H. Federley, "Ans och vård åt de friska barn," in *Barnens by* (Helsingfors: A.B.F. Tilgmanns tryckeri, 1926), 8-10; H. Federley, *Samfundets moderspremiering och dess syfte* (Helsingfors: Samfundet folkhälsan i Svenska Finland, 1946), 127-35.

50. H. Federley, "Belöningar för berömlig modersgärning," *Barn och Ungdom. Nordisk socialpedagogisk tidskrift* (1926): 1-7.

51. H. Federley, "Ans och vård åt de friska barn," in *Barnens by* (Helsingfors: A.B.F. Tilgmanns tryckeri, 1926), 8-10.

52. See, for example, M. Klinge, *Vihan veljistä valtiososialismiin: Yhteiskunnallisia ja kansalllisia näkemyksiä 1910- ja 1920-luvuilla* (Porvoo: Werner Söderström OY, 1972), 45-56.

53. H. Federley, "Det sjunkande födelsetalet ett varningstecken," *Församlingsbladet*, no. 7-8 (1924).

54. L. Ringbom, "Rashygieniska syften och mål," *Åbo underrättelser*, 20 February 1923.

55. H. Federley, "Folkhälsan och rashygien," *Nylänningen* (1933): 15-16.

56. "Harry Federley 70 år," *Hufvudstadsbladet*, 22 March 1949; "Professor Federleys död," *Hufvudstadsbladet*, 14 November 1957; interview with Professor Esko Suomalainen, 6 June 1987.

57. H. Federley, "I sterilisationsfrågan," *Tidskrift utgifven av Stiftelsen för psykisk hälsa* 7, no. 1-2 (1934).

58. H. Federley, "Degenerationsfaran och dess avvärjande genom sterilisation," *Finlands Röda Kors* (1927): 6-21; H. Federley, "Sterilisering i rashygieniskt syfte," *Medicinska Föreningens Tidskrift*, no. 9 (1929): 223-37; H. Federley, "Ärftlighetslära och rashygien," in *Hälsa och sjukdom* (Helsingfors: Söderström & Co Förlagsaktiebolag, 1930), 239-310; H. Federley, "I sterilisationsfrågan," *Tidskrift utgiven av Stiftelsen för psykisk hälsa* 7, no. 1-2 (1934): 1-16; H. Federley, "Sterilisaatiokysymys ja sen kehitys Suomessa," *Suomen Punainen risti*, no. 3 (1935): 55-60; H. Federley, "Rashygieniska synpunkter på oss vår framtid," *Finlands Röda kors*, no. 4 (1935): 1-6; H. Federley, "Ras, rasbiologi och raspolitik," *Nya Argus*, no. 17 (1935): 223-27.

59. Federley received sixteen letters from Herman Lundborg, fifteen letters from Alfred Mjöen, twenty-one letters from Otto Mohr, thirty-eight letters from Fritz

Lenz and three from Alfred Ploetz (Papers of Harry Federley, Helsinki University Library).

60. Fritz Lenz to Harry Federley, 19 December 1917, Papers of Harry Federley, Helsinki University Library.

61. Fritz Lenz to Harry Federley, 30 December 1929, Papers of Harry Federley, Helsinki University Library.

62. Federley had asked Lenz about his opinion on Mjöen and Lundborg. Lenz wrote: "Was ihre Bemerkungen über die Rassenhygieniker betrifft, muss ich Ihnen leider Recht geben. Mjoen ist ein recht zweifelhafter Gewinn. Auch was Sie über Lundborg sagen dürfte wohl zutreffen. Aber trotzdem habe ich ein Eindruck, dass die Rassenhygienische Bewegung sich wissenschaftlich mehr und mehr klärt" (Fritz Lenz to Harry Federley, 3 March 1924, Papers of Harry Federley, Helsinki University Library).

63. "Tvillingsforskning: Arv och miljö, Prof. Federleys rasbiologiska föreläsningar," *Upsala Nya Tidning,* 25 October 1934; "Arvsanlagen och kriminaliteten: Nya resultat av tvillingsforskning, Professor Federleys föreläsningar om tvillingsforskning," *Nya Dagligt Allehanda,* 25 October 1934. Cf. H. Federley, "Brottsligheten som biologisk företeelse. Föredrag hållet den 7, januari 1934 under den bekämpande avbrottsligheten anordnande föredragsveckan i Helsingfors," *Psykisk Hygien,* no. 1-2 (1935): 21-30.

64. E. Suomalainen, *Kromosomitutkimuksen ja klassillisen perinnöllisyystieteen aika 1923-1949* (Helsinki: Institutum Geneticum, Universitas Helsingiensis, 1983), 14-23.

65. Interview with Professor Esko Suomalainen, Helsinki, 6 June 1987.

66. "Harry Federley ordförande i Samfundet folkhälsan i Svenska Finland," *Svenska Pressen,* 7 October 1940; "Folkhälsan får institutet för ärftlighetsforskning," *Hufvudstadsbladet,* 2 April 1942; "Svenskt institut för ärftlighetsforskning," *Svenska Pressen,* 1 April 1942.

67. J. Tegengren, "Finland: En hälsning till 20-årige," *Allsvensk Samling,* 6 June 1921.

68. L. Ringbom, "Rashygieniska syften och mål," *Åbo Underrättelser,* 20 February 1923.

69. H. Andersson, "Ett svenskt statsinstitut för rasbiologi: Dess tillkomsthistoria," *Finska Läkaresällskapets Handlingar* 62-63 (Helsingfors: Finska Läkaresällskapet, 1921).

70. "Rotuhygieniasta," *Helsingin Sanomat,* 31 July 1921.

71. Tiitus [pseud.], "Mieltäkiinnittävä ajatustenvaihto 'ruotsalaisesta rotupuhtauoesta' eli mitä yksi riikinruotsalainen lääkemies voi itsestänsä ja muista ajatella," *Helsingin Sanomat,* 7 October 1922; B. Gripenberg, *Drömmen om folkviljan* (Helsingfors: Holger Schildts förlag, 1918).

72. E. Böök, "Kysymys naisten yötyön kieltämisestä teollisuudessa: 'Ennemmin tai myöhemmin on ryhdyttävä tähän rotuhygieniseen toimenpiteeseen,'" *Helsingin Sanomat,* 7 March 1929.

73. V. Annala, "Virkamiehistön nykyinen palkkaus ja rodun huonontuminen," *Helsingin Sanomat,* 7 September 1928.

74. A. von Bonsdorff, *Om vården av andesvaga barn i Finland*, Meddelanden utgivna av socialministeriet i Finland 21 (Helsingfors: Valtioneuvoston kirjapaino, 1925).

75. H. Federley, "Rodun terveyttä parantavat yhteiskunnalliset uudistukset," *Sosiaalinen Aikakauskirja*, no. 5 (1924): 375-91; H. Federley, "I sterilisationsfrågan," *Tidskrift utgiven av Stiftelsen för psykisk hälsa* 7, no. 1-2 (1933-34): 1-16.

76. Committee for Legalising Eugenic Sterilisation. Other Countries 1929-1932, Papers of the Eugenics Society, London University College, Eug/ D 208; Memoranda concerning various laws. Dr. J. Crowley Board of Control, Papers of the Eugenics Society, London University College, Eug/ D 226.

77. Aatos Lehtonen had visited hospitals for mentally ill in Germany during three months in 1913. Later he visited the mental hospitals in Stettin, Dresden, Colditz, Leipzig, Nermsdorf, München, Berlin, and Stralsund (Lääkintöhallitus, Matkakertomukset 1896-1925, National Archives of Finland).

78. Väinö Mäkelä followed keenly discussions on laws of sterilization in various countries. In 1907, 1911, 1924-25, 1929, and 1930-32 he made professional study tours to Germany, in 1929 to Sweden, in 1930 to Austria and in 1938 to Norway. He did research on schizophrenia in the 1930s and published a book on the subject, *Die Psychopatologien der Schitzophrenie*, in 1936.

79. Komiteanmietintö [Committee Report], no. 5 (Helsinki, 1929).

80. When the committee report was published, Federley sent a copy to Herman Lundborg, deploring the fact that the Finnish state ties had not for reasons of economy published it in Swedish although the major bulk of it had already been written in Swedish (Harry Federley to Herman Lundborg, 19 May 1929, Papers of Herman Lundborg, Uppsala University). The Finnish committee report stated that the number of sterilizations performed under the law in the United States was 8,515, until 1 January 1928. Of these, 4,517 were performed on men, and 3,998 were performed on women. The majority of cases (5,820) were reported in California (Komiteanmietintö [Committee Report], no. 5, 17).

81. Komiteanmietintö [Committee Report], no. 5.

82. A. J. Palmén, "Kysymys vajaakelpoisten sterilisoimisesta maassamme," *Sosiaalinen Aikakauskirja*, no. 11 (1933); A. J. Palmén, "Komiteanmietintö vajaakelpoisten sterilisoimisesta," *Duodecim*, no. 11 (1929): 957-63.

83. The Parliamentary Publications of Finland [henceforth P.P.], Vuoden 1934 valtiopäivät, Hallituksen esitys Eduskunnalle sterilisaatiolaiksi, no. 112, 14 [Government bill on sterilization].

84. "Lakimääräistä sterilisoimista ei puolleta," *Uusi Suomi*, 5 May 1929; "Tylsämielisten, mielisairaiden ja kaatumatautisten sterilointi ehdotetaan säädettäväksi vapaaehtoiseksi," *Uusi Suomi*, 7 May 1929; "Lakimääräistä sterilisaatiota ei puolleta," *Ilkka*, 6 May 1929; "Sterilisoimista koskeva lakiehdotus valmis: Komitea ei puolla lakimääräistä sterilisointia, Steriloimisluvan antaa lääkintöhallitus," *Helsingin Sanomat*, 7 May 1929; "Lain määräämää sterilisointia ei puolleta: Vaadittava itse henkilön tai hänen holhoojansa ehdotus," *Sosialisti*, 6 May 1920;

Maskuliini [pseudon.], "Rikosko äitiyttä vastaan? Ajattelemisen aihetta työläis-naisille," *Työläis- ja talonpoikaisnaisten lehti*, no. 4-5 (1929).

85. E. Böök, "Heikkomielisten hoito," *Huoltaja*, no. 14 (1929): 233-38.

86. E. J. Horelli, "Sterilisoimiskysymyksestä I," *Vankeinhoito*, no. 10 (1929): 166-67.

87. E. J. Horelli, "Sterilisoimiskysymyksestä II," *Vankeinhoito* (1929): 12-13.

88. A. J. Palmén, "Komiteanmietintö vajaakelpoisten sterilisoimisesta," *Duodecim*, no. 11 (1929): 957-63.

89. "Tiedonantoja ulkomailta: Sterilisoimiskysymys," *Sosiaalinen Aikakauskirja*, no. 4 (1929): 200-2.

90. W. L. Telkkä, "Tanskan steriloimislaki," *Vankeinhoito*, no. 11 (1929): 190-91.

91. "Sterilisointikysymys Ruotsissa" (Extract from the Swedish Sociala Meddelanden)," *Sosiaalinen Aikakauskirja*, no. 10 (1929): 535-36.

92. E. Ehrnrooth, "Perinnöllisyydestä ja sen vaikutuksesta erinäisten mielisairauksien syntyyn," *Sielunterveysseuran aikakauslehti*, no. 1ʳ (1929): 1-11; "Sterilisoimiskysymys Pohjoismaissa: Erittäinkin Norjan oloja silmällä pitäen," paper of Henr. Ouren presented at the social philanthropic conference in Helsinki 4-6 July 1930, *Huoltaja*, no. 2 (1931): 23-29, no. 3 (1931): 44-47.

93. Promemoria from the Board of the Association for Mental Health, 11 April 1928; Promemoria from the head of Perttula Reformatory to the Ministry of Social Affairs, 11 April 1928; Promemoria from the Association of Schools for Retarded in Finland to the Council of the Finnish Government, 30 November 1929; peti-tion from the Mannerheim League for the Welfare of Children to the Finnish Government, 10 December 1929; letter from the Ministry of Social Affairs to the Ministry of Education, 9 May 1930, published as a supplement to Komiteanmietintö, no. 5 (1929); Einar Böök, "Onko vajaamielisten hoidon jär-jestämistä koskevan kysymyksen selvittely tarpeellinen," *Huoltaja*, no. 23 (1932): 410-14.

94. Advertisement for subscription, *Sielunterveysseuran aikakauslehti*, no. 1-2 (1933): 2.

95. R. Hedman, "Yhteiskunta ja vajaaälyiset," *Sielunterveysseuran aikakauslehti*, no. 31 (1931): 9-21.

96. "Vajaaälyisyys sosiaalisena kysymyksenä: Katsauksia," *Huoltaja*, no. 10 (1931): 192-95.

97. S. E. Donner, "Lausunto sterilisoimiskysymyksestä," *Sielunterveysseuran aikakauslehti*, no. 2 (1931): 9-21.

98. I. Kalpa, "Mielisairauksien ja sielullisten häiriötilojen periytymisestä ja periytyviin mielisairauksiin kohdistuvista ehkäisytoimenpiteistä," *Sielunterveysseuran aikakauslehti*, no. 1-2 (1932).

99. R. Hedman, "Sielunterveys ja kansanterveys," *Sielunterveysseuran aikakauslehti*, no. 1-2 (1932): 20-26.

100. "Psykiatrisen perinnöllisyysbiologian saavutusten merkitys käytännölliselle eugeniikalle," paper of Professor Rüdin presented at the Congress of Mental Hygiene in Bonn 21 May 1932, *Sielunterveysseuran aikakauslehti*, no. 3 (1932): 3-14.

101. "Avioliittoneuvonta ja sukupuolihygienia," *Sielunterveysseuran aikakauslehti*, no. 4 (1932): 3-11.

102. "Tietopuolinen oppijakso mielisairaanhoidossa," paper of Professor Ietscher presented at the Congress of Mental Hygiene in Bonn 21 May 1932, *Sielunterveysseuran aikakauslehti*, no. 1-2 (1933).

103. A. J. Palmén, "Rodun huonontuminen vaatii toimenpiteitä. Kysymys vajaakelpoisten sterilisoimisesta," *Terveydenhoitolehti*, no. 2 (1934): 28-30.

104. "Sterilisoimislain tarpeellisuus," *Huoltaja*, no. 6 (1933): 121-22.

105. "Sterilisoimiskysymys meillä ja muualla: Saksan uusi sterilisaatiolaki," Report of the German Sterilization Law, *Huoltaja*, no. 1 (1934): 18-19; "Ehdotus sterilisoimislaiksi Ruotsissa," (Proposal for a Sterilization Law in Sweden,) *Huoltaja*, no. 9 (1934): 196; "Ruotsin mielisairaiden sterilisoimista koskeva laki," *Sosiaalinen aikakauskirja*, no. 11 (1934): 700-1.

106. H. Federley, "Brottsligheten som biologisk företeelse: A paper read during the Crime Prevention Week in Helsinki, 13 July 1934," *Psykisk Hygien*, no. 1-2 (1935): 21-30.

107. The papers by Ley and Kinberg were published in *Sielun terveys*, no. 4 (1935).

108. H. Federley, "Sterilisoimiskysymyksestä," *Sielun terveys*, no. 1-2 (1935): 10-17.

109. B. Honkasalo, "Sterilisoinnista," *Sielunterveysseuran aikakauslehti*, no. 1-2 (1934): 5-33.

110. P. Mustala, "Mitä rikollisuuden vastustamisessa olisi otettava huomioon," *Sielunterveysseuran aikakauslehti*, no. 1-2 (1934): 34-38.

111. K. Neuman-Rahn, "Rengas rikollisuuden ehkäisytyössä," *Sielun terveys*, no. 1-2 (1935): 23-29.

112. V. Mäkelä, "Mitä voimme tehdä tulevien sukupolvien henkisen terveyden kohottamiseksi," *Sielun terveys*, no. 1 (1936): 11-13.

113. V. Mäkelä, "Die Sterilisations- und Kastrationsgesetzgebung Finnlands," *Archiv für Rassen- und Gesellschaftsbiologie* 31 (1937): 420-50.

114. "Pakollinen sterilisaatio: Vaarallinen lakiehdotus," *Tulenkantajat*, 6 October 1934; "Kaksi tunnettua lääkäriä sterilisaatiolainsäädännöstä," *Tulenkantajat*, 30 October 1934.

115. "Merkintöjä," *Soihtu*, no. 3 (1935): 45.

116. K. Pohjola, "Sterilisoimislaki," *Suomen nainen*, no. 1 (1935).

117. "Alaikäisten ja nuorten henkilöiden suojeleminen sukupuolisilta väkivallanteoilta," *Huoltaja*, no. 8 (1933): 151-53.

118. "Lasten ja nuorten suojeleminen siveellisyysrikoksilta: Eduskunta hyväksynyt toivomusaloitteen," *Ajan Suunta*, 17 February 1934.

119. "Ihmisrodun jalostaminen," *Toveritar*, no. 3 (1934): 28.

120. K. W. O. "Eduskunnan työkaudelta," *Naisten ääni*, no. 10 (1935): 10-11.

121. R. Jalas, "Mielisairaus ja köyhyys," *Huoltaja*, no. 8 (1931): 137-40.

122. R. Jalas, "Syntyväisyyden säännöstelystä," *Huoltaja*, no. 22 (1935): 469-76.

123. R. Jalas, "Muutama sana steriloimisesta ja sterilisoimislaista," *Kotiliesi*, no. 7 (1935): 270-71.

124. Köyhäinhoitotilasto 1932, *Suomen Virallinen Tilasto* 21 (Helsinki: Central Statistical Office of Finland, 1935), 15 [The Official Statistics of Finland].

125. P.P., Vuoden 1934 valtiopäivät, Hallituksen esitys Eduskunnalle sterilisaatiolaiksi, no. 112 [Government bill on sterilization].

126. P.P., Vuoden 1934 valtiopäivät, Talousvaliokunnan mietintö, no. 11 [Report of the Economy Committee of the Parliament].

127. A member of the Finnish Parliament, Oskari Reinikainen, criticized the bill on the sterilization act because the proposal was born of the draft of one private specialist (P.P., Speech of Reinikainen in the session of the Parliament, 11 December 1934).

128. P.P., Speech of the minister of the interior, Yrjö Puhakka, in the session of the Parliament, 11 December 1934 and Speech of Bruno Sundström in the session of the Parliament, 11 December 1934.

129. P.P., Speeches of Karl Wiik and Bruno Sundström in the session of the Parliament, 11 December 1934.

130. P.P., Speeches of Bruno Sarlin, Karl Wiik, Eero Rydman, Oskari Reinikainen in the session of the Parliament, 22 February 1935.

131. P.P., Speeches of Reinhold Swentorzetski, Vilho Kivioja, Mikko Ampuja, in the sessions of the Parliament, 11 December 1934, 22 February 1935, and 5 March 1935.

132. Fritz Lenz to Harry Federley, 7 December 1935, Papers of Harry Federley, Helsinki University Library.

133. H. Federley, "Prof. Lassilas angrepp på steriliseringslagen" The Institute of Genetics, Papers of Harry Federley, Helsinki University; The Sterilization Act of 13 June 1935, The Statute Book of Finland; H. Ryömä, "Sterilisoimislaki," *Huoltaja*, no. 10 (1935): 201-5; A. J. Palmén, "Suomen sterilisoimislaki," *Sosiaalinen aikakauskirja*, no. 7 (1935): 431-33.

134. "Sterilisoimislaki," *Suomen Poliisilehti*, no. 15 (1935): 339.

135. The Sterilization Act of 13 June 1935.

136. "Sterilisoimislaki vahvistettu: Lääkintöhallitus käsittelee säädetyssä järjestyksessä kaikki sterilisoimistapaukset," *Suomen Sosialidemokraatti*, 14 June 1935; "Sterilisoimislaki vahvistettu," *Helsingin Sanomat*, 14 June 1935; "Sterilisoimislaki: Tasavallan presidentti vahvisti sen eilen," *Ilkka*, 14 June 1935.

137. Sterilisoimislain täytäntöönpanomääräysten muuttamista ja täydentämistä varten asetetun komitean mietintö, no. 16 (Helsinki, 1944) [Committee Report, Proposal on Castration Act].

138. C. A. Borgström, *Tillämpningen av lagen om sterilisering i Finland 13.6.1935- 30.6.1955 kastreringarna obeaktade,* Bidrag till kännedom av Finlands Natur och Folk 103 (Helsingfors: Finska Vetenskapssocieteten, 1958).

139. Fritz Lenz to Harry Federley, 24 May 1939, Papers of Harry Federley, Helsinki University Library.

140. Borgström, *Tillämpningen av lagen om sterilisering i Finland 13.6.1935-30.6.1955 kastreringarna obeaktade,* 59-57. Bidrag till Kännedom av Finlands Natur och Folk 103 (Helsingfors: Finska Vetenskapssocieteten, 1958).

141. Ibid., 86.

142. Ibid., 188.

143. G. Bock, "Racism and Sexism in Nazi Germany," in *When Biology Became Destiny: Women in Weimar and Nazi Germany*, ed. R. Bridenthal, A. Grossmann and M. A. Kaplan (New York: Monthly Review Press, 1984), 271-96.

144. Anomusdiaarit, Lääkintöhallitus, National Archives of Finland [National Board of Health, Register for applications]. On intelligence tests and on the inheritance of intelligence, see P. D. Chapman, "Schools as Sorters," in *Applied Psychology and the Intelligence Testing Movement, 1890-1930*, ed. L. M. Terman (New York: New York University Press, 1988), 30-31.

145. A. Myrdal and G. Myrdal, *Kris i befolkningsfrågan* (Stockholm: Albert Bonniers förlag, 1934). See also A. Kälvemark, *More Children of Better Quality? Aspects on Swedish Population Policy in the 1930's*, Studia Historica Upsaliensia 115 (Uppsala: Almqvist & Wiksell International, 1980); R. Lento, *Väestöpoliittisen ajatustavan synty ja tähänastinen kehitys Suomessa Väestöpolitiikkamme taustaa ja tehtäviä: Väestöliiton vuosikirja I* (Porvoo: Werner Söderström OY, 1946), 41-63.

146. A. Nieminen, *Väestökysymys entisinä aikoina ja nykyään* (Porvoo: Werner Söderström OY, 1941), 35-66.

147. Väestöliitto 1941; Ohjelma, Säännöt, "The Population and Family Welfare Federation Program Rules," *Väestöliiton julkaisuja*, no. 1 (Helsinki: Väestöliitto, 1942).

148. L. Pihkala, "Kulttuurin mittapuu," Jyväskylä maakunta-arkisto, Papers of Lauri Pihkala, Jyväskylä Provincial Archives.

149. R. Lahti, "Vuoden 1970 abortti-, sterilisaatio- ja kastraatiolainsäädäntö," in *Festskrift utgiven i anledning av Juristklubben Codex' 30-års jubileum* (Helsinki: Juristklubben Codex, 1970), 88-96.

150. P. P., Hallituksen esitys kastroimislaiksi ja sterilisaatiolaiksi HE 59/1948 [Government bill on castration and sterilization].

151. Sterilisaatio-, kastraatio- ja aborttilaki (1950) [Act on sterilization, castration and abortion].

152. Lahti, "Vuoden 1970 abortti-, sterilisaatio- ja kastraatiolainsäädäntö," 88-91.

153. P.P., Hallituksen esitys kastraatiolaiksi H 58/1948 [Government bill on castration].

154. B. A. Salmiala, "Onko pakkokastratio oikeus- ja kulttuurivaltiossa hyväksyttävä reaktiomuoto rikoksen seurauksena?" *Defensor Legis*, no. 2-4 (1951).

155. R. Lahti, "Vuoden 1970 abortti-, sterilisaatio- ja kastraatiolainsäädäntö," 96-97.

156. Ibid., 69-73.

157. P.P., Hallituksen esitys sterilisaatiolaiksi 105/1969 [Government bill on sterilization]; Hallituksen esitys kastraatiolaiksi 106/1969 [Government bill on castration].

158. P.P., Laki raskauden keskeyttämiseksi 104/1969 [Government bill on abortion].

159. P. Weindling, *Health, Race and German Politics*, 215-30.

Conclusion: Scandinavian Eugenics in the International Context

Nils Roll-Hansen

Two waves of interest in eugenics affected Scandinavia, much like those in Britain.[1] The first wave peaked just before World War I, the second in the 1930s and 1940s. Eugenics was a significant issue of social policy and there was extensive public interest in the topic. Eugenics organizations, however, were weak. It was an area for expertise rather than democratic politics. Sweden was the only country with a national eugenics society. In the other countries various organizations with social causes took on some of the same tasks, for instance, the Association of Public Health in Swedish-speaking Finland, and there were groups of active people doing propaganda for the cause, such as Mjöen's Consultative Eugenics Committee of Norway. This loosely organized movement was most active and visible during the first wave. Its zenith was reached with the establishment of Herman Lundborg's Institute for Race Biology in Uppsala in 1922. But it was during the second wave that eugenics achieved its most striking results in the Nordic countries, namely, the sterilization laws of the 1930s.

At the beginning of the century physical anthropology, with its concept of race, formed the theoretical core of eugenics. The Nordic countries, especially Sweden, had a leading international position in this discipline. This first phase has been characterized as "mainline" eugenics in distinction to the "reform" eugenics[2] typical of the 1930s and 1940s. Mainline and reform views overlapped in time. The first emphasized racial differences and relatively simple forms of inheritance for socially important characteristics in humans. The second was antiracist and based on more sophisticated genetic theory.

In Scandinavia as in other European countries before World War I there appears to have been little doubt that Europeans saw themselves as superior to other people, in particular to blacks. Notions about biological inheritance were vague. More or less explicitly Lamarckian views on heredity were generally accepted, implying that the characteristics an individual acquired during his lifetime were to some extent inherited by his offspring.

The distinction between mainline and reform eugenics has been criticized for obscuring the real historical dynamics in the evolution of eugenics. One recent account of the relationship between American and German eugenics during the Nazi period defines racism as discrimination between groups of people. Differences between types of eugenics in terms of their attitudes to ward Nazi population policies is admitted but the account agrees with the idea that all eugenics is inherently racist and that the ultimate consequences of mainline and reform eugenics were often the same.[3] The effect of such an inclusive definition of racism is to downplay the difference between support and opposition to Nazi population policies.

Genetics as a special scientific discipline with a precise and systematic theory about biological inheritance was formed only during the first decade of the twentieth century. The core of classical, often called "Mendelian," genetics was the concept of the genetic factor, the gene, and the distinction between genotype and phenotype. The central formula of classical genetics was "phenotype = genotype + environment."[4] Or, in other words, the individual organism is the product of an interaction between inherited genetic factors and the environment, two aspects equally essential to the development of the organism. With these concepts a theoretical basis was laid for a more precise analysis and assessment of the influence of specific hereditary and environmental factors under varying circumstances.

The second wave of eugenic interest, developing in the 1920s and 1930s, included antiracist sentiments and demands for more precise and specific knowledge on how heredity affects the properties of organisms. The critical attitude toward the assumptions of the old mainline eugenics represented a renewal of the "social contract" of the movement. Reform eugenics became linked to birth control and other progressive social causes. Inspiration for the rejection of racism came from the democratic and socialist egalitarian ideologies of the period and from growing scientific knowledge about biological inheritance. There was no instant impact of the new insight through genetic research. It took time before new knowledge of human heredity had been convincingly established, systematized, and popularized. Only then was it fully effective in undermining eugenic policies such as sterilization.

After World War II eugenics acquired a reputation for being a politically conservative or reactionary movement. But the close link between eugenics and the movement for social reforms is now well established.[5] In particular, eugenic sterilization was an integral part of the social welfare state that emerged in the 1930s and 1940s. In Denmark, for example, the first government commission to consider sterilization and other eugenic measures was established just after the accession of the first Labor government in 1924. Leading in the effort to work out and implement eugenic policies was the minister of justice and later of social affairs, K. K. Steincke. As a result of these efforts in 1929 Denmark was the first Nordic country to have a sterilization law. This social democratic belief in eugenics continued up to the 1950s.

The Scandinavian accounts also show how eugenics was closely integrated with respectable scientific research. The participation of geneticists in the introduction of the sterilization laws in the 1930s as well as in their later evaluations and revisions demonstrates the scientific respectability of a moderate eugenics. Some of the most prominent geneticists, however, doubted there would be any significant positive effects of eugenic sterilization. Otto Lous Mohr in Norway in the 1920s and 1930s held sterilization to be ineffective eugenically, and saw contemporary eugenics generally as a problematic movement with many socially reactionary features. But he accepted the Norwegian sterilization law and the practice of sterilizing the mentally retarded, insane, etc., on social grounds. Gunnar Dahlberg in Sweden held a similar view. Other geneticists were partisans of eugenic sterilization, such as the Finn Harry Federley, the Swedes Nils von Hofsten and Arne Müntzing, and the Dane Tage Kemp. As head of an institute for human genetics and the organizer of the First International Congress of Human Genetics in Copenhagen in 1956, Kemp played an important international role in the period after World War II.

Nevertheless, there is no doubt that eugenics deserves its reputation as fertile ground for pseudoscientific propaganda. From early on, some geneticists made continuous efforts to uphold sound criteria of scientific evidence and argument in the debates over eugenics, often with moderate success. The debate and the polarization among supporters of eugenics were sharpest in Norway, where Jon Alfred Mjöen was the foremost figure of mainline eugenics, with a prominent position in the international eugenics movement. On the other side, criticism growing out of socialist and democratic ideology as well as accumulating scientific knowledge had a strong proponent in Otto Lous Mohr. The professional genetic experts among Norwegian biologists and medical doctors were organized in the Genetics Society which kept Mjöen ostracized from 1915 until his death in 1939. In the other Nordic countries there was less polarization and Mjöen was to some extent accepted by professional geneticists such as Federley in Finland and Lundborg in Sweden. He was even able to persuade the skeptical Wilhelm Johannsen, the most internationally prominent geneticist in Scandinavia, to join the International Federation and become a contributor to Mjöen's journal, *Den Nordiske Rase* (The Nordic Race).

The introduction of sterilization laws in the Nordic countries in the 1930s was carried by the ideology of reform eugenics, at least on the expert side. In public debates more mainline and partly racist views were still influential. The idea of a superior Nordic race had appeal to the broad public, especially in Sweden and Norway. Denmark was more continental and relaxed with respect to the Nordic idea, while Finland was divided due to its own internal conflict between Swedish and Finnish speakers. The latter were regularly thought of as belonging to the Baltic rather than the Nordic race.

Medical doctors had a professional interest in eugenics and played a central role in developing its policies and practices. They were in charge of psychiatric hospitals and institutions for the mentally retarded, and their expertise was needed for sterilization, both for the screening of cases and the operations. The standard term for eugenics in the Nordic countries was the equivalent of German "Rassenhygiene," which pointed to its place within a general program for social hygiene.

While sterilization laws were introduced in several states in the United States during the first wave of mainline eugenics around World War I, no European national government introduced such laws in this period. Only with the wave of reform eugenics were such laws introduced in Europe, and then only in Northern Europe, mainly in countries with a Lutheran state church. When the sterilization laws finally came they met very little public opposition. There was apparently a broad consensus that such moderate measures were necessary. In the Parliaments only very few voted against them. In Norway the unanimity was greatest with only one protest vote. In Finland with its recent civil war there were fourteen, mostly socialist left-wing politicians who saw sterilization as an attack on the labor class. The Finnish committee report of 1929, which formed the basis of the law, was considerably more restrained than the actual law passed in 1935. In the early 1930s there was increasing concern about the growth of crime and about an increase in the number of the mentally retarded. During the Finnish so-called Crime Prevention Week in January 1934 most of the organized public lectures dealt with eugenics.

Prevention of sexual crimes was one motive for sterilization. It was presumably easier for the popular sentiment to accept such mutilating interventions on criminals who deserved punishment. Women's organizations were particularly active in sending petitions to support the sterilization laws, often referring to the need for preventing sexual crime. Official documents frequently found it necessary to stress that sterilization as punishment was not

Table 1. Sterilizations in Scandinavia, Estimations

Country	Period	Number of Sterilizations	Population 1950
Denmark (excl. medical ind.)	1929-1960	ca. 11,000	4,281,000
Finland (excl. medical ind. 1951-1960)	1935-1960	ca. 4,300	4,030,000
Finland (incl. medical ind.)	1935-1960	ca. 17,000	—
Norway (excl. medical ind.)	1934-1960	ca. 7,000	3,280,000
Sweden (excl. medical ind. 1942-1960)	1935-1960	ca. 17500	7,042,000
Sweden (incl. medical ind.)	1935-1960	ca. 38,900	—

Source: Denmark: T. Kemp, *Arvehygiejne: Festskrift udgivet af Köbenhavns Universitet i anledning af Universitetets Årsfest 1951* (Copenhagen: Köbenhavns Universitet, 1951); G. Koudahl, *Om Vasectomi med Sterilisation for Yje* (Copenhagen: Munksgaard, 1967). Finland: C. A. Borgström, *Tillämpningen av lagen om sterilisering i Finland 13. 6. 1935-30. 6. 1955 kastreringarna obeaktade* (Helsingfors: Finska Vetenskapssocieteten, 1958); *Public Health and Medical Care*, The Official Statistics of Finland XI, 1950-1961. Norway: K. Evang, *Sterilisering etter lov av 1. juni 1934 om adgang til sterilisering m. v. h.* (Sarpsborg: F. Verding, 1955); The Norwegian Parliament, Government Bill 1976/1977 no 46, "Om lov om sterilisering m.v." Sweden: *Sveriges Offentliga Statistik: Allmän Hälso- och sjukvård* (Stockholm: Statistiska centralbyrån, 1935-1976).

Note: Statistics are not easy to compare due to differences in the statistical material. E.g., figures on Norway refer to *granted* sterilizations. In Denmark, it was estimated that some 80 percent of the women who were sterilized around 1960 underwent the operation on medical grounds

acceptable. It is a sign of the importance of the connection to crime prevention that sterilization applications in Sweden were handled by the Board of Health's Forensic Psychiatry Committee until 1947. Only then were they taken over by the Social Psychiatry Committee. In Norway the sterilization law of 1934 was prepared by the government's commission for criminal law. Still, the number of sterilizations carried out on sexual criminals was small in all the Nordic countries. Relatively few castrations were performed, most of them in Finland where eugenic sterilization in general came later and lasted longer than in the other Nordic countries. One reason for this delay was the strong Finnish involvement in World War II with large numbers of casualties. In all four Nordic countries the great majority of eugenic sterilizations was on the mentally retarded. This was the group that most clearly stood out as a target for eugenic sterilization.

The predominance of women among the sterilized—in the Swedish case more than 90 percent—must also be underlined. The strong imbalance between the sexes is of course not accidental, but shows that the history of eugenics must be written not merely as a history of science and pseudoscience; the implementation of the sterilization laws was not gender neutral. Further research, which explicitly addresses the question of gender, is necessary to explain how and why women became the primary object of the Scandinavian sterilization programs. One hypothesis, proposed by scholars in women's history, suggests that eugenics reflected male norms, something which our studies do not contradict. Thus, when male scientists and physicians defined the standards of biological and social normality, a sterilization policy concerned with deviancies and differences made women per se the focal point.

In Denmark, Sweden, and Norway there was a rapid drop in the number of sterilizations of the mentally retarded and insane from the middle of the 1940s through the 1950s, with Finland a little behind. This drop seems to indicate a phasing out of eugenic sterilization due to declining support for eugenic policies.[6] The decline of eugenics corresponds to what appears to have taken place in other countries.[7] Support for eugenics declined gradually after World War II, a major factor clearly being the experience with Nazi population policies. Nevertheless, those who had promoted eugenics in the 1930s largely held on to their convictions into the period after 1945. This was certainly the case with geneticists of a liberal or socialist political bent, such as J. Huxley, J. B. S. Haldane, or H. J. Muller in England and the United States or H. Nachtsheim in Germany.[8] In Scandinavia key medical or biological experts like Tage Kemp (Denmark), Nils von Hofsten (Sweden), C. A. Borgström (Finland), and Karl Evang (Norway) all argued for eugenic sterilization of the mentally retarded well into the 1950s.

Decrease in eugenic sterilization did not imply a decrease in the total number of sterilizations, however. First, there was change from eugenic indications to medical. In Sweden this tendency is particularly marked. Second, there was a trend toward using sterilization as a means of contraception. The steadily increasing number of sterilizations in Norway during the postwar period until the 1970s is due to this development. It had been strongly emphasized in Norway from the introduction of the law in 1934 that sterilization should be voluntary as far as possible. The old socialist and eugenic enthusiast Johan Scharffenberg, for instance, wanted freedom for everybody who wished to be sterilized. The Norwegian law set limits, however, by demanding a "worthy reason." But in the post-World War II period this was gradually given a more liberal interpretation. When a new Norwegian law was introduced in 1977 explicitly stating that for any person with full legal rights sterilization was a matter between patient and doctor, this was only a formalization of a practice already instituted. In Sweden a less liberal attitude seems to have dominated. The Swedish Population Commission in 1936 found the idea that every person should be free in all respects to determine the use of his or her own body to be "an extremely individualistic view."[9] All the Nordic sterilization laws of the 1930s assumed that permission for sterilization had to be given by government authorities. It was illegal to perform sterilization without permission. But under the new sterilization laws introduced in the 1970s the principle of individual freedom to decide was accepted as a matter of course for sterilization. This resulted in a large jump in the number of registered sterilizations in Sweden. The number had reached a level of about 2,400 around 1950 and then declined to 1,500 in 1974. When the new sterilization law was introduced in 1975 it rose abruptly to nearly 10,000 in 1980.

The principle of free individual choice was frequently emphasized in debates and reports leading up to the Scandinavian sterilization laws. But for persons without full legal rights the right of application was transferred to their guardian or the institution where they lived. This gave ample room for more or less compulsory procedures. Regulations of 1947 from the Swedish Board of Health assumed that a person without legal rights would be informed and asked for consent. If he did not agree the operation could still be carried out, though not "with the use of physical force."[10] There were also various kinds of pressure exerted, both on those who had and those who did not have full legal rights. For instance, sterilization could be set as a condition for leaving an institution, for getting an abortion, or for permission to get married. But, as already pointed out, there was a gradual strengthening of the right of the patient, especially from the 1950s on.

From an international perspective the comparison of the Nordic countries with Germany is particularly interesting. The cultural links were traditionally close. Among other things there was a common background in the Lutheran church. Up to 1933 the development of eugenics in Germany and Scandinavia was quite similar. For instance, all these countries had well-developed traditions of public medical service as a background for eugenic policies, in contrast to England and the United States. But under the Nazi regime German eugenics diverged. Racist ideas which had little support even among the biological scientists who cooperated with the Nazis were made the basis of government policies. The practice of sterilization used means of coercion and physical force that were not accepted in Scandinavia. Yet racist tendencies were also present in Scandinavia, even at the government level. For instance, Jewish refugees from central Europe had great difficulty in getting into the Nordic countries in the late 1930s. Thus, whereas mainline eugenics influenced Nazi German politics, the Scandinavian development took another turn. Mainline eugenics still attracted attention and affected immigration policy. Population policy, on the other hand, was formed by reform eugenics.

The different developments of eugenics in Scandinavia and Germany provide a useful background for evaluating the doctrine of continuity in the development of eugenics in Germany. The continuity of German eugenics from the Weimar Republic, through the Nazi period, and into the era after World War II, has been emphasized by Gerhard Baader.[11] The history of German eugenics by Peter Weingart, Jürgen Kroll, and Kurt Bayertz[12]also emphasizes continuity rather than change. The events of the Nazi period are seen as a natural, more or less necessary, result of the eugenic doctrines of the earlier era. This tendency is taken to an extreme by K. H. Roth, who attributes to genetic science a collective responsibility for the eugenic policies of the Nazi regime. He describes geneticists as a "power elite" (*herrschaftselite*) who formulated a program for world domination (*weltmachtprogram*) and applauded Nazi population policies at the outbreak of World War II toward the end of August 1939. The criticisms of Nazi race policies from liberal and socialist biologists such as J. Huxley, H. J. Muller, J. B. S. Haldane, O. L. Mohr, G. Dahlberg, etc., have little importance in Roth's view.[13] The British historian of science Paul Weindling, on the other hand, concludes that the "Nazi takeover marked a fundamental change in the course of German eugenics." He emphasizes the role of racial theories as the basis for Nazi population policies.[14] Both goals and means were quite different from those of Scandinavian governments.

There is no doubt that scientific institutions such as the Kaiser Wilhelm Institute for Anthropology, Human Heredity and Eugenics cooperated with the Nazi regime from 1933 throughout World War II. But as Paul Weindling has argued, there was a definite change in the dominant attitudes and lines of work of the institute after the Nazi takeover in 1933: "Attention to the composition of the Institute's staff, and to the social responsibilities of the Institute does not support any thesis of direct and uninterrupted lines of bureaucratic or ideological continuity. Intense pressures had to be exerted on the biologists in order to integrate them into the new order."[15]

The force of the comparison between Germany and Scandinavia can be increased by taking into consideration the different situations of the four Scandinavian countries during World War II and the different developments of sterilization practices. Finland was the first country to be drawn into the great war when it was attacked by the Soviet Union at the end of November 1939. The sudden drop in the number of sterilizations in this country was clearly a result of the war and the great loss of young men. This war experience was also the main reason for the slow development of sterilization practices in Finland. Both Norway and Denmark were occupied by Germany in April 1940. While the Danish government was cooperative and a continuity of internal politics and administration was upheld, the Norwegian government resisted and fled to England while the Germans set up a puppet Nazi regime in Norway. In Denmark there appears to have been little change in the number of sterilizations during the occupation. But in Norway the Nazi government introduced a new and more radical sterilization law which led to a large increase in the frequency of eugenic sterilizations. Sweden was not directly involved in the war. A new sterilization law was introduced in 1941 promoting greater efficiency in sterilization. The numbers shot up and reached a peak around 1944.

Considering the Scandinavian sterilization laws and the practice that was built on them, it seems that a liberal democratic tradition with emphasis on the rights of the individual provided for a moderate law and practice. Leading experts such as Dahlberg and Mohr who doubted any positive eugenic effects of sterilization, were strong proponents of such a political tradition and had considerable influence on the formulation of the laws. This comparison of eugenics in Germany and Scandinavia suggests that it was short-term political changes rather than a fundamentally different German social and cultural development, a German "Sonderweg," that led to the realization of Nazi eugenic policies.

We also note that it took time before the experience with Nazi racial and population policies affected eugenic policy in the Nordic countries very much. It was some years after World War II that eugenic sterilization had its most rapid decline. The decline of eugenics in Scandinavia appears to have other causes beyond revulsion against the events in Germany. For instance, the change from collectivistic to individualistic attitudes in the ethics of procreation had begun long before World War II. This change was no doubt stimulated by the experience with Nazism, but it was not dependent upon it. It was a development with many other driving forces as well.

A similar slowness in the decline of eugenics has been noted for France. William Schneider writes that the experience with the Fascist regime of Vichy and its pursuit of more radical eugenic policies during World War II "did not, however, permanently discredit eugenics." There was much more continuity of eugenics in France than in Germany or the United States.[16]

The Scandinavian material indicates that before World War II there was a general support for eugenics of some kind. There was a wide spectrum of opinions as to how ripe human genetics was for such social application and what measures were in harmony with other important social goals and accepted moral norms. But right across the political spectrum there was a general favorable attitude toward a mild eugenics policy. In Europe it was in culturally conservative groups, such as the Catholic Church, that a more consequential opposition to eugenics was found. And the countries where those groups were weakest introduced the sterilization laws. While campaigns for sterilization laws succeeded in Scandinavia, they failed both in England and in the Netherlands.[17] Main factors in the failure of the British campaign for the introduction of sterilization were "the strength of the Catholic lobby and the unwillingness of the National Government to run the risk of adopting a contentious piece of legislation," wrote G. R. Searle.[18]

The Nordic countries, plus Estonia,[19] were the only European countries that introduced sterilization laws in the 1930s under democratic regimes. Germany did not have a sterilization law until after the Nazi takeover. What was so special about the Nordic countries? They all had Lutheran state churches, a relatively homogeneous culture, and a relatively egalitarian social structure. Strong labor parties cooperated with strong labor organizations and were winning government power that was to last more or less continuously for the next half century. The Scandinavian model for the welfare state was well on its way. The sterilization laws and the way they were managed—moderate, well-organized, with loyal participation and little protest—is a symptom of the special character of the social and cultural conditions that existed in the Nordic countries in this period.

The history of eugenics raises the issue of the relationships between science and politics, knowledge and values, with special force. It is, as Mark Adams has pointed out, a particularly suitable topic for elucidating the complex interaction of so-called internal and external factors in science.[20] The technological and economic, or more generally instrumental, use of science has in recent decades dominated our conceptions of how science affects society. In the case of eugenics, however, the ideological influence seems to have been more important. It was by influencing the formation of social aims and attitudes that science in this case made its impact, not by introducing new and more efficient techniques. In other words, science had a normative and enlightening rather than an instrumental social role.

Political considerations and experiences, in particular experience with the population policies of Nazi Germany, obviously influenced the eugenic views of geneticists and probably also their judgments on controversial scientific issues, such as the effect of race crossings or the pace of genetic degeneration. William Provine has argued, for instance, that in the post-World War II period geneticists revised their theories on race crossings to "fit their feelings of revulsion" rather than because of "new compelling data."[21] Diane Paul has argued likewise that the collapse of reform eugenics after World War II was due to political and ideological factors. It was certainly not "by developments internal to science during this period."[22] Though the phrases "new compelling data" and "during this period" indicate a somewhat restricted and perhaps overly empiricist view of what constitutes growth of scientific knowledge, Provine and Paul are surely right in pointing out the profound ideological and political influence on scientific thinking in this case.

The story of eugenic sterilization has been told to teach us that "human rights must not be hidden away in an inaccessible system of expertise or an incomprehensible social system."[23] The events in Scandinavia as well as in Germany show that scientific knowledge and expert judgment is not sufficient to secure a sane policy, but that a liberal and democratic political system can promote restraint on extreme applications of science to programs of social policy. The ideal of a value-free and purely factual science was used by some scientists to justify their accommodation to Nazi policies. On the other hand, the Scandinavian developments also demonstrate how growing knowledge about human genetics had an important effect on the development of eugenic policies. Though social and political controversies set problems for research, it is a scientific task to clarify what the facts are. And this clarification can have important political consequences. It was hardly obvious that race crossing could not be detrimental or that there could not be a considerable genetic degeneration in the course of a few generations. If the facts of human biology had turned out to have been different, our judgments about right and wrong politics could also have been quite different.

The history of sterilization in the Nordic countries provides an interesting case of interaction of scientific knowledge and political ideology in the development of social policies. The gradual accumulation of knowledge of genetics, in particular human genetics, from the early years of the twentieth century until eugenics faded out in the 1960s, was essential in setting premises for the political debates and decisions. But there was also an underlying view of the relation between science and politics which linked eugenics to the development of the welfare state that was so typical of the Nordic countries in the middle decades of the twentieth century. In continuation of the enlightenment view of science, social and economic planning based on science was seen as the motor of social progress. We tend in hindsight to see many pernicious effects of this enthusiasm for planning. It represented a superstition in science and human reason. But even if the traditional ideals of central planning have wilted, the reliance on science in forming our social and economic systems has not disappeared. Due to the growth of science, not least social science, and the decline of other institutions, such as religion, it may be greater than ever before. Thus the description and analysis of the role of science in the rise and fall of the welfare state is a topical theme. And eugenic sterilization appears as a promising research site. The studies in this book can only pretend to give a preliminary account. A more extensive and precise investigation of each of the Nordic countries with a follow-up on developments up to the present time would provide more material for interesting comparative analyses. One question that needs pursuing is the nature and significance of the differences between mainline and reform eugenics. More generally a comparison of eugenics in Scandinavia and Germany appears particularly well suited for a sophisticated analysis of the interaction between science, ideology, and politics.

NOTES

1. G. R. Searle, "Eugenics and Politics in Britain in the 1930s," *Annals of Science* 36 (1979): 159-69.
2. For a description of "mainline" and "reform" eugenics, see Searle, "Eugenics and Politics in Britain in the 1930s," 166; and Daniel Kevles, *In the Name of Eugenics* (New York: Alfred A. Knopf, 1985), 88, 173.
3. S. Kühl, *The Nazi Connection: Eugenics, American Racism, and German National Socialism* (New York and Oxford: Oxford University Press, 1994), 72.
4. The concept of the "gene" as well as the distinction between "phenotype" and "genotype" was introduced by the Danish geneticist W. Johannsen (N. Roll-Hansen, "The Genotype Theory of Wilhelm Johannsen and Its Relation to Plant Breeding and the Study of Evolution," *Centaurus* 22 [1978]: 209-35). The botanical institute of the University of Copenhagen owns a silent movie of Johannsen coming to his institute. To express his main theoretical accomplishment he writes this formula on the blackboard.
5. See, for example, L. Graham, "Science and Values: The Eugenics Movement in Germany and Russia in the 1920s," *American Historical Review* 52 (1977): 1133-64; M. Freeden, "Eugenics and Progressive Thought: A Study in Ideological

Affinity," *The Historical Journal* 22 (1979): 645-71; Searle, "Eugenics and Politics in Britain in the 1930s"; D. Paul, "Eugenics and the Left," *Journal of the History of Ideas* 44 (1984): 567-90.

6. Most likely, other factors were also important for the quick decline in steriliza-tions of the mentally retarded in the 1950s. For example, it should be investigated what role the introduction of new methods of contraception played.

7. See, for example, Paul, "Eugenics and the Left," 585-90.

8. U. Deichmann, *Biologen unter Hitler: Vertreibung, Karrieren, Forschung* (Frankfurt & New York: Campus, 1992), 276-80.

9. G. Broberg and M. Tydén, *Oönskade i folkhemmet. Rashygien och sterilisering i Sverige* (Stockholm: Gidlunds, 1991), 189.

10. Ibid., 140-43.

11. G. Baader, "Das 'Gesetz zur Verhütung erbkranken Nachwuchses'—Versuch einer kritischen Deutung," in *Zusammenhang. Festschrift für Marielene Putscher*, vol. 2, ed. O. Baur and O. Glandien (Cologne: Wiemand Verlag, 1984), 865-75.

12. P. Weingart, J. Kroll, and K. Bayertz, *Rasse, Blut un Gene. Geschichte der Rassenhygiene in Deutschland* (Frankfurt: Suhrkamp Verlag, 1988).

13. K. H. Roth, "Schöner neuer Mensch," in *Der Griff nach der Bevölkerung*, ed. H. Kaupen-Haas (Nordlingen: Delphi Politik, 1986), 14-15, 19, 25-26. A more detailed analysis of these German accounts of the relation between eugenics and human genetics is found in N. Roll-Hansen, "Eugenic Sterilization: A Preliminary Comparison of the Scandinavian Experience to that of Germany," *Genome* 31 (1989): 894-95.

14. P. Weindling, *Health, Race and German Politics between National Unification and Nazism, 1870-1945* (New York: Cambridge University Press, 1989), 9.

15. P. Weindling, "Weimar Eugenics: The Kaiser Wilhelm Institute for Anthropology, Human Heredity and Eugenics in Social Context," *Annals of Science* 42 (1985): 315.

16. W. H. Schneider, *Quality and Quantity: The Quest for Biological Regeneration in Twentieth-Century France* (New York: Cambridge University Press, 1990), 286, 291.

17. For events in the Netherlands, see J. Noordman, *Om de kwaliteit van het nages-lacht. Eugenetica in Nederland 1900-1950* (Nijmegen: SUN, 1989).

18. Searle, "Eugenics and Politics in Britain in the 1930s," 168.

19. Estonia was also a Lutheran country with a language close to Finnish and tradi-tional cultural ties to Finland and Sweden.

20. M. Adams, "Towards a Comparative History of Eugenics," in *The Wellborn Science: Eugenics in Germany, France, Brazil, and Russia*, ed. M. Adams (New York and Oxford: Oxford University Press, 1990), 217-31.

21. W. B. Provine, "Geneticists and the Biology of Race Crossing," *Science* 182 (1973): 796.

22. Paul, "Eugenics and the Left," 587.

23. Broberg and Tydén, *Oönskade i folkhemmet*, 190.

Selected Bibliography

General Works

Adams, M. "Towards a Comparative History of Eugenics." In *The Wellborn Science. Eugenics in Germany, France, Brazil, and Russia*. Ed. M. Adams. New York and Oxford: Oxford University Press, 1990.

———., ed. *The Wellborn Science: Eugenics in Germany, France, Brazil, and Russia*. New York & Oxford: Oxford University Press, 1990.

Allen, G. "Geneticists, Eugenics, and Class Struggle." *Genetics* 79 (1975).

———. "Geneticists, Eugenics and Society: Internalists and Externalists in Contemporary History of Science." *Social Studies of Science* 6 (1976).

———. "The Eugenics Record Office at Cold Spring Harbour, 1910-1940: An Essay in Institutional History." *Osiris* 2nd series, 2 (1986).

Baader, G. "Das 'Gesetz zur Verhütung erbkranken Nachwuchses': Versuch: Einer kritischen Deutung." In *Zusammenhang: Festschrift für Marielene Putscher*. Vol. 2. Ed. O. Baur and O. Glandien. Cologne: Wiemand Verlag, 1984.

Barker, D. "The Biology of Stupidity: Genetics, Eugenics and Mental Deficiency in the International War Years." *British Journal for the History of Science* 22 (1989).

Bock, G. "Racism and Sexism in Nazi Germany." In *When Biology became Destiny: Women in Weimar and Nazi Germany*. Ed. R. Bridenthal, A. Grossmann, and M. A. Kaplan. New York: Monthly Review Press, 1984.

———. *Zwangssterilisation und Nationalsozialismus: Studien zur Rassenpolitik und Frauenpolitik*. Opladen: Westdeutscher Verlag, 1986.

Chapman, P. V. "Schools as Sorters." In *Applied Psychology and the Intelligence Testing Movement, 1890-1930*. Ed. L. M. Terman. New York: New York University Press, 1988.

Deichmann, U. *Biologen unter Hitler: Vertreibung, Karrieren, Forschung*. Frankfurt & New York: Campus, 1992.

273

Farral, L. "The History of Eugenics: A Bibliographical Review." *Annals of Science* 36 (1970).

Freeden, M. "Eugenics and Progressive Thought: A Study in Ideological Affinity." *The Historical Journal* 22, no. 3 (1979).

Graham, L. "Science and Values: The Eugenics Movement in Germany and Russia in the 1920s." *American Historical Review* 52 (1977).

Kevles, D. J. *In the Name of Eugenics: Genetics and the Uses of Human Heredity.* New York: Alfred A. Knopf, 1985.

Kühl, S. *The Nazi Connection: Eugenics, American Racism, and German National Socialism.* New York and Oxford: Oxford University Press, 1994.

Lilienthal, G. *Der "Lebensborn e. V.": Ein Instrument nationalsozialistischer Rassenpolitik.* Stuttgart: Gustav Fischer Verlag, 1985.

Ludmerer, K. M. *Genetics and American Society: A Historical Appraisal.* Baltimore: The Johns Hopkins University Press, 1972.

MacKenzie, D. "Eugenics in Britain." *Social Studies of Science* 6 (1976).

————. *Statistics in Britain 1865-1930: The Social Construction of Scientific Knowledge.* Edinburgh: Edinburgh University Press, 1981.

Markowitz, G. E. and D. Rosner. "Doctors in Crisis: Medical Education and Medical Reform during the Progressive Era 1895-1915." In *Health Care in America: Essays in Social History.* Ed. S. Reverby and D. Rosner. Philadelphia: Temple University Press, 1979.

Mayr, E. *The Growth of Biological Thought.* Cambridge: The Belknap Press, 1982.

Muller, H. J. *Studies in Genetics: The Selected Papers of H. J. Muller.* Bloomington: Indiana University Press.

Müller, J. *Sterilisation und Gesetzgebung bis 1933.* Husum: Matthiesen Verlag, 1985.

Müller-Hill, B. *Tödliche Wissenschaft: Die Assonderung von Juden, Zigeunern und Geisteskranken 1933-1945.* Hamburg: Rowohlt, 1984.

————. "Genetics after Auschwitz." *Holocaust and Genocide Studies* 2 (1987).

Noordman, J. *Om de kivaliteit van het nageschlacht: Eugenetica in Nederland 1900-1950.* Nijmegen: SUN, 1989.

Nowak, K. *"Euthanasie" und Sterilisierung im "Dritten Reich."* Göttingen: Vandenhoech & Ruprecht, 1978.

Numbers, R. L. "The Fall and Rise of the American Medical Profession." In *Sickness and Health in America: Readings in the History of Medicine and Public Health.* Ed. J. W. Leavitt and R. L. Numbers. Madison: University of Wisconsin Press, 1985.

Paul, D. "Eugenics and the Left." *Journal of the History of Ideas* 44 (1984).

Pick, D. *Faces of Degeneration: A European Disorder c. 1848-c. 1918.* Cambridge: Cambridge University Press, 1989.

Proctor, R. N. *Racial Hygiene: Medicine under the Nazis.* Cambridge: Harvard University Press, 1988.

Provine, W. B. *The Origin of Theoretical Population Genetics.* Chicago: Chicago University Press, 1971.

———. "Geneticists and the Biology of Race Crossing." *Science* 182 (1973).

Reilly, P. R. "The Surgical Solution: The Writing of Activist Physicians in the Early Days of Eugenical Sterilization." *Perspectives in Biology and Medicine* 26 (1983).

———. *The Surgical Solution: A History of Involuntary Sterilization in the United States.* Baltimore: The Johns Hopkins University Press, 1991.

Roll-Hansen, N. "The Genotype Theory of Wilhelm Johannsen and its Relation to Plant Breeding and the Study of Evolution." *Centaurus 22* (1978).

———. "The Progress of Eugenics: Growth of Knowledge and Change in Ideology." *History of Science* 24 (1988).

———. "Eugenic Sterilization: A Preliminary Comparison of the Scandinavian Experience to that of Germany." *Genome* 31 (1989).

———. "Geneticists and the Eugenics Movement in Scandinavia." *British Journal for the History of Science* 22 (1989).

Roth, K. "Schöner neuer Mensch." In *Der Griff nach der Bevölkerung.* Ed. H. Kaupen-Haas. Nordlingen: Delphi Politik, 1986.

Schneider, W. H. *Quality and Quantity: The Quest for Biological Regeneration in Twentieth-Century France.* Cambridge: Cambridge University Press, 1990.

Searle, G. R. *Eugenics and Politics in Britain, 1900-1914.* Leyden: Noordhoff International, 1976.

———. "Eugenics and Politics in Britain in the 1930s." *Annals of Science* 36 (1979).

Stepan, N. L. *"The Hour of Eugenics": Race, Gender, and Nation in Latin America.* Ithaca & London: Cornell University Press, 1991.

Weindling, P. "Weimar Eugenics: The Kaiser Wilhelm Institute for Anthroplogy: Human Heredity and Eugenics in Social Context." *Annals of Science* 42 (1985).

———. *Health, Race and German Politics between National Unification and Nazism, 1870-1945.* Cambridge: Cambridge University Press, 1989.

Weingart, P. "Eugenik—Eine angewandte Wissenschaft: Utopien der Menschenzüchtung zwischen Wissenschaftsentwicklung und Politik." In *Wissenschaft im Dritten Reich.* Ed. P. Lundgreen. Frankfurt: Suhrkamp, 1985.

————. "The Rationalization of Sexual Behavior: The Institutionalization of Eugenic Thought in Germany." *Journal of the History of Biology* 20 (1987).

Weingart, P., J. Kroll, and K. Bayertz, *Rasse, Blut und Gene: Geschichte der Eugenik und Rassenhygiene in Deutschland.* Frankfurt: Suhrkamp, 1988.

Weiss, S. "Wilhelm Schallmayer and the Logic of German Eugenics." *Iris* 77 (1986).

————. "The Race Hygiene Movement in Germany." *Osisis* 3 (1987).

————. *Race Hygiene and National Efficiency: The Eugenics of Wilhelm Schallmayer.* Berkeley: University of California Press, 1987.

Wiseman, S., ed. *Intelligence and Abilitiy: Selected Readings.* Harmondsworth: Penguin Books, 1967.

Denmark

Andersen, F. E. "Diskurs og Discrimination." *Agrippa* 3 (1982).

Hansen, B. S. "Eugenik i Danmark: Den Bløde Mellemvej." *Niche* 4 (1984).

Kemp, T. *Arvehygiejne: Festskrift udgivet af Københavns Universitet i anledning af Universitetets Årsfest 1951.* Copenhagen: Københavns Universitet, 1951.

————. "Address at the opening of the First International Congress of Human Genetics." *Acta Genetica et Statistica* 6 (1956/57).

————. "Genetic-Hygienic Experiences in Denmark in Recent Years." *The Eugenics Review* 49 (1957).

Kirkebæk, B. *Abnormbegrebet i Danmark i 20. erne og 30. erne med Særlig Henblik på Eugeniske Bestræbelser og Særlig i Forhold til Åndssvage.* Copenhagen: Danmarks Lærerhøjskole, 1985.

————. "Staten og Den Åndssvage 1870-1935: Fra Filantropi til Kontrol." *Handicaphistorie* 1 (1987).

————. *Da de Åndssvage blev farlige.* Copenhagen: Socpol, 1993.

Koudahl, G. *Om Vasectomi med Sterilisation for Øje.* Copenhagen: Munksgaard, 1967.

Le Maire, L. *Legal Kastration i Strafferetslig Belysning.* Copenhagen: Munksgaard, 1946.

Mohr, J. "Human Arvebiologi og Eugenik." In *Det Lægevidenskabelige Fakultet, vol. 7, Københavns Universitet 1479-1979.* Ed. J. C. Melchior, et al. Copenhagen: Københavns Universitet, 1979.

Schmidt L. H. and J. E. Kristensen, *Lys, Luft og Renlighed: Den Moderne Socialhygiejnes fødsel.* Copenhagen: Akademisk Forlag, 1986.

FINLAND

Aimo Halila. *Suomen naisvoimistelu ja urheiluseurat vuoteen 1915: Suomenkielisten miesvoimistelu ja urheiluseurojen synnystä, perustajien yhteiskunnallisesta koostumuksesta ja emäaseuroista.* Historiallisia tutkimuksia 53. Helsinki: Finnish Historical Society, 1959.

Borgström, C. A. *Tillämpningen av lagen om sterilisering i Finland 13. 6. 1935-30. 6. 1955 kastreringarna obeaktade.* Bidrag till kännedom av Finlands Natur och Folk 103. Helsingfors: Finska Vetenskapssocieteten, 1958.

Hietala, M. "The Diffusion of Innovations: Some Examples of Finnish Civil Servants' Professional Tours in Europe." *Scandinavian Journal of History* 8, no. 1 (1983).

————. *Services and Urbanization at the Turn of the Century: The Diffusion of Innovations.* Studia Historica 23. Helsinki: Finnish Historical Society, 1987.

————. "Berlin und andere Grosstädte als Vorbild für die Selbstverwaltungen von Helsinki und Stockholm um die Jahrhundertwende." In *Blicke auf die deutsche Metropole.* Ed. Gerhard Brunn and Jürgen Reulecke. Essen: Reimar Hobbing, 1989.

————. "Innovaatioiden ja kansainvälistymisen vuosikymmenet." In *Tietoa, taitoa, asiantuntemusta: Helsinki eurooppalaisessa kehityksessä 1875-1917,* vol. 1, Historiallinen Arkisto 99:1/Helsingin kaupungin tietokeskuksen tutkimuksia 1992:5:1. Helsinki: Finnish Historical Society/Helsingin kaupungin tietokeskus, 1992.

Kallenautio, J. "Kieltolaki ja sen kumoaminen puoluepoliittisena ongelmana." *Alkoholitutkimussäätiön Julkaisuja* no. 31 (1979).

Kemiläinen, A., M. Hietala, and P. Suvanto, eds. *Mongoleja vai Germaaneja? Rotuteorioiden suomalaiset.* Historiallinen Arkisto 86. Helsinki: Finnish Historical Society, 1985.

Klinge, M. *Vihan veljistä valtiososialismiin: Yhteiskunnallisia ja kansalllisia näkemyksiä 1910- ja 1920-luvuilla.* Porvoo: Werner Söderström OY, 1972.

Lahti, R. "Vuoden 1970 abortti-, sterilisaatio- ja kastraatiolainsäädäntö." In *Festskrift utgiven i anledning av Juristklubben Codex' 30-års jubileum.* Helsinki: Juristklubben Codex, 1970.

Mäkinen, T. "Yhdysvaltojen ja Suomen välisten tieteellisten kontaktien kehitys 1917-1970." Unpublished Master's thesis, Department of History, University of Turku, 1980.

Paasivirta, J. *Finland and Europe: The early years of independence 1917-1939.* Helsinki: Finnish Historical Association, 1988.

Portin, P. and A. Saura. *The Impact of Mendel's work on the development of Genetics in Finland.* Folia Mendeliana 20, Acta Musei Moravie. Brno: Moravske Musei Moravie, 1985.

Saarinen, H. "Studien und Bildungsreisen von Finnen nach Berlin 1809-1914." In *Miscellanea.* Ed. A. Tammisto, K. Mustakallio and H. Saarinen. Studia Historica 33. Helsinki: Finnish Historical Society, 1989.

Salmiala, B. A."Onko pakkokastratio oikeus- ja kulttuurivaltiossa hyväksyttävä reaktiomuoto rikoksen seurauksena?" *Defensor Legis* no. 2-4 (1951).

Suomalainen, E. *Kromosomitutkimuksen ja klassillisen perinnöllisyystieteen aika 1923-1949.* Helsinki: Institutum Geneticum, Universitas Helsingiensis, 1983.

NORWAY

Aasen, H. S. *Rasehygiene og menneskeverd: Nasjonalsosialismens steriliseringslov av juli 1942,* Institutt for offentlig retts skriftserie no. 4/1989. Oslo: 1989.

Dalcq, A. M. "Notice sur la vie et l'œuvre de M. O. L. Mohr: Correspondant étranger." *Academie royale de médecine de Belgique* 7 (1967).

Evang, K. *Sterilisering etter lov av 1. juni 1934 om adgang til sterilisering m. v. h.* Sarpsborg: F. Verding, 1955.

Gogstad, A. Chr. *Helse og Hakekors: Helsetjeneste og helse under okkupasjonsstyret i Norge, 1940-45.* Bergen: Alma Mater Forlag, 1991.

Langfeldt, G. "Psykiatriske arbeidsoppgaver i etterkrigstiden." *Tidsskrift for den Norske Laegeforening* 65 (1945).

Lavik, N. J. *Makt og galskap.* Oslo: Pax, 1990.

Longum, L. *Drömmen om det frie menneske: Norsk kulturradikalisme og mellomkrigstidens radikale trekløver, Hoel—Krogh—Verland.* Oslo: Universitetsforlaget, 1986.

Mohr, T. *Katti Anker Möller: En banebryter.* Oslo: Tiden, 1968.

Nordby, T. "Profesjokratiets perioder innen norsk helsevesen: Institusjoner, politikk og konfliktemner." *Historisk Tidsskrift* (1987).

Nordby, T. *Karl Evang.* Oslo: Aschehoug, 1989.

Roll-Hansen, N. "Den norske debatten om rasehygiene." *Historisk Tidsskrift* (1980).

———. "Eugenics before World War II: The Case of Norway." *History and Philosophy of the Life Sciences* 2 (1980).

Seip, A.-L. "Politikkens vitenskapeliggöring: Debatten om socialpolitikk i 1930-årene." *Nytt Norsk Tidsskrift* 6 (1989).

Slagstad, R. "Prövingsretten i det norske system." *Nytt Norsk Tidsskrift* 6 (1989).

Waaler, G. H. "Professor, Dr. med. Otto Lous Mohr: Vitenskapsmannen." *Det Norske Videnskaps-Akademi i Oslo: Årbok 1967.* Oslo: Universitetsforlaget, 1968.

SWEDEN

Bennich-Björkman, L. "Så tuktas en argbigga: Den svenska steriliseringspolitiken." *Kvinnovetenskaplig tidskrift* no. 2 (1992).

Broberg, G. "Linnaeus as an Anthropologist." In *Linnaeus: The Man and His Work.* Ed. T. Frängsmyr. Berkeley: University of California Press, 1983.

————. "Lamarckismen i Sverige." *Lychnos. Lärdomshistoriska samfundets årsbok 1988.* Uppsala: Almqvist & Wiksell International, 1988.

————. "Rasbiologiska institutet: Tillkomståren." In: *Kunskapens trädgårdar: Om institutioner och institutionaliseringar i vetenskapen och livet.* Ed. G. Broberg, G. Eriksson, and K. Johannisson. Stockholm: Atlantis, 1988.

Broberg, G. and M. Tydén. *Oönskade i folkhemmet: Rashygien och sterilisering i Sverige.* Stockholm: Gidlunds Bokförlag, 1991.

Carlson, A. *The Swedish Experiment in Family Politics: The Myrdals and the Interwar Population Crisis.* New Brunswick: Transaction, 1990.

Curti, M. "Sweden in the American Social Mind of the 1930s." In *The Immigration of Ideas: Studies in the North Atlantic Community. Essays presented to O. Fritiof Ander.* Ed. J. I. Dowie and J. T. Tredway. Rock Island, Illinois: Augustana Historical Society, 1968.

Forssman, H. "Sterilisering och befolkningspolitik." *Socialmedicinsk tidskrift* 35, no. 4 (1958).

Freiburg, J. "Counting Bodies: The Politics of Reproduction in the Swedish Welfare State." *Scandinavian Studies* 65, no. 2 (1993).

Hammar, T. *Sverige åt svenskarna: Invandringspolitik, utlänningskontroll och asylrätt 1900-1932.* Stockholm: Caslon Press, 1964.

Hatje, A. *Befolkningsfrågan och välfärden: Debatten om familjepolitik och nativitetsökning under 1930- och 1940-talen.* Stockholm: Allmänna förlaget, 1974.

Heymowski, A. *Swedish "Travellers" and their Ancestry.* Studia Sociologica Upsaliensia 5. Uppsala: Almqvist & Wiksell, 1969.

Hirdman, Y. *Att lägga livet tillrätta: Studier i svensk folkhemspolitik.* Stockholm: Carlssons, 1989.

Hofsten, N. von. "Steriliseringar i Sverige 1935-1939." *Nordisk Medicin* 7, no. 34 (1940).

————. "Steriliseringarna och aborterna." In *Medicinalväsendet i Sverige 1813-1962.* Ed. W. Kock. Stockholm: Nordisk bokhandel, 1963.

————. *Steriliseringar i Sverige 1941-1953.* Socialmedicinsk tidskrifts skriftserie 28. Stockholm: Socialmedicinsk tidskrift, 1963.

Jackson, W. A. "The Making of a Social Science Classic: Gunnar Myrdal's *An American Dilemma.*" *Perspectives in American History,* New Series 2 (1985).

Johannisson, K. "Folkhälsa: Det svenska projektet från 1900 fram till 2:a världskriget." *Lychnos. Årsbok för idéhistoria och vetenskapshistoria.* Uppsala: Swedish Science Press, 1991.

Kälvemark, A. *More Children of Better Quality? Aspects on Swedish Population Policy in the 1930's.* Studia Historica Upsaliensia 115. Uppsala: Almqvist & Wiksell International, 1980.

Koblik, S. *The Stones Cry Out: Sweden's Response to the Persecution of the Jews 1933-1945.* New York: Holocaust Library, 1988.

Lindberg, H. *Svensk flyktingpolitik under internationellt tryck 1936-1941.* Stockholm: Allmänna förlaget, 1973.

Lindström, U. *Fascism in Scandinavia 1920-1940.* Stockholm: Almqvist & Wiksell International, 1985.

Lööw, H. *Hakkorset och Wasakärven: En studie av nationalsocialismen i Sverige 1924-1950.* Göteborg: Avhandlingar från Historiska Institutionen i Göteborg, 1990.

Misgeld, K., K. Molin and K. Åmark, eds. *Creating Social Democracy: A Century of the Social Democratic Labor Party in Sweden.* University Park: The Pennsylvania State University Press, 1992.

Myrdal, G. *Historien om An American Dilemma.* Stockholm: SNS förlag, 1987.

Olsson, L. *Kulturkunskap i förändring: Kultursynen i svenska geografiböcker 1879-1985.* Malmö: Liber, 1986.

Palmblad, E. *Medicinen som samhällslära.* Göteborg: Daidalos, 1990.

Qvarsell, R. *Utan vett och vilja: Om synen på brottslighet och sinnessjukdom.* Stockholm: Carlsson, 1993.

Söder, M. *Anstalter för utvecklingsstörda: En historisk sociologisk beskrivning av utvecklingen.* Vols. 1-2. Stockholm: Ala, 1979.

Southern, D. W. *Gunnar Myrdal and Black-White Relations: The Use and Abuse of "An American Dilemma" 1944-1969.* Baton Rouge: Louisiana State University Press, 1987.

Svanberg, I., ed. *I samhällets utkanter: Om "tattare" i Sverige.* Uppsala Multiethnic Papers 11. Uppsala: Centre for Multiethnic Research, 1987.

Tydén, M. and I. Svanberg. "I nationalismens bakvatten: Hur svensken blev svensk och invandraren främling." In *Bryta, bygga bo: Svensk historia underifrån.* Vol. 2. Ed. G. Broberg, U. Wikander and K. Åmark. Stockholm: Ordfronts förlag, 1994.

INDEX

A

B